LSE GENDER INSTITUTE

DEBATING GENDER, DEBATING SEXUALITY

D0543021

DEBATING GENDER, DEBATING SEXUALITY

Edited by
NIKKI R. KEDDIE

NEW YORK UNIVERSITY PRESS
New York and London

NEW YORK UNIVERSITY PRESS
New York and London

Copyright © 1996 by New York University
All rights reserved

Library of Congress Cataloging-in-Publication Data
Debating gender, debating sexuality / edited by Nikki R. Keddie.
p. cm.
Includes bibliographical references.
ISBN 0-8147-4654-3 (cloth : alk. paper).—ISBN 0-8147-4655-1
(pbk. : alk. paper)
1. Sex role. 2. Sex. I. Keddie, Nikki R.
HQ75.D42 1995
305.3—dc20   95-36785
                        CIP

New York University Press books are printed on acid-free paper,
and their binding materials are chosen for strength and durability.

Manufactured in the United States of America
10 9 8 7 6 5 4 3 2 1

Contents

Introduction
Nikki R. Keddie   ix

I. Debates on Women and Gender

A. Procreation and Female Oppression

Procreation: The Substance of Female Oppression in Modern
Society
   Part One: The True Proletariat   5
   Part Two: Feminism and the Spirit of Capitalism   25
Nicky Hart

Juliet Mitchell Responds to Nicky Hart   49
Juliet Mitchell

Procreation and Women's Rights: A Response to Nicky Hart   52
Elizabeth Fox-Genovese

Nicky Hart Replies   61
Nicky Hart

B. Culture

A Culturalist Critique of Trends in Feminist Theory   73
Ruth H. Bloch

Gender Analysis and Social Theory: Building on Ruth Bloch's
Proposals   101
Barbara Laslett

Culture as an Object of Knowledge   114
Sandra Harding

Response to Sandra Harding and Barbara Laslett   120
Ruth Bloch

C. WELFARE

Gender, State, and Society: A Debate with Theda Skocpol   129
Linda Gordon

Soldiers, Workers, and Mothers: Gendered Identities in Early
U.S. Social Policy   147
Theda Skocpol

Response to Theda Skocpol   174
Linda Gordon

D. MARXISM AND WOMEN'S HISTORY

Is Marxism Still a Useful Tool of Analysis for the History of
British Women?   181
Deborah Valenze

Marxism and Women's History: African Perspectives   193
Iris Berger

Response to Valenze and Berger   208
Philippa Levine

E. THE UNDEBATED

Life-Story, History, Fiction: Reflections on Simone de
Beauvoir's Wartime Writings   217
Susan Rubin Suleiman

The Male's Search for a New Identity   238
Theodore C. Kent

II. SEXUALITY: FREUD, FOUCAULT, AND AFTER

A. FOUCAULT AND SEXUALITY

Is Foucault Useful for Understanding Eighteenth and
Nineteenth Century Sexuality?   247
Roy Porter

Sexuality and Discourse: A Response to Roy Porter on
Foucault   268
Mark Poster

B. FREUD, SEXUALITY, AND REPRESSED MEMORY

The Assault on Jeffrey Masson   277
Roy Porter

Response to Roy Porter's "The Assault on Jeffrey Masson"   296
Jeffrey Moussaieff Masson

Missing the Point about Freud   301
Frederick Crews

Response to Frederick Crews's "Missing the Point about
Freud"   312
Jeffrey Moussaieff Masson

On the Abuses of Freud: A Reply to Masson and Crews   315
Jeffrey Prager

Reply to Jeffrey Prager   324
Frederick Crews

Contributors   329

INTRODUCTION

NIKKI R. KEDDIE

Gender and sexuality have been among the most debated subjects both within and outside of academe in the past three decades.
The rise of a new wave of feminism—often dated from the publication
of Betty Friedan's *The Feminine Mystique* in 1963—was soon accompanied by a rising interest in women's and gender studies. The contemporary use of the word *gender* (hitherto mainly used for grammati-
cal purposes) to express an understanding of sexual identities as
socially constructed signified a shift in modern conceptions of sexuality. Within the broad feminist movement, there arose a diversity of
views regarding the roles of men and women in society, past and
present, and also regarding the paths women and men might follow to
attain the goal of greater equality of opportunity for the sexes.

A number of debates central to feminism may be grouped
around the emphasis on equality (or similarity) versus difference between genders. The wave of feminism that began in the 1960s stressed
gender equality, with the implicit or explicit assumption that boys and
girls should be brought up the same, that men and women should be
encouraged to have the same educations and jobs, that they should
share child rearing and housework equally, and that to call for maternity (rather than parental) leave or special protections for women was
more harmful than helpful to women. Egalitarian feminists in the
United States were more concerned with passage of the Equal Rights
Amendment (despite the fact that many of its provisions were by then
covered by law) than they were with mobilizing for parental leave,
better schools, or child care. Egalitarian feminism, especially in its
early years, tended also to be directed toward girls and women who
had access to professional education and jobs. For working-class
women the prospect of jobs was often less than liberating. The great
expansion of female employment that began in the 1960s, which owed
more to the demands of the job market and the fall or stagnation in
male salaries than it did to feminism, did not always bring with it the

satisfaction that many egalitarian feminists had expected. Many jobs paid little and required few skills; and the issues of child care and other family and social problems overall remained critical. On the other hand, the major opening of a variety of more desirable jobs to women was a significant gain.

Opponents of the egalitarian trend may be classified into at least two other groups: (1) those who did not necessarily stress sex difference, but argued that women lose time and wages because of childbirth and child raising, and that women's and children's needs require special attention as a result, regardless of whether education and politics are working to make the sexes more equal; and (2) those who stress the special features of women on such bases as psychological tests, recording of speech, or biological tests. Recent brain research, for example, seems to show differences between male and female brains (and may even—however controversially and tentatively—suggest differences between the brains of homosexuals and heterosexuals).

The differences between those who stress male-female similarity and those who emphasize differences in life patterns between men and women are addressed in the section by Nicky Hart, Juliet Mitchell, and Elizabeth Fox-Genovese.

How then can one best approach gender differences? During much of this century a materialist perspective held the day, based on a belief that the material organization of societies is the basis for their intellectual and cultural organization and also, ultimately, for the differential treatment of the sexes. Marxist and other materialist views tied the role of women in society to property relations and to the desire of men or of whole kinship groups to guarantee inheritance in the family line. Once men and families had significant property to pass on, they felt a need to be sure that their children really were theirs. This led to a variety of measures to assure women's virginity at marriage and "fidelity" thereafter. Similarly, the more public roles of women in modern times as well as class differentiation among women were explained primarily on the basis of changes in the material base of society.

The decline in the intellectual popularity of Marxism and other basically materialist views has been accompanied by a shift away from Marxist or quasi-Marxist feminism. Among the new approaches that developed was the culturalist one expressed in this book by Ruth Bloch. The culturalists draw on cultural anthropology's view of culture not as exclusively characteristic of elites but as an interrelated expression of all elements of society, and they apply a similar view to the study of women. In particular they deny that any material base is a privileged cause of other cultural phenomena. Barbara Laslett and Sandra Harding debate Bloch from an intermediate position. The continued vitality and contribution of the Marxist approach to women's history is upheld in the articles by Iris Berger and Deborah Valenze, but treated more skeptically in the response by Philippa Levine.

If the first two debates concern outlooks centering on women today, that between Theda Skocpol and Linda Gordon deals with an aspect of gender history that does, however, like most studies of gender history, have profound implications for today. The history of women and gender is perhaps the most flourishing branch of women's studies, and has produced a great variety of work critical to our understanding of history as a whole.

SUMMARIZING THE GENDER DEBATES

Nicky Hart begins the book by arguing that more attention should be given to childbirth and early child care as sources of women's inferior position and lower income, both of which continue to exist in capitalist societies despite the recent extensions in women's formal rights. She suggests that the equality of job opportunities emphasized by many feminists cannot provide a basic solution to the continuing problem of inequalities. In the second part of her article Hart emphasizes that those feminists who deny the special role of procreation in the lives of women do women a disservice, as they encourage all women to compete on what has to be an uneven playing field and discourage policies that could give needed consideration to mothers and children.

In commenting on Nicky Hart's paper, Juliet Mitchell supports Hart's stress on procreation and motherhood, but says she is wrong in her solutions and conclusions, to which she suggests alternatives.

Elizabeth Fox-Genovese criticizes Hart for her individualism and for stressing public responsibility only to biological mothers, rather than to children, which would involve a social program different from the one Hart suggests. Hart responds to the two critiques by defending and clarifying her basic positions.

Addressing another set of gendered questions, Ruth Bloch's "A Culturalist Critique of Trends in Feminist Theory" surveys major trends in feminist thought, noting many significant achievements in the last three decades, but criticizing a variety of schools for neglecting or understating the importance of culture. She believes that Marxist and related schools of thought as well as postmodern ones overstress material causation at the expense of a sophisticated understanding of culture, defined mainly in its broad anthropological sense.

Both Barbara Laslett and Sandra Harding accept some of Bloch's points but think she tends to separate culture as a primary causative factor when what is needed in order to understand gender and other questions is to integrate culture with material and other factors. Laslett in particular presents an alternative path for understanding women and gender that is also applicable to other social issues, and that she believes should interest even those who may think they have no special interest in feminist theory. Bloch responds that her critics have not properly understood, or at least addressed, her actual arguments.

In a discussion of an important recent book by Theda Skocpol, Linda Gordon limits her comments to points of disagreement while noting briefly that she also has many points of agreement. Gordon finds that Skocpol, like some other authors, mentions gender only regarding women and not when dealing with men; that she almost omits discussion of class; and that she uses quantitative evidence that adds little or nothing to her argument. Skocpol responds that Gordon has misunderstood or misstated many points. Skocpol stresses that her book reveals how widespread government aid to various classes of people was even before the New Deal, contrary to the myth of American backwardness in this regard. Skocpol believes she has shown what kind of women's and other organizations were important in achieving such government support, and also how they could be effective before women could vote. She relates her findings to current political controversies involving women and children. Skocpol also criticizes

Gordon's ideas and methodology—criticisms that Gordon, in her response, says are based largely on misreadings of her work.

In the section of undebated (but still provocative) articles, Susan Rubin Suleiman reevaluates Simone de Beauvoir on the basis of recently published writings and arrives at a more comprehensive and less harshly judgmental view than some recent French writers.

Finally, Theodore Kent tells you everything you wanted to know about gender, especially from the viewpoint of the male (from spiders to Robert Bly), but probably never thought to ask.

DEBATES ON SEXUALITY

The second part of the book, covering approaches to sexuality, broadly conceived, also represents a number of key debates. Like studies of women and gender, the study of sexuality has developed rapidly in recent decades, though it has a longer history going back at least to the late nineteenth century. As with gender studies, studies of sexuality have both a historical-theoretical aspect and a concern with current issues, and these two often interpenetrate. Many of the current intellectual controversies over sexuality revolve around two figures who have engendered both disciples and opponents and are still regarded by many as key to any understanding of sexuality: Sigmund Freud and Michel Foucault, the chief subjects of the debates in this book. Both discuss the major issue of sexual repression. How should their work be interpreted? Are their theories, in general, correct and illuminating or misleading and harmful?

Roy Porter's article on Foucault's *History of Sexuality* compares some of the key assertions of that work with what has been empirically established by other recent scholars regarding sexual ideas and practices in Europe in the eighteenth and nineteenth century. Porter suggests that Foucault's theories simply cannot be supported by historical fact. If we are concerned with verifiable reality, the emperor, he argues, has no clothes. Mark Poster, much more favorably disposed toward Foucault's work, objects to Porter's type of empiricism and suggests that Porter does not know how to read a text, or at least not the one he discusses here.

Beginning a more extended debate centering on recent approaches to Freudian views of sexuality, Porter assesses the views of Jeffrey Masson, utilizing especially literature that has appeared since the publication of Masson's important book, *The Assault on Truth*. Porter believes that aspects of Masson's persona have led to his ideas being taken less seriously than they deserve. Porter thinks Masson has revealed important faults in Freud's methods and beliefs, but that recent scholarship and the questioning of some reports of child abuse cast doubt on aspects of Masson's theses. Masson's suggestion that Freud abandoned his belief in the reality of seduction by fathers because it was so unpopular seems to Porter to ignore the equal unpopularity of his subsequent theory of early childhood sexuality. Also, recent literature indicates that patients did not volunteer reports of early childhood incidents, which were largely Freud's constructions. Finally, Porter thinks scholars should place psychiatry more firmly in its social surroundings and concentrate less on questions of individual sexuality.

Masson responds on several points by emphasizing that he did not stress Freud's motivation but presented it as a hypothesis. He adds that Porter and others who assert that Freud's later theory of childhood sexuality would have been at least as unpopular as his earlier seduction theory have never checked to see if this is true. Masson reviews the literature of the period and shows that in fact Freud's view of childhood sexuality was far better received than is usually assumed, and it was welcomed in contrast to the seduction theory. Masson calls for more serious research rather than polemic.

In a further response Frederick Crews strongly criticizes both Masson and Freud and accuses Roy Porter of equivocating in his discussion of them. Crews and Masson make opposite assertions on the important and current topic of repressed memories of child abuse. The controversy regarding Freud, repressed memory, and related questions continues with an article by Jeffrey Prager in which he sees both Masson and Crews as excessive in their criticisms of Freud and proposes reasons for their hostility. Crews objects to Prager's approach and defends his position.

These discussions of Freud include points important to the position of women and gender relations, including Freud's theories of seduction and sexually charged relations between parents and children; the question of whether Freud's women patients actually told him what he later said; and the discussion of child abuse and repressed memory.

The articles suggest the wide range of current discussions of gender and sexuality, as well as the disagreements that are current in these discussions. Newer scholarship has begun to deal both with men and with homosexuals of both sexes, without whom no complete discussion of gender relations is possible.

Scholarship to date has more agreed-upon points than a work stressing debates can emphasize. Most scholars would agree, for example, that the study of women and gender is important and should enter into the general consciousness; that dominant ideologies have exaggerated the weaknesses and inferiorities of women and have justified male dominance; and that women (as well as men) of different classes, colors, and nationalities often see their interests and the nature of their lives quite differently. There is less concern than before about whether women and men are "basically" identical or different, as even egalitarians seem less concerned than they once were over findings, say, of female-male brain differences. Nearly all would agree that much that passes for sex difference is largely cultural, but that biological differences that affect behavior are also significant. As in other fields of study, these major areas of general agreement are often and unfortunately overlooked given the more dramatic nature of disagreement.

This general agreement does not include many in the religious and secular right, who tend to have a more traditional approach to women's proper roles. Even here, however, there is a significant difference between how most conservatives would have talked about women's roles before 1960 and how they talk about them today. Today they tend to acknowledge many of women's problems and potentialities in a way they would not have done before. Hence, even when disagreements are major it must be realized that once women's positions became a central point in public debate, even those who proclaimed themselves hostile to feminist ideas were in many ways influenced by them. Although this book, and the journal *Contention* from which its essays were taken, can deal with only some of the many important debates on this subject, its debate format crystallizes major discussions and disagreements and should encourage further thought and discussion.

PART ONE

DEBATES ON WOMEN AND GENDER

A. PROCREATION AND FEMALE OPPRESSION

PROCREATION: THE SUBSTANCE OF FEMALE OPPRESSION IN MODERN SOCIETY

PART ONE : THE TRUE PROLETARIAT

NICKY HART

Pluck from under the family all the props which religion and morality have given it, strip it of the glamour true or false, cast around it by romance, it will still remain a prosaic, indisputable fact that the whole business of begetting, bearing and rearing children, is the most essential of the nation's businesses. If it were not done at all, the world would become a desert in less than a century.

Eleanor Rathbone [1]

FEMALE OPPRESSION AND THE MYSTIQUE OF HUMAN PROCREATION

The "business" of making new human beings, thereby ensuring the maintenance of a continuous flow of population through the social fabric, is the most mundane yet the most essential of all *social* activities. It is women's work; it is taken for granted work; it is unpaid work. Yet human beings are *the* material substance of social life, without them society could not exist, the institutions of collective life would wither away, economy and culture would dissolve and no more provide the endless source of fascination, not to mention well paid employment, for the intelligentsia. Yet the "business" of procreation is ignored in modern economics and a marginal even a non-issue in both classical and contemporary social theory.

The mystique of procreation is not confined to the intelligentsia. Indeed, the same group takes its cue from the broader cultural tendency of associating God, nature, or the modern physician with the creation of the *viable* infant. I emphasize viability because before the late nineteenth century, the bulk of procreative effort did not result in viable additions to the human race. When left to God or nature, human creation was an extremely chancy business. In the more salubrious environment of modern industrial society, procreative labor has become highly efficient primarily for reasons connected to the improved material and social position of the childbearing sex, though the allied professions of obstetrics and neonatal pediatrics have enhanced their reputation by associating themselves with this progress.

For most of recorded history, the practical result of the mystique of procreation has been the widespread cultural norm of discrimination against females and especially their nutritional neglect. In the modern era, it is manifested in the tendency to equate infant viability with high tech medical supervision and intervention and in the persisting ideology of procreation as natural and non-remunerated behavior.

From a public health perspective, the mystique of procreation is both dangerous and culturally absurd. The idea of God or nature as the principal author of life has justified the material neglect of the second sex, legitimized unrestrained access to women's procreative capacities, and provided a spiritual excuse for high reproductive waste. The same ideology distracts public concern away from the fact that the creation of a stream of healthy, viable infants depends upon the material conditions of their procreation. If any empirical evidence ever pointed to the dysfunctions of culture, the norms of female neglect underwritten by the mystique of divine or natural creation must take the prize. Ultimately, these beliefs entail a disregard for human survival irrespective of sex, for the impoverishment of the childbearer diminishes the chances for creating a stream of *viable* male and female infants. Cultures of male preference are therefore fundamentally illogical; the creation of healthy, viable men cannot be achieved except in the bodies of healthy, well grown, and adequately nourished women.[2]

Procreative labor includes the connected activities of conception, infant nurturance and the early training of new human life. In developed industrial societies with low rates of fertility, the minimum time demands of maintaining the membership levels of the social order are more concentrated than in earlier epochs. The time "needed" for the creation of two human beings from conception to the age of five by the same individual is less than a decade. This allows around three years between births and up to six years before part of the responsibility for daily supervision and education is transferred to public institutions. Clearly, this timetable may be lengthened according to individual discretion or shortened by the purchase of substitutes for direct parental care, an option more available and acceptable to those with greater economic resources to control the labor relationship thereby established. The economically privileged also enjoy the option of seeking private education for their offspring to cushion and delay the transition to the public sphere of social life.

This paper seeks to restore the labor process of procreation to the agenda of contemporary social, economic and political theory. Part One — "The True Proletariat" — sets out to underline the *social* character of procreative labor, to identify the heavy costs it entails for women, and to raise the question why this most *vital* of all human work has been left out of classic theories of social relations. It concludes with a discussion of the comparability of class and gender as forms of stratification. Part Two — "Feminism and the Spirit of Capitalism" — examines the place of procreation in contemporary feminist theory. With only a few exceptions, I argue, the female intelligentsia, partly through an internal logic and partly through its inheritance from nineteenth century social thought, has failed to develop a theory which gives sufficient emphasis to the social relations of procreation in the formation of gender inequality. I conclude with a discussion of the implications of bringing procreativity to center stage for a politics truly geared to women's material and social interests.

THE COSTS OF CREATING THE HUMAN MATERIAL OF SOCIAL LIFE

Creating new human life is a costly material process. The developing fetus remains in utero for a lengthy spell, drawing for continuous sustenance upon the material resources (energy, nutrition, and labor) of its mother. Its gestation also entails substantial opportunity costs for the mother, costs extended and elaborated by the extreme physiological dependency of the infant. After parturition, the fact that the mother's body represents the source of ideal nourishment for the neonate increases both the length of infant dependency and the probability that the principal full-time parent will be the same person who bore the child. Sentiments of love and possession may also act to "bond" mother and infant and to increase the difficulty of dividing the associated tasks of childbearing and child rearing in any analytical perspective. Theories promulgating optimal approaches to management of infancy abound in the late twentieth century, among them those which advocate the collectivization of child care principally as a route to female emancipation. This paper analyses the recorded costs of procreative labor for the childbearing sex *not* on the basis of future theoretical scenarios but on the basis of recorded empirical experience.

Throughout history, the material ingredients of human reproduction have been supplied by the female of the species (in part literally channeled through her body), more often than not in conditions of material hardship. I have analyzed their history elsewhere and provide only a brief summary here.[3] Procreation involves the connected sequence of conception, gestation, parturition, lactation, infant care and early socialization. Before the twentieth century, much of the resources routinely invested in these connected activities were wasted. I emphasize that these resources were supplied by the mother, and in the case of food, from a culturally defined ration which took no account of procreative labor. Vital registration (births and deaths but not stillbirths) was a governmental innovation of the first industrial century, and the period provides the first nearly accurate data base for measuring infant and early childhood mortality in the pre-modern era.[4] The recorded rates indicate less than half of full term live-born mid-nineteenth century infants surviving to adulthood to become productive or reproductive members of the human community. This estimate refers only to live-born infants. It excludes procreative attempts which resulted in stillbirth at full term, or in spontaneous or induced abortion. As these also consumed maternal investments, they must also be included in any estimate of the full count of reproductive waste in the pre-modern and early industrial era and the costs that this entailed for women.

These costs cannot be seen as the outcome of unvarying female biology. High rates of reproductive casualty are not intrinsic to human biology. In the modern era, they are correlated with maternal undernutrition, closely spaced births, and cultures of female subordination, conditions widespread in the "world we have lost".

The ancient and pre-modern demographic regime of low life expectancy, excess female mortality, and low reproductivity characterized societies marked by material, in particular nutritional, scarcity.[5] Food is the raw material of human tissue and the fuel of human action; it is a *vital* ingredient of human procreation. Everything we know about its distribution before the twentieth century indicates that the brunt of scarcity was shouldered by women.[6] The material scarcities of pre-industrial communities affected the wellbeing of all except the rich. However, social norms exacerbated the procreative consequences of food scarcity. The childbearing sex, lacking control (for normative as much as technical reasons) of their bodies, were systematically deprived of the vital resources for the support, let alone the creation, of new life.[7]

High rates of fertility and infant death ensured that the procreative equipment of women was continuously employed from the mid twenties (delayed marriage being the customary mechanism of family planning in pre-modern Europe) to the forties. This unrelieved sequence carried major costs for women, costs which seldom appear in historical "bookkeeping". In human societies, norms of male privilege are almost as universal as the incest taboo. They make sense in belief systems which mystify human creation, converting a mundane material process to one authored by a holy spirit capable of energizing the female procreative equipment with supernatural resources. The demographic consequences of the mystique of procreation have received scant attention from scholars. Systematic inequality in the distribution of food, particularly protein food, is explained and justified by reference to the greater calorific needs of the laboring male. The material consequences for the procreating female are never addressed and do not appear as a factor in demographic, economic, or even most epidemiological history.

The public health consequences of differential female neglect are obvious. By the twentieth century, they were increasingly recognized in the preference accorded to the pregnant or lactating woman in the allocation of wartime rations. In the Dutch Hunger Winter of 1944-45 for example, the expectant mother was singled out as being especially deserving of additional rations.[8] This policy must be viewed as revolutionary against the standard cultural norms of most of human history and the critical judgement of historians.

The single best indicator of the material burdens of procreative labor in the pre-modern era is the diminished vitality of the female of the species. Before the modern era, excess female mortality was normal.[9] It remains so today in most contemporary pre-industrial populations. Though Engels pronounced the development of private property as the decisive factor in the origins of patriarchal society, paleo-demographic records reveal excess female mortality in his imagined matriarchal era. The same evidence casts doubt on the idea that early Goddess worship proves there was material equality between the sexes.[10]

By contrast with earlier epochs, in every modern industrial society women outlive men. Indeed, the development of excess male mortality or, alternatively viewed, of increased female vitality is so systematically connected to industrialization as to merit inclusion among the key features of the demographic transition. It is only amid twentieth century material plenty that any potential physiological superiority of the female is revealed. In the "world we have lost" the evidence suggests that the material demands of procreative labor alongside other female work and norms sanctioning female deprivation took their toll in the diminished stature, vitality, and durability of the female body and consequently in massive rates of reproductive waste.[11]

There is now little nutritional scarcity in the industrialized world but procreation continues to be an under-valued activity in the late twentieth century, undervalued by society and by much of the male and female intelligentsia alike. In developed societies, where the civic status of the childbearing sex has been substantially raised by any historic standard, the costs of procreating the next generation are still borne by women with little social and no economic reward. It is no accident that women and their dependents are disproportionately poor in the advanced societies. It results from the unpaid status of procreative labor. In a world where almost every other form of human activity has its price, the most vital work of all is performed for free.

One contemporary version of the mystique of procreation is the belief that unsupported mothers can and should "conjure up" the material means to raise their children without financial aid and despite their acknowledged handicaps in their labor market. Like any other "indigent", an unsupported mother may be able to claim a citizen's right to a minimum subsistence, but this does not entail any special recognition or reward for her procreative labor. She obtains help by virtue of poverty, not "occupational" responsibility. Outside Scandinavia, the poverty of children in single parent families is fatalistically accepted — a fact of nature, not society. Surely there is nothing natural about the feminization of poverty. It comes about because of cultural values which assign definite material rewards to the labor characteristically performed by men, and none to the vital work performed by women.

The opportunity costs of maternity in one modern society have been carefully estimated by Heather Joshi.[12] She shows (for the UK in the third quarter of the twentieth century) that the cumulative loss of earnings resulting from the creation of two new human beings is equivalent to about half the average male lifetime income. Her calculations separate the effect of being female from maternity. Her hypothetical British woman born in 1946, would have earned $354,954 had she borne two children at ages 25 and 28. These lifetime earnings are cumulated through an assumed work career (from 15-59 years) involving 8 years of full-time absence from wage labor and 10 years of part-time paid employment. The total compares with $579,505 for a childless women of the same birth cohort. The comparable male recorded lifetime income is $754,488. The earnings gap between an average male and a maternal female was therefore more than $350,000, with $167,040 accounted for by gender (the difference between the male and the childless female). Maternity and all it entails accounted for a more substantial share of the depressed economic status of women than female gender itself. These losses accumulate through absence from wage work on account of childbearing. They are not the result of the depressed value of female labor, dual labor markets, "diminished human capital" — the issues which attract attention in analyses of female labor markets. No amount of tinkering with legislation to change the terms of gender inequality in wage and salary employment will affect the opportunity costs of engaging in the procreation of new human life.

Joshi's calculations indicate that motherhood can reduce participation in wage employment over the lifetime by 33%. This is only part of the cost of bearing children. To this must be added the fringe benefits and supplementary financial rewards of being a fulltime and continuous member of the paid labor force. Disrupted occupational careers and reliance on casual earning opportunities which fit with a domestic timetable leave mothers with reduced pension benefits increasing their probability of poverty in old age.[13] Add the fact that bearing the next generation also engenders responsibilities to care for and support it through the vagaries of unmarried parenthood, separation and divorce to get closer to the full economic disadvantages of engendering the next generation.

I quote Heather Joshi because her work embodies a superior *conceptual* means of depicting the economics of gender inequality in contemporary society. Though her figures illustrate the volume of time that one particular generation of British women invested in the creation and early socialization of their children, their importance lies in the focus on the dialectics of procreative and productive labor in women's lives. The absence of other similar analyses is testimony to the failure to theorize procreation as a fundamental barrier to the full incorporation of women in the formal occupational structure. No doubt women could reduce the time lost from paid labor. Leaving aside those with resources to pay for personalized substitute care, the life career space devoted to procreativity might be reduced by greater reliance on institutionalized child care. Who is to say what the irreducible minimum time for the procreation of a new human being by the direct producer should be, and how much choice and sheer material necessity might structure any observed statistical pattern? This is a question I shall return to in the second installment of this paper.

Wage and salary differentials (issues of comparable worth) and occupational segregation, which occupy pride of place in contemporary analyses of the *economics* of sexual inequality, constitute only a minor part of women's material status. The accumulation of economic inequality through the developmental cycle of domestic life is *the* principal material cause of women's second class status. *Lifetime* income and pension inequalities of the kind pioneered by Joshi give a much more accurate picture of the totality, the true level of monetary deprivation associated with the non-remuneration of childbearing. The dearth of research evidence structured by comparable analytical frameworks testifies to the theoretical vacuum in the conventional understanding of women's economic status.

Even this is only one side of the coin. The average cost of raising a child from conception to the end of full-time education in the USA was estimated in 1980 at between \$100,000 and \$140,000.[14] The significance of these expenditures must be set against current trends in family formation and disintegration. The increasing trend of unmarried birth (in the US from 5.3% in 1960 to 20% in 1990) and the rising incidence of divorce (from 258 per 1000 marriages in 1960 to 490 in 1980) have created a substantial number of single parent, female headed families. The U.S. Census Office estimated in 1980 that the majority (60%) of children would spend some part of their childhood living in a one-parent family. These households are at special risk of poverty for several reasons. The single household head's opportunities for paid employment are constrained by domestic responsibilities; the same individuals are exposed to gender discrimination in the labor market and their households may contain a more unfavorable ratio of dependents. Add the very low level of child support from divorced, separated, and unmarried fathers to glimpse the enormous economic risks faced disproportionately by female parents. Weitzman's study of divorced parents offers a glimpse of what this means in practice — a year after separation, the living standards of the average mother are reduced 40%; those of the father are raised 70%[15] Being male, irrespective of marital or parental status, has been deemed a qualification for a family wage. Being the actual but female head of a dependent family attracts no special treatment or financial compensation from employers. At stake is not merely paternal indifference to the material needs of children. Though writers who envisage social progress occurring through the agency of the "traditional" proletariat might sense discomfort at the apparent lack of financial commitment to their children by divorced male workers, the fundamental problem is *systemic*. The material process of creating new human life is neither valued nor rewarded in most advanced industrial societies. Whatever else is needed to reduce social and economic inequality, the most essential task for women is to politicize procreation, to redefine it culturally as the most vital work of human society and to redistribute economic rewards accordingly.

THE FORM AND THE SUBSTANCE OF GENDER INEQUALITY

The cultural innovation of costing and thereby determining the worth (profitability) of human labor according to a monetary scale was termed *formal rationality* by Max Weber.[16] He distinguished the new accounting (economizing) mentality of market capitalism from *substantive rationality*, in which the calculation of the means and ends of material survival is submerged in social relationships. The formal quality of rationality is marked by the shearing away of cultural impediments to reveal means/ends calculation as a naked and precise activity. *Formal* rationality is therefore rationality reduced (or elevated) to its essential *form* or in the contemporary idiom, its *structure*. *Substantive* rationality by contrast is submerged and disguised by the *substance* it seeks to manage and protect.

In Karl Polanyi's expression, it is "embedded" in the social order and governed by affective norms and behavior.[17]

The triumph of formal rationality over the conduct of social life was the source of Max Weber's "disenchantment of the world," the substitution of expressive motivation by a narrow instrumentality, leading ultimately to the bureaucratization of social life on a massive scale. Weber's pessimism about the march of formal rationality was both reinforced and countered by Karl Polanyi, who emphasized the extreme artificiality of humanity as Homo Economicus and of the self-regulating market as an autonomous and workable system for satisfying human needs. The model of capitalism embodied in the core of classical, neo-classical, and derivative forms of political economy rests on a falsity: the belief that a market for land and labor is a viable and self-correcting process. Polanyi argues that self regulation is a myth, that the market is an artificial structure, imposed on humanity through self-conscious political innovation, and perpetuated through political management and enforcement. The myth of self regulation is matched by the fictitious commodity status of the key constituents of market exchange: land (the natural environment), labor (humanity) and money (symbol of confidence in the political order). The conversion of these *substances* to an exchangeable *form (commodities embodying a profit element)* cannot be achieved without laying the basis for their ultimate destruction. In Polanyi's memorable words:

> The important point is thus: labor, land, and money are essential elements of industry, they also must be organized in markets; in fact these markets form an absolutely vital part of the economic system. But labor, land and money are obviously not commodities, the postulate that anything that is bought and sold must have been produced for sale is emphatically untrue in regard to them. In other words, according to the empirical definition of a commodity, they are not commodities. Labor is only the name for a human activity that goes with life itself, which in its turn is not produced for sale but for entirely different reasons, nor can that activity be detached from the rest of life, be stored or mobilized; land is only another name for nature which is not produced by man; actual money, finally is merely a token of purchasing power which as a rule is not produced at all, but comes into being through the mechanism of

banking or state finance. None of them is produced for sale. The commodity description of labor, land, and money is entirely fictitious.[18]

More than any other theorist, Polanyi delineated the deformities of social relations in the elevation of formal economic logic to an organizing principle of social life. Though he was not motivated by any desire to understand the causes of gender inequality in the twentieth century, his critique of classical and modern political economy and of complementary social theory offers more insights for the development of a feminist materialism than any other author. To put it more candidly and quite against the orthodox flow, a chapter of Karl P. is worth a volume of Karl M. in the search for an understanding of the material causes of and potential solutions to female subordination in contemporary capitalism.

The relevance of Polanyi for the analysis of gender inequalities lies in his insistence on the *social* character of the substance of social life. The central feature of the social substance is procreation, the creation of the fictitious commodity, *labor*, the maintenance of the continuous flow of humanity without which there would be no society, no intelligentsia, no social theory. It is precisely because the "business of begetting, bearing and rearing children" lies embedded in the untheorised substance of life that Polanyi's work is so relevant for understanding gender inequality.

Childbearing is attenuated and arduous work but it takes a form which sets it apart from more conventional forms of capitalist labor. In a market society, the value of labor is realized in the sale of its product. This entails a process of abstraction — goods and services must be separated from the producer if the value of the human labor they embody is to be reckoned and rewarded. This is why the commodity is defined as the product of abstracted or alienated labor, as a thing produced for sale. Clearly, the creation of human life does not fit easily into this paradigm; human beings are not things, they are not produced for sale and the idea that they might be is an anathema to the majority of people. The creation of human life, for all the rationalization and medicalization that surrounds it in the late twentieth century still remains the most spontaneous and unforced of human activities and perhaps the source of greatest life satisfaction for a very large number of people.

Though children, the product of procreative labor, have so far proved too awkward to be technically or ethically adapted to the universe of cash nexus exchange, women in industrial societies continue to maintain the flow of population despite the economic hardship they suffer in the process. The mentality of formal rationality has made some inroads into the procreation domain. In industrial societies, most families are now planned and the timing and phasing of successive births are controlled with markedly beneficial results. However, there is still formidable resistance to the full rationalization of procreation, as the heat of the abortion debate in the USA reveals. The strategic use of the rallying call "Pro-Choice" in the pro-abortion movement captures the difficulty. The female population cannot be easily divided into those for or against abortion. Between these two clear commitments are many women who do not actively oppose abortion yet feel a considerable unease at the use of purely rational criteria in the extinction of fetal life.

Procreation remains embedded in the substance of social life. Of all the activities vital to social and economic survival, it has held out longest against the commodity form. The science of pre-natal engineering is in its infancy and perhaps to the general relief, human conception, pregnancy, and birth continue to be processes largely within the control of ordinary people, surrounded by notions of "natural right" and among the last truly charismatic events to punctuate an increasingly impersonal human existence.

This leads me to the central theoretical argument of this paper and to the appropriate terminology for its expression. The subordination of women in modern society has a material and a substantive origin. It is rooted in the fact that one, perhaps the most, essential of all social activities, the procreation of new human life, has so far resisted the commodity form and therefore escaped the attention of economic rationalism and its theoretical heirs.

The social and economic upheaval that inaugurated industrial capitalism created a separate economic sphere for the social activity called production. This sphere (the formal sector) was set apart from the rest of society both in the intellectual imagination (classical political economy) and in the organization of everyday life. The sexual division of labor was not created by industrialism, but the partition and consequent reconceptualization of procreative labor as a non-productive activity was — hence Rathbone's title *The Disinherited Family*. The commodification of human labor created a new measure of social value — the money wage, which would henceforth become the measure of the social worth of individuals. Human activities not articulated to the new scale of values would increasingly appear as voluntaristic, leisure pursuits restricted to a backstage area of social life: in feminism, the private sphere; for Polanyi, the substance; and in the popular imagination, nature.

The founding fathers of economic science could not be accused of neglecting the question of human reproduction and its relationship to economic life.[19] Their discipline was born out of demographic concerns, and shaped in its infancy by Malthusian issues. However, as the division of intellectual "labor" gradually abstracted questions of economy, society, and demography into specialisms, the economics and social relations of procreation got mislaid in that vacuous left luggage locker of intellectual history called nature. Nature emerged as the terrain of the untreated substance: in the case of procreation, a vital prerequisite of social life governed by norms, customs, and power relations, yet presumed to be outside the sphere of the social.

Nineteenth century social theory accepted this view. To Marx, Weber, and Durkheim the mother/child relation was founded in and governed by nature and therefore outside the proper sphere of *social* relations. This unanimity alongside their opposed positions in other respects testifies to the opaque masculine logic which defined the theoretical field. As Weber himself might have put it: the construction of social theory like all forms of social action was motivated and shaped in the "course of its direction" by the meaning of the social actor, in this case "meaning" for the male theorist.[20] The relationships of men in society articulated by the capitalist division of labor and orchestrated by the logic of formal rationality emerged as the material core of society, the essence of social organization, the proper object of the sociological imagination. Broadening this theoretical perspective to incorporate the material experience of women as well as men carries important consequences for social theory, as the final section of this paper will indicate.

PROCREATIVE AND PRODUCTIVE LABOR :
PRIVILEGE AND OPPRESSION IN THE SOCIAL
RELATIONS OF CLASS AND GENDER

This paper argues that the social subordination of women in modern society is rooted in the absence of an institutional mechanism for social reciprocity in the most vital of all social activities — the creation of new human beings. It happens because the product of procreation cannot be easily alienated from the direct producer — the mother. In societies which have allowed the market a determining role in the estimation of social worth, only those human activities fully capable of being transformed to commodity form (purchasable goods and services) can be valued. Procreative labor does not lead to the production of saleable commodities. New human beings are not for sale, they belong to the direct producers with ownership enshrined in the natural rights of parents. In pre-industrial societies, these rights were monopolized by men. Industrial capitalism has witnessed a major expansion of the concept of the mother's natural rights, the clearest empirical evidence that it is dubious to conflate to the modern era with all past civilizations under the single term "patriarchal".

The idea that procreative labor is inherently alien to a market culture would not be accepted by all. Some might argue that the "sacralization" of the child is very much a contemporary phenomenon,[21] that in the "world we have lost," the creation and dispensation of human beings was surrounded by more pragmatic considerations. Leaving aside the institution of slavery in which the procreative labor of "out groups" is systematically expropriated, early modern history is replete with examples of at least some aspects of procreative labor being paid its price. The widespread resort to wet nursing at least in France, the sale of child labor and the Japanese system of human brokerage all serve as proof that the commodity may not be not entirely foreign to the sphere of human procreativity. Moreover, in the late twentieth century, prenatal engineering holds out the prospect of womb hire and surrogate parenthood as a potential means of commodity procreation. Who could conceivably make use of a personal service of this character? Only the rich. The costs of paying someone else to bear a child, not to mention the medical costs of "delivery" are prohibitive for the mass of the population.

The prospect of commodity procreation is surrounded by formidable ethical barriers. To date, only in the U.S.A., the most unfettered market system, has surrogate parenthood succeeded in challenging moral and legal opposition, and even there it is a practice of last resort, sought only by the infertile and frequently even then the subject of legal dispute. The majority continue to look upon procreation as a highly personal human action performed for love, not money, and in the context of kinship rather than the cash nexus. This motivation is the predominant reason that the industrial mother continues in Eleanor Rathbone's memorable words to be: "A little lower than the angels, . . . a little higher than a serf."[22]

Aversion to the idea of commodity procreation is undoubtedly linked to the desire of women to nurture their own children, to observe their growth and full development. The era of industrial capitalism undoubtedly increased the opportunity for maternity and the duration of childhood. In the developed world it produced an unprecedented leap forward in life expectancy, all but eliminating the grief of child mortality. It recast the social and ultimately the legal basis of parenthood, expanding a mother's rights over her children. It has also been accused of celebrating motherhood as a means of ensnaring women in a subservient economic role. Looked at from this latter vantage point it might be concluded that capitalist society, for all its material and political benefits, is ultimately antagonistic to the childbearing sex because it lacks a mechanism to pay for the generation of new human life. In truth, industrial capitalism left procreation out on a branch line of social development, severed it from the increasingly monetarized reward structure of social life, and obscured it from the gaze of the intelligentsia.

To hold the idea that the elevation of commodity production as the material basis of social life is the contemporary cause of the economic degradation of procreative labor is not to see class and gender as collateral forms of social stratification. For Marx, class was a form of social inequality built upon the alienating and expropriating character of the commodity. Recasting the wage employment in a more enlightened form as a pathway to the distributive value system of the social order carries rather different conclusions. The creation of commodities is literally socially valued labor; the creation of human beings is inconsequential by the same yardstick. Forms of labor excluded from the wage/salary nexus, are simultaneously excluded from the process of social validation.

This argument can also serve to explain the survival of the appearance of patriarchy through the transition from feudalism to capitalism. In the long pre-capitalist era (99% of human history) when the value of labor was not reckoned by the cash nexus, processes of production and reproduction were submerged in the substance of collective life. Gender was a preeminent though unremarkable axis of social stratification with its roots in a patriarchal social order. As the material and institutional base of patriarchal privilege withered in the face of market forces, male domination was re-constituted on a different base, on the foundation of commodified labor. The survival of ancient patriarchy in modern times is therefore an illusion. Men retained power over women through the transition to market capitalism through their privileged command over the means of livelihood. This in turn emerged from their structural relation to the entitlement system of market capitalism. This new source of power is economic, not ideological — the feudal norms of patriarchy would gradually founder on the rocks of economic pragmatism and market-sponsored individualism.

In the perspective of this paper, masculine domination in the late twentieth century has a naked material character — it is not significantly upheld by cultural norms. It is not, in the Weberian sense, a form of "legitimate domination," it carries no significant moral imperative.[23] Quite the contrary, the capitalist era has witnessed a continuous assault and whittling down of the institutional fabric of male privilege. As Hannah Gavron could put it even in 1965:

> . . . the legal position of the woman today is greatly
> improved as compared with one hundred years ago, partic-
> ularly within marriage where the husband has lost his
> proprietary rights over his wife's person, and property, has
> become liable to proceedings for divorce and the custody
> of children, must leave his deserted wife undisturbed in the
> matrimonial home and may not exercise the common law
> right of reasonable chastisement which is now grounds for
> divorce. Indeed the emancipation of married women has led
> to the creation of a new legal personality — "the married
> man".[24]

The theoretical explanation of female oppression offered in this paper has neither need of nor recourse to the ideological concept of patriarchy. It is also quite specific to modern forms of social organization based upon industrial capitalism. This form of social life has delivered mortal blows to pre-modern ideologies legitimating the subordinate social position of the childbearing sex. It has sponsored ideologies of female liberation and continues to enlarge educational and occupational opportunities for women. Its mechanisms contain the means of eradicating all forms of patriarchal privilege and of increasing the kinship autonomy of male and female wage laborers alike. Against this contemporary reality, women remain the second sex because they possess the physiological equipment for replenishing the species. Though they had much to gain from the new system of livelihood, the model of citizenship it spawned would ultimately disqualify because procreative labor would not fit into an occupational system organized by the cash nexus. The childbearing sex became the true proletariat of modern capitalism - offered the lowest rung of citizenship in exchange for their procreative labor. There is not any doubt that those who choose *not* to activate their procreative powers achieve the highest degree of economic and social equality with men.

By this line of reasoning the social relations of production and procreation, otherwise class and gender, are opposed forms of social stratification. To consider them otherwise is to assume a natural unity of interest between men and women, to submerge the identity (social, political, economic) of the childbearing female in that of her male breadwinner.

The portrayal of the liberating qualities of the commodity gels with the tendency in contemporary feminism to equate wage employment with female liberation. While conventional industrial sociology (at least during the Keynesian age) conveys an image of the commodity status of human labor as exploitative and alienating, much contemporary feminist thought identifies it as the sine qua non of *adult* fulfillment. The same inference flows from evidence of demographic change at the birth of the industrial capitalist era. There is little doubt that the spread of new income-generating opportunities in late eighteenth century England enabled more people to marry and set up their own adult establishments at an earlier age.[25] This initial stimulus to the modern rise of population in the first industrial nation may be recast as the beginning of not only a new mode of human exploitation but also of a new system of entitlements, a new opportunity structure, which over time would systematically discriminate against the childbearing sex.[26]

The idea of wage employment as a source of entitlement, widely recognized by early nineteenth century observers, lies untheorized at the root of the widespread feminist assumption that participation in commodity production is the only means of achieving adult autonomy in a market society.[27] This belief has been reinforced in the post war era by the "discovery" that gender divisions are cultural artefacts, social constructions of patriarchal culture with no firm anchor in sexual physiology. Anti-essentialism and a view of the labor market as the prime site of liberation are the structural frame of late twentieth century feminism. I contend that this causal theory with its embedded agenda for female emancipation is ultimately fallacious and self-defeating. I elaborate why in part II. Here I anticipate the main conclusions: The assumption that wage employment is *the* remedy for female oppression is linked to a specific diagnosis of the female condition and a pejorative image of womanhood. Unfettered access to wage employment is offered as *the* means of achieving individuality, of becoming a person in one's own right, of severing the affiliate bonds of kinship that tie people together in a community that services human needs without counting the cost. A prerequisite of this gender-free future is the destruction of the prevailing sexual division of labor and the neutralization of sexual biology. Ideally this would be accompanied by the elimination of the vocation of motherhood as an exclusive actual or potential dimension of the female persona and the transformation of procreation into a more rationalized process, perhaps ultimately even a sphere of commodity production or whatever the equivalent under public provision or control. If effective (and it is a big if), this would involve more than a complete triumph of the "spirit of capitalism" over the conduct of social life, it would also entail the dissolution of the immemorial female and her substitution by a neutered subject on a preemptive male commodity model. Is there a kind of female masochism in this feminist utopia?

(To be continued)

NOTES

I would like especially to express my gratitude to the insightful empirical scholarship and advice of Heather Joshi and to the steadfast encouragement and critical suggestions of Nikki Keddie. The following also offered valuable comments/criticisms — Ruth Bloch, Regina Morantz-Sanchez, Parminder Bachu, Carrie Menkel-Meadow, Hannah Kully, Ruth Miikman, Linda Gordon, Joan Waugh, Ivan Light, Perry Anderson and Michael Mann. Not all the above would wish to be associated with the fundamental thrust of my argument.

1   Eleanor Rathbone, *The Disinherited Family* (London: Allen and Unwin, 1924), p. X.
2   The nutritional neglect of female infants is the most demographically significant form. Twentieth century research in reproductive epidemiology has repeatedly shown the that the scope for reducing rates of

procreative casualty through the supplementary feeding of pregnant or lactating mothers is minimal.

3   Nicky Hart, "Female Vitality and the History of Human Health," paper presented to Third Congress of the European Society of Medical Sociology, Marburg, October 1990.

4   William Farr, *Vital Statistics: A Memorial Volume of Selections from the Reports and Writings of William Farr*, edited for the Sanitary Institute of Great Britain by Noel Humphreys, with an Introduction by Mervyn Susser and Abraham Adelstein (New Jersey: New York Academy of Medicine Library. History of Medicine Series, No. 46, Metuchen, 1975).

5   Mark N. Cohen, *Health and the Rise of the Civilization* (New Haven: Yale University Press, 1989). See also by same author "Population Pressure at the Origins of Agriculture" in Stephen Polgar (ed.), *Population, Ecology and Social Evolution* (The Hague: Mouton Publishers, 1982).

6   See e.g. Joan Thirsk, ed., *The Agrarian History of England and Wales Volume VI 1750-1850* (Cambridge: Cambridge University Press, 1967), 729-30.

7   Amartya Sen, *Poverty and Famines: An Essay on Entitlement and Deprivation*, (Oxford: Clarendon Press, 1981). See also by same author "More Than 100 Women Are Missing," *New York Review of Books*, December 20, 1990.

8   See G.C.E. Burger, H.R. Sandstead, J.C. Drummond eds. *Malnutrition and Starvation in Western Netherlands Part II* (The Hague: General State Printing Office, 1948), p. 265 and 270-71. See also Nicky Hart, "War, Famine, Fertility and Mortality: Lessons from the Dutch Hunger Winter" (forthcoming).

9   See, e.g., Lawrence Angel, "Health as a Crucial Factor in Changes from Hunting to Developed Farming in the Eastern Mediterranean," in Mark N. Cohen and George J. Armelogos eds., *Paleopathology at the Origins of Agriculture*, (London: Academic Press, 1984). See also Nicky Hart, "Class *and* Gender in the History of Infant Mortality: Recasting the Biological Factors in Reproductive Epidemiology" (forthcoming).

10   Riane Eisler, *The Chalice and the Blade* (San Francisco: Harper and Row, 1988) reconstructs pre-historic European society as a non oppressive partnership between men and women.

11   Hart, "Female Vitality" p. 23

12   Heather Joshi, "The Cost of Caring." in Glendinning and Millar, *Women and Poverty in Britain.* (Brighton: Harvester Press, 1987).

13   Heather Joshi, *Sex, Equality and the State Pension* (London: Birkbeck College Discussion Papers in Economics, 1989).

14   Viviana Zelizer, *The Pricing the Priceless Child* (New York: Basic Books, 1985).

15   Leonore Weitzman, *The Divorce Revolution: The Unexpected Consequences for Women and Children in America* (New York: The Free Press, 1985).

16   Max Weber, *The Theory of Social and Economic Organization* (translated by A.M. Henderson and Talcott Parsons) (London: Collier Macmillan, 1964), p. 184-5.

17   Karl Polanyi, *The Great Transformation: The Political and Economic Origins of Our Time* (Boston: Beacon Press, 1957).

18   Polanyi, *Great Transformation*, 72.

19   Rathbone, *Disinherited Family*, 7-8.

20   Weber, *Economic and Social Organization*, 150.

21   Zelizer, *Pricing*, 21.

22   Rathbone, *Disinherited Family*, 54.

23   Weber, *Social and Economic Organization*, 56-77. See also Herbert Goldhammer and Edward Shils, "Types of Power and Status," *American Journal of Sociology*, XLV, 2 (1939), 171-182.

24   Hannah Gavron, *The Captive Wife* (Harmondsworth: Penguin 1966).

25   A.J. Wrigley and R. Scofield, *The Population History of England 1541-1871: A Reconstruction*, (Cambridge: Cambridge University Press, 1981). See also J.A. Goldstone, "The Demographic Revolution in England: A Re-examination," *Population Studies* 49 (1986), 5-33.

26   Sen, *Poverty and Famines*, Polanyi anticipated Sen's interpretation — see *Great Transformation* 60.

27   Ivy Pinchbeck, *Women Workers and the Industrial Revolution*, (London: Virago Press Ltd., 1981), 313.

PROCREATION: THE SUBSTANCE OF FEMALE OPPRESSION IN MODERN SOCIETY

PART TWO: FEMINISM AND THE SPIRIT OF CAPITALISM

NICKY HART

PROCREATION AND THE FORM AND SUBSTANCE OF SOCIAL REALITY

Procreation is the *substance* of female subordination in the late twentieth century. Substance denotes a sphere of social activity free of the rationalizing forces of market capitalism.[1] In their procreative labor, women continuously regenerate the living material of society. This work is vital but unpaid because capitalist production abstracts livelihood from the substance of social life. In consequence, the average childbearer forfeits opportunities for wage or salary employment which reduce her lifetime earnings and pension prospects to about 50% of their potential.[2] This is the principal cause of women's economic vulnerability and, as the experience of being part of a single parent household increases, it is also the reason why the percentage of children in the poverty population has doubled in recent years.

Greater access to paid employment among mothers of pre-school children offers no complete solution. Infant care *cannot* be confined to the interstices of wage employment. Institutionalized child care during working hours is a highly partial solution and not necessarily attractive or financially feasible, except where the "rewards" of employment are high. Where the option is semi- or unskilled work, we cannot assume that mothers of infants would choose *continuous* wage work except from sheer financial necessity. Even then, out of sight is rarely out of mind: a committed parent cannot give undivided attention or ambition to work abstracted from family duties. This is undoubtedly why most mothers prefer part time work close to home.[3] Equal pay for equal work can only guarantee economic equality to child-free men and women; it does not eradicate the costs of bearing and rearing children.

Why have most social theories failed to conceptualize the social relations of procreation as an axis of inequality? Sociological orthodoxy is imprisoned by the rationalizing logic of capitalism. Conceiving social reality as relations mediated by the institutions of the formal economy, procreation, a "natural" process, was theoretically irrelevant to the great theorists. Part I opposed this restricted vision of social life. The process of stratification in capitalism has a dual structure: the relations of procreation distribute access to the means of generating livelihood; the relations of production shape the distribution of rewards. Life chances are thus stratified by a dual system of entitlement and exploitation. The story of exploitation is well rehearsed in social theory, that of entitlement less so, though elements emerge when Keynesian ideas feature in discourses of class struggle.

Systematic inequalities of class and gender arise out of the interaction of the relations of production and procreation, though orthodox theory privileges the only former as the organizing principle and dynamic of society. As the individuating force of market capitalism crushes and sweeps away the cultural substance of kinship, the stratifying potential of the latter will increasingly be impressed on the sociological imagination.

The search to understand the persistence of gender inequality in industrial democracies highlights in one form the most critical political issue facing the future of humankind. How far can society permit the substance of social life (human beings and the human habitat) to be ravaged by the rationalizing forces of market capitalism? Where are the sources of resistance? How do they find political expression? Can they be galvanized into a coherent movement to challenge the terms of political discourse on the site where human reason finally makes its stand and calls a halt to the destructive logic of industrial capitalism?

Ignorance of the stratifying potential of the social relations of procreation is encouraged by the tendency to mystify human procreation, to see the creation of new life as an autonomous natural sequence or one initiated and managed by divine or supernatural will. The product of the human mind, social theory is always subject to some influence by the personal circumstances and cultural understandings of the author. This was the fate of nineteenth century theories of industrialism as their authors depicted the processes shattering the traditional society they knew by focussing on the future of man- — *not* womankind. The result was a conceptual myopia of the first order. Blind to the links between the form and substance of newly emerging industrial capitalism, Marx and his contemporaries mistook an abstracted process of livelihood for the social whole.

Some versions of contemporary feminism repeated these errors of theoretical judgment seeing only the *formal* image of social reality and thereby adopting male standards of political, economic, and social citizenship. In its conviction that the passageway to liberation was illuminated by the logic of formal rationality, even socialist feminism became the unwitting prophet of the *spirit of capitalism* as the ideal dissolvent of gender. Ironically, this legacy of Engels upholds profit and the protestant work ethic as a new life discipline for an emotionally unruly childbearing population. In elevating the wage worker as the "female elect," much of the feminist intelligentsia came, by default, to discredit the immemorial work of their own sex. Following the lead of classical theory, they abandoned procreation to a pre-social "natural" backwater, accepting that its social relations caused no more than a ripple on the surface of real material life — the production of saleable goods and services.

ANTI-ESSENTIALISM AND CONTEMPORARY FEMINISM

Modern feminism is a *plural* movement with sectarian divisions. Even "movement" is a misnomer, for feminism is more a state of mind than a coherent collectivity with shared beliefs. Thus I differentiate popular feminism as a loose ideology espoused by many contemporary women from the ideas of the feminist intelligentsia engaged in constructing theory and an agenda for emancipation.

Popular feminism entails a commitment to social and economic justice for women in manifold ways, from the natural childbirth movement with its celebration of the mother-child bond through the birth and suckling experience to the claim that mothers in the military who have signed up to kill and be killed should not be exempt from combat at the risk of orphaning their kids. This broad spectrum has room for a diversity of ideas, and agendas for change abound.

My critique is focussed on the academic discourse of postwar feminism and its primary fault line demarcating the boundary between conviction and uncertainty that gender is socially constructed and *not* determined by sexual biology. Feminists disloyal to the anti-essentialist creed are a diverse collection of agnostics and fundamentalists, among whom the latter perceive sex as an irresolvable source of *social* antagonism. I argue that anti-essentialism is unnecessary to a progressive feminism and that an emphatic commitment to the absence of essential difference is itself a sign of analytic weakness and over-dependence on conventional masculinist wisdom. It is also linked to a regressive version of the claim to social equality and therefore ineffective, even counterproductive, as the foundation of a practical strategy for improving the material position of the childbearing sex.

On the question of whether sexual difference carries *inevitable* social consequences, I am an agnostic. I use *"childbearing sex"* as no mere description but as an analytical term to underline a formidable and empirically verifiable *essential* difference between the sexes. Women possess the physiological equipment to replenish the human substance of society. I do not know how far this impinges on the average woman's motivation to enter the traditional male domains of occupational life. I do know that it severely interferes with their ability to do so on the same terms as non-childbearers. The transformation of the occupational structures of advanced industrial societies has reduced occupational gender differences linked to physiological differences of, e.g., muscularity. Even before the explosion of tertiary sector jobs, women had demonstrated the capacity to substitute for men when needed in heavy industrial work. The issue is not whether women are capable of performing men's work, but whether most want to do so as a priority.

Sex differences of occupational aptitude are irrelevant to the claim for social equality; if they exist, they have no necessary bearing on the distribution of social, political, moral, and economic worth. Thus, to understand in order to struggle to correct *structured* social inequality, it makes no difference whether men and women are essentially the same or different. What matters is the *social arrangements* that give form and meaning to oppressive hierarchies. A truly progressive feminism must root out the *structural* causes of women's social inferiority, not seek to erase femininity in order that women may compete in an otherwise antagonistic environment. The crucial problem for the economic emancipation of *all* women is to change the environment not the woman — this cannot be achieved without raising the economic and social value of work traditionally associated with women. The identification of entry to male occupational domains on male terms as liberation legitimizes the idea that women's unpaid work is intrinsically worthless and unnecessary.

I exempt from the critique that follows academic feminist work which does not raise anti-essentialist sentiment to an organizing theoretical principle. This excludes versions of Marxist and radical feminism which give some causal primacy to sexuality and/or procreativity. I confess admiration for and disappointment with radical feminism, which broke free of masculinist dependency only to develop theories which fail to distinguish biology and social structure. The economic subordination of women is a feature of *social organization*; it is not an inevitable product of sexual physiology. Sexual difference is not an irretrievable barrier to the establishment of social organization built on mutual tolerance and interdependency.

This demarcates my approach from both essentialism and antiessentialism. Both are united by the mistaken inference that if essential differences exist, this must constitute the very stuff of gender inequality and therefore nothing can change. This underlies Lynn Segal's recent critique of radical feminism.[4] The argument is a non-sequitur. Essential difference need not be associated with power and subordination nor does it necessarily imply a static relationship between the sexes. The industrial era has witnessed revolutionary change in the social meaning of male and female physiology as factors of social organization. The same era proves that the persistence of a division of labor built upon sexual physiology has not prevented a massive improvement in women's legal and political rights and invalidates the belief that inequality is inevitable if sex and gender are related. To maintain clarity I employ the term *anti-essentialist feminism* as the target of my critique.

ANTI-ESSENTIALIST FEMINISM AND THE CLAIM
TO SOCIAL EQUALITY

Anti-essentialist feminism is more than an academic theory; it is an ethical creed for the ideal female. Here liberal and socialist feminism finds common ground in the conviction that wage (or preferably) salaried employment is *the* fundamental condition of female liberation with pro-creation recast as a unisex and quasi-leisure activity of private life. This ideal fuels the theoretical imagination in tautological fashion. If salvation can be had in the labor market, the source of female oppression must be obstacles to equal access to wage employment. Emphasis on dual labor markets, occupational segregation, the wage gap, and the documentation of patriarchy in the workplace in feminist analyses of *economic inequality* between the sexes bears testimony to the belief that the solution to the woman question will be found where Engels predicted, on the social terrain where *real* work is performed and paid for.[5]

This vision is confined by the belief that freedom involves further extensions of formal rationality over women's lives; with the *Spirit of Capitalism* invading the female psyche and eclipsing the private space for social action borne out of love and kinship. The purpose of the anti-essentialist creed is immediately obvious. If gender is artificial there is no rationale for discrimination in employment — male and female become socially interchangeable units rationalized and ready for the capitalist process. This is the simplest means of erecting a liberal claim to sexual equality — equality on the grounds of fundamental similarity.

The alternative claim to social equality — that human beings are not identical but that difference is not a legitimate basis of *social* valuation is more difficult to construct and harder to implement. This principle argues that a society resting on the claim of *structured* social equality, if it is to make good on its own ideological claims, must devise means to share power and resources equally among *all* citizens. The principle of equality despite difference carries particular implications for inequality arising out of sexual physiology. If the irrefutable *essential* difference between the childbearing and the non-childbearing sex is *systematically* connected to the distribution of social worth and economic reward, then we have a prima facie case for indicting the society for failing to uphold the legal, and in the USA, constitutional, principle of equal treatment.

I stress *systematically* to emphasize the institutional foundation of gender inequality. Economic and political inequalities are the property of social organization — of norms and institutions — they are not eternally given in the substance of human beings. Inequalities between men and women in modern America are *systematically replicated* because they are built into social structure. Their removal requires more than a superficial remodel of "social actors"; it requires *restructuring*.

The two claims to equality are logically linked to two strategies of social mobility. Equality on grounds of *no essential difference* seeks a route to social mobility via a structure of equal opportunity to the entitlement system of market capitalism. Impediments in the path of individuals, e.g., patriarchal gender attitudes, must be eliminated to ensure equal access to sexually undifferentiated *individuals*. Differences of occupational merit can then be fairly sifted and hierarchically ordered by the market through processes of recruitment, promotion, and differential reward. If gender is dissolved, sexual division should not be a feature in the occupational class structure that emerges from the labor market.

This version of the claim to social equality legitimizes class privilege through the demonstration of meritocracy. It accepts the validity of competitive hierarchy provided the opportunity structure is free of discriminatory practices. It is based on the concepts of an undifferentiated humanity and an unencumbered individual who can transcend the absence of financial and cultural capital in his or her formation.

The equality despite difference claim to social justice requires a transformative approach to social hierarchy — *"From each according to his capacity, to each according to his need."*[6] Difference is acknowledged in the goal of creating a cooperative society tolerant of difference and ordered by a model of economic and political citizenship, not market competition. Upward mobility in this claim to equality is collective, not individual, entire group promotion rather than escape hatches for the "talented." This involves more than tinkering with promotion channels in a hierarchical social structure; it requires new structural mechanisms of defining social worth and meeting needs. The masculinist counterparts of the two appeals to equality are, respectively, liberalism and socialism.

THE MYSTIQUE OF PROCREATION IN
ANTI-ESSENTIALIST FEMINIST DISCOURSE

The mystique of procreation is pervasive in anti-essentialist writings as manifested in the failure to credit the significance of procreative work for women themselves, to devalue its importance for society at large, to trivialize the barriers to the continuous participation of mothers in wage employment:

> If we choose to regard these events as 'biological liabilities' of the female condition, then we have to ask how we weigh up their social implications. . . . Is a planned pregnancy for a thirty five year old woman more or less disruptive to her working life than an unplanned heart attack for a man of the same age? Is eighteen months of lactation more or less restrictive than a bout of chronic ulcerative colitis?[7]

These sentiments capture the anti-essentialist mood perfectly. In Michele Barrett's view, the creation of new life need carry no more significance for women's authentic experience and identity than a bout of ulcerative colitis. If we accept this, we may also believe that collective facilities for 24 hour infant care are a realistic and effective means to extinguish maternal responsibility, that reducing the age of entry to the public sphere to the first birthday might be a desirable goal for the mass of unliberated women.

There is no evidence that most women share this vision of what having children means. In an increasingly bureaucratized world, procreation remains among the last forms of social action initiated for purely non-utilitarian motives. Why do women do it? In anti-essentialist constructions, mothers often appear by default as victims or cultural dupes conceiving children either at the behest of a conjugal patriarch or mindlessly to serve the interests of capitalist class or pronatalist state.[8] Is this credible? Is it not more likely that modern women choose to bear children out of the desire to exercise their human capacities to the full? Moreover, most do so in full knowledge and possession of contraception, which they use to space and limit births. For the most part, modern childbirth is neither accidental nor forced. If a woman in the US today wants a child-free life career, the procreative imperative does not stand in her way. Even so, the majority elect to bear two children.

This demographic reality lies at the heart of the woman question today and must be confronted in any plausible theory of gender inequality. It raises two important questions. The first, addressed in Part I, concerns the material nature of procreation: how substantial is the effort required to maintain the flow of population? The second involves the significance of procreative biology in the female identity: how important is the connected sequence of conception, gestation, childbirth, and infant nurturance among the valued and purposeful experiences in the average female lifetime? Can childbirth be easily divided from the motivation to nurture the newcomer, to be part of, and to witness the achievement, of their full physical and intellectual potential? Why would a woman undergo the physiological discomforts of pregnancy and parturition only to produce clients for institutional care? Finally, can the empirical evidence that most women still choose to become mothers and to invest the creation of new life with significance for their social identities be written off as irrelevant in constructing causal theories of gender inequality?

These questions are excluded from the discourse of anti-essentialist feminism because procreation is virtually a taboo in theories dedicated to demonstrating the mutual autonomy of sex and gender. The fear of biological essentialism paralyzes contemporary feminism, as Michele Barrett's words once again reveal:

> Although it is important for feminist analysis to locate the question of biological difference, the slide into biological reductionism is an extremely dangerous one. It is regressive in that one of the early triumphs of cross cultural feminist work — the establishment of distinction between sex as a biological category and gender as a social one — is itself threatened by an emphasis on the causal role of procreative biology in the construction of male domination. . . . In practice too, such an analysis may lead to a feminist glorification of supposedly female capacities and principles and a reassertion of separate spheres for women and men.[9]

Serious analysis of the social relations of procreation is the casualty of this posture because it underlines the correspondence between sex and gender, an association passionately denied by many contemporary feminists.[10] So orthodox is the denial that essentialist positions have taken on the mantle of the radical. For the majority, procreation is too close to a crude notion of nature to be theorized for what it is. To recognize that societal survival depends on the distinctive biological characteristics of the female body and that this gives rise to structured relations which underpin the subordination of women is to risk falling into the murky waters of biological essentialism. The flaw in this reasoning is the failure to distinguish *gender* from *gender inequality*. Structured *inequality* is socially constructed whether or not it is biologically based. Lack of essential difference is neither a prerequisite of a sexually egalitarian society, nor does it guarantee equality.

Anti-essentialism is a major stumbling block in the development of a truly liberated feminist imagination. In the present state of technology, there is no denial that procreation requires a female body. But because theoretical recognition of the biological capacities of the female body as an instrument of human labor draws a direct link between sexual physiology and the female social identity, anti-essentialism is forced to redefine childbearing as a limited biological function easily severed from the total process of making a new social being. Beyond the discrete process of expelling the fetus, anti-essentialism recognizes no further barriers to the reincorporation of the new mother in wage employment. With procreation fractured and childbearing despatched as a medical episode, child rearing becomes a non-sex specific activity, and therefore, a non-feminist issue. This unreal vision of procreation, reshaped according to alienated and bureaucratized principles, lies at the heart of the anti-essentialist recipe for female liberation. It is exactly the scenario that Sheila Kitzinger, a leading spokesperson for natural childbirth feminism struggles to resist:

> I would not suggest that one should approach childbirth on the wings of a pseudo-mysticism which might collapse at the crucial moment, nevertheless to anyone who thinks about it long enough, birth cannot simply be a matter of techniques for getting a baby out of one's body. It involves one's relationship to life as a whole, the part one plays in the order of things; and as the baby develops and can be felt moving inside, to some women, annunciation and incarnation, seem to become facts of their own existence.[11]

This representation of childbirth as a labor of love — spiritual, sensuous and life-affirming — must be anathema to those convinced of the lack of essential difference between the sexes. This is why, with the exception of writers like Adrienne Rich, feminists are rather tight-lipped regarding natural childbirth, a decidedly female movement intent on challenging the forces of formal rationality, bureaucracy, and the medicalized commodity of the creation of life.[12] The possibility that a new mother might freely allocate her time according to non-utilitarian motives does not fit with anti-essentialist visions of a brave new future with its male production bias. To deny its immense potential significance in the emergent adult female identity, the experience of becoming and being a mother is typically portrayed as even *less fulfilling, less creative, less responsible* than even the most exploited forms of wage employment:

> At present, reproduction in our society is a sad mimicry of production. Work in a capitalist society is an alienation of labor in the making of a social product which is confiscated by capital. But it can still sometimes be a real act of creation, purposive, and responsible, even in conditions of the worst exploitation. Maternity is often a caricature of this. The biological product, the child, is treated as if it were a solid product. Parenthood becomes a kind of substitute for work, an activity in which the child is seen as an object created by the mother in the same way as a commodity is created by a worker. Naturally the child does not literally escape but the mother's alienation can be much worse than the worker whose product is appropriated by the boss. No human being can create another human being. A person's biological origin is an abstraction.[13]

These inferences are empirically unsubstantiated. If they were not, they could neither cast the creation of new life as an autonomous biological process, nor conclude that "fit and virtuous" people could emerge in the absence of committed and careful parental care. The devaluation of motherhood in Juliet Mitchell's above version of the mystique of procreation represents a failure to credit, perhaps even an ignorance of, the contribution of women to the rise of modern life expectancy. The extension of the average lifetime from four to almost eight decades is the clearest indicator of material progress in the capitalist era. It is mostly the result of sharp declines in infant and child mortality recorded only from the very end of the nineteenth century. Why did twentieth century, and, in particular, working class, children, become so much healthier than their predecessors?[14] Many factors contributed, among them the development of a protected and closely supervised childhood with the emergence of the child's alter ego — the specialized parent.[15] Resourceful parenting (in practice, mothering) remains a major ingredient of infant and child vitality, a profound *source* of social and health inequality and an important factor transmitting privilege and underprivilege between the generations. Only a theory abstracted from empirical evidence can dismiss the contribution of twentieth-century mothers to the revolution in human vitality and denounce their role as merely an ideological ploy to entrench the patriarchal privileges of male breadwinners.

Devaluation of the mother reappears in representations of housewives as parasitic and unnecessary. It is widespread in accounts which exaggerate the extent of pre-industrial occupational equality in order that the modern mother may be held up as an artefact of twentieth century patriarchy.[16] Housework, with procreation submerged, is an unnecessary elaboration designed to keep women at home and preserve the male monopoly of wage employment — real work. The Philippe Aries's thesis that the concept of childhood is a post-enlightenment phenomenon is offered as proof of the artificiality of the maternal instinct and bolstered by claims that pre-industrial children were not children at all, but rather miniature adult servants who earned their keep.[17] The high infant and child mortality of the pre-industrial era (with the wastage of maternal effort and resources it manifestly entailed) is left off the balance sheet of the sexual division of pre-industrial labor. Even materialist feminists discount the health consequences of closely spaced pregnancies and the mortal risks of self inflicted abortion for the health and vitality of pre-modern women and their capacity to contribute in "real" material life.

The denial of women's domiciliary contribution to material progress in the twentieth century is the result of the glorification of production as the only worthwhile form of human praxis. For Marxist and socialist feminism it leads to some notable contradictions. The advocacy of uninterrupted wage employment as *the* pathway to female emancipation challenges Marx's theory that commodity labor is a denial of species being, an alienation of the individual from the essentially human capacity to exercise mental creativity in work. From this perspective, the evidence of writers loyal to historical materialism, willing the fracture and abstraction of human creation to liberate women as commodity producers is more than a trifle ironic. If the division of labor and the expropriation of the inanimate commodity from the worker represents alienation, how much more so the abstraction of childbearing from the total process of nurturing the development of a new human being.

The feminist version of the mystique of procreation is profoundly insulting to the twentieth-century mother and dismissive of her achievements. In producing a feminism which patronizes ordinary women: caricaturing their role, devaluing their work, challenging their intelligence as active decision makers, it is theoretically misguided and politically divisive. Surely it is up to feminism to question, not condone, the masculine evaluation of women's worth. What most women need is economic resources, economic recognition and economic power in respect of their maternal responsibilities. It is only against a background of economic parity between the sexes that valid sociological investigation of the meaning and rewards of parenting as work can be carried out.

In glossing the *meaning* of the reality of what most women actually do in their lives, anti-essentialism misses a series of critical questions about the human condition in capitalist civilization and female resistance to the motor of capitalist rationality. Why do women willingly allow emotional commitments to their children to override the wage earning instinct? Why do they remain only semi-conscious that "time is money?" Why do they resist the appeal of the labor market as *the* universal site for the search for authentic self? Only Freudo-feminists seriously ask why women sacrifice economic self-interest to make children.

PSYCHOANALYTIC FEMINISM AND
ANTI-ESSENTIALIST FALLACY

Gynocentric Freudo-feminism isolates maternal *motivation and behavior* as the cause of women's captivity in the private sphere of family life.[18] Exemplified in Nancy Chodorow's work, this approach accepts the social relations of procreation as the cause of women's *social* inferiority and pinpoints the mothering psyche as the mechanism perpetuating gender inequality. Chodorow shows less allegiance to Freud than to Winnicott. She depicts the scope of personality development as the opportunity to differentiate infant self from other.[19] Women mother because they were themselves mothered by a same sex parent and deprived of an early opportunity to *objectify* ego boundaries. Conversely, males do not develop a maternal psyche because they were mothered by a different sex parent against whom they could identify themselves as an autonomous person. Chodorow narrowly escapes essentialism — mothering is neither an inborn trait nor a socially learned behavior; it is more an anachronistic predisposition born out of the sexual dynamics of the mother-child relation.

While sexual physiology seems to carry some causal weight in the formation of the "handicapped" female psyche, the approach is firmly anti-essentialist. This is revealed in the solution proposed to overcome female social inferiority — Chodorow's call for the destruction of the sexual division of labor is intended to transform motherhood, as far as is feasible, into sexless parenthood (she assumes two parents on hand and willing to share the work). Her analysis, motivated and shaped by the anti-essentialist perception of the *ideal* female, is driven by the search to uncover the cause of the propensity to mother in order to prove it artificial and therefore remediable.

Gynocentric feminism conceptualizes the social relations of procreation in modern capitalism as a problem of psyche, not economy. The primary aim is to liberate women from overidentification with child rearing, not to raise the social status and economic rewards of domiciliary work. The emphasis on equal parenting flows from the recognition of the economically underprivileged and socially despised nature of the work to be shared. Like other anti-essentialists keen to dissolve maternity as a distinctive feature of the female persona, the gynocentric school recognizes the danger of advocating a substantial economic rehabilitation of mothering — this might discourage women from disowning childrearing as a valued sphere of female *social* action.

Women who look after other people's children are among the most exploited in modern society. If the value of this work were recognized and paid for at realistic levels, most mothers of pre-school children would have little financial incentive to work for wages full time. Let us be clear about the choice. Modern motherhood is not a full-time, five decade tour of duty. It is a single phase of a diversified life career interspersed with other identities and activities. The issue is, how should it be defined, valued, managed? If a substantial redistribution of income to the childrearing population could be achieved, how would the mass of ordinary women react? My guess is that a substantial number would take a welcome respite from full-time wage earning by paying themselves, not someone else, to look after their own infants. In two parent families, the "appointed mother" could well be male, but the trend in single parenthood indicates that the main beneficiaries of any change would be overwhelmingly female. In circumstances of financial parity, we must ask whether the conventional sexual division of labor matters. Indeed, if procreative labor were properly rewarded, who is to say that the proverbial sisters would want to share with men? And why should they? After centuries of performing the work with no social or economic thanks, why, when its vital nature is finally validated, should they willingly open the door to male, or for that matter, professional female, competition? Certainly a substantial financial upgrade in the rewards for procreative work offers the surest strategy for dissolving the traditional sexual division of labor and persuading the average male to look upon child care as an "enriching" occupational experience. The goal of Freudo-feminism — restructuring the male psyche — is much more likely to be accomplished through financial rehabilitation of the labor of mothering rather through mere exhortation to anti-essentialist principles.

IN SEARCH OF AN ADEQUATE FEMINIST CONCEPT OF REPRODUCTIVE RIGHTS

The social goals of anti-essentialist feminism require only minimal political effort because the social forces of capitalist rationality are on the same ideological side. The market will eventually produce the "female elect"; it will erode non-monetary motivation and bring the principles of commerce into every sphere of human existence. Meanwhile, feminism can act out a seemingly progressive politics in the struggle to defend and extend women's *reproductive rights*.

The concept of *reproductive rights* associated with the anti-essentialist claim to equality is actually a code for neutralizing female biology — women's liberation entails liberation from the female body and the effects of its procreative capacity. This leads to a minimalist definition of reproductive rights involving little more than free access to the means of preventing conception or birth at full term plus the unelaborated *childcare*.

In the USA, *reproductive rights* usually means the defence of abortion legalistically defined as the protection of the right to *privacy*. A widely-read feminist history of the struggle for birth control in America, *Woman's Body, Woman's Right*, captures the sentiment of private property in this individualist concept of reproductive rights — since the site of procreation is female personal property, the decision to initiate or terminate fetal life must rest with the owner.[20] This enshrines a view of procreation as a private activity which sits awkwardly with the associated demand that childcare should be a public responsibility.

The "New Feminists" who sustained the political struggle for women's rights in inter-war Britain offered an alternative and broader vision of reproductive rights. Their intellectual inspiration was Eleanor Rathbone whose analytic tour de force *The Disinherited Family* represented a decisive break with, and critique of, masculinist political economy.[21] Rathbone theorized procreation as dignified human labor, vital to society yet the source of female social inferiority. She called for public recognition and economic rewards for childbearing and child rearing. Almost alone among twentieth-century feminists, Rathbone is a role model of intellectual ingenuity *and* unswerving political activism. Unlike most contemporary career feminists on Women's Studies faculties, Rathbone was no conference theorist. She theorized the necessity for eradicating the cultural norm of the male breadwinner and spent much of her life establishing the political apparatus to achieve her beliefs. Yet, with few exceptions, her extraordinarily gifted intellectual work and political achievements rarely appear in feminist discourse; she is not identified among the founders of feminism, and her theoretical work is specifically excluded from the corpus of feminist knowledge transmitted in modern universities.[22]

Rathbone's concept of reproductive rights was marked by empathy with the motivation and consciousness of the average woman. She understood the material conditions of women whose daily routines involve the living and organizing of not one but up to three or more lives — their own and their offspring's. What concept of reproductive rights would serve the material interests of this average woman and thereby bring her procreative labor to a rewarding conclusion? At the minimum, the public resources to ensure that each new human being she brings into the world will have the opportunity to develop to the optimum of their physical and intellectual potential. Reproductive rights for primary parents, who are overwhelmingly female and who will still be so for the foreseeable future, must be broadly cast, encompassing public investment in facilities for children: education, health care, and income maintenance alongside a redistribution of income to those who rear future generations. Surely these must be the authentic feminist political issues for the coming century.

That a more restricted interpretation of reproductive rights dominates modern feminism is revealed in how much easier it is to raise consciousness and mobilize feminist action over access to abortion (*the* modern feminist issue) than over the lack of primary medical care for US children, reckoned currently at up to one quarter of the child population. It is conspicuous that the very term reproductive rights stresses the control of procreativity with very occasional forays against involuntary sterilization but *not* financial redistribution to underwrite the financial costs of childbearing and childrearing — the twenty four hour a day, twenty four years per child responsibility. The gap reflects the distance between a view of procreation as a biological liability versus a socially vital and potentially creative female experience.

Contraception is of fundamental importance to the gains women have made in the twentieth century. But the contraceptive revolution did not eliminate motherhood or the desire to experience it for the majority of women. A minimalist concept of reproductive rights must alienate the mass of women for whom the creation of new life holds a greater significance than orthodox feminism allows. Any movement which claims the right to speak for women as a whole must respect the potentiality that what women do in their lives reflects their active choice, that engagement with motherhood arises out of authentic desires, that it still offers more fulfillment than unbroken service as a sales assistant in a department store.

POLITICS AND THE REPRESENTATION OF WOMEN'S INTERESTS

For all the greater equalization of education, occupational training and access to jobs, women are still primarily responsible for creating and maintaining the next generation. Greater access to wage employment has produced more work and less free time, with no improvement in economic well-being or political power.[23] Moreover, current trends in single parenthood in the US suggest that the economic position of the childbearing sex and their offspring could get worse in the decades ahead if government fails to address the problem. The well-being of US children in the twenty-first century is inextricably tied to the economic status of their mothers; it ought to be the leading issue in any progressive politics which seeks to represent the interests of women.

Current trends cannot be understood as the outcome of class inequality as the term is conventionally employed. Indeed, the contemporary experience of women and children in a highly developed market society like the US brings the conceptual limitations of class theory into sharp relief. Class was developed to comprehend the exploitive dimensions of industrial capitalism for wage-employed men. The same conceptual language ignores a fundamental and dialectical feature of capitalism, that it constitutes both a system of entitlement and exploitation.

The entitlement system of capitalism privileges the unencumbered individual; it systematically discriminates against people with kinship commitments and obligations. This is not new; even in the heyday of the male breadwinner, economic well-being was always crucially a function of marital status and family size rather than the volume of surplus value extracted from the worker. The anti-social character of capitalism cannot be understood through its own abstract operations. It is rooted in the gap between the *form* of the capitalist economy and the needs of the human *substance* of social life. The immediate casualties of capitalism are the un- or partially incorporated, not fully fledged wage-employed citizens. And let no one delude themselves that those with unrestricted access to wage employment opportunities are likely candidates to lead a social and economic revolution in the interests of all or to reveal the fundamental crises for human existence spawned by capitalist civilization at the turn of the twenty-first century.

Women's claim for economic and social justice cannot be confined to reforms of the labor market. Procreation is too substantial to be an after work activity. As much as anyone, the female intelligentsia is guilty of maintaining the mystique of procreation. In the scramble to prove that men and women are essentially the same, the burden of procreative work is ignored, minimized, and devalued. This is the fatal fallacy of anti-essentialist feminism — the inability to see that the childbearing sex will never achieve social and economic parity while the work of creating and caring for new human beings remains discredited, devalued, and deprived of legitimate resources. Women are not the same as men. Only they possess the capacity to regenerate the species and as long as this is true, the social relations of procreation will be a formidable source of economic and social cleavage.

I do not underestimate the significance of racial discrimination and class inequality in worsening the plight of the second sex; but the gender component of social inequality merits theoretical analysis on its own terms. I believe that women of all races and colors have more to gain from united action than by making political demands through segmented ethnic or racial movements. A female civil rights movement to demand economic redistribution for women's procreative labor is the best hope to enhance the position of women in the twenty-first century. It also the means of revitalizing and humanizing the discourse of democratic politics.

The case can be made on the grounds of social justice and the *distinctive* character of women's citizenship rights. It can also be argued that the present system no longer works. In early industrialization, the bonds of kinship were seen as a sufficient means of articulating the economic needs of the family within the capitalist market through the male breadwinner. This system had evident shortcomings emphasized by a number of writers. Today, the male breadwinner system no longer gives even the semblance of being workable. After decades of exposure to the individuating forces of market society, industrial workers of all ages increasingly fail to recognize the kinship obligations which previously circulated at least some part of the wage from earners to non-earners. Children no longer expect to support their parents and a surprising number of fathers feel no imperative to support their dependent children. The feminization of poverty is the visible effect. The time to devise policies for broadening the definitions of entitlement to a share in the fruits of social production has long since arrived.

Procreative labor, in other words, responsible loving parenthood, is vital for society and needs to be validated with appropriate economic rewards and related compensations. To install this as a political belief requires a change of consciousness in the voting public and especially its female component.[24] Women must revalue their contribution to social life so long disguised by a vision of work imprisoned in the discourse of formal rationality. They must organize collectively to demand economic justice and a fair share of national income for themselves and the next generation. Against these goals, the removal of barriers restricting the access of the qualified child-free female candidates to high, medium, or low status employment are chicken feed.

What is the most appropriate way to redistribute income to the childbearing population? I have space for only a few suggestions. Federal and state governments already recognize the basic needs of households. Every year up to $100 billion is redistributed through indiscriminate mortgage interest relief, a policy that does more to gratify the domiciliary ambitions of the middle and upper classes than to satisfy the basic housing needs of low income families. This represents a sizeable pool of revenue for alternative social uses. At the very least, a more politically defensible policy could allocate mortgage relief by size of household, or even by the

ratio of wage earners to dependent children or retired adults. Persuading
the electorate of the justice of such a reallocation would clearly be a
delicate matter but should not deter those committed to greater economic
equality between the sexes from opening a political debate on the means
of financing a redistribution of income to households with dependent
children.[25]

There is more scope for manipulating tax revenue as an instrument
of social policy. The current practice of allowing family households to file
an exemption for every child is a *relatively* regressive mechanism of
redistribution because it benefits only taxpayers and especially high earners. Also, in channeling the benefit disproportionately through the male
breadwinner's hands, tax exemptions do more to validate fatherhood than
motherhood. In part, these limitations are recognized by politicians who
have recently advocated tax credits of up to $1000 for every child to
equalize and uprate the value of public funds redistributed to households
with children.

Such transfers offer one means of upholding the living standards
of family households; but to take account of the full financial costs of
parenthood, bolder initiatives must be considered. Why not a lifetime tax
exemption designed to compensate the opportunity costs of bearing and
rearing children? Such a tax benefit could be invoked at any time in
woman's wage working career (after childbirth) or made transferable to a
male parent who shoulders the direct responsibility for a child's upbring-
ing. Allied to other incentives aimed at encouraging opportunities for
part-time work (e.g. national health insurance to relieve employers of the
responsibility for financing medical care) plus increased public investment
in facilities and services for children, tax policy can play an effective role
in redistributing resources to the predominantly female population responsible for overseeing the growth and development of the next generation.
But this is not a sufficient means of guaranteeing the economic security of
the childbearing population. To the extent that procreative work is incompatible with continuous wage employment, other policy instruments are
necessary to underwrite the economic autonomy of the primary parent.
Universal allowances paid direct with no means test are probably the most
effective and equitable means to secure the objectives of cultural reform
elaborated in this paper.[26] They redistribute income from non-childbearing
to childbearing units in the population at the time of greatest need and they
serve simultaneously as a means of cultural validation for society's most
vital work. Non-means tested, they do not discourage wage employment

and once installed, they serve as an object of political struggle, a vehicle to engage the political consciousness and action of women.

The retreat from anti-essentialism offers further advantages to the development of a progressive feminist politics. A telling statement of feminism's problems to date has been the failure to mount an effective challenge to the male domination of national politics. The tiny representation of women in national legislatures outside of Scandinavia must surely be the product of deep structural obstacles which conventional feminist wisdom has failed to uncover. If men and women are essentially different and if this difference carries substantial economic and social implications, it follows that a system of political representation which is overwhelmingly dominated by men will never represent the interests of the childbearing population. To secure the economic and political reforms necessary to create a social foundation for sexual equality, feminists must consider whether it is necessary to mount a political campaign to secure equal representation of men and women in national legislatures and to require political parties to offer the electorate equal numbers of male and female candidates for political office.

The articulation of distinctive citizenship rights for women on the basis of their vital contribution to social life and the opportunity costs entailed has never been made in the US.[27] The majority of the feminist intelligentsia has upheld a model citizenship tailored for men and has consequently demanded the social and political conditions which would allow women to achieve equality on men's terms. The consequences have been negative for nearly all but an elite of professional women. Working mothers labor for longer hours at their two roles, aid to unsupported mothers and children remains tainted by the stigma of charity, female presence in the corridors of power continues to be negligible, and the legitimate economic interests of the childbearing sex and their offspring are virtually absent from political discourse. There is no evidence that the wage employment route out of the private sphere engenders political action on the part of women. The idea that class is *the* basis of political consciousness and that incorporating women into classes would be a means of their mobilization has not born fruit. Wage-employed single mothers are the most exploited section of the community and there is no political or theoretical voice to represent their *distinctive* claims as citizens. My guess is that the absence of women from political leadership reflects the absence of the claim that their truly "vital" contribution to social life is a serious economic and political issue. In other words, it reflects the continuing

mystique of human procreation, the belief that children arrive spontaneously at very little cost to the direct producer. It is only when the extreme
falsity of this idea is recognised, and political action to redress its consequences achieved, that we may truly envisage the social emancipation of
women.

NOTES

1   See Part I. My approach draws on the insights of Karl Polanyi, *The
Great Transformation: Political and Economic Origins of Our Time* (Bos-
ton: Beacon Press, 1957) and Eleanor Rathbone, *The Disinherited Family*
(Bristol: Falling Wall Press, 1986)

2   Based on the British cohort born in 1946. See Part I for references.

3   Sweden is a valid context for examining the employment preferences of mothers. With a small wage gap, income redistribution to households with children and exemplary public provision of childcare, Swedish
mothers record the highest levels of part-time work in the OECD.

4   Lynn Segal, *Is the Future Female?* (London: Virago, 1989).

5   The *uniqueness* of Joshi's approach (see part I), which isolates the
economic significance of mothering suggests a general reluctance to
conceive the problem in this way.

6   Karl Marx, *Critique of the Gotha Programme* (New York: 1933).

7   Michele Barrett, *Women's Oppression Today: Problems of Marxist
Feminist Analysis* (London: Verso, 1980), 75.

8   Harold Garfinkel, *Studies in Ethnomethodology* (New Jersey:
Prentice Hall, 1967), p. 68.

9   Barrett, *Women's Oppression*, p. 13.

10   See the response to Alice Rossi, "A Biosocial Perspective on
Parenting," *Daedalus* 106 (1977) 2, 1-31; Harriet Engel Gross et al.,
"Considering 'A Biosocial Perspective on Parenting,' *Signs* 4 (1979) 4,
695-717.

11   Sheila Kitzinger, *The Experience of Childbirth* (Harmondsworth:
Penguin, 1962),15.

12   See Adrienne Rich, *Of Woman Born: Motherhood as Experience
and Institution* (New York: W.W. Norton, 1976).

13   Juliet Mitchell, *Women: The Longest Revolution* (London: Virago 1984), 33.

14   In the words of new feminist Maude Royden (circa 1919): "A woman who bore a child, or many children, ran a household, and brought up a family fit and virtuous, was still only an arrested man and a perpetual minor, but a woman who can clip tickets in a tramcar is recognised at once as a superwoman - in other words, a man." Quoted (p.51) by Suzy Fleming in her edited introduction to the 1986 edition of *The Disinherited Family*.

15   Working class infants shared in the spectacular twentieth century gain in life expectancy. They did so, in no small measure, through the resourceful efforts of their mothers who, by every empirical indicator, restriced their own diet to feed their children. See Nicky Hart, "Gender and the Rise and Fall of Class Politics," *New Left Review* 175 (1989), 19-47. I address the social and economic causes of modern rise of life expectancy in *Life Chances and Longevity* (London: Macmillan, forthcoming).

16   See Harriet Bradley, *Men's Work, Women's Work* (Minneapolis: University of Minnesota Press, 1989) 33-42.

17   Ann Oakley, *Housewife* (Harmondsworth: Penguin, 1976), 26-27. For the Aries thesis, see Philippe Aries, *Centuries of Childhood* (London: Jonathan Cape Ltd., 1962).

18   Miriam Johnson, *Strong Mother, Weak Wives* (Berkeley: California University Press, 1988), makes the apt distinction between "gynocentric" and "phallocentric" approaches within psychoanalytic feminism.

19   Nancy Chodorow, *The Reproduction of Mothering: Psychoanalysis and the Sociology of Gender* (Berkeley: University of California Press, 1978). See also David Winnicott, *Playing and Reality* (New York: Basic Books, 1978).

20   Linda Gordon, *Women's Body, Women's Right: A Social History of Birth Control* (New York: Grossman Publishers, 1976).

21   See Suzy Fleming's introduction to the new edition of Rathbone's *Disinherited Family* for a discussion of New Feminism.

22   See, e.g., Sheila Rowbotham, *Hidden From History* (London: Pluto Press, 1973).

23   See Victor Fuchs, *Women's Quest for Economic Equality* (Cambridge: Harvard University Press, 1988).

24   The success of the elderly as a political lobby is evidence of the potential power of a constituency in the private sphere· A mere 11% of the US population, they comprise a third of the active electorate. Over the last

few decades their political activism has helped to secure a substantial redistribution of income from the youngest to the oldest members of the community.

25   Tax credits are fixed sums deducted from the sum of tax payable, unlike tax exemptions which are deducted from taxable income. The "Gore-Downey" proposal (see, e.g. "Papa's little deduction". *Newsweek* June 17th 1991 p.47) would convert the current tax exemption into a tax credit of $800 for each child. A commission headed by Sen. John D. Rockefeller has proposed a more generous credit of $1000 per child to be paid to parents irrespective of their employment and tax status. (see *Los Angeles Times*, June 23 and 25, 1991).

26   Fuchs, *Women's Quest* links several indicators of malaise in the US child population to women's increased labor force participation and endorses European family allowances as one means of redress. See also Mary Ann Mason, *The Equality Trap* (New York: Shuster and Simon, 1988).

27   Silvia Hewlett, *A Lesser Life* (New York: Warner Books, 1987), concludes that the position of most women (in her perspective, the pre-dominantly middle income strata of the US population) has deteriorated during the feminist era. She finds US welfare policy (compared to Europe) hostile to women and accuses feminism of failing to represent women's real needs and interests. See also, by the same author, *When The Bough Breaks: The Costs of Neglecting Our Children* (New York: Basic Books, 1991).

Juliet Mitchell Responds to Nicky Hart

Nicky Hart throws down the gauntlet to a number of feminist positions. Her own cuts across the usual division of feminists who argue that men and women are similar and should be treated the same. Hart's contention is that men and women are different and should be treated the same. In Hart's thesis, the critical distinction that separates women and men is women's unique ability to procreate: this, she argues, should be rewarded (paid) in the same way as mankind's ability to produce.

Without doubt, Nicky Hart is right to highlight the central importance of motherhood for feminism and adversely to criticize those of us, myself very much included, who failed (and worse) to do so or who too simply diffused it into "shared parenting." However, her solution leaves me more, not less, worried. I think that Hart misunderstands the socialist-feminist emphasis on productive work — at least she does not understand what I personally understand by it. This has to do not with the wage, but with the possibility of collective action.

Doubtless many of us oversimplified the issue by seeing entry into production as a *pre*-condition for women's liberation, yet in terms of social equity, let alone social change, surely it is more retrograde to see the solution as financial remuneration, not as productive work. The demand for a living wage must always take a vanguard position, yet in and of itself the wage has no power whatsoever to change the social structure. The wage is the result but not the cause or condition of social change.

The liberating potential of production is not the wage but the community of workers. *Inherent* within the industrial worker's situation is the end of individualism and the rise of the collectivity. Collectives can be created from "outside" as in nations, races, ethnic groups, collective farms, women. In this case, the initial task is to find the lowest common denominator of identity, the so-called essence that defines the difference from all other groups. These constructed collectives can be forces either of reaction or of progress. By distinction, however, the inherently collective nature of industrial work makes it, at least in theory, potentially necessarily progressive because ultimately its future should be the future of all. It is for women's place in that future that socialist-feminists are fighting. In the field of industrial production, though, the distinction between the sexes may be (and ususally is) preserved for extrinsic, not intrinsic, reasons — i.e., it has to do with "motherhood" as Hart demonstrates, but this factor operates from outside production itself. The entry into production on equal terms with men (the "same as" men) was never more than a *pre*condition of women's liberation. After that all the conditions specific to the differences of women remain; hence the creation of a *constructed* collective: feminism.

This same non-distinction of men and women within production has been transposed by feminists to the very different field of reproduction in the notion of "shared parenting." In reacting against this tendency by privileging motherhood as women's different sphere, Hart, I believe, is touching on a real problem, but once more, her "solution" leaves me more, not less, worried. O.E.D. "*procreate*: to beget, generate, produce offspring." And Noah begat . . . but Nicky Hart writes, "Women are not the same as men. *Only* they possess the capacity to regenerate the species . . ." "Women possess the physiological equipment to replenish the human substance of society." Although Hart's argument is about the socioeconomic place of childbearing and motherhood, a neo-primitivism (or late technocratism) seems to underlie it. This is a dualistic holism in which while Adam delves and hunts or produces, Eve procreates either immaculately or impregnated by steams, saplings, or computers.

A dualistic holistic vision would seem to be merely the flip-side of the atomization of late capitalism that Fox-Genovese highlights in her critique of Hart. Economic atomization, social single parenting, ideological unisex and psychological fantasies of parthenogenesis have their inversion in a totalizing vision of absolute sexual division. It is important that the difficult question of the social place of motherhood, which is historically variable, does not collapse into the timeless mystique of earth-motherdom.

Most, but by no means all, men and women can and do procreate. The distinction between women and men is not that one procreates and the other produces or any other particular opposition one might select; but that one is not the other. What distinguishes women is that they are not men (and vice-versa); therefore the key difference must be within each area. In this instance *within* the field of procreation — the difference in the social and psychological place of fathers and of mothers.

In the late capitalist family, or in the lack of it, do we have the condition (as we do in production) in which there is no intrinsic reason to distinguish men and women either in heterosexuality or paternity and maternity? Does the social form no longer need to rest on an interpretation of biological differences in reproduction just as it no longer needs to rest on interpretations of differences of biological strength between men and women in work or warfare? In different idiom, this is the question that Mary Wollstonecraft raised some two hundred years ago. That it can be a question indicates that it is a possibility.

Elizabeth Fox-Genovese has outlined a number of the scenarios which any implementation of Hart's proposal entails and I agree with this critique. Not, of course, that failure to envisage a solution necessarily invalidates an analysis. But in this instance the fantasies one can evoke about implementation do relate simply and strictly to Hart's thesis. When mothers have felt themselves united as mothers within a social class either regressively as in "right-to-life" movements or progressively as in bread riots or peace movements they have been collectively effective. Industrialization converted the atomized peasant into a communal worker; what conditions could do the same for motherhood? Certainly not a wage which must either ignore or respect, but certainly in no way change, class, race, and ethnic divisions; nor, in a structural way could it transform the relationship of women to men.

Nicky Hart's position has a vocal history within the Women's Movement in our own time. The question was debated on both sides in the active campaign in Europe of "wages-for-housework." A history of the arguments about the place of motherhood in feminist thought and politics would be an important starting point for this central, recurrent and deeply difficult question. Although I would argue against much of her analysis, I do not disagree with Nicky Hart's emphasis on the importance of the social place of motherhood. I am very glad she has reopened the issue so forcefully.

PROCREATION AND WOMEN'S RIGHTS:

A RESPONSE TO NICKY HART

ELIZABETH FOX-GENOVESE

"Women," Nicky Hart insists, "are not the same as men." Women bear children; men do not. On this obvious — if too frequently ignored — biological fact, Hart mounts a sweeping challenge to contemporary social theory, notably what she calls anti-essentialist feminism. Mainstream academic feminism has woefully ignored this fact, assuming that the road to female "liberation" necessarily leads through full incorporation into the capitalist labor market, and it has thereby sold out the true needs and desires of the vast majority of women. The core of Hart's argument lies in her contention that procreative labor constitutes "the material and substantive" foundation of women's subordination. Late capitalist society has stripped away the cultural justifications for male domination, exposing its naked materialist character. Women remain the second sex because of their capacity to bear children. The bearing and rearing of children, rather than sex per se, accounts for most of the difference between men's and women's earnings. Hart bases her argument on calculations of the income that women who bear and rear children forego during their lifetimes. Women who do not bear children do not forego that income and, accordingly, their total earnings do not differ dramatically from those of men. In her view, these figures invalidate the arguments of those who emphasize systemic bias against women in the labor market, including labor market segmentation. Social theorists, including most feminists, have blindly persisted in looking to class relations and the organization of labor markets as the primary source of women's inequality. Theory thus abstracts from the substance of women's oppression.

Hart's ambitious argument cuts a broad swath: a spirited defense of Karl Polanyi as the analytic superior of Karl Marx; a resounding attack on the capitalist division of labor and the logic of formal rationality as the alpha and omega of modern social theory; a defense of the role of mothering in the improved health and life expectancy of modern populations; an insistence that procreative labor is inherently alien to the culture and logic of the market; a dismissal of the notion that equal access to wage labor can mitigate women's oppression; an impatient critique of psychoanalytic feminism for attempting to eliminate the consequences of sexual difference; and more.

There is much here that compels attention and much more that remains obscure and dubious. Of course Hart is right on the main point: Women's reproductive capacities — their irreducible differences from men — cannot simply be collapsed into existing theoretical models. Here we have what is becoming widely acknowledged among even academic socialist feminists, whose complacency about the interchangeability of women and men Hart deplores, as the "equality-difference" dilemma. How, that is, can a humane society protect women's difference as women without curtailing their access, as individuals, to equality.[1] Since Hart does not explicitly engage the preliminary debates among feminist theorists about the tension between equality and difference, her blanket dismissal of academic feminists risks appearing high-handed.[2]

The debate over the respective claims of equality and difference runs like a fault line through the center of academic feminism, and one side of that debate forcefully emphasizes the importance of differences between women and men. It is hard to think of a more influential feminist book than Carol Gilligan's *In a Different Voice*. But Gilligan is far from alone in emphasizing the ways in which women differ from men.[3] Hart departs from the other proponents of difference primarily in her insistence on procreation as a specific form of labor and her rejection of ensuring women's equal participation in the labor market as an adequate solution to women's economic inequality. In this respect, Hart's primary target remains the socialist feminists who do, somewhat uncritically, remain tied to the goal of establishing women's functional equality — virtual interchangeability — with men. But even they are considerably less consistent than Hart suggests, and more than occasionally edge off into a conception of women as "different."

In some respects, Hart unfairly simplifies the position of those she is criticizing in order to highlight the originality of her own position. And in one essential respect, she remains much closer to them than she is prepared to acknowledge. For Hart never criticizes the underlying individualist premises that account for some of the most intractable contradictions in various tendencies in feminist theory. Any serious attempt to square the circle of equality and difference must begin with a critique of the radical individualism that advanced capitalism is fostering. Hart remains silent on the question of individualism and her persistent devotion to "equality" even suggests that she remains fundamentally loyal to individualist premises. To follow her argument to its logical conclusion is to acknowledge women's rights as individuals to bear and rear children at public expense. This reading of her argument may well horrify her, but it follows directly from her premises.

Hart gets into logical difficulties by trying to establish the value of procreative labor without taking adequate account of the social context within which it is performed. The strength of her position lies in the argument that theorists have tended to relegate reproduction to the realm of nature and, accordingly, to refuse to recognize it as (unpaid) labor that entails not merely its own cost, but the impressive costs of raising infants to adulthood.[4] In Hart's view, the persistent failure to pay women for years spent in bearing and rearing children, compounded by the costs of the rearing, more than accounts for the "feminization" of poverty. The solution to this massive injustice does not lie in improving mothers' access to paid labor but in remunerating them for refraining from it during their children's early years. She further insists that those who advocate policies to allow mothers to behave more like men are generalizing from the atypical preferences of professional women. Most women, if given the choice, would prefer to stay home with their children, enjoying one of the few — if not the only — voluntary, creative, and life-affirming occupations left in our society.

Hart scores heavily in signaling the all-too-frequently unacknowledged gap in the experience and goals of women of different classes and races. She could have scored yet more heavily had she noted that many professional women are also showing an unforeseen preference to stay home with their children. Experience suggests that many, if not most, mothers feel a special bond to the infants they have born and suckled, and a special satisfaction in sharing and guiding their children's early development. But not all women enjoy caring for small children, and some do abuse them. Many women who have very young children desperately crave some relief from them and welcome an opportunity to engage in some work outside the home, if only to interact with other adults. Above all, Hart remains distressingly vague on who is to pay for procreative labor and on what terms. Her passing suggestions about tax transfers do not begin to engage the most difficult problems.

Hart must know that she would find warm support for her defense of motherhood among many conservatives. She must also know that conservatives invariably combine the defense of motherhood with a passionate defense of the family. But families, to say nothing of fathers, do not figure in Hart's account. As a result, she leaves the strong impression that she intends to claim motherhood as a woman's individual right that society must respect and, especially, support.

The ability to specialize in procreative labor, as Hart acknowledges, has been a fragile possibility directly associated with the development of capitalism. What she does not explicitly explore is the extent to which it has also been associated with the hallmark of capitalism: a bourgeois individualism, grounded in absolute private property. Thus Hart seriously shortchanges the complexities of historical development. Even before the emergence of capitalism, and certainly thereafter, most mothers have combined reproductive and productive labor, and to the extent that some have not it has largely been a question of class privilege. Specialization in procreative labor has normally depended upon an individual man's ability and willingness to pay for it. Men have paid women to be mothers. And when men have been unwilling or unable to do so, women have tended to have abortions, commit infanticide, abandon or give up their children for adoption, or struggle along the best they could.

The gradual emergence of motherhood as a specialized occupation can, to draw upon Hart's favorite theorist, Karl Polanyi, usefully be seen as its disembedding from the substance of life. In this respect, the emergence of "motherhood" has followed the same path and timetable as the emergence of capitalism, from which it cannot be separated. Like the emergence of capitalism, the disembedding of "motherhood" has been an uneven process, but in our own time it has entered a new phase in which the occupation of mothering has been virtually stripped of the other forms of domestic labor with which it had long been associated. The accelerated commodification of subsistence has decisively undercut most of the remaining pockets of use value — of non-wage labor. It has long been more economical to buy than to make bread. Today it is arguably more economical to buy than to make meals. The work that women long combined with mothering has lost most of its value, or, to put it differently, has become a luxury. By the same token, the possibility of engaging in it has become a privilege. Participation in the labor market may well leave much to be desired, but, for better or worse, it has become the primary — if not the exclusive — way to contribute to our economy as a whole. Without doubt, the most demeaning, deadening, and alienating forms of wage labor cry out for reform or restructuring, but Hart never claims that the public subsidy of motherhood will accomplish that result. She merely proposes to relieve mothers of the obligation to perform it during their children's early years.

The common denominator between the degradation of labor and the degradation of motherhood lies in the accelerated atomization of our society. The world of multinational corporations has scant, if any, need for the traditional norms and institutions of civil society. The accelerated commodification of every day life has coincided with a near total collapse in the social norms that protected at least some women against the more debilitating consequences of their own reproductive capacities. The proliferation of divorce, as Hart notes, has virtually liberated men from the obligation to support women and children. The collapse of what many view as repressive sexual norms, combined with the improved standards of health and nutrition, has liberated children to have children. The growing acceptance of single motherhood is virtually liberating men from any stake in children at all.

Hart believes that specialization in motherhood has constituted one of the great benefits of capitalism, not least because it has demonstrably resulted in the improved health and longevity of children. No doubt. But it would be difficult to divorce the benefits of mothers' close supervision of and engagement with their children from such other benefits as smallpox vaccinations and pasteurized milk. And what are we to attribute to the role of universal public education as it emerged? Or to higher standards of cleanliness? Or to improvements in public and private health? For many children, mothers indeed proved the implementers of these general advances. For some they did not. The point is that the specialized mothering which Hart defends occurred within a specific social context. She is now proposing to provide it with public rather than private support.

Let us, for purposes of argument, agree that children do constitute the primary resource of society and a pressing matter of public concern. Let us even, again for purposes of argument, agree that the immediate care of a small group of children by a single individual may constitute the optimal means of preparing them to participate effectively in an advanced technological society. On what basis do we then agree that the biological mother, independent of the biological father, should be entitled to perform that labor at public expense? And if we could agree to that much, how would we then agree upon the private, or individual, rights that a mother should enjoy?

Take the delicate issue of such purportedly private rights as abortion and the use of drugs during pregnancy. If children were recognized as a matter of primary public concern and if biological mothers were being supported to raise them, would it be in the public interest to permit abortion? What if the public — however defined — determined that it were in some cases and not in others? What if the "public" determined that a woman's use of drugs during pregnancy raised the cost of caring for the children after birth to unacceptable levels? What if the "public" determined that the use of alcohol or tobacco during pregnancy posed unacceptable risks? What if the "public" began to protect its "interest" in the way in which individual biological mothers raised their children? What if the "public" determined that it was not in its interest for a woman to bear more than a specified number of children — as in China — or that it was in its interest for a woman to bear the maximum number of children — as in Nazi Germany?

What, under such conditions, are we to make of women's private rights as mothers? If children are defined as a social responsibility, should not the public, which supports them, have some rights in the conditions of their bearing and rearing? Hart does not begin to consider such questions. In this respect, she falls into precisely the same implicit defense of individualism as those she opposes.

It is especially telling that Hart never seriously entertains the question of fathers' possible interests in their children. If we are to build a social theory and public policies on the basis of reproductive biology, should we not also attend to fathers' rights and responsibilities? No, men can not bear or suckle children. But they can give them bottles, diaper them, hold and cuddle them, play with them, comfort them, care for them during illness, and in countless other ways contribute to their wellbeing and development. Many believe that women are better suited to these activities and responsibilities than men, as Hart herself apparently does. But if the care of small children constitutes one of the most rewarding experiences in the modern world, it is not clear why men should be excluded from it. Hart does not adequately explain whether she regards women's care for small children as a natural consequence of biology, or as socially or psychologically preferable, and if so why. If she is arguing that children need the care of their biological mothers specifically, not just the care of some loving individual, she must give her reasons. If she is arguing that children need the care of a female rather than a male individual, she still must giver her reasons. In the case of the death of a child's natural mother, would she prefer to see the child raised by its father or by a female caretaker?

Hart insists that the recognition of gender difference does not necessarily lead to the acceptance of "gender inequality," which, unlike simple gender difference is socially structured. Unfortunately, she does not adequately explain how the two are to be separated. The extent to which Hart views motherhood as a biological or a social role carries portentous consequences. If motherhood were to be acknowledged as a respected and well-paid occupation, why should men not be permitted to engage in it as they might be encouraged to engage in nursing or elementary school teaching? And if it is recognized as an especially important role, why should it not be primarily performed by people who are real specialists, in the manner of nannies who move from one job to another when the children in their charge are ready to go to school? If, conversely, it is viewed as a predominantly biological role, then should not women's acceptance of their biological destiny begin with the first stirrings of their adult sexuality? Hart suggests nothing of the sort and, intentionally or not, conveys the impression that she might well support the liberation of women from the consequences of their biology with respect to sexual pleasure and intellectual training, thereby granting them virtual equality with men. Or does she propose to raise girls differently than boys?

In the end, Hart is arguing that women are economically unequal to — do not earn as much as — men because of the time that they spend in unpaid procreative labor. To redress that inequality, she proposes public support of women for their procreative labor. To ensure that public support, she urges women to unite across class and racial lines to establish a strong political presence. Baldly stated, her position reduces to an argument for a transfer of funds from men and women who are not mothers to women who are mothers within the existing system. The position rests on the chilling assumption that women as mothers have an individual right to raise and control the children they bear without the interference of the children's fathers or the society that supports them. It thus (perhaps unintentionally) reinforces the narrowest view of individual right and social atomization. And, at its most macabre, it could even be read to defend the rights of mothers at the expense of the interests of children.

I warmly concur with Hart that children are our most pressing social responsibility and that they are being woefully short-changed. I also believe that the most effective way to defend their interests is to encourage the view that their welfare constitutes a public responsibility. Meeting that responsibility assuredly entails enhanced support for those who are entrusted with primary responsibility for their care, who may well be their biological mothers. But I am not sure that it is theoretically consistent or socially desirable to ground sweeping policies on the assumption that biological mothers necessarily constitute the only appropriate custodians of small children, much less that biology gives women an unquestioned right to extensive public support. If we take the perspective of the needs of children and the needs of society as a whole, it is quite possible to imagine alternatives. Children might well thrive with a massive and flexible program of daycare that included choices between putting children in nurseries or in private homes and especially, included decent standards and wages for daycare workers. Comprehensive national health insurance, including pre- and post-natal care for women and children is essential. Benefits for part-time workers and more flexible work hours would provide mothers with important supports that did not necessitate their dropping out of the labor market entirely. And what about related policies for fathers? Why should men not be able to leave work early in order to pick children up at daycare and spend a few hours with them?

Hart, broad theoretical claims notwithstanding, has taken the easy way out: leave everything as it is and simply support biological mothers for a period of specialized mothering. She thus reinforces rather than criticizes the atomized individualism grounded in the capitalist market into which our social institutions are collapsing. In failing to criticize the assumptions of individualism, Hart is effectively advocating its further acceleration. But if children are to be treated as women's private concern, why should society in general, much less men in particular, continue to pay taxes for their support?

NOTES

1   In *Feminism Without Illusions: A Critique of Individualism*
(Chapel Hill: University of North Carolina Press, 1991), I have attempted
to explore some of the implications of this dilemma.
2 The Sears case, in particular, prompted some soul-searching among many
who had assumed that women primarily needed equality with men. See,
in particular, Alice Kessler-Harris, "The Just Price, the Free Market, and
the Value of Women," *Feminist Studies* 14, 2 (Summer 1988): 235-50;
Ruth Milkman, "Women's History and the Sears Case," *Feminist Studies*
12, 2 (Summer 1986); and Joan Wallach Scott, "Deconstructing Equality-
Versus-Difference: Or the Uses of Poststructuralist Theory for Feminism,"
Feminist Studies 14, 1 (Spring 1988): 33-50. Some of the most interesting
work on the problems is being done by feminist legal scholars, especially
Jennifer Nedelsky, "Reconceiving Autonomy: Sources, Thoughts and
Possibilities," *Yale Journal of Law and Feminism* 1, 1 (Spring 1989): 7-36;
Martha Minow, *Making All the Difference: Inclusion, Exclusion, and
American Law* (Ithaca, N.Y.: Cornell University Press, 1990). And for
some of the main philosophical issues, see, Elizabeth Wolgast, *The Gram-
mar of Justice* (Ithaca, N.Y.: Cornell University Press, 1987).
3   Sara Ruddick, *Maternal Thinking: Toward a Politics of Peace*
(Boston: Beacon Press, 1989); Mary O'Brien, *The Politics of Reproduction*
(Boston: Routledge and Kegan Paul, 1981).
4   Notwithstanding Hart's commitment to taking account of the experience of women of different classes, one can only assume that the figure
of $100,000 to $140,000 which she advances reflects middle class rather
than working class, much less underclass, experience.

Nicky Hart Replies

Capitalism contains stronger forces of individualism than solidarity. This judgement unites my approach with that of Elizabeth Fox-Genovese notwithstanding her hostile reaction; it is also the principal division between myself and Juliet Mitchell.

Mitchell has made truly pathbreaking contributions to the "Woman Question." Her work has been an inspiration for many and even those who do not agree with the balance of her conclusions will readily acknowledge the original part she has played in shaping the arena of second wave feminist discourse. I do not share her vision of the route to female emancipation and I believe she underestimates the extent of my critique. I understand perfectly well her belief that raised consciousness, political bonding, and class organization are supposed to be crucially engendered by wage employment. I just don't believe it. Her orthodox interpretation is far too unimaginative about the power of culture and community beyond the workplace in shaping and maintaining collective sentiments.[1] It also overestimates the potential of the relations of production for nurturing social, as opposed to sectional, interests. When organized labor has fought for wider social equalities, other contingencies, like male suffrage, have been necessary to broaden the collective consciousness.[2]

I learned what socialism means in the rural Welsh community where I grew up. My mother was my tutor; she taught me the conditions that engender socialist consciousness, she made me a passionate believer long before I read the orthodox theory of how socialist commitment is supposed to be born. Did Juliet Mitchell learn socialism from direct experience as wage laborer? I doubt it. To defend her own understanding, she must do better than merely restate the orthodox productivist theory. Where is the evidence that the relations of production have the potential she claims for them? How does her theory cope with steady decline of support for working class parties during the era of married women's unprecedented entry into "industrial work?" If shared occupational experience is the stuff of common and progressive political consciousness and action, why have right wing parties ruled unchallenged during the nineteen eighties? In the U.S., the decade which saw the mother of small children emerge as the fastest growing component of wage employment, has also seen turnout at national elections slump to around 50%, dipping even lower among the younger cohorts who register the highest rates of female participation. Meanwhile the policies of Thatcher and Reagan, which starve the public services on which children's growth and development depend, have triumphed. Well paid professional women have been little touched by these developments — they do not rely on medicaid or even public education for their children, if they have them. The majority of mothers in the U.S., working or otherwise, have witnessed a steady decline in the willingness of public authorities even to maintain resources for decent standards of compulsory education.

It is the material situation and motivation of this majority of women that a progressive feminist politics must address. This is why I reject Elizabeth Fox-Genovese's advice that I could adjust my argument to "... score even more heavily with professional women." Feminists have been scoring disproportionately with this group, who have more means than do most women to make realistic life career choices. The political shortcomings of feminism are rooted in the inability to see beyond the life circumstances and aspirations of professionally qualified women. This is also why academic feminists have attracted the charge that they are the female equivalents of white male race and class supremacists.

To this feminists have hurriedly responded with research on race *and* gender, but we cannot escape the fundamental contradiction of our privileged status. In large measure, second wave feminism has been institutionalized, incorporated in the academic curriculum and thereby freed of the need to be politically accountable to a female constituency outside the universities. Professionalization has involved the elaboration of an increasingly esoteric discourse removed from the bread and butter concerns of most women. Against this backdrop, Juliet Mitchell "worries" about my proposal to redistribute income to the childbearing population.

Like Fox-Genovese, she misreads a central element of my argument. I did not argue that women should be paid for procreation in "... the same way as mankind's (sic) ability to produce." On the contrary, I specifically argued against commodification — I am against turning childbearing into a wage earning occupation. Public financing of procreative labor should be organized to preserve its affective and voluntary impulse. Redistributive child support transfers should be related to need, they should *not* be received as a wage paid for specific services rendered because it is not possible to "clock" parental work.

I reject in the strongest possible terms the whole section of Fox-Genovese's critique which represents me as advocating that "biological mothers" ought to be primarily responsible for children. This misinterpretation leads to a whole catalogue of misleading and irrelevant conjectures about my argument; it also detracts from a discussion of the fundamental issues. I made no prescriptions about the desirable sex of the primary child raiser. Nor did I doubt that domiciliary infant care, where chosen, would ever be more than a small component of a life career in which wage employment would predominate. I argued, at some length, that child raising is a *social* activity whose costs (opportunity and direct) should be met out of the public purse in a way that enables primary parents to exercise self determination over the process of their children's growth and socialization. For some, self determination may involve payment for substitute care. I estimated that many parents when relieved of the opportunity costs might well elect to take either a full or part time domiciliary sabbatical for the period of their children's infancy; I did not say that they ought to. In the matter of infant care I am definitely pro-choice.

Financial redistribution can facilitate the use or creation of cooperative child care initiatives. The point is to provide a citizenship transfer which allows primary parents, whatever their occupational class, to *choose* for themselves how much direct involvement they invest in rearing their children, and offsets the enormous additional costs involved in supervising their full development to early adult life. Though I did not *prescribe* the sex of the primary child raiser, I did point out that on current evidence, most beneficiaries would be female.

Fox-Genovese's fears about the scope for repressive state intervention in family life that would be unleashed by this initiative are unfounded. They are fueled by a failure to differentiate between "welfare" payments and universal transfers. There is no reason why a *universalistic* redistribution of national income to households with children should lead to any increased public surveillance of parents. The majority of middle and upper class U.S. households are already the beneficiaries of universal benefits in the form of mortgage interest relief. The U.S. government redistributes more than $100 billion annually to individual mortgagees. In doing so, it does not place any conditions on how the benefit is used. The money may be spent to install swimming pools, wet bars or bedrooms with mirrored ceilings. Why assume that redistributive policies targeted specifically at child raisers rather than home owners would unleash a spate of totalitarian repression? Europeans have distributed universal child benefits for almost half a century with no implication of increased public surveillance over, and very little success in increasing the fertility of, recipients. The prospect of restricting reproductive rights is currently much greater in the U.S. than in Europe.[3]

Scare-mongering about the repressive powers of the state involved in any attempt properly to compensate primary parents for their procreative work is a smear tactic which has *no* empirical precedent.[4] Repressive governments have never required the excuse of financial accountability to justify coercion. The ability of public powers to act against the people is a matter of political activism or quiescence. It is a red herring to raise these fears as if they were peculiarly attached to a redistributive social wage and not the product of an institutional framework which fails to guarantee the rights and freedoms of citizens. Fox-Genovese should know this since, in *Feminism without Illusions*, she has used the same argument to defend public censorship of pornography.[5]

There is no doubt that social policies have the potential, like the market itself, to shape social structure and human behavior. To the extent that innovative social policies are the product of raised political consciousness and action, they also have tremendous power to lift community morale. The extension of social wage initiatives in the sphere of procreation could, would, and undoubtedly should seek to shape reproductive choice. In France such initiatives have always had a pro-natalist slant — large families have benefited disproportionately; in Sweden, the benefit is unrelated to family size but designed to encourage part-time maternal wage employment. Shaping voluntary action through *universalistic* policy instruments is not the same as coercive intervention in people's lives or bodies.

I have to admit some puzzlement at the hostility of Elizabeth Fox-Genovese. I share her view, expressed in *Feminism Without Illusions*, that individual rights are rooted in social arrangements and I believe we are united in the belief that the solidifying tendencies of the self-regulating capitalist market are puny beside its powers of individuation. So where do we differ? One insight may be gleaned from her inference that I should be horrified by her representation of my argument as ". . . an acknowledgement of women's rights to bear and rear their children at public expense." I was surprised at her choice of terms which for me betray a conservative Benthamite mentality — a belief that the creation of children must be a privately financed undertaking. Only the principle of less eligibility can, in her words, ". . . protect women from the more debilitating consequences of their own reproductive capacities." These sentiments are compatible with the further observation that "It is especially telling that Hart never seriously entertains the question of father's possible interests in their children." Fox-Genovese appears to believe that the issue of father's rights is inseparable from financial obligation. She seems to object to the extension of a social wage to the primary parent (i.e., the mother) because this would increase her autonomy and decrease her dependence upon the pater familias. In other words, Fox-Genovese invokes the utilitarian principle that fathers' rights should be built on financial obligation, that the bonds of modern kinship must be woven with cash.

She is right, I am horrified — not by her exposure of my argument but by her terminology. I found it extraordinary that a feminist could present a proposal to redistribute income to households with children, a tried and tested tool of poverty prevention among women and children, as a device to increase individualism. Does Fox-Genovese really believe that any government subsidy could ever fully compensate for the work of modern parenthood? Does she not realize that parental work requires love and self sacrifice — substantive not formal rationality? Her view betrays an ignorance of what parenthood entails, what it means, what it costs, and it strengthens my conviction that reshaping social life to meet women's material interests is too important a task to be left to academic feminism.[6]

In calling for a revaluation of the social value of primary parenting, I made the unremarkable observation that the overwhelming majority of primary custodial parents are female and it is they who bear the largest opportunity cost for their parental duties. My case rested on the observation that the conventional system of providing for the livelihood of families is breaking down. The cracks are evident and, unlike Fox-Genovese, I believe the old system is beyond repair and is also the fundamental source of women's relative social marginality and economic deprivation. With 60% of children now spending at least part of their childhood in single parent households, the most pressing need is to build an institutional fabric which systematically underwrites the costs of child raising. Fox-Genovese offers lip service to this view but she gives no guidance on what is to be done. My mistake, it appears, was to offer remedies.

Fox-Genovese is wrong in portraying my proposed reform as merely a transfer to support mothers during their children's infancy. The feminist redistribution of income I proposed is more fundamental. It involves: i) Direct financial allowances for custodial parents; ii) Lifetime compensation through tax benefits for the opportunity costs of primary parenting; iii) Generous public provision of educational, health, and recreational facilities and services for primary parents and children. This is my recipe for separating gender difference from gender inequality. If I did not make it clear enough before let me do so now. The social subordination of women in the late twentieth century has both a material and an institutional base. There can be no guarantee of equality between childbearing and non-childbearing people as long as the costs (and I mean all the costs) of raising children are borne overwhelmingly by women. It is all very well to argue that men and women *should* share parental responsibilities; the fact is that in the real world, they do not. I dealt with practical realities not, with feminist visions of shared parenting which may or may not come to pass. If parents are to be supplanted by "real specialists" in the manner conjectured by Fox-Genovese, I for one would prefer that this occur through a politically conscious process and not through a market driven "business" of creeping professionalization. The risks of coercive intervention in family life would be more enhanced by the emergence of a new professional class of child rearers claiming to know better than the natural parents, than they would by the simpler and fairer measure of income redistribution.

To claim that the form of my defense of motherhood would find warm support among conservatives is incorrect. Conservatives are overwhelmingly against substantial redistribution of income to vulnerable economic groups — they would undoubtedly prefer to deliver support (if any) in the form of professionally based services which would enable people to "help themselves." Anti-essentialist feminism endorses this view in its drive to impose the protestant work ethic on women; when it comes to child care, most feminists are not pro-choice. Among socialist feminists as Mitchell makes clear, exposure to the discipline of the production process is a prerequisite for political enlightenment; only the intelligentsia can appreciate the need for socialism without prior exposure to wage slavery.

Servicing the needs of other human beings without thought of profit is the basis of both modern parenthood and social democracy. It is highly appropriate that the public/ private division of these sentiments should be dissolved by enabling public resources to flow into the private sphere — to socialize parenthood by underwriting its costs while leaving this most meaningful human praxis in the hands of ordinary people. I agree that not all women like looking after small children, but since being a good parent is not an innate predisposition, many people become effective parents by trial and error. The process of acquiring the skills of parenting offers the best antidote I know to self-centered individualism. If Fox-Genovese understood the selflessness required for effective parenthood, she would not equate my position with expanding the ethic of individualism.

Though Mitchell allies herself with Fox-Genovese's critique, her position is built on completely different premises. Fox-Genovese's refrain, here, and in her book, *Feminism Without Illusions*, is a pessimistic reaction to the atomization spawned by the capitalist market. For Mitchell, the process deplored by Fox-Genovese is a necessary and progressive ingredient, "at least in theory" to establish the "lowest common denominator of identity." This is why socialist feminism fights for women's right to be included in the great atomization experience. Fox-Genovese, by contrast has literally no illusions that the traditional dynamic that Mitchell clings to is anything other than a destroyer of collective sentiments and responsibilities. She dreams of reconstructing "community" in form and spirit, but there is a conceptual vacuity in her vision. Indeed if anyone is "distressingly vague," it is she on the question of what the revitalized communities of late twentieth century capitalism would actually look like and how they would work. There is a sociological naivety in her accusation that a politics of redistribution (including the activism needed to initiate and sustain it) would have the effect of adding to, rather than subtracting from, market-sponsored individualism. If she examined these issues in a more dialectical spirit, she might glimpse the socially progressive dimensions (for her own project) of political activism to redistribute income to child-raising households. To raise political consciousness of the *social* character of procreation, to redistribute income on the grounds of need and to be part of communities which are as much organized to support human beings without thought of personal gain as they are to the consumption of commodities, is to erect a community where social relationships take precedence over material things.

The claim that my support of equality entails a fundamental loyalty to individualist premises is without logic. I restate: equality of opportunity in an unfettered capitalist market is a myth — a myth with the purpose of legitimizing individual inequality. Modern citizenship in its most progressive forms entails a commitment to equality of outcome — in effect a commitment to compensation for the systematic inequalities generated by market capitalism. The most appropriate point in the lifetime to safeguard individuals from the effects of the market is childhood and the most appropriate managers of redistributed resources are parents who spend part of every day in selfless service of others.

Equality of outcome can serve to uphold equality of opportunity in its most progressive sense. Universalist income redistribution to child-raising households and high quality educational, health and recreational public facilities can bring a truly progressive meaning to the idea of individual freedom as *material freedom* for full physical and intellectual development. But the institutional mechanisms required to bring true equality of opportunity into reality themselves involve a limitation on selfish individualism and the encouragement of communal responsibility. To achieve these ends requires political energy, organization, and the use of collective power to restrain that other freedom sponsored by the self-regulating market. In all this the accountable state must play a primary role. For some this raises the specter of civil society crushed by the all-powerful state; but there is nothing inherently virtuous about civil society. The future of human freedom depends upon the state's being made the conscious instrument of civil society; only the state can orchestrate economic redistribution and a just measure of income equality, which has to be the fundamental condition of a progressive civil community. At all costs we must avoid romanticizing the virtues of the "free association" in the restricted civil social space granted by an advanced capitalist market.

NOTES

1   Nicky Hart "Gender and the Rise and Fall of Class Politics," *New Left Review* 175 (1989): 19-47.

2   See chapter 18 in Michael Mann *The Sources of Social Power* Volume II *The Rise of Classes and Nations 1760-1914*, (New York: Cambridge University Press, 1992).

3   The political pressure for introducing family allowances in Europe was undoubtedly aided by the declining birth rate and the hope that some measure of redistribution to offset the costs of raising children would increase fertility, but this has not happened.

4   Government funded professions, like the academic salariat, are the beneficiaries of public largesse. The state hands over resources and allows the academic community an enormous discretion in how the funds are dispersed. It is highly subsidized, yet protected by a charter of academic freedom. Why should not child rearers be treated in the same way? I do not doubt that it would require a formidable effort of political mobilization, yet the test of feminism's political potential must be its ability to increase awareness of women's true interests and organize effectively for *real* change. The goals of feminism require nothing short of a fundamental reorientation of social organization and economic priorities. The struggle for women's rights cannot be confined to making space within the labor market and enforcing comparable worth. See David Lockwood "Class, Status, Gender," *Gender and Stratification*, Rosemary Crompton & Michael Mann eds., (Cambridge: Polity Press, 1986), pp. 11-22.

5   Elizabeth Fox-Genovese *Feminism Without Illusions: A Critique of Individualism* (Chapel Hill: University of North Carolina Press, 1991), p. 111.

6   Here and in *Feminism without Illusions* , Fox-Genovese employs the structural functionalist sex role paradigm to refer to the disembedding of motherhood — what Parsons or Smelser would have called role differentiation. My own understanding of the force of Polanyi's insight is quite different. Polanyi made the crucial distinction between formal and substantive economics. For him incorporation in formal social life involves entry to the sphere of capitalist accounting — of market relations. Parenthood, in particular, motherhood, has never achieved this status in any marked degree; the economic marginality of single parents is the result. I

do not follow the logic of Fox-Genovese's argument about the disembedding of motherhood; she draws on abstracted Marxist terminology to depict the commodification of domestic labor — but still finds it useful to refer to motherhood as disembedded. Though she may find this language instructive, hers is an idiosyncratic interpretation and, in my view, seriously misunderstands the purpose of Polanyi's great insight.

B. Culture

A Culturalist Critique of Trends in Feminist Theory

RUTH H. BLOCH

Perhaps the most fundamental claim of modern feminism is that anatomy is not destiny. With few exceptions, feminists blame society, not the body, for producing women's subordination. Yet in rejecting biological arguments, feminists have faced a formidable theoretical problem: what is it about society that explains the position of women?[1] This essay explores some of the most common answers that have been given to this question, arguing that one of the very strengths of feminist theory — its refusal to accord the anatomical difference of sex the ability to determine social life — has itself encouraged what may in fact be an equally fallacious intellectual tendency. The rejection of biology as the source of gender relations has fostered contrary, but similarly reductive explanations, based instead on wealth and power.

Most recent feminist theorists have tried to resolve a theoretical problem of their own: how can women's distinctive social position be explained if not biologically? In the following pages, I will attempt to clarify what I mean by the term "culture," itself one of the most widely appropriated and misunderstood concepts in social science. Indeed, a striking feature of feminist theory, like most social thought, is precisely its extensive invocation of the term. The view that gender relations are "cultural" has been a standard cliché of the anti-biological argument. The very term "gender" — as distinguished from "sex" — has derived its widespread appeal from its supposedly cultural definition. As a cultural rather than purely physical fact, "gender" is meant to refer not merely to the male and the female but to the contingent and variable symbols that define masculinity and femininity within a particular social group. In my view, however, this cultural perspective has not gone far enough. Within some feminist theory it even threatens to subvert itself. For, while gender is often *defined* as cultural, it is not itself typically *understood* culturally. Feminist theorists too often reduce culture, and with it the cultural symbolism of gender, to the material relations of class or some other self-interested assertion of power by one group over another. The subjective meaning that men and women attribute to gender identity becomes in this view essentially the result of false consciousness or (in a non-Marxist variation) instrumental manipulation. Lost from such an understanding is the way that gender becomes socially meaningful and articulates with other common structures of meaning. Nor is this limited conceptualization of culture and gender merely a narrowly academic problem. It is an important theoretical flaw that diminishes our appreciation of how feminism might work to change the world.

Feminist practice has been, in this respect, far ahead of feminist theory. The new wave feminists of the late 1960s and 1970s started with the subversive cry, "the personal is political" and sought to transform the subjective meanings of being female or male. At the beginning, feminist activism consisted largely of participation in consciousness-raising groups and emotionally-wrought confrontations with men in political organizations, families, and intimate relationships. While ritual bra-burning was a sensationalist media fabrication, women affected by the movement often altered their public appearance — rejecting skirts, bras, and cosmetics and usually no longer shaving their armpits and legs. To be sure, most participants may have only superficially understood their actions as a struggle against confining stereotypes and the behaviors of specific men. What was to them simply being "open" and "natural," however, amounted to defining a cultural code of their own. The underlying significance of the practice of the women's liberation movement was to identify and transform that aspect of culture that we have since come to call gender. New wave feminists of the 60s and 70s perceived themselves as enmeshed in a variable system of meanings, both internalized within and imposed from outside, that defined sex roles, images of men and women, and sexuality.

The concept of culture, while not explicitly invoked by feminist activists in the 1960s, was simultaneously being refined by symbolic anthropologists. Clifford Geertz, Mary Douglas, Victor Turner, Claude

Levi-Strauss and others drew on older traditions of social theory to describe many of the symbolic structures and ritual behaviors that define collective life. A basic feature of this developing perspective was its insistence on the causal autonomy of culture. It consequently objected to Marxist and other attempts to reduce an ideological "superstructure" to an underlying "base" of material relations. Myths, symbols, rituals, and other structures of collective meaning emerge, according to this view of culture, from the creative interaction of older cultural traditions, contemporary conditions, and human practice. Culture, in other words, both constrains and enables social actors, just as it is experienced simultaneously as internal and external to the individual.

This basic definition and theory of culture, while familiar enough to "culturally-oriented" social scientists, has been in my view too much overlooked by feminists theorizing the subject of gender. With some qualifications and revisions, the understanding of culture developed within symbolic anthropology in the 1960s still has potential for feminism. It can help, for example, to illuminate the way popular definitions of femininity — such as the idea of women as nonviolent and responsive to others — have been both experienced as oppressive and refashioned as a basis of feminist solidarity. From this perspective, much of the work of the women's movement can be seen as specifically cultural, involving at once iconoclastic challenges to conventional definitions of femininity and the creative construction of new ones. Even the open expression of non-monogamous and lesbian sexuality and the common restructuring of domestic obligations of women and men are not merely efforts to express natural impulses or to equalize work. They are, as significantly, cultural acts reformulating gender definitions of sexuality and labor. Despite significant differences among feminists, such practices have forged a new common meaning — a new, feminist variation of American culture has come into being. This cultural work of feminism continues, of course, even today. Although stripped of much of the effervescence and utopianism of the sixties and early seventies, it still takes place within women's studies programs, in public demonstrations of pro-choice activists, in the work of women artists and theologians, and in innumerable encounters of everyday life. The myriad of ways that individual women seek to live up to shared ideals of independence, equality, and social responsibility are themselves testimony to the continuing cultural impact of the women's movement.

Yet for reasons largely idiosyncratic to left-wing academic thought, feminist theory has rarely reflected on this cultural dimension of feminist

practice.[2] Scholars, like other feminists, have been engaged in this process
of cultural transformation, but they have rarely deemed culture something
to theorize about. In the 1970s a few feminist academics, most notably
anthropologists and historians, applied a culturalist perspective to their
own research on other times and places.[3] During the same period feminist
literary critics concerned to expose patriarchal views of women or to
underscore the "unifying voice in women's literature" also took an essentially culturalist approach in their explorations of intellectual context.[4]
Generally, however, these studies stopped short of generating a broader
theory of gender as culture.[5] Anthropological theories' of culture tendency
to overlook conflict and change provides one explanation for this neglect.
A second reason is the residual Marxism of much feminist social science,
which favors material over cultural analysis. A third is the tendency of
many feminist scholars in the humanities to focus on the specific cultural
productions of writers and artists without investigating the concept of
culture itself or drawing a clear connection between the meanings of texts
and the processes of social change. Yet a fourth reason why feminist
theorists have tended not to concentrate on gender as culture stems from
the practical exigencies of the feminist movement itself. Its "cultural
work" notwithstanding, the main legal and reform agenda of the movement
has been, of course, to end discrimination against women. Feminist intellectuals have therefore been inclined to conceive of women not as cultural
agents or symbols but as the victims of social institutions representing
tangible power and wealth.

　　　With the infusion of French poststructural theories into the American academic left, the concept of culture has seemingly taken on a new
life. The center of gravity with the world of social theory has in the past
decade shifted from political economy and sociology to literary criticism
and philosophy. Among contemporary feminist intellectuals it is the
poststructuralist literary critics and philosophers who have come the
closest to insisting on the importance of gender as a cultural construction.
In contrast to the relatively static and consensual theories of earlier cultural
anthropologists, poststructuralists describe culture as unstable and contradictory, a perspective that is more amenable to radical interpretation, as
shown by the influential example of Michel Foucault. But, for all the
sophistication and insight of this now popular kind of cultural criticism,
its advocates tend either to lack a theory of social change or else to resort
to a materialist one. While they insist on the centrality of culture to human
experience, they deny its causal autonomy in relation to other oppressive

structures like class and race. Of course, radical poststructuralists would in general resist this distinction — claiming that race and class are themselves cultural constructions — but when it comes to explaining historical variation and change (a task few attempt) they do not practice what they preach.[6] Indeed, whereas Marxist critics of poststructuralism find fault with what they take to be its abstract idealism, I would question its often implicit materialism and interest-driven view of humanity. As I will elaborate below, the influence of poststructuralism has merely reinforced a tendency among feminist theories to reduce gender to inequalities of wealth and power.

For all these intellectual and political reasons, feminists have for the most part overlooked the benefits of a non-reductive theory of culture. While feminism was launched with the self-empowering slogan "the personal is political," it has too often produced theories in which the personal itself is no more than a shallow reflection of impersonal structures of power. The net effect of such theorizing is to divest "gender" both of intrinsic meaning — of subjectivity — and explanatory value. Definitions of masculinity and femininity become epiphenomena, the extension of structures of domination and oppression which typically come down to class and, more recently, race. If we understand culture as the system of meaning that expresses collective needs and ideals that go beyond the utilitarian pursuit of power, then culture has only a precarious place within feminist theory, especially outside the humanities. The result is that such human motives as curiosity about the natural world, the appreciation of beauty, the desire for intimacy, or the quest for spiritual experience have been in effect eliminated from feminist analysis of society. The basic fact that men tend to dominate women seems to justify a preoccupation with the dimension of domination alone. Even when connections are drawn between definitions of gender and other aspects of culture like science, religion, and art, the common denominator between them typically is power. Drawing from Marxism and poststructuralism alike, feminists tend to conceive of culture as the reflection of dominant interests. Gender occupies a subservient position in an analytic hierarchy that situates power, not meaning, on top.

By presenting a brief survey of the main developments in feminist theory in the last twenty-five years, I aim to give substance to these general criticisms. During this period there has been a continuous interaction between neo-Marxist materialism in various forms and a series of sexual, psychoanalytic, and linguistic theories, none of which has gained clear

ascendancy. What fundamentally unites writers of varying persuasions is
their common enlistment in the feminist project of defining gender as a
non-biological social fact. Even though many feminists concede that
biology is a partial source of gender distinctions, others insist that our
understanding of biology is itself constructed by gender difference.[7] Virtually all agree that the task of feminism is to look at society, not nature,
for it is only as social actors that we can hope to transform gender relations.

How feminists analyze the social conditions of womanhood has
varied greatly. Some conceptualize the distinctive position of women in
terms of the social inequality of the sexes, others in terms of the attitudinal
and psychological differences between them. Some stress the negative
effects of oppression, others the positive attributes of female identity or
"sisterhood." The non-Marxists have generally countered (or at least
supplemented) an emphasis on capitalism and class relations with arguments for the importance of male sexual domination, the process of identity
formation in early childhood, and the social imperatives of language.
Neither Marxism nor its major theoretical alternatives has, however,
advanced a social theory of gender that gives primacy to culture as more
than an instrument of oppression (or, conversely, as resistance to oppression). While feminist theorists have gone to great lengths to explore the
positive and negative valences of equality and difference, the central
proposition that gender is both an aspect and a product of a wider cultural
system has been largely ignored. A look at the evolution of feminist social
theory since the late 1960s reveals the cost of this neglect.

EARLY FEMINIST SOCIAL THEORY: CAPITALISM
VS. PATRIARCHY

In the first decade of feminist debate, the main contending theories
of society were socialist feminism and the theory of patriarchy, both of
which focused on the problem of inequality. Although some early works
of feminist protest, such as Betty Friedan's *The Feminine Mystique* and
Kate Millett's *Sexual Politics*, exposed the cultural manifestations of
female oppression, those theorists who sought instead to unravel the social
causes of gender inequality typically failed to consider gender as culture.
Rather, the argument between the contesting patriarchy and socialist
schools turned on the extent to which female subordination was caused by

men, as a sex, and the extent to which it stemmed from the more impersonal dynamics of the capitalist system.[8] The oldest debate within contemporary feminist theory, this discussion has gone through many subtle permutations and continues to resonate today. Catherine MacKinnon's recent treatment of pornography and rape develops the earlier perspective of patriarchal theory by advancing the view that violence and domination are inherent in male heterosexuality. In her memorable words, "Sexuality is to feminism what work is to marxism: that which is most one's own, yet most taken away. . . . [As] the organized expropriation of the work of some for the benefit of others defines a class, workers, the organized appropriation of the sexuality of some for the use of others defines the sex, woman."[9] If theorists of patriarchy like MacKinnon would underscore the contrast between feminism and Marxism, a neo-Marxist perspective dating back to the late 60s has also retained its vitality through years of debate. The socialist feminist assertion that female oppression flows from capitalist class relations still can be heard in such diverse and important works of the 1980s as Nancy Hartsock's *Money, Sex, and Power*, Alison Jaggar's *Feminist Politics and Human Nature*, and Christine Stansell's *City of Women*.[10] For all the differences between patriarchy and Marxist theories, they come together in asserting the primacy of material categories — respectively, the biological fact of sex and the economic one of capitalism.[11] Both neglect the importance of gender symbolism in its own terms.

WOMEN'S "CULTURE" AND WOMEN'S PHYCHE

In the mid-1970s, these two competing theories of women's oppression were joined by a new set of arguments that emphasized the particularities of "women's culture." The word culture here refers not to broad patterns of meaning that construct notions of femininity but to a loose mixture of moral, psychological, and ideological characteristics that bind women together as a social group. Inasmuch as myths and symbols were the focus of analysis, as was frequently the case in literary and religious studies, such examinations of culture were typically confined to descriptions of notions of femininity itself. Aside from the view that cultural definitions of women could be either oppressive or emancipatory, thus serving the interests of either dominant patriarchal or subordinate feminist groups, little effort was made to explain the causal origins of myths and symbols of femininity. That these myths and symbols could be explained with reference to other myths and symbols (which may not have been specifically about women) went against what was a more socially reductionist grain. For this literature tended to uphold what came to be called "women's culture," understood as a set of beliefs that reflected the distinctive and concrete experience of women as women. Attention shifted from inequality to difference, and with this change in perspective came a closer look at the common features of womanhood.

Many different kinds of writers involved in this redefinition of feminist scholarship turned to the study of the special characteristics of women's social and familial relationships. In American history these concerns gave rise to groundbreaking studies of nineteenth-century female friendship, women's education, and voluntary associations by scholars like Nancy Cott, Carroll Smith-Rosenberg, and Kathryn Kish Sklar.[12] In the field of literary criticism the work of Patricia Meyer Spacks, Elaine Showalter, Sandra Gilbert, and Susan Gubar uncovered the literary history of neglected women writers and revealed ways that their texts challenged the prevailing gender ideology.[13] The view that women have distinctive forms of expression found substantiation in the more explicitly theoretical works of feminist psychoanalysis, most notably that of Nancy Chodorow's description of mother-daughter relationships, followed by Carol Gilligan's survey of female moral values.[14] Taken together, all these disparate works powerfully reinforced a sense of the common experience and values of women. Their accounts of this common "women's culture," however, were not themselves cultural but descriptive and psychoanalytic. What, if anything, produced the distinctive qualities of femininity other than the apparently near-universal dynamics of family life and the division of public and private spheres, remained unexplored.

The emerging interest in women's subjectivity and community in the English-speaking world received reinforcement from an infusion of French feminist theory in the late 70s and early 80s. Asserting the existence of an intrinsic femininity in polar opposition to male-dominated social life, French feminists pushed the notion of a "women's *écriture*" in a more radical direction. Similarly grounded in psychoanalytic ideas about the primacy of mother-infant bonds, these writers advanced a powerful, at times utopian and primitivist, vision of women set in contrast to the destructive force of phallogocentric language and civilization. The widely read novel *Les Guérillères* by Monique Wittig perhaps best exemplifies this tendency within French feminism in its vivid portrayal of an ideal society of revolutionary and erotic women.[15] In America this visionary quality, if not all the theoretical underpinnings, also found expression in the radical female-separatist works of Mary Daly and Andrea Dworkin.[16] For all their often acute and inspiring insights into the difference between women and men, however, in this work the sources of the difference usually remain decidedly vague. Only a few of the proponents of "women's culture," most notably Mary Daly in her early theological writings, have sought to analyze femininity and masculinity in specifically cultural terms.

Because of their tendency to take gender difference for granted, many feminists who have insisted on women's distinctive identity and culture have proven vulnerable to the charge of implicit biological determinism, or what is commonly disparaged as "essentialism."[17] For, their critics object, if women's subjectivity is distinctive, what is the ultimate source of this difference from men if not women's bodies? And if it is women's bodies, what is our hope for feminist social transformation? Although some theorists like Chodorow at least partly answer such objections by pointing to interactive processes of identity formation rather than to bodily essences, the nagging question of social causality remains. Those most inclined to celebrate distinctive female attributes have tended to avoid the issue of causality altogether. Instead of analyzing "women's culture" as a cultural formation with its own internal structure and history, the advocates of "women's culture" tend to accept it as a given, as generated by the chronic facts of biology, female mothering, or oppression. Even though most of them would strenuously reject the "essentialist" label, they have little in the way of an alternative social theory to offer. The closest a few of them get is a sophisticated reworking of psychoanalytic theory. Yet, however powerful these insights into individuals and families may be, psychoanalysis in and of itself can say very little about broader social patterns, historical changes, or variations among different groups.

Politically, moreover, the implication of some of the work emphasizing gender difference is that women's particular values and roles are socially beneficial in relation to the patriarchal order and that, for this reason, they need not be fundamentally reformed. Instead of pursuing what one recent polemicist has called "the equality trap," these writers suggest that women need instead to receive more appreciation and reward for what they have traditionally been and done. Nicky Hart's case in *Contention*, nos. 1-2 for state compensation to mothers is but one variation of this argument. For all her disagreements with Hart in *Contention*, no. 3, Elizabeth Fox-Genovese's own *Feminism Without Illusions* advances a similar polemic against individualistic feminism by linking justice for women to the revitalization of traditional social structures like the family and local community organizations. Although Fox-Genovese specifically denounces "the siren calls of nostalgic and utopian communitarianism" and calls for a "new vision" of communities, the conservative implications of her desire to "protect" sex and gender "asymmetry" have not been lost on liberal, egalitarian feminists who are still pressing for the full inclusion of women into male bastions of wealth and power.[18] In perhaps the most publicized egalitarian attack on "difference" theory, the journalist Susan Faludi goes so far as to categorize prominent feminist writers like Carol Gilligan and Betty Friedan as part of a backlash against feminism, in the company of men like Ronald Reagan and George Bush.[19]

Feminist theorists stressing the social, moral, and psychological differences between women and men have also proven vulnerable to accusations that they have falsely generalized from their own culture to others. Following on the heels of African-American literary critics like Hortense Spillers and Barbara Smith, for example, Elizabeth Spelman, in her recent book *Inessential Woman*, forcefully argues that the effort to define a distinctive women's culture or voice falsely universalizes from the experience of privileged white women.[20] This case against elite white essentialism and its universalizing implications has been further reinforced by post-Kuhnian developments in studies of sexuality which point to the culturally specific and historically variable understanding of the body itself.[21]

POSTSTRUCTURALISM AND THE PROBLEM OF "OTHERNESS"

The critique of essentialism has gained increased strength with the rise of poststructuralist theory since the early 1980s. A key text in this transition was Gayle Rubin's 1975 article "Traffic in Women" in *Toward an Anthropology of Women*. By distinguishing between the economy and the sex/gender system as separate elements of social organization, Rubin turned a feminist revision of both Freud and Levi-Strauss against biological determinism and Marxist feminism.[22] Rubin made a strong case for the autonomy and causal role of the sex/gender system in the genesis of women's oppression, stressing its origins in culturally variable kinship systems rather than in nature itself. Separating herself clearly from both the Marxist emphasis on capitalism and the patriarchy theorists' emphasis on male aggression, Rubin drew inspiration from the structuralist psychoanalyst Jacques Lacan to cast a clear light on the artificial role of the incest taboo in shaping sexuality and gender. Unlike more recent poststructuralists who have similarly drawn on Lacan to emphasize the conventionality of gender, however, Rubin, while calling for a "revolution in kinship" and the end of the oedipus complex, largely ignored the role of culture in producing and sustaining gender.[23] For Rubin the sex/gender system was historically rooted in the reproductive needs of the species and the social need for human reciprocity and exchange — needs that, in her view, modern society no longer requires antiquated kinship systems to fill. Since the appearance of Rubin's essay, poststructuralists rallying behind the phrase "the social construction of gender" have concentrated more on the cultural system of language and symbols that continue to shape and perpetuate gender distinctions even in the modern world.

As part of a feminist variation on the broader intellectual phenomenon of "the linguistic turn," these writers have increasingly shifted away from categorizing woman as a sex to concentrating on the cultural representations of sexual difference and attitudes toward femininity and masculinity.[24] The recent outpouring of poststructuralist feminist theorizing has been marked by the influence of Foucauldian and deconstructionist literary theory, concentrating its attention on symbols and ideologies. French feminist theorists such as Luce Irigaray and Hélène Cixous, who through Jacques Lacan formed a bridge between poststructural linguistics and psychoanalysis, have contributed greatly to this phase of theoretical development.

The shift in focus from women as a social group to gender as a symbolic construction also highlights the importance of cultural diversity. According to the postmodern perception that our knowledge is structured by language, it is no longer possible to think of the category of "woman" as fixed or given. The appeal of this insight from a feminist point of view is that it opens the door to the possibility of limitless change. It also makes room for the contributions of third world women and American women of color whom earlier feminist scholars had largely ignored. The detaching of gender from anatomy has opened to view multiple variations on the themes of women and men. "Woman" itself became a positional term, in the words of the poststructuralist feminist Luce Irigaray, "the possibility, the place, the sign of relations among men."[25] Defined not in relation to female biological difference but in relation to its oppositional term "man," "woman" (much like "black" or "lower class") constitutes a marker of "otherness."

While poststructuralism has pointed to the cultural variability of gender, an unintended effect of emphasizing "difference" has been to undermine the analytical significance of "gender" itself. In such accounts of social life, gender ceases to be a determining variable. Conceptually and politically, the solidarity of women across class and racial lines has become increasingly problematic. If women no longer have something in common by virtue of being women — if, instead, we are broken into distinct groups by virtue of the multiplicity of the positions of "otherness," especially in relation to class, ethnic, or racial identities — why bother theorizing about sex or gender at all? Instead, increasing attention is given to the task of describing variations and differences among women and exposing conflicts between them.[26] To young feminist intellectuals of the late 60s and 70s the very perception of sexual inequality seemed tremendously illuminating. Now, however, the tendency is to shy away from generalizations. Sensitivity to difference leads to an endless fragmentation of social groups, to a focus on groups defined only partly by gender, and to an understanding that gender itself is variously constructed by other social characteristics. Every woman's situation is virtually unique, defined by particularities of economic organization, political structure, and national or minority groups.

To a degree, the logic of this approach runs against the very effort to explain the condition(s) of women. Indeed, in keeping with postmodernist skepticism about theories of causality, feminist scholars have increasingly denied any intention of providing systematic explanations. As the postmodernist psychoanalyst Jane Flax surveys the fragmented field of knowledge: "The very search for a cause or 'root' of gender relationships or, more narrowly, male domination may partially reflect a mode of thinking that is itself grounded in particular forms of gender or other relations in which domination is present. Perhaps 'reality' can have 'a' structure only from the falsely universalizing structure of the dominant group."[27] A recent feminist literary anthology similarly begins with the disclaimer, "one never arrives at a point where one can fix — or has a fix on — the questions and answers; far from arriving at definitive solutions, the cumulative effect of reading and writing here is of resistance to certainty and stasis."[28] A major thrust of feminist accounts of the Enlightenment and modern science has been to challenge the premises of western rationalism on the grounds of its inherently masculinist bias.[29] Within the academic disciplines it is, not surprisingly, historians and literary critics who are the most comfortable with this reaction against traditional social science methodology. Historical and literary scholarship both characteristically avoid generating abstract or general laws. Historians, trained to concentrate on particularities, customarily insist on the specificity of time and place. Literary critics likewise traditionally focus on the details of individual texts. The recent movement in literature toward historical analysis known as the "new historicism" combines the particularities of text with the particularities of context. Understandably, highly publicized attacks on feminist scholarship in *The New York Review of Books* have come from within the same fields of social history and literary criticism in which feminists have gained the most strength.[30]

Despite all the feminist critiques of western rationalism, however, the impulse towards explanation and generalization remains strong. It typically lurks beneath the surface of the word "social" in the standard incantation "the social construction of gender." Although "social" is by one definition an umbrella term that encompasses all nonbiological features of human life, by another, originally Marxist definition, it refers essentially to class relationships. In left-wing discourse generally, phrases like "social structure," "social relations," and "social conflict" usually still signify the organization and dynamics of class. Today, in the post-Marxist world of Michel Foucault and Pierre Bourdieu, culture is rarely explained by class alone, but by the more sweeping invocation of a context of domination and oppression. Such a perspective remains tied, however, to a critique of capitalism and liberal democracy.

For Foucault this oppressive social context of culture is subsumed under the rubric of power. Despite the centrality of discourse in his theory, discourse is not understood as an independent cultural formation but as the means to gain, justify, and preserve power. The concept of power itself, while in ordinary language an elusive one with multiple resonances, for Foucault finally boils down to the exercise of force: "Nothing is more material, physical, corporeal."[31] Similarly, Lacanian psychoanalytic theory, by connecting language and civilization with the domination of the phallus in the oedipus conflict, links culture to power. In contemporary feminist theory we see clear resonances of such ideas. Scholars with a radical poststructuralist orientation typically interpret ideology, and with it the symbolic representations of gender, as both a symptom and an agent of domination. Stressing what she calls the legitimizing function of gender, for example, Joan Scott asserts that "gender is a primary field within which or by means of which power is articulated."[32] Judith Butler, who indicts Lacan, Foucault, Wittig and other icons of poststructuralist feminism for their implicitly naturalist assumptions about the body, follows them in her view of culture as constructed by power — in this case the power of dominant heterosexuality. Gender is, as she puts it, "an illusion . . . maintained for the purposes of the regulation of sexuality within the obligatory frame of reproductive heterosexuality."[33] The metaphorical language in which such interpretations of gender symbolism are enmeshed — "regulation," "contestation," "deployment," "site," "field," "territory" — suggests an analogy between cultural formations and the actions of a police state.[34]

To a surprising degree, given Foucault's own antipathy towards Marxism, the hierarchical relations that many poststructuralist feminists see gender as expressing are still class relations and the oppressive imperatives of a capitalist economy. Gayatri Chakravorty Spivak, a leading proponent of Third World feminist deconstructionism, insists "that the practice of capitalism is intimately linked with the practice of masculinism."[35] The residual materialism of feminist poststructuralism is similarly exemplified in the work of Mary Poovey, an English literary critic who acknowledges her simultaneous debt both to Marx and Foucault. As she sums up her social theory of literary production, "the conditions that produce both texts and . . . individual subjects are material in the ever elusive last instance."[36] Far from implying a fundamentally different historical analysis, the Foucauldian elements of her criticism differs from traditional Marxism only in its insistence on the "elusiveness" of this material last instance.

GENDER AND THE RACE/CLASS ANALOGY

The view that gender is a symbolic screen for material power relations helps to explain why feminist intellectuals in America so readily draw an implicit analogy between gender, class, and race. Implied in this trilogy of terms, of course, is the comparability of these categories. Although the specific litany "race, class, and gender" has been increasingly invoked in the context of recent debates over multiculturalism, this equation is hardly new. Marxist and socialist feminists in the 1970s pointed to the similarities between the condition of women and that of the proletariat, stressing the parallel features of wage slavery and unpaid housework, of alienation and sexual objectification, of production and reproduction. Nancy Hartsock's idea of a "feminist standpoint," which rested on the analogy with Marx's proletariat, further extended this perspective.[37] There is, in addition, the old tradition within American feminism, going back to the abolitionist influence within the first women's rights movement in the nineteenth century, of drawing parallels between the oppression of women and blacks. Despite the fact that black feminists have at times objected to this equation, arguing that it obscures the unique position of black women, to this day the analogy remains a common rhetorical feature of feminist thought.[38] Academic feminists who argue for the three-factor analysis of race, class, and gender often stress the similarity of the status of racial minorities, workers, and women. In the words of historian Gerda Lerner, "Race, class, and gender oppression are inseparable; they construct, reinforce, and support one another."[39] For some writing within a neo-Marxist framework, this similarity consists of overlapping material inequalities.[40] For others, however, for whom gender has come to mean a set of symbolic constructions that vary by class and racial group, gender is not only presented as analogous to class and race but as virtually reducible to them.

In both neo-Marxist and poststructuralist work, then, gender is retreating into the dependent position it assumed in earlier discussions of the female body: it is becoming an empty vessel which is filled with the residues of other kinds of domination. The feminist Foucauldian perspective that analyzes gender symbolism as a tool of oppression suffers from the same weaknesses as the older theories of Marxism or patriarchy. So do the still more recent efforts to draw from the work of Jurgen Habermas in order to root modern gender definition in the rise of a "bourgeois public sphere." The literary critic Rita Felski, for example, in her argument against the radical claims of *l'écriture féminine*, advances a model of a "feminist counter-public sphere" explained by the context of "late capitalism" and its "bourgeois" character.[41] Felski rightly insists upon the "relative autonomy" of art within society. But while "art" is for her essentially genre, narrative, and other formal literary conventions, "society" — which in her view unavoidably conditions art — seems driven by the dynamics of class and oppression alone.

Are social conceptions of gender no more than reflections of more "objective," that is, presumably material, structures of political and economic inequality? For all the greater sophistication implied in the "linguistic turn," the cultural analysis of gender too frequently echoes early feminist ideas of woman-as-victim. Only now, instead of woman being the victim of patriarchy or of capitalism, the victim is the very concept of gender-as-culture. Even where gender is still defended as a primary factor in social life, it typically refers to the social conditions of being male and female, not to symbolic life. In their recent synthesis of the history of European women, for example, Bonnie Anderson and Judith Zinsser assert that "gender has been the most important factor" shaping women's lives, overriding all other differences such as class, region, or epoch.[42] Yet, after a preliminary chapter describing ancient intellectual traditions that justify the subordination or, less frequently, the empowerment of women, the remainder of their lengthy narrative disregards cultural definitions of gender in preference for social history. Cultural views of women, they argue, "changed remarkably little over time," an assertion hinging on a definition of culture that is concerned with the issues of subordination and empowerment alone.[43]

This impasse can be overcome only by developing a broader and specifically culturalist perspective. Feminist critiques of poststructuralism, however, have actually argued in completely the opposite way. Rather than suggesting other ways of analyzing culture, they have objected to the very emphasis on the ideological components of gender, calling for renewed attention to the "social" lives of women instead. This critique originates from a materialist position that insists on the primacy of concrete experience as against the purportedly abstract and merely ideational notions of gender. Related to this objection are the complaints of many social scientists and social historians that to study gender symbolism instead of "real women" is to privilege an elite. Yet the cultural understanding of gender, with its rejection of the view that women comprise an easily definable social group, neither inherently discounts the subjective experience of actual women nor necessarily values one class over another. These problems, as difficult as they may be, are methodological and empirical rather than theoretical. The real issue at stake is how one analyzes the experience of any social group. Beneath the argument that the study of "real" women is more valuable than the study of gender there lies the claim that women's experience is fundamentally constructed by material relations of wealth and power, not by symbolic systems.

Ironically, feminist poststructuralists often concur with their chief critics on this very point. Far from truly privileging the cultural over the material, they typically derive gender from the dynamics of class and racial domination. In a revealing recent debate between Linda Gordon and Joan Scott, Gordon accuses postmodernist scholarship of being too remote from the social realities of women's oppression to be truly political; Scott defends the recent scholarship by pointing out the singular preoccupation of feminist poststructuralism with matters of power.[44] Regardless of who had the better of this argument, neither writer questioned the postmodernist premise that culture essentially embodies power relations. The construction of gendered meaning in response to demands for spiritual fulfillment, aesthetic pleasure, or the anxieties of human existence are either ignored or treated as epiphenomena of a "more real" driving force that is Nietzchean in character: it is a reflection of the quest of theologians, artists, and philosophers for increasing their prestige and the domination of their race or class.

To challenge this reductive perspective on culture raises immediate questions about the study of gender. Is gender more than a metaphor for power? If so, what does it signify? The claim that gender is not solely the product of unequal relations of subjection and domination rekindles some of the issues in the literature on women's culture and subjectivity that first arose in the mid-70s. That literature had taken issue with feminist Marxist and patriarchal theories for denying agency to women. It advanced the view that distinctive features of women's roles and values are produced not simply by male or capitalist oppression but by women themselves and that, as such, these values are often commendable. The strident objection to such work as romanticized, universalizing, and essentialist put this initial response to dominational theory on the defensive. Recent efforts to particularize and relativize have further eclipsed a vision of "women's culture" and, along with it, the notion that the symbolism of women and femininity involves something other than the dynamics of oppression.

Feminist theorizing has, in other words, come close to throwing out the baby with the bath water. To recognize the centrality of culture, with all its changes and variations, need not imply that culture is primarily reflective of power. The more voluntaristic insights of "women's culture" need to be incorporated into the more recent discursive analyses of gender. Without making claims about women's inherent nature, we can see ways in which conceptions of gender have coded broader cultural perspectives on human interconnectedness. This is particularly obvious in conceptions of pregnancy and birth, nursing and childcare, and erotic relations. Cultural constructions of these activities, such as the sentimental image of motherhood and the belief in romantic love, are, to be sure, partly about unequal power. But they are also about the permeability of boundaries between human beings and the pleasures and satisfactions, as well as the sufferings and disappointments, of intimacy. This is perhaps especially evident in the speech and writings of women, although not exclusively so. The meanings associated with maternal nurturance and sexual attachment are by no means universal. As symbolic structures, motherhood and love obviously vary a great deal in their content and associations. Inasmuch as such symbols represent the human capacity for relational identification with another, however, they encode a dimension of social life as universal as the dynamics of power. Even gender symbols that signify destruction or self-contained isolation — e.g., the witch, the monk, the cowboy — speak to the same set of underlying relational issues.

To emphasize relations and boundaries as reference points for the cultural construction of gender dovetails with the insights of feminist psychoanalytic theorists who have been influenced by object relations theory. In their discussions of human development, they, too, stress the importance of relationality as opposed to the power dynamics associated with the castration complex. As Nancy Chodorow makes clear in her essay "Psychoanalytic Feminism," this is where feminist Lacanian and object relations theories diverge. Whereas for Lacanians such as Juliet Mitchell "there can be no experiences not generated by male dominance nor can there be a femininity defined in itself," Chodorow and other object relations feminists "see women's relational qualities as desirable and more fully human than masculine autonomy."[45] Yet even among object relations feminists there has recently been a notable shift towards defining gender in terms of power. The most conspicuous example is Jessica Benjamin's *The Bonds of Love*, in which intimate human relations are defined by the dynamics of domination. Jane Flax similarly suggests that the power of men over women is virtually the only universal feature of gender definition: "The actual content of being a man or woman and the rigidity of the categories themselves are highly variable across cultures and time. Nevertheless, gender relations so far as we have been able to understand them have been (more or less) relations of domination."[46] If even non-Lacanian psychoanalytic theorists have become increasingly taken with the postmodern view of human relations as structured by power, it is partly because psychoanalysis can provide no alternative theory of culture. Even those psychoanalytic theorists who, like Chodorow, insist on the importance of relationality see gender as a product of individual, psychological relationships rather than the patterned interrelationships of culture. An idea of culture as providing symbols and values that impinge upon, rather than reflect, the formation of gender identity within families is foreign (if not necessarily antagonistic) to psychoanalytic thought. The question of how individual identity articulates with collective systems of meaning is one that feminist psychoanalysts have yet to explore.

The analysis of gender as the cultural representation of human interdependency and relationality does not preclude the analysis of it as the representation of power. Both sets of perceptions are true. They are even in a sense connected to each other: to be interdependent is still to be in part dependent, and therefore to be vulnerable to the exercise of power. To argue that feminist theorists need a stronger theory of culture is not to imply that cultural analysis would necessarily concentrate on interrelationality instead of inequality. Oppressive exercises of wealth and power are rendered socially meaningful by an independently structured cultural system; as such, they need to be better understood as cultural acts rather than taken for granted as a function of human nature, male nature, or capitalism. A cultural analysis of the meanings of gender would address the social problem of gender inequality without reducing it to either individual psychodynamics, political struggle, or class relations.

A recognition of the cultural embeddedness of gender need not imply a static view of history that divests women and men of agency. Cultures change at least as much as material structures of wealth and power, and it has always been an implicit goal of feminism to effect cultural as well as political and economic change. This is, indeed, a case where theory needs to catch up with praxis. Instead of advancing theories that render this cultural work at best epiphenomenal, at worst irrelevant, feminist intellectuals should be theorizing its importance to social change.[47]

TOWARDS A CULTURALIST FEMINIST THEORY

This essay has attempted to offer constructive criticism of major recent trends in feminist theory. Like many feminist poststructuralists, I am advocating a theoretical perspective on society that emphasizes the symbolic analysis of gender. I take issue, however, with the materialist theory of causality of radical poststructuralists who define gender symbolism as a product of race, class, or power. There are, I have argued, at least two key elements to an alternative, more culturalist theoretical undertaking.

The first is the recognition that gender symbolism tends to be at least as much about interconnectedness as about power. Integral to this assertion is a view of human beings as driven not merely by utilitarian interests but by existential questions of meaning. The social purpose of gender definitions within various cultures is to interpret such human qualities as mutual dependency and the mysteries of procreation at least as much as to justify structures of domination. Precisely how gender is defined varies by time, place, and social group; such cultural variations in gender meaning at once transcend and inform the life experience of individuals.

The second element of a culturalist feminist theory is the insistence that gender is embedded in wider systems of meaning. The interpretation of gender difference is not an isolated and independent component of a given culture, but one that intersects with many other ways that people address fundamental questions about human experience. The definition of gender is a part of a larger cultural whole and is therefore fundamentally structured by broader religious, aesthetic, and scientific concerns.

Many empirical demonstrations of these two elements of a culturalist feminist theory exist in the scholarly literature, although they rarely receive theoretical elaboration. To chose an illustration from my own area of study, changing gender definitions in the early modern West in the sixteenth and seventeenth centuries were closely tied to the Reformation of Christianity. To understand the historical emergence of the widespread view of women as morally superior to men (a critical development of the eighteenth century that still reverberates today), one must appreciate how popular ideas about human salvation increasingly elevated the role of emotions in religious experience. Although historians have sought to interpret this development differently — for example, by connecting the ideal of motherhood to the separation of home and work associated with industrialization, or to the political experience of women in the American Revolution — such perspectives inadequately account for the earlier timing, symbolic content, and trans-Atlantic character of the symbolic redefinition.[48]

To save the cultural analysis of gender from being merely a dependent variable of class or race or power, feminist scholars need to look more closely at other kinds of social contexts, at religious beliefs, aesthetic and narrative traditions, scientific and moral thought. Too many academic specialists still view such cultural phenomena as religion, literature, folklore, art, philosophy, and science as either separate from a hypostatized "society" or as a product of it. As feminist scholars of religion and science like Caroline Bynum, Donna Haraway, and Evelyn Fox-Keller have begun to show us, these are arenas of cultural expression in which the symbolic and gendered meaning of human relationships are most clearly defined by men and women alike.[49] Feminist theory would do well to utilize such empirical building blocks in the construction of a more systematic and self-conscious culturalist analysis of gender.

By interpreting culture as an index to meaning, we can begin to understand gender as no more exclusively a function of race, class, or power than of biology. It is structures of meaning that provide the framework both for debates over anatomical differences and for struggles over sexual power. Most feminist theory to the contrary, materialism is not the only "social" alternative to biologism. A stronger theory of culture, in which gender symbolism receives analysis in its own terms, would help to free us from being caught between the Charybdis of materialism and the Scylla of biology. Only when the cultural dimension of society is taken more seriously will we be able to lend new and deeper meaning to the popular phrase among feminist intellectuals, "the social construction of gender."

NOTES

I would like to thank Joyce Appleby, Anne Lombard, Anne Mellor, Carrie Menkel-Meadow, and Debora Silverman for their helpful readings of an earlier draft.
1   The recent debate in *Contention* over Nicky Hart's article also addresses this issue. As Juliet Mitchell, Elizabeth Fox-Genovese, and others have pointed out, some of the reproductive processes that Hart regards as given, such as the mother's primary role in childrearing, others

would view as the products of society and subject to feminist transformation. See Nicky Hart, "Procreation and Women's Oppression," *Contention*
1 (Fall 1991) and 2(Winter 1992); Juliet Mitchell and Elizabeth Fox-Genovese replies in *Contention* 3 (Spring 1992).

2   There are some fine studies of the women's liberation movement,
most notably Alice Echols, *Daring to be Bad: Radical Feminism in
America, 1967-1975* (Minneapolis: Minnesota University Press, 1989),
but they do not take this theoretical perspective.

3   See, for example, the examples and discussion of the "culturalist"
approach within social anthropology in Sherry B. Ortner and Harriet
Whitehead, eds., *Sexual Meanings: The Cultural Construction of Gender
and Sexuality* (New York: Cambridge University Press, 1981). Among
historians, Natalie Zemon Davis, "Women on Top," in *Society and Culture
in Early Modern France* (Stanford: Stanford University Press, 1975);
Carroll Smith-Rosenberg, "The Female World of Love and Ritual," and
other essays in *Disorderly Conduct: Visions of Gender in Victorian America* (New York: Oxford University Press, 1985).

4   Most notably, Kate Millett, *Sexual Politics* (Garden City, New
York: Doubleday, 1970); Elaine Showalter, *A Literature of Their Own:
British Women Novelists from Bronte to Lessing* (Princeton: Princeton
University Press, 1977).

5   One notable but much criticized exception is Sherry Ortner's
classic article "Is Female to Male as Nature is to Culture?" *Feminist
Studies* 1 (Fall 1972): 5-31. Ortner presented a structuralist cultural analysis of dualistic and hierarchical symbols of men and women. The static
and deterministic implications of her analysis aroused objections from
other feminists. For example, see Carol P. MacCormack, "Nature, Culture,
and Gender: A Critique," in MacCormack and Marilyn Strathern, eds.,
Nature, Culture, and Gender (Cambridge: Cambridge University Press,
1980), pp. 1-25, and Ludmilla Jordanova, "Natural Facts," in her *Sexual
Visions: Images of Gender in Science and Medicine between the Eighteenth and Twentieth Centuries* (New York: Harvester Wheatsheaf, 1989),
pp. 19-41.

6   The Foucauldian tendency to explain racist cultural formulations
by referring to a material context of "power" has become increasingly
common. See, for example, David Theo Goldberg, "The Social Formation
of Racist Discourse," in Goldberg, ed. *Anatomy of Racism* (Minneapolis:
University of Minnesota, 1990), pp. 295-318.

7   For works on opposite ends of this spectrum, see Jean Bethke Elshtain, *Public Man, Private Women: Women in Social and Political Thought* (Princeton: Princeton University Press, 1981), and Judith Butler, *Gender Trouble: Feminism and the Subversion of Identity* (New York: Routledge, 1990).

8   For example, Shulamith Firestone, *The Dialectic of Sex: The Case for Feminist Revolution* (New York: Morrow, 1970); Juliet Mitchell, *Woman's Estate*, (New York: Pantheon, 1971); Susan Brownmiller, *Against Our Will: Men, Women, and Rape* (Washington: Simon and Schuster, 1975); Zillah R. Eisenstein, ed., *Capitalist Patriarchy and the Case for Socialist Feminism* (New York: The Monthly Review Press, 1979); Annette Kuhn and AnnMarie Wolpe, eds., *Feminism and Materialism: Women and Modes of Production* (Boston: Routledge and Kegan Paul, 1978); Lydia Sargent, ed. *Women and Revolution: A Discussion of the Unhappy Marriage of Marxism and Feminism* (London: Pluto Press, 1981).

9   Catherine A. MacKinnon, *Towards a Feminist Theory of the State* (Cambridge: Harvard University Press, 1989),p. 3.

10   Nancy Hartsock, *Money, Sex, and Power: Toward a Feminist Historical Materialism* (New York: Longman, 1983); Allison Jaggar, *Feminist Politics and Human Nature* (Totowa, N.J.: Rowman and Allenheld, 1983); Christine Stansell, *City of Women: Sex and Class in New York, 1789-1860* (New York: Knopf, 1986). Other excellent works in this neo-Marxist, socialist feminist tradition include: Gayle Rubin, "The Traffic in Women," in *Toward an Anthropology of Women*, ed. Rayna Rapp Reiter (New York: Monthly Review Press, 1975), pp. 157-210; Heidi Hartman, "The Unhappy Marriage of Marxism and Feminism," in Sargent, ed. *Women and Revolution*; Sheila Rowbotham, Lynne Segal, and Hilary Wainwright, *Beyond the Fragments: Feminism and the Making of Socialism* (London: Merlin Press, 1979); Linda J. Nicholson, *Gender and History: The Limits of Social Theory in the Age of the Family* (New York: Columbia, 1986); Linda Gordon, *Heroes of Their Own Lives: The Politics and History of Family Violence, Boston, 1880-1960* (New York: Penguin, 1988); Jeanne Boydston, *Home and Work: Housework, Wages, and the Ideology of Labor in the Early Republic* (New York: Oxford University Press, 1990).

11   For a recent comparison of the theories of patriarchy and Marxism, see Sylvia Walby, *Theorizing Patriarchy* (Cambridge: Blackwell, 1990).

12   Kathryn Kish Sklar, *Catharine Beecher: A Study in American Domesticity* (New Haven: Yale University Press, 1973); Nancy F. Cott, *The Bonds of Womanhood* (New Haven: Yale University Press, 1977); Smith-Rosenberg, "Female World of Love and Ritual."

13   Patricia Meyer Spacks, *The Female Imagination* (New York: Knopf, 1975); Showalter, *Literature of One's Own*; Sandra Gilbert and Susan Gubar, *The Madwoman in the Attic: The Woman Writer and the Nineteenth-Century Literary Imagination* (New Haven: Yale University Press, 1979).

14   ¨ Nancy Chodorow, *The Reproduction of Mothering: Psychoanalysis and the Sociology of Gender* (Berkeley: University of California Press, 1978); Carol Gilligan, *In a Different Voice: Psychological Theory and Women's Development* (Cambridge: Harvard University Press, 1982). Also see Juliet Mitchell, *Psychoanalysis and Feminism*, (New York: Pantheon, 1974); Jean Baker Miller, *Toward a New Psychology of Women* (Boston: Beacon, 1976); Sara Ruddick, *Maternal Thinking: Towards a Politics of Peace* (Boston: Beacon, 1989); Mary Belenky, Blythe Clinchy, Nancy Goldberger, and Jill Terrle, *Women's Ways of Knowing: The Development of Self, Voice, and Mind* (New York: Basic Books, 1986); Dorothy Dinnerstein, *The Mermaid and the Minotaur* (New York: Harper and Row, 1976); Nell Noddings, *Caring: A Feminine Approach to Ethics and Moral Education* (Berkeley: University of California Press, 1984).

15   Monique Wittig, *Les Guérillères*, trans. David Le Vay (Boston: Beacon Press, 1969). Luce Irigaray, *This Sex Which Is Not One*, trans. Catherine Porter with Carolyn Burke (Ithaca: Cornell University Press, 1985); Irigaray, *Speculum of the Other Woman*, trans Gillian C. Gill (Ithaca: Cornell University Press, 1985); Toril Moi, ed., *The Kristeva Reader* (New York: Columbia University Press, 1986); Toril Moi, *Sexual/Textual Politics: Feminist Literary Theory* (London: Methuen, 1985). Also see selections by Hélène Cixous, Julia Kristeva, Luce Irigaray and others in Elaine Marks and Isabelle de Courtivron, eds., *New French Feminisms: An Anthology* (Amherst: University of Massachusetts, 1980).

16   Mary Daly, *Beyond God the Father: Toward a Philosophy of Women's Liberation* (Boston: Beacon, 1973); *Gyn/Ecology: The Metaethics of Radical Feminism* (Boston: Beacon Press, 1978); Andrea Dworkin, *Woman Hating* (New York: Dutton, 1974).

17   Several critics of Gilligan made this point in the commentaries in *Signs* 11 (1986): 303-333 and *Feminist Studies* 11 (1985): 149-161. The conflicting and problematic meanings of "essence" itself are explored in

Diana Fuss, *Essentially Speaking: Feminism, Nature, and Difference* (London: Routledge, 1989).

18   Elizabeth Fox-Genovese, *Feminism Without Illusions: A Critique of Individualism* (Chapel Hill: University of North Carolina, 1991), p. 54. For a scathing critique, see Ellen DuBois, "Illusions Without Feminism," *The Nation* 254 (Jan. 20, 1992): 57-60.

19   Susan Faludi, *Backlash: The Undeclared War Against American Women* (New York: Crown, 1991).

20   Elizabeth V. Spelman, *Inessential Woman: Problems of Exclusion in Feminist Thought* (Boston: Beacon Press, 1988). For a similar perspective among literary critics and women's historians, as well as efforts to rectify the imbalances, see Judith Newton and Deborah Rosenfelt, eds. *Feminist Criticism and Social Change: Sex, Class, and Race in Literature and Culture* (New York: Methuen, 1985), and Ellen Carol DuBois and Vicki L. Ruiz, eds. *Unequal Sisters: A Multicultural Reader in U.S. Women's History* (New York: Routledge, 1990).

21   For example, Suzanne J. Kessler and Wendy McKenna, *Gender: An Ethnomethodological Approach* (Chicago: Chicago University Press, 1978); Emily Martin, *The Woman in the Body: A Cultural Analysis of Reproduction* (Boston: Beacon, 1987); Thomas Laqueur, *Making Sex: Body and Gender from the Greeks to Freud* (Cambridge: Harvard University Press, 1990); Butler, *Gender Trouble.*

22   Gayle Rubin, "Traffic in Women."

23   Ibid., p. 199.

24   On the broader phenomenon of the "linguistic turn," see, for example, the discussion and works cited in John Toews, "Intellectual History after the Linguistic Turn," *American Historical Review* 92 (October 1987): 879-907.

25   Irigaray, *Sex Which is Not One*, p. 186.

26   See, for example, Nancy Hewitt, "Beyond the Search for Sisterhood: American Women's History in the 1980s," *Social History* 10 (1985): 299-321; Stansell, *City of Women*; Gordon, *Heroes*; DuBois and Ruiz, eds. *Unequal Sisters.*

27   Jane Flax, *Thinking Fragments: Psychoanalysis, Feminism, and Postmodernism in the Contemporary West* (Berkeley: UC Press, 1990), p. 28.

28   Linda Kauffman, ed., *Gender and Theory: Dialogues in Feminist Criticism* (New York: Basil Blackwell, 1989), p. 5.

29   The literature making this point is increasingly large. For a few examples, see: Elizabeth Fee, "Is there a Feminist Science?" *Science and Nature* 4 (1981): 46-57; Carolyn Merchant, *The Death of Nature: Women, Ecology, and the Scientific Revolution* (New York: Harper and Row, 1980); Evelyn Fox Keller, *Reflections on Gender and Science* (New Haven: Yale University Press, 1985); Sandra Harding, *The Science Question in Feminism* (Ithaca: Cornell University Press, 1986); Ruth Bleier, *Science and Gender: A Critique of Biology and Its Theories on Women* (Oxford: Pergamon Press, 1984); Genevieve Lloyd, *The Man of Reason: "Male" and "Female" in Western Philosophy* (Minneapolis: University of Minnesota Press, 1984); Carole Pateman, *The Sexual Contract* (Stanford: Stanford University Press, 1988).

30   Lawrence Stone, "Only Women," *New York Review of Books* 32 (April 11, 1985): 21-22, 27; Helen Vendler, "Feminism and Literature," *New York Review of Books* 37 (May 31, 1990): 19-25.

31   Michel Foucault, "Body/Power," in *Power/Knowledge*, ed. Colin Gordon (New York: Pantheon Books, 1980), pp. 57-8.

32   Joan Wallach Scott, *Gender and the Politics of History* (New York: Columbia University Press, 1988), p. 45.

33   Butler, *Gender Trouble*, p. 136.

34   I owe this insight to an observation of Lucy White of the UCLA Law School during a discussion of poststructuralist feminist theory.

35   Gayatri Chakravorty Spivak, *In Other Worlds: Essays in Cultural Politics* (New York: Methuen, 1987), p. 107.

36   Poovey, *Uneven Developments: The Ideological Work of Gender in Mid-Victorian England* (Chicago: University of Chicago Press, 1988), p. 17.

37   Nancy C. M. Hartsock, "The Feminist Standpoint: Developing the Ground for a Specifically Feminist Historical Materialism," in Sandra Harding and Merrill B. Hintikka, eds. *Discovering Reality: Feminist Perspectives on Epistemology, Metaphysics, Methodology, and Philosophy of Science* (Boston: D. Reidel, 1983), pp. 283-305; Also see Harding, *Science Question*, pp. 136-196; Dorothy E. Smith, "Sociological Theory: Methods of Writing Patriarchy," in Ruth A. Wallace, ed., *Feminism and Sociological Theory* (Newbury Park, Calif.: Sage Publications, 1989), pp. 34-64.

38   Deborah K. King, "Multiple Jeopardy, Multiple Consciousness: The Context of a Black Feminist Ideology," *Signs* 14 (1988): 42-72; Audre Lorde, *Sister Outsider: Essays and Speeches* (Trumansburg, New York:

Crossing Press, 1984), pp. 114-123; Patricia Hill Collins, *Black Feminist Thought: Knowledge, Consciousness, and the Politics of Empowerment* (Boston: Unwin Hyman, 1990).

39   Gerda Lerner, "Reconceptualizing Differences Among Women," *Journal of Women's History* 1 (Winter 90): 116.

40   See, for example, Bonnie Thornton Dill, "Race, Class, and Gender: Prospects for an All-Inclusive Sisterhood," *Feminist Studies* 9 (Spring 1983): 131-150; Karen Brodkin Sacks, "Toward a Unified Theory of Class, Race, and Gender," *American Ethnologist* 16 (1989): 534-50.

41   Rita Felski, *Beyond Feminist Aesthetics: Feminist Literature and Social Change* (London: Hutchinson Radius, 1989), p. 8. For Felski's repeated use of the adjective "bourgeois" to describe and to modify the noun "society," see especially pp. 155, 159-60, 164-67. Other excellent recent studies that draw (in my view too much) on Habermasian categories are Joan Landes, *Women and the Public Sphere in the Age of the French Revolution* (Ithaca: Cornell University Press, 1988) and Nancy Fraser, *Unruly Practices: Power, Discourse, Gender in Contemporary Social Theory* (Minneapolis: University of Minnesota Press, 1989).

42   Bonnie S. Anderson and Judith P. Zinsser, *A History of Their Own: Women in Europe from Prehistory to the Present*, 2 vols. (New York: Harper and Row, 1988), I: xv.

43   Ibid., p. xvii.

44   The Joan Scott-Linda Gordon exchange is in *Signs* 15 (1990): 848-859.

45   Nancy Chodorow, *Feminism and Psychoanalytic Theory* (New Haven: Yale University Press, 1989), pp. 189-190. Also see Miriam Johnson on "expressiveness," *Strong Mothers, Weak Wives: The Search for Gender Equality* (Berkeley: University of California Press, 1988).

46   Flax, *Thinking Fragments*, p. 23.

47   Judith Butler, who calls for the performance of stylized "acts" that challenge gender conventions, is in this respect close to the mark. Yet without a broader theory of culture she both exaggerates the individual's freedom to improvise independently of broader systems of meaning and sells short the ability of collective as well as individual feminist "acts" to change conventional gender definitions. *Gender Trouble*, esp. pp. 128-141.

48   Compare the interpretations of Gerda Lerner, "The Lady and the Mill-Girl: Changes in the Status of Women in the Age of Jackson," *Mid-Continent American Studies Journal* 10 (1969); Nancy F. Cott, *The Bonds of Womanhood: Woman's Sphere in New England, 1780-1835* (New

Haven: Yale University Press, 1977); Mary Beth Norton, *Liberty's Daughters: The Revolutionary Experience of American Women, 1750-1800* (Boston: Little, Brown, & Co., 1980); Linda Kerber, *Women of the Republic: Intellect and Ideology in Revolutionary America* (Chapel Hill: University of North Carolina Press, 1980); and Ruth H. Bloch, "The Gendered Meanings of Virtue in Revolutionary America," *Signs* 13(1987): 37-58.

49   None of these writers advances my particular theoretical position, but their works can in part be seen as empirical demonstrations of this argument. See especially Caroline Walker Bynum, *Jesus as Mother: Studies in the Spirituality of the High Middle Ages* (Berkeley: University of California, 1982); Bynum, *Holy Feast and Holy Fast: The Religious Significance of Food to Medieval Women* (Berkeley: University of California Press, 1987); Evelyn Fox Keller, *A Feeling for the Organism: The Life and Work of Barbara McClintock* (San Francisco: Freeman, 1983); Keller, *Reflections on Gender and Science;* Donna Haraway, *Primate Visions: Gender, Race, and Nature in the World of Modern Science* (New York: Routledge, 1989).

Gender Analysis and Social Theory:

Building on Ruth Bloch's Proposals

BARBARA LASLETT

Ruth Bloch has made a compelling argument for feminist theory to be more attentive to culture. Culture, and the ideas, representations, and institutions through which it is constituted are, in my view, important to contemporary theoretical debates — feminist included — about social structure, human agency, and their intersection in concrete and specific historical contexts. And I strongly agree with Bloch that social action is shaped by goals and motives that cannot be reduced to material interests or the search for political power alone.

Bloch's suggestions about what the content of a cultural theory of gender would include — underlying issues of relatedness and the relationship between gender and the larger systems of meaning of which it is a part — are certainly good starting places. There are, I think, other basic building blocks of such a theory — one that comes to mind immediately is desire and/or pleasure — and I will elaborate on this idea later in this essay. But there is one other point that I would like to discuss first because it seems central to a social theory of gender — whether it focuses primarily on cultural, materialist, political, and/or psychological phenomena.

It seems to me that in trying to counter what she sees as the reductionism of most contemporary feminist theory, Bloch has fallen into some of the same intellectual pitfalls she criticizes. In particular, I have in

Contention, Vol. 2, No. 3, Spring 1993

mind her tendency, when arguing against theories that press for a materialist and/or political theory of gender relations and in arguing for a cultural theory of gender, also to argue that they can and should be separated from each other — that it is possible to construct an autonomous theory of culture. I will take issue with that idea, and will suggest some of the dangers of pursuing it.

My argument is twofold: Precisely because cultures are social phenomena, they are located and reproduced in institutions — although with varying degrees of organizational complexity in different societies, different historical periods, and different cultural arenas. As a consequence of this institutional embeddedness, cultures (or any other social phenomena) cannot be understood apart from the organizational, political, and material conditions — more generally, the structural context, in which they exist. In addition, social actors produce and reproduce cultures within these contexts and in so doing perpetuate and change them. Social actors are the agents of continuity and they are the agents of change. From this perspective, the idea of an autonomous theory of culture — one that abstracts culture from the social structure and social actors who construct it within a historically specific context — needs to be questioned.

Second, the wish to build a cultural theory that is abstracted from material, political, and organizational relations also runs the danger of fostering inappropriate causal hierarchies in our explanations. If economic organization has some essential logic, some universal essence apart from the context in which it is found and apart from the social actors who construct it (positions that some versions of Marxist and Weberian theory would argue), and if political life and organizational forms have some intrinsic qualities and universal features (as some writers on the relative autonomy of the state and/or bureaucracy would argue), then we will, I fear, be prone to formulate our arguments about them in terms of questions like: which one is more basic than the other? Which one continues to have an effect when the effects of the others are controlled? (A rhetorical formulation that is common in the quantitative wings of the social sciences.) Such questions lead to intellectual controversy over the analytic power of one or another approach to theorizing gender that is contrary to the anti-reductionist spirit and message of Ruth Bloch's argument.

To be against reductionism in general, however, does not mean that multi-causality is always present or that causal hierarchies are never appropriate. Whether or not they are is a question to be asked about any empirical event or phenomenon of interest. Nor does anti-reductionism mean that the use of "controlling" metaphors and devices do not have some heuristic advantages for some kinds of questions. But, although we always use them both, rhetorics and devices cannot substitute for careful and nuanced conceptual work. What we need is good social theory that takes account of structures, cultures, and agents — not one that emphasizes one or another of these elements. It may be the case that, for analytic and technical purposes, we may separate components of a given research topic or of a given explanation from each other. I will elaborate on this point in a minute. But such practical considerations — considerations that reflect the finite time, energy and capacities that we have as human beings — should not blind us to the overlapping and contingent nature of the phenomena we study.

There is a formal division of labor in academia (at least in American colleges and universities, but certainly not restricted to them) that is usually manifested in administratively (and often budgetarily) distinct departments. In the social sciences, this departmental structure differentiates, for instance, history, sociology, political science, economics, and anthropology, among others. And students of these subjects learn different skills, different literatures, different professional and intellectual norms. They develop what Kai Erikson called "disciplinary reflexes."[1] And in the process of socialization that goes on in graduate schools and in intellectual professions, people also develop different identities — they learn to be historians, sociologists, anthropologists, economists, etc. This institutionally-based differentiation can be very useful in preparing scholars with the technical skills — in statistics, in field work, in archival research, in languages — that we need to do our work, especially in the contemporary intellectual world that includes so many different places and periods for study.

But it would be a mistake, in my view, to treat this particular institutional arrangement as if it were essential to the intellectual process itself. The existence of historical sociologists like myself, or cultural historians such as Ruth Bloch, suggests that scholars can address questions conventionally raised in disciplines different than the ones in which we were trained and with which we identify. It is unhelpful, I think, to take a position that essential differences exist between these discourses, despite the different "reflexes" that training in one or the other of them might foster and despite their organizational differentiation. It is unfortunate that Bloch identifies cultural theory with anthropology — or, rather, identifies anthropology as the discipline that has been most directly concerned with culture in the social sciences and, indeed, defines culture as "myths, symbols, rituals and other structures of collective meaning," i.e., as anthropologists have done. In this regard, the growth of "cultural studies" as a field of inquiry is informative. What is called "cultural studies" in the United States today can be found in English and in History departments. But it can also to be found in departments of Sociology, Communication Studies, American Studies, Film Studies and, occasionally, in Schools of Music, to name a few. Our intellectual work is not fostered, I think, by a tendency to identify culture with a single discipline. And although I doubt that Bloch would press for a strong form of such an identification, her argument appears to do so implicitly through the examples and definitions that she uses.

Yet, institutional differentiation is real and is the focus of struggles over whether subjects such as Women's Studies, Chicano Studies, etc. should be academic programs or departments — or exist at all as administratively distinct units. But they often do have concrete institutional form within contemporary American universities and they often face competition with other units for resources and status, competition which is especially intense when funding is scarce. The sociologist of science, Tom Gieryn, has argued that the creation of intellectual boundaries is fostered by competition between fields of knowledge as they vie for both material resources and status.[2] It is quite understandable if, in the process of competition, advocates of one discipline or another emphasize its perspective and the knowledge that it generates as more "basic" in understanding some social phenomenon than another. Some Marxists argue for the primary importance of class relations and economic organization and some microeconomists do the same about the primacy of the market. Some feminists argue for the primary importance of sexuality, gender relations, or the social organization of procreation. Some political scientists argue for the primary importance of political institutions and power relations. And some literary scholars and postmodernists argue for the primary importance of textuality and linguistic forms. But this emphasis on difference, born out of historical contingency, competition for material resources and the technical skills needed to do different kinds of intellectual work, should not lead us to conclude that there are some essential differences between these institutionally differentiated intellectual projects.

Nevertheless, competition between ideas and perspectives exists, although the severity and consequences of competition vary historically. This has, unfortunately in my view, resulted in a tendency to argue for a hierarchy of causes in our theoretical work and, with it, for a hierarchy of disciplines. Early in its history, for instance, August Comte argued that sociology was at the top of that hierarchy; I think some historians have also made that claim for the discipline of history. And the intellectual imperialism of economics is easy to observe. The recent emphasis in postmodernism on language and on literary theory, and its application to what have, traditionally, been domains of the social sciences is another example of a similar kind of move. While this is not an appropriate place to elaborate on the point, a question about the place of competition and the emphasis on competing "interests" in the organization and culture of academic life in the United States cannot be separated from the organization and culture of its economic and political life. But neither can it be reduced to them.

Now, I am not asserting the need for a "de-departmentalization" of higher learning, or for knowledge always to be pursued in an inter- or multidisciplinary way. The disciplinary format may be as good a system as many others to prepare people for participation in scholarly debates and as a way to shape those debates. (Of course, legitimation of disciplinary and inter/multidisciplinary scholarship makes it possible to benefit from both approaches.) While any institutionalization runs the risk of entrenchment and resistance to change, culture that is not institutionalized is in danger of being too quickly superseded. Doing serious intellectual work takes time and trials; institutionalized standards supply some common criteria for the acceptance or rejection of new knowledge and new perspectives. But contention is a regular part of scholarly discourse as well, and this contention is also connected to competing interests. In the intellectual world, struggles are not only over ideas.

Here I want to say a bit about the concept of "interests." Bloch argues, rightly I think, that the concept of "interests" has achieved an unusually and, unfortunately, prominent place in academic discourse today, especially although not exclusively in the social sciences. But "interests" have a dual meaning. On the one hand, the word refers to something thought to be of benefit, as "in my interest." This is the way I have just used the concept, as in "competing interests." On the other hand, the term also implies something that is intellectually engaging, something "interesting." Different people may, for a wide range of reasons — psychological, autobiographical, historical, political, and intellectual — see different subjects as interesting, as engaging their attention. If this is the case, then we need to understand why certain intellectual questions and practices become interesting while others do not.

In the past few years, in the context of studying the history of sociology in the United States early in this century, I have argued that the development of a quantitative, objectivist and empirical sociology after World War I is explained, in part, by changing gender relations in the late nineteenth and early twentieth centuries; that changing gender relations made this kind of sociology both "interesting to" and "in the interest of" the second generation of mostly male, mostly white, American sociologists.[3] But it is the second meaning of "interests" that is more commonly used today in much theoretical and interpretive debate in the social sciences. A contemporary example of this practice can be found in the microeconomic models of Gary Becker, the recent recipient of the Nobel Prize in Economics, which have been particularly influential in the development and spread of rational choice theory in sociology.

From this perspective, a single metric is seen as appropriate to compare the similarities — or exchange value — of, for instance, purchasing a new car as against having a child. The "value" of cars and children is transformed into a single metric that makes their comparison "rational." (Using the rhetoric of "rationality" to describe choices that ignore the multiple meanings of the terms that are compared should not be allowed to pass without comment.) Differences between the two choices — the ways in which cars and children are phenomena whose meaning and value are constructed varyingly by historically and socially located social actors — are treated as "preferences" that the model chooses to ignore. They interfere with its elegance, its simplicity. In this way of thinking, parsimony rather than complexity is valued. So too are generalization and abstraction as against specificity and contextualization. Parsimony as a criterion for accepting or rejecting explanations — i.e., that, all other things being equal, theories that rely on fewer principles are superior to those that rely on more — is widely accepted in the social sciences, at least in their quantitative wings. But it is not restricted to them. Ruth Bloch's critique is so important to contemporary intellectual debate precisely because of the hegemony of ideas about theory-building that value simplicity over complexity, that focus on one dimension of social life such as "interests" — regardless of the distortions such an emphasis may foster.

One of the arguments in favor of this approach to intellectual work is that a competitive, exchange model — a marketplace — of ideas produces the best results. This is not an argument with which I agree. I do not think that a zero-sum approach to higher learning, scientific knowledge, etc., fosters useful debate or facilitates the "discovery of truth" — especially not when such debate is closely tied to our social status. But I also do not see intellectual controversy that is not built on strict competition for prestige or power as necessarily pallid or a weak version of one that is. People involved in academic debate can, and do, have strong, indeed passionate, disagreements over ideas even when they are not instrumental to other purposes. But when our professional and intellectual status and our material well-being, our sense of personal efficacy and our political power — within our disciplines, and, sometimes, within the wider society in which we live — depend on how we fare in the "marketplace of ideas," we will be encouraged to create intellectual hierarchies. We will tend to inflate the importance of our own discipline and our own ideas and to devalue the contributions of others or the reliance of our ideas on those of others.

In some instances, creating intellectual hierarchies that pit one explanation against another in a zero-sum framework may be appropriate. As a general epistemological stance, however, I do not believe it is. The emphasis on "parsimony" in social science explanations that is often used to justify such practices should no longer be accepted uncritically. While I do not know much about the history of this idea, or how and why it came to be adopted as doctrine in many parts of the social sciences, it is unclear to me that it continues to hold out promise for advancing our intellectual practices. Given some recognition of the importance of diversity in social experience and social organization, how can we claim that parsimony is, in and of itself, of value.

The increasing hegemony of power — of political and economic "interests" — as a central theoretical concept in contemporary feminist theory that Bloch identifies reflects, I think, ideas about theorizing constructed by the mostly male, mostly white social theorists whose voices have, until recently, thoroughly dominated academic discourse. To be part of that discourse, even some feminist theorists have succumbed to its conceptual framings. But this hegemony also reflects a zero-sum model of competition for the resources within our institutions of higher learning and within our cultural institutions more generally. Yet competition is not an illusion and, indeed, it is particularly strong at the present time in the United States when the value and resources to pursue one's intellectual interests (in the second sense of the word) are being hotly contested. That may explain (at least in part) why so much passion and energy are expended in academic politics and why academic disciplines often make jurisdictional, boundary-making claims for themselves. But I think that Ruth Bloch's argument implicitly takes too seriously the disciplinary divisions that exist today in American academia. Although they have become formalized in modern institutions of higher learning, and their spokespersons make declarations about their unique intellectual importance, we need to be aware of the dangers of taking such advocacy too much at face value.

Yet, even though I do not share with Ruth Bloch a belief that it is possible to construct an "autonomous theory of culture," I do think there is a core to gender relations that differentiates them from other types of social relationships. I therefore agree that we need to be attentive to "the importance of gender symbolism in its own terms." But what might these terms be? In a work currently in progress, Nancy Chodorow speaks of gender identity as necessarily including, among other things, cultural and emotional interpretations of genitality and genital and reproductive difference. This definition suggests, and I agree, that a relationship between sex and gender is inescapable. The meanings of that relationship, however, and of the components that comprise it depend on the context of meanings that are shaped by historically specific structures, cultures, and actors. From this perspective, the task of feminist theory is to develop, in more complex and nuanced terms than has been the case to date, a theory for understanding variation in the relationship between sex, gender, and other aspects of social life, be they psychological, cultural, material, and/or political. I have some suggestions about how this might be done.

First, we need to rethink the gendered division of labor. The assignment of some tasks to men and others to women, and the identification of some institutions as women's domains and others as men's, has been recognized in some social theory — both functionalist and Marxist. The newly available literature on women's history, however, has sensitized us to the historical specificity of this division of labor and the complex dialectic through which it has been changed. Structural economic changes in 19th century America, for instance - the decline of domestic production, the rise of a market economy - increasingly took middle-class men out of their homes and left women within them. And this spatial arrangement was buttressed by an ideology of separate spheres and a rhetoric about white, middle class women and men's different natures. This had not been common earlier when family economies had dominated production and when women and men both contributed to economic production, although usually in different ways. And while religious beliefs of the time recognized gender distinctions and did not see women and men as equal, ideas about gender had not been dichotomized nor had women and men been conceptualized as qualitatively different from each other. As we have learned from Ruth Bloch's scholarship, "Women were measured against essentially the same standard as men and were judged worthy of a position one rung beneath." In the eighteenth and nineteenth centuries, in contrast, sexual divisions came to be seen more in terms of "qualitative, horizontal distinctions between the sexes."[4] But Ruth Bloch has demonstrated many times in her own scholarship that we cannot adequately understand the changing beliefs about gender without contextualizing them in the economic and political relationships of the time.[5] Similarly, we cannot adequately understand the emerging capitalist class relations in late eighteenth and early nineteenth century Britain without taking into account changing ideas about masculinity and femininity.[6] Class and gender were inextricably intertwined in both of these instances.

The gendered division of labor affects social action as well as social structure. When gender roles are dichotomized and are defined in terms of qualitative differences between women and men, and when social institutions, such as families and work places, support such definitions, social action is likely to be gendered — to be socially defined as feminine or masculine. Changes in the gendered division of labor in the United States from the eighteenth and into the nineteenth and early twentieth centuries — middle class white women's increasing, and increasingly exclusive, responsibility for child rearing, middle class white men's increasing, and increasingly exclusive, responsibility for family breadwinning — affected what people did, what they thought, and how they related to each other. The explanations for these changes are multidimensional. While it may be useful to ask how aspects of cultures relate to the larger system of meaning of which they are a part, contextualization in the concrete social, political and cultural institutions is also critical to understanding the meanings that they have to social actors.

Second, sex and gender are related to social structure and human agency in ways that go beyond the gendered division of labor. And although it may be especially easy to see the social structuring of sexuality in contemporary times — sexual and gay liberation, AIDS and controversies over the control of procreation immediately come to mind — sexuality has always been socially organized. Theoretically less recognized, perhaps, than the ways that social institutions shape sexuality, is the relationships of sex and gender to human action. Family relationships, sexual identity and sexuality itself, for instance, can provide powerful motives for human actions and gender relations are central to understanding them. Furthermore, sexual energy and sexual meaning can be attached to social phenomena that are not related to sexuality or gender in any obvious manner at all. And the sexual nature of that energy gives some actions, but not others, a particular charge, a particular emotional power, as in the meaning of occupational activity and success for men's gender and sexual identity. Thus, while an occupation has no intrinsic connection to masculinity or femininity, it can take on such meaning under given historical circumstances — a dynamic that can be widely seen historically and in the contemporary world in, for instance, the tenacity of sex segregation in the paid labor force.

Third, gendered meanings — particularly, I think, in modern times, the issue of gender identity (achieving masculinity and femininity) — are often part of, if not central to, the ways in which social institutions and cultural forms are constructed. In the United States, the family began to be viewed as a feminine domain and the work place a masculine one in the nineteenth century and that was accompanied by a way of thinking about them in terms of qualitative differences between women and men. This can also be seen in our intellectual pursuits — in the development and gendering of ideas about hard and soft science, hard and soft methods, hard and soft fields of inquiry.[7] While this process can reasonably be seen as part of the competition between newer and older intellectual practices, it has resulted in an intellectual culture that uses dangerous, simplistic and, too often, gendered dichotomies to describe knowledge and its pursuit.

If feminist theory is to become more nuanced and more adequate to the intellectual purposes to which it can be put, and if new empirical work continues to support our present understanding of the importance of gender to both social structure and human agency, it suggests that material, organizational and political contexts are fundamentally shaped by sex and gender relations. These relationships engender our social meanings and our social institutions. The engendering of intellectual work is, of course, neither universal nor static. It can be quite open and contingent. We do the engendering — although not under conditions of our own choosing but under conditions that we inherit from the past, as Marx so succinctly put it in the *Eighteenth Brumaire of Louis Bonaparte*. Thus, although we can change the engendering of our pursuits, such change will be no simple matter. Too much personal and social history is invested in the current arrangements. Too many interests and too much of what is interesting to us is involved in its present form. Change, although possible, will not occur without contention or without powerful resistance from many quarters.

Which brings me back to the second meaning of intellectual "interests" that I referred to earlier and the connection of sexuality, pleasure, and desire to them. I suggested that passion will always be a part of intellectual work and that scholarly debate will always be based on contention. This is the case, I believe, not only because new ideas inevitably contest older ones in terms of empirical evidence, theoretical acuity and technical advances in knowledge but also because contention among intellectuals is often more than intellectual. For some of us, intellectual work, intellectual interests (in the sense of things that are interesting to us) and our identities as intellectuals are fueled by what Nancy Chodorow is calling "the power of feelings," and reflect the emotional construction of our own autobiographies. Among people who care about them, ideas are rarely neutral.

In the history of Western thought, there has been a continuing argument about the need to replace emotion and magical thinking with rationality and objectivity in the pursuit of knowledge. Max Weber's essay on "Science as a Vocation" comes to mind as one of the canonical statements on this topic, at least in the social sciences. But to define the "calling" of science in terms that require us to hold our commitments at a distance from the scholarship we do misses the positive relationship of emotional, political, and personal commitments to intellectual work. While the scientific tradition that Weber's name is often used to justify recognizes that politics, for instance, may shape the questions we choose to work on, it considers only in negative terms how values affect the research process itself. But this position ignores an essential part of why intellectual work gets done. Our emotions provide the energy to go on with a project even when the going gets tough. To see only as negative the relationship of commitment to our scholarship is to ignore part of what makes a question interesting to us and why we work hard to answer it well.

As I have been writing this essay, I have also been reading a collection of short stories by women crime writers who have as their main characters female sleuths. In "Murder Without a Text," by Amanda Cross (aka Caroline Heilbrun), Leo Fansler, the nephew of Kate Fansler — Cross' female sleuth — says in response to his aunt's comment about his involvement in his cases (he is a public defender), "I'm always involved; that's why I am so good at what I do and why it's interesting."[8] Exactly my point!

We need to rethink our understanding of intellectual life and to create a set of norms and structures for its pursuit that acknowledges the positive side of commitment. Caring emotionally about the scholarship we do can be a source of intellectual bias. But it can also foster our commitment to finding the best answers to the questions we ask. Emotion, the search for pleasure, and the desire associated with our efforts to achieve rewards and recognition are part of the intellectual process. But that process is not fueled only by the search for power or control, or for social status, much as those motivations may also be part of the process. To understand the culture of intellectual life, we also need to understand the emotions — including pleasure — that such work can provide, although goodness knows the way higher education, and worklife in general, in the United States is organized often makes it hard to experience the pleasure.

Max Weber's arguments about modern science need to be broadened to include a positive as well as a negative view of commitment. A feminist theory of culture can help us in that regard by drawing attention to the relationship of gender, sexuality, and pleasure to academic and scientific ideas and practices. But such a cultural theory of knowledge cannot be meaningfully constructed as autonomous from the political, economic and emotional character of the institutions in which it is practiced and from the actors that shape these practices. Neither can a cultural theory of gender.

NOTES

1   Kai Erikson, "Sociology and the Historical Perspective," *American Sociologist:* 5, 4 (1970):331-38.
2   Thomas F. Gieryn, "Boundary-work and the Demarcation of Science from Non-science: Strains and Interests in Professional Ideologies of Scientists," *American Sociological Review* 48 (December 1983):781-795.
3   Barbara Laslett, "Unfeeling Knowledge: Emotion and Objectivity in the History of Sociology," *Sociological Forum* 5, 3 (1990):413-433; "Biography as Historical Sociology: The Case of William Fielding Ogburn," *Theory and Society* 20 (1991):511-538; "Gender In/And Social Science History," *Social Science History* 16 (Summer 1992):177-195;

"Gender and The Rhetoric of Social Science: William Fielding Ogburn and Early 20th Century Sociology in the United States," to appear in *The Rhetoric of Social History*, edited by Jeffery Cox and Sheldon Stromquist (forthcoming).

4   Ruth H. Bloch, "Untangling the Roots of Modern Sex Roles: A Survey of Four Centuries of Change," *Signs: Journal of Women in Culture and Society* 4 (Winter 1978):237-252.

5   Ruth H. Bloch, "The Gendered Meanings of Virtue in Revolutionary America," *Signs: Journal of Women in Culture and Society* 13 (Autumn 1987):37-58.

6   Lenore Davidoff and Catherine Hall, *Family Fortunes* (Chicago: University of Chicago Press, 1987).

7   Laslett, ops. cit.; also Linda Gordon, "Social Insurance and Public Assistance: The Influence of Gender in Welfare Thought in the U.S., 1890-1935," *American Historical Review*, 97 (1992):19-54.

8   Sara Paretsky, ed., *A Woman's Eye* (New York: Dell Publishing, 1991).

Culture as an Object of Knowledge

SANDRA HARDING

Ruth Bloch's project of producing a more complex and useful theory of culture is badly needed. Feminist theories of gender, like other social theories, have suffered from apparently having to choose between explanations of gender as an epiphenomenon of nature (of sex), or of the political economy ("materialism", "power and wealth"), or as a fully autonomous symbolic system that floats free of any systems or contingencies in nature and social structure.

Bloch argues persuasively for the good consequences of such a project. However, I am not persuaded that she is yet conceptualizing either gender or symbolic systems in a sufficiently complex or accurate way that would give an adequate account either of the terrain that other feminist theorists have tried to map or of how humans use gender dichotomies to give meaning to borders and interconnections (the topic in which she is most interested). As long as theorists think that they have to *choose between* explaining material structures, structures of meaning, or natural patterns, or that they must *choose between* accounting for gender, race, class or sexuality, the consequences of their choices will distort our understanding of nature and social relations. The trick is to develop theoretical frameworks that reject these distorting choices; however, it is not clear to me that Bloch's proposal really intends to do so. I will briefly develop my argument here by focusing on three points where I find her account problematic.

DID EARLY FEMINIST ACTIVISM CONSIST
LARGELY OF "DEFINING A CULTURAL CODE"?

Bloch argues that feminist practices were far ahead of feminist theory in that they were concerned primarily "to transform the subjective meanings of being female or male." Certainly, consciousness-raising groups and confronting the sexism of individual men in political organizations, families, and intimate relationships were very important to early feminist activists. I, for one, found them extremely illuminating and energizing! However, to characterize the feminism of the late 1960s and the 1970s as concerned primarily to "define a cultural code" through consciousness-raising and individual confrontations seriously distorts the projects of the vast majority of activists of this period, and devalues the important consequences of their attempts to change social institutions and practices.

Bloch's account erases the fact that the women's movement emerged at least as much from the Civil Rights movement as it did from resistance to the "feminine mystique," and that even resistance to the feminine mystique had far broader goals than to transform social meanings, however important that was. These women (and men) and the thousands who shortly joined them organized women workers within unions and founded new ones, and they succeeded in removing residual formal and informal barriers to women's equality in housing, education, and access to financial credit. They liberalized divorce laws, began the work that would issue in comparable worth legislation, founded the women's health movement, organized for reproductive rights, generated the anti-violence against women movement that set up hundreds of rape crisis centers and battered women's shelters, and redefined sexual harrassment as a violation of women's civil rights. They worked within Third World development projects and in anti-militarism and ecology movements to insist on the importance of women's concerns. They created the first courses and programs in women and gender studies, which began the long project of shifting the center of knowledge from the masculine to the human. They organized formal and imformal women's political caucuses across the country which are finally succeeding in getting women into decision-making positions in public office. And they began forging alliances across borders of class, race, ethnicity, and sexuality to combat the ethnocentrism and elitism of many scholars and political movements.

This history must be remembered or it becomes mysterious, as it is in Bloch's account, why the mainstream of feminist theorizing, which has tried to learn from and be useful to the practices of the women's movements, would be concerned with social structure. The majority of feminist activities were fundamentally struggles not against individual men but against sexist and androcentric institutions, including both their practices *and meanings*. They were also directed against other social tendencies — such as racism, imperialism, class exploitation and compulsory heterosexuality — that invest in and profit from sexism and androcentrism. All of this history disappears in Bloch's early account, to surface briefly only some pages later in the phrase "the main legal and reform agenda of the movement." While Bloch's report of the preoccupations of much early feminist theorizing as between "patriarchy vs. socialist schools" and her characterization of liberal feminists as concerned only to press "for the full inclusion of women into male bastions of wealth and power" contains some truth, it distorts the relation between feminist theory and the list of feminist projects noted above which have engaged the energies of liberal, radical, and socialist feminist theorists for more than two decades.

This historical erasure is important not only because it omits a realistic context for reviewing feminist theorizing, but also because it leads Bloch to a more limited understanding of gender than many theorists today work with. They do not think it necessary to choose between thinking of gender as material structure or as systems of meaning.

GENDER: SYMBOLIC, STRUCTURAL, INDIVIDUAL

Readers may have noticed that I am avoiding the term "culture." This is because the term is used by different disciplines and theoretical approaches with widely varying meanings, and also because I think we can talk about the causal role of symbolic systems such as gender meanings without insisting as Bloch does that this is the only legitimate reference for the term "culture."

Gender appears in many different forms within social relations, as I have argued elsewhere.[1] First, it appears as an ancient and widespread system of dichotomous meanings that assigns femininity and masculinity to objects and processes that have no literal connection to human biological differences. Thus ships and nations are often coded feminine, and mountains on the moon are coded masculine. (We can ask: how will our belief and behavior change now that hurricanes are coded alternately masculine and feminine instead of only feminine or — a possibility refused — as gender-neutral?) Second, gender also appears, obviously, as one important element in individual identity, and, third, it appears as a component of social structure. The latter is constituted by the gender division of labor or, more generally, activity. Some societies are more gendered than others in the structural sense that they assign a greater proportion of human activity by gender. The gendered meanings that these activities have can and do vary immensely. Gender may well appear in additional forms, but these three clearly are important in that they have obvious and, as we are learning from feminist scholarship, not so obvious but nevertheless significant, effects on the social and natural worlds.

I was first led to appreciate the importance of gender's multiple appearances in reflecting on historian Carolyn Merchant's comment in *The Death of Nature: Women, Ecology and the Scientific Revolution* (New York: Harper and Row, 1980) that the rise of misogynous gender-symbolism at the birth of modern science in Europe did not reflect the direction of structural social change (though it contributed to causing it subsequently). It was exactly when women began filling more varied social roles (as Queen of England, as activists in the Protestant reform movements in northern Europe, etc.) that scientific and political rhetoric became more male supremacist. Changes in gender symbolism and in gender structure were going in opposite directions, at least initially. This is not to say that this system of gender meaning is autonomous from gender structures, but rather that their causal relations are complex and historically specific.

Thus it seems to me that Bloch's discussion denies the two-way causal relation of meaning systems to social structure when she insists that gender must refer only to "contingent and variable symbols" and criticizes feminists for focusing on "power, not meaning." Power is created in part through meanings, and, in turn, generates meanings. Symbols, social structures, and individual identities are not autonomous but complex interactive aspects of social relations. We need analyses of how they interact, whether in support of or in resistance to each other. It seems to me that Bloch's account sometimes recognizes this, but that in the heat of criticizing excessive materialists and some poststructuralist tendencies it often retreats to proposing that gender is only autonomous meanings.

GENDER, RACE, CLASS, SEXUALITY: ALWAYS
MUTUALLY CONSTRUCTING AND MAINTAINING

My final problem with Bloch's project arises from my conviction that gender is not only parallel to and used as an analogue for class, race, sexuality, ethnicity and such other highly influential features of social relations. It is also in another relation to them: they construct, permeate, and maintain gender just as it, in turn, shapes these other social features. Bloch's failure to come to terms with this point is indicated by her quotation of Gerda Lerner and citation of Patricia Hill Collins to support her own statements that the oppressions of women and blacks are parallel and that this "analogy remains a common rhetorical feature of feminist thought."

In the first place, the claim about parallel oppressions refers to race and gender *structures* at least as much as it does to race and gender meanings, but any analogy, such as the race/gender one, is only a system of *meanings* (powerful though these be). Social structures are not meanings; they *carry* different meanings for different groups.

However, my main point is a different one. While Lerner and Collins of course are aware of the structural parallels and borrowed meanings that partially constitute relations between race and gender, they are in fact concerned with a quite different matter: "Race, class and gender oppression are inseparable; they construct, reinforce and support one another," as Lerner asserts in the passage Bloch quotes. Thus, racism is a resource used to bring about race-specific forms of gender oppression; male supremacy is a resource used to shape gender-specific forms of race oppression, etc. This "mutual aid" that racism and sexism supply to each other is achieved in a variety of ways. Public policies, for example, can legislate one reproductive policy for Aryans and another for Jews so that motherhood comes to have radically different structures and meanings for women in the two "races." Political analysts have pointed to similarly oppositional race and class constructions of mothering in 1980's U.S. government policies that advanced pro-natalism for middle-class women and a variety of anti-natalist exhortations and regimens for poor women and single mothers "living off welfare." To take another familiar example, Sojourner Truth asked the white women's suffrage advocates "Ain't I a Woman, too?" even though slavery placed very different requirements on her womanhood from what it required of white womanliness.

This more complex way of understanding hierarchically organized social structures, meanings and identities is called "matrix theory." No doubt it will require some fine-tuning; but in its broad outlines it offers powerful resources for understanding gender, race, class and other structural relations as complex *relations* that are continually defined and redefined in terms of each other. Moreover, matrix theory directs attention to how men, too, are situated in a determinate gender location, and whites in a determinate race location, in any particular social structure. "Men (and whites) are made, not born," one could say (with apologies to Simone de Beauvoir). They are "made" through continual contests over the cultural meanings given to social structures and identities, through the institutions constructed to preserve or destroy cultural meanings and individual identities, and through the identities individuals choose for themselves amongst the possibilities made available by the existing array of cultural meanings and institutions.

In conclusion, Bloch's project of generating a more empirically and theoretically satisfactory account of gender as a historically varying way of giving meaning to boundaries and interconnections will be welcome indeed. A maximally adequate account will require attention to the two-way relations between these meanings and the varying social structures (and prevailing forms of individual identity) that both make possible and also limit these meanings. And it will require attention to the resources that race, class, sexuality, and ethnicity provide for these constructions of gender. Now there is a program for a serious "culturalist."

NOTES

1   Sandra Harding, "Chapter 2. Gender and Science: Two Problematic Concepts," *The Science Question in Feminism* (Ithaca: Cornell University Press, 1986), pp. 30-57.

Response to Sandra Harding and Barbara Laslett

RUTH BLOCH

I am in the awkward position of agreeing with much of what my critics have to say and yet finding their criticisms curiously off base. On the one hand, both of them profess to agree with my criticisms of feminist theory, and to proceed merely to offer refinements upon it. On the other hand, they both directly criticize my central thesis. Thus, while I welcome their apparent sympathy for my undertaking, I must politely refuse to accept it. Because I believe their characterization of my position is wrong, I find their extensions and revisions of my argument out of place.

Much of what Harding and Laslett have to say is unobjectionable enough, although, to my way of thinking, beside the point. Certainly I am in accord with Harding's view that the first wave of contemporary feminism was much more than an effort to define a cultural code. I, too, applaud the numerous practical, social and legal accomplishments of women's activism during the past twenty-five years, although I think Harding wishfully exaggerates the cross-class, multi-racial base of the movement. I never meant to "erase" this history of achievement — which is to say that I never intended my essay to offer a comprehensive account of the history. Rather, by pointing to the countercultural sides of feminism, my intention was to highlight a far less visible and enduring aspect of the movement. The cultural qualities I identified not only go far to explain the energy and spirit of feminism, especially in its "charismatic" early phase, but are also embedded within even the most concrete features of its reform agenda. It is for this reason that we must resist the common tendency to shrug off the early, countercultural features of the feminist movement as trivial and or (especially in retrospect) embarrassing. It is this dimension of our history that is in is greater danger of being "erased" than the one Harding indignantly seeks to protect. It is she, not I, who is drawing a misleading dichotomy between the "symbolic" and the "real."

I can also easily accept many of Barbara Laslett's observations about the organization of academic life. I, too, applaud interdisciplinary work and believe that we are at a point when the institutional boundaries between departments in universities are being redefined. I also agree that conflicts between intellectual approaches are partly a matter of power (or "interests" in the instrumental sense) and partly a matter of the freedom to pursue intellectual passions (or "interests" in the expressive sense). One contribution I would make to her formulation, however, is to add the concept of "culture" to what she calls "passion" and "desire." The affective qualities of intellectual engagement are, for traditionalists and innovators alike, partly derived from extra-individual systems of meaning. Yet Laslett apparently takes desire/sexuality to be unmediated by meaning, as do most psychoanalysts. There is certainly more that could be said in response to her remarks about disciplinary knowledge, but I find the subject only tangentially related to the content of my essay. The link between these comments and my essay seems to be Laslett's view that my argument privileges anthropology in the hierarchy of disciplines. This is not my position, for reasons I will elaborate below, despite my acceptance of much that she has to say about competition between academic fields.

More to the point are the criticisms made by both Laslett and Harding about the way that I define culture and my plea for its autonomy. On the one hand, I acknowledge at the outset of my essay that culture is a frustratingly vague and elusive term with multiple referents and usages. On the other, I explicitly seek to address this difficulty by employing the term in a relatively specific way. That is, I define the concept of culture as a symbolic system of meanings, a definition derived primarily from scholarship in the field of cultural anthropology. This is not to say, as Sandra Harding apparently believes, that I think there is no other "legitimate reference" for the term, or that, as Barbara Laslett implies, I have in mind a "hierarchy" of academic disciplines with anthropology on top. I would have thought it was obvious that I was identifying an interdisciplinary theoretical tradition: the cultural anthropology of the 1960s itself drew upon such sources as linguistics, semiotics, and narrative theory; poststructuralism, a widely interdisciplinary movement, shares an interest in the internal, symbolic workings of culture. Neither of my critics demonstrates why a more expansive or inclusive use of the term culture would advance a better theoretical agenda.

Sandra Harding prefers to avoid the term altogether. But when she does attempt specifically to define gender, her concept of gender symbolism — i.e. what I would call the cultural dimension — strikes me as remarkably limited. Indeed, the only examples she offers are the ways ships, nations, and, formerly, hurricanes are named as females. Other than this limited linguistic phenomenon, gender for Harding devolves into the non-symbolic: 1) a component of individual identity (apparently uninfluenced by socially-determined symbolism) and 2) the gender division of labor (regarded as structural rather than symbolic). Whatever the merits of such conceptual distinctions, nowhere in her schematic definition of gender is what I call the "cultural" taken into account. Her notion of symbolism is so narrow that the broader and deeper ways that human beings symbolize concepts of masculinity and femininity are eliminated along with the term culture.

Both Sandra Harding and Barbara Laslett insist that in social life the "cultural" cannot be separated as an "autonomous" influence. As an assertion about the empirical realities of human experience, I couldn't agree more. This misplaced objection to my argument boils down to the truism that all parts of a whole are related to one another — or, to employ some of the terms that my critics themselves use, that culture is not independent of institutions, social structures, individual and racial identities, and so on. But as writers we do not pretend to reproduce society in all its bewildering complexity and disorder. Even if that were possible, such a complete and accurate description would have dubious intellectual interest or value. Instead, we strive to interpret society and even, with luck, partially to explain it. No matter how hopelessly interfused the cultural, the social, and the psychological may be in reality, we work to distinguish them in analysis. Nor is anything inevitable or sacred about these categories; they are themselves artificial constructs of the culture of academic social science. One may be able to imagine alternatives. Yet the terms carry enough common meaning to be serviceable in scholarly communication and, regardless of their inherent value, these or similar categories are essential to the analytical enterprise.

Without such analytic distinctions and without "hierarchical" judgments about the relative importance of different influences in different situations, we could never hope to trace the relationships that Laslett, Harding, and I, wish to explore. Relationships presuppose separable parts, and understanding such relationships requires comparison. Barbara Laslett passingly acknowledges that this "analytic and technical" process may be "appropriate" at times, but she and Sandra Harding both imply that a truly anti-reductionistic understanding of society could and should dispense with it. I think not.

By the "autonomy" of culture, then, I do not mean that in actual society culture is empirically independent from, or has determinate power over, the other classic variables of social-scientific thought. In real life, culture is mixed together with other structures like organizations, economic systems, politics, and family systems — as well as with psychological variables like desire, whether sexual or otherwise. When I insist on the autonomy of culture I insist on its autonomy in an analytical, theoretical sense. Analytic autonomy is the only way to maintain "relative autonomy" empirically. That is, if culture is not viewed as having independence from economy or polity, it cannot be seen as interacting with them in an "equal" way, either in history or in social scientific analysis. To deny its autonomy in this analytical sense is to shortcircuit all genuine attempts to study the relationships between culture and other features of society.

Finally, culture is a "social structure" just as surely as are the other categories of analysis that typically receive the name. To pose "structure" as the antinomy of "culture" — a strategy to which both my critics subscribe — is to discredit the causal value of culture; it depicts culture as somehow unreal and therefore incapable of motivating or inhibiting social action. For culture to achieve analytic autonomy, attention needs to be given to its internal structure: symbolic systems, codes, narratives, rituals, theologies, ethics, salvational paths, and so on. Insofar as action is guided by meaning, it is channeled via these structural patterns rather than by material exigencies as such. The internal structure of culture, just like the internal structure of the economy, can never be seen unless it is "abstracted" in precisely the manner to which Barbara Laslett objects.

As far as our understanding of gender relations is concerned, my argument is, first, that too much attention has been given to relations of interest and power and too little to the ways that gender definitions address problems of meaning. Interpretations of masculinity and femininity, and hence the active construction of gender differences, are motivated by existential as well as utilitarian concerns. Second, I call for more cultural (not only psychological) analysis of the way that gender definitions serve to encode the key existential issue of human interdependency. I contrast the issue of interdependency to the more routinely considered one of domination and subordination. Third, I insist that the meaning given to these relations must be seeing as "imbedded in wider systems of meaning," which means that there is an initial, internal reference of cultural patterning. Finally, I see the need to reattach the cultural dimension of gender to other structural (and psychological) variables: "How gender is defined varies by time, place, and social group . . ." This hardly seems like an emphasis on the autonomy of culture from the rest of society. It is an effort, rather, to add complexity to our understanding and to increase our emphasis on the importance of culture in relation to more material variables. Only in this way can the mutual conditioning my critics call for actually take effect.

Of course, the notion that symbolic understandings impinge upon the structure and organization of social life is hardly a new idea. My point is that, when it comes to feminist theory, it has hardly been investigated. We have remarkably few accounts of how gender symbolism has contributed to shaping what Barbara Laslett and Sandra Harding refer to as institutions and social structures. Feminist theorists — even those post-structuralists most associated with "idealist" cultural analysis — have been quick to reduce culture to interests and power. Indeed, while Barbara Laslett and Sandra Harding concede this point, their misinterpretations of my argument for "cultural autonomy" suggest that they don't understand the ramifications of what they think they accept. Most left-wing social scientists (and feminists are no exception) are more comfortable emphasizing the material than the symbolic. This can be seen, unfortunately, in the real difficulties that my critics have in theorizing culture in their illustrations. For, despite their best intentions, they actually end up treating culture in the very reductionist ways that I (and they, ostensibly) agree must be overcome.

Sandra Harding, as I have already noted above, prefers to avoid the term culture, relegating the "symbolic" to a most superficial and indeterminate status. While "gender appears as a component of social structure," the latter "is constituted by the gender division of labor." The division of labor, one assumes, should be considered to be only economic or political, for it is continually associated with "structural." Culture relates only to names, not to social structure. Nor can there be any relation, for Sandra Harding never relates it to powerful cultural movements, institutions, or social patterns. Culture, in short, is accorded no analytic autonomy and is given no internal structural basis. Matrix theory, or any other approach that attempts to interweave parts of society like gender and race, must, in my view, have a theory of culture that is complex enough to get beyond the simple fact of reinforcing oppressions. I am not discounting the fact that such reinforcing oppressions exist, but am arguing that the cultural components of gender and racial identities require separate as well as combined analysis. Such an approach is missing in Harding's critique.

Similarly, Barbara Laslett's brief historical sketch of the gendered division of labor in nineteenth-century America privileges the causal factor of "structural economic changes." It was "the decline of domestic production, the rise of a market economy" which, in her view, "increasingly took middle-class men out of their homes and left women within them." This arrangement was "buttressed" by an "ideology of separate spheres" and by "rhetoric" about different male and female natures. She claims, in other words, that the economic occurred in its own terms and created the gendered split; ideology, rhetoric, or meaning followed in a buttressing way. This sort of analysis does not give action an interpretive dimension, only a utilitarian one. It does not connect, but severs, gender from other traditional domains of meaning. It does not restore empirical interdependence, but produces a typical structural emphasis in which gendered meanings follow, and are expressly subordinated to, the "context" of economic facts. While Barbara Laslett generously acknowledges a debt to my own work, she fails to appreciate the underlying differences in our interpretations. I stress changes in systems of meaning — particularly religious transformations — which, far from merely following upon economic patterns, actually made an independent contribution to them. It was cultural systems of gender meanings, interacting with other forces, that led early industrial life to take on such a dramatically gendered form.

I am afraid that my critics' illustrations of their own theoretical positions, in other words, only serve to underscore the urgency of the criticisms I have made. Culture is not something that feminist theorists understand, despite the fact that those most committed to non-reductive analysis present themselves as being open to including it. Because my critics do not recognize the depth and the pervasiveness of the problem, they can accept my argument even while they dismiss its substantive claims. The refinements and alternatives they offer are, to my way of thinking, either off the point or, worse, examples of what needs to be criticized and changed in the ways that we think about the social role gender plays.

C. Welfare

Gender, State and Society:
A Debate with Theda Skocpol

PROTECTING SOLDIERS AND MOTHERS (CAMBRIDGE:
HARVARD UNIVERSITY PRESS, 1992)

LINDA GORDON

In the spirit of *Contention*, Theda Skocpol and I agreed to debate about different approaches to welfare history. We decided to organize our discussion around my review of her book and her response, and it is a challenge and a pleasure for me to engage in this exchange with a scholar of Skocpol's high caliber. This background explains the construction in what follows of a deliberately polarized argument. In our interpretations of the development of public provision in the Progressive era and after, and in our political leanings regarding social policy today, I suspect that we agree far more than we disagree. For example, we position the Social Security Act as the product of a history of welfare policy, not as a *de novo* result of the Depression. We both find that organized white women reformers had a substantial influence on this history. We both attribute significance to absences, noting missed opportunities in the early twentieth century. But the purpose of this exchange is to identify and explore intellectual differences so as to reveal the assumptions behind dissimilar approaches and the complexities of historical interpretation. Hence, this is not a general review or even a review essay trying to offer a balanced characterization of the book. It is an essay focused exclusively on substantive and methodological differences.

For over a decade, Theda Skocpol has been making an important contribution to historical sociology in building a theory and practice of incorporating the state into explanatory problems. Labelled sometimes with Skocpol's phrase "Bringing the State Back In," sometimes as a "new institutionalism," the perspective expresses a critique of social-history and historical-sociology work that exaggerates societal and understates political influence. Her influential paradigm stimulated both emulation and criticism. Last fall she published a book, *Protecting Soldiers and Mothers*, on the development of social policy (what I would call welfare policy) from the Civil War pensions to the Sheppard-Towner Act of the 1920s. In it she not only offers a developed example of the influence of politics—in what she now calls a "polity-centered" analysis — but also the first book-length treatment of the history of US social policy to grant appropriate attention to the woman-dominated stream of welfare activism.[1] It is a significant book.

I pursue only a few of many possible debates that I might have with Theda Skocpol.[2] I object, first, to her (usually implicit) theory of gender and of women's participation in social-policy history, and second, to her polity-centered explanations. I also argue with one aspect of her method — specifically, with the use of explanatory methods that apply precise and quantitative comparisons to inappropriate material and thus produce falsely precise answers.

I.

Protecting Soldiers and Mothers argues that there were several lines of welfare development in the post-Civil War U.S., including a paternalist and a maternalist, and that the latter was more influential early in this century: "A fundamental question addressed in this book is why maternalist forces promoting social policies for mothers and women workers were considerably more effective in U.S. politics during the early 1900s than were paternalist forces that simultaneously worked for the enactment of policies targeted on male wage-earners" (p. 56). The paternalist line derived from the Civil War veterans' pensions, about which Skocpol has published extensively, arguing that these became a massive program of public provision, peaking long after the War. At the turn of the twentieth century, the scale of the Civil War pension program was comparable to that of some European social insurance programs. During the Progressive era, Skocpol argues, some reformers expected that these pensions could be transformed into a general program of old-age and health insurance for workers, but this did not occur. Workmen's compensation was the only victory of this paternalist approach. Other opportunities were lost, paradoxically, *because* of the Civil War pensions: the strong political party system of the late nineteenth century had captured the administration of those pensions in its patronage net, and in the Progressive era, reformers were above all concerned to overcome the "corruption" of patronage democracy (p. 355). Reformers were thus hostile, Skocpol argues, to any public social provision because they feared it could not be administered "cleanly" but would enlarge the power of the party machines. Workmen's compensation was an exception because it required only a reworking of existing state functions, not an extension of them (p. 296).

A maternalist line of development, pushed by a variety of women's organizations such as the Congress of Mothers and the Federation of Women's Clubs, was the only welfare strategy able to get around the reformers' fear of the inevitable corruption of public assistance. The major victory of the maternalist women reformers was the state and local mothers' aid (sometimes known as mothers' or widows' pensions) laws of the 1910-20 period. The momentum of the maternalist line continued even in the 1920s, through the influence of the U.S. Children's Bureau (established in the Department of Labor in 1912), with the maternal and infant health education program inaugurated by the short-lived Sheppard-Towner Act, 1921-29. Unfortunately, the maternalist dynamic was stopped in the late 1920s, when Sheppard-Towner was repealed and the Children's Bureau weakened by an alliance of the American Medical Association, the Public Health Service and President Hoover's conservative supporters.

This history functions for Skocpol as an argument for "bringing the state back in." Reacting against a stream of historical sociology that ignores state structures, Skocpol's work for over a decade has emphasized politics. This book features state actors who represent a point of view usually ignored, she charges, in society-centered analyses such as those that rest on class or gender. And it argues the influence of state capacity and political arrangements in limiting or conditioning various successes and failures. For example, she emphasizes how a women's mode of doing politics — through nonpartisan membership organizations with the ability to mobilize local affiliates — worked because it took advantage of existing state patterns. Women used existing state agencies, such as the juvenile courts or investigatory hearings of state legislatures. Because of the relation between women's organizations and the state, a relation largely outside party politics (women could not yet vote), these organizations were well suited to lobbying state legislatures and courts on nonpartisan bases. Because they were nonpartisan and because state capacity was undeveloped, the bureaucracy relatively small, their own labor could accomplish some of what the state could not, such as collecting social data for expert reports. The success of workmen's compensation and the failure of public old-age or health insurance were also primarily influenced by state capacity — the lack of a professional bureaucracy and reliable civil service control at a crucial moment of reform made Progressives worry about the corruption that, they believed, would accompany government provision.

Skocpol's new definition of the state — what she now calls the polity — includes the influence of a variety of civic organizations, prominently including women's groups, on mothers' pensions and the Sheppard-Towner Act. She brings in the important role of the unions, mainly AFL unions, challenging the common conclusion that all unions were opposed to public insurance. She shows that many state and local unions were more positive towards public social insurance. The major reason for this national/local difference, she argues, was that state federations were in some ways more political than the national AFL, as it was primarily at the state level that unions had political influence.

In this discussion she makes a contribution to the scholarship arising from the question, why did the US have no Labour or Social Democratic Party? Her argument runs as follows: she places some weight on the fact that craft unions more than industrial ones thought they could protect their members' interests best through workplace and market action (p. 217). Mainly, however, she emphasizes state factors. One was the lack of proportional representation in the U.S., so that third-party candidates usually ended up getting no representation despite a substantial popular vote. This constitutional aspect of the U.S. state tended to confirm organized labor's suspicion of the value of electoral politics (p. 221). Making it more difficult for unions to influence one of the two major parties was the decline of the competitive party system and its replacement in some areas by a regional system of one-party rule (such as the "Solid South") (p. 223). The main obstacle, she argues, to politicized unions was the power of the courts to stop legislation, creating bitterness within the unions and forcing them constantly to defend themselves against the state. Another consideration was labor's certainty that public insurance would be administered in a manner hostile to union interests by a professional elite; union experience with one such elite — judges — was extremely negative (p. 228).

II.

These brief distillations of Skocpol's narrative may be enough to indicate its richness in detail and its coherence as an argument. The book fails, however, to create a satisfying explanation of the construction of social provision in this period, and even its description and narrative of what happened lacks precision. A major reason for these faults is the systematic exclusion of social-structural power relations, such as class and gender, from her analysis.

I am aware that the book's subtitle is *The Political* [i.e., not social or economic] *Origins of Social Policy*. Skocpol writes that she tries not to substitute political for social determinism, but to show how political and social factors combine (p. 47). This is not what she does. Instead, she continues a vacillation that has characterized her work on social policy: her general statements are often reasonable, modest, even to the point of insignificance: asserting that the state matters. (In this book she shows and explains lucidly how past state policy influences new policy several times, notably in a fine discussion of "policy feedback" [pp. 57-60].) But in the actual narration of historical process her implicit premise often shifts, until she is resting on the claim that the state is all that matters, and society is excluded from explanations.

Still, this book is more open to social-structural and social-movement influence than her previous work on social policy. I think it likely that making women visible required examining the social realm since, until recently, women were legally excluded from state office and power. It is a marker of this shift that in *Protecting Soldiers and Mothers*, Skocpol changes her claim about what matters from state to "polity." She does this rather mysteriously, as her only explanation of the shift is in a footnote attributing the new nomenclature to political scientist Peter Hall. Instead of a discussion of the state/polity difference, historical and/or theoretical, we get simply a list of the kinds of processes involved, which include "the 'fit' — or lack thereof — between the goals and capacities of various politically active groups, and the historical changing points of access and leverage allowed by a nation's political institutions" (p. 41).

Thus one induces what "polity" means and how it differs from "state" by the context, by what Skocpol actually considers in the book. Polity is evidently broader than state and includes not only those who hold government jobs and offices, not only those who participate in electoral and other official state-organized processes, but also those connected with civic organizations who pressure or lobby government or politicians. Polity-centered explanations can include the impact of some civic organizations — a premise without which there would be virtually no women in policy history. Moreover, the shift in paradigm allows Skocpol to meet the criticisms of many scholars who pointed out how much was excluded from her previous work. But the result of this shift may have been to evacuate her very argument, or at least to reduce it to a weaker formulation — that one should not leave the state out of explanations of policy development, but that other influences are also significant. For example, her conclusion with regard to the mothers' aid laws passed in most states between 1910 and 1930, for example, is exactly that which earlier historians have drawn — that the most influential factor was the women's movement. Theoretically speaking, there is no longer anything in her approach that distinguishes it from the approaches of many of her critics.

But while her amendment to her state-centered claims brings social movements back into the force field, it continues to leave out social structure. Without any discussion of the power differentials between men and women, rich and poor, white and Black, WASPs and immigrants, the various civic organizations are reduced to pressure groups competing on a presumably level field. Moreover, her lens picks up formal organizations but not informal policy influences from social movements or shifts in popular consciousness. Her discussion of key woman-dominated organizations takes place without a context that would help us understand the source of their influence — a context that ought to include, for example, the state of the women's-rights movement, of consciousness about women's sexual and marital rights, so that we can place the ideology of these organizations in their universe of discourse.

The problems begin from the outset of the book with Skocpol's failure to produce any adequate definitions of what she means by "paternalist" and "maternalist." This failure exemplifies ways in which Skocpol's approach to the influence of gender is undeveloped in relation to the theoretical level of much scholarly gender analysis today. In the introduction she seems to be distinguishing merely between policies for male workers and others for women and children — hardly an adequate definition (p. 2). In the middle of the book she suggests that paternalism involves policies created by "elite males, bureaucrats and national political leaders" doing things "*for* members of the working class" and aimed at shoring up the breadwinning position of the male wage earner (p. 314). But policies and advocates she calls "maternalist" equally fit this definition: the maternalists were elite, dedicated to providing what they believed was good for the working class, and mainly in agreement on the necessity of shoring up the male breadwinner as head of family.[3] She might have done well to listen more seriously to Mrs. G. H. Robertson of the National Congress of Mothers, whom she quotes remarking that " 'our government should be maternal, some may prefer to call it paternal, there is no difference.' " (p. 357)

At one time women's-studies or gender scholars assumed that male/female were inevitably a binary set of opposite principles, and that women had unique and universally similar perspectives, but no longer. Skocpol's immersion in the debates about the relative influence of state and society is not matched by familiarity with scholarly debates about gender. The book has a gender consciousness that would be bizarre if it were not, alas, still common. To Skocpol as to many others, gender means female. Part III of the book, about the maternalist stream, is couched in terms of gender. In Parts I and II, about the Civil-War pension and paternalist streams, I found gender mentioned in only one sentence. We learn that the key actors in the pension and welfare campaigns were men, but nothing about the gendered content of their vision and practice. She considers the male actors influenced by their state and professional positions, never by their positions as men (or by their class position, of which also more below). Thus, the chapter on veterans' pensions never takes up the implications of the fact that this was primarily a male benefit, nor does the discussion of the dispensation of welfare by party bosses. The one sentence, tacked on to the end of a paragraph, mentions that nineteenth-century political parties created rituals and symbols of manhood, with no analysis of the implications of this fact.

There was also a time when women's-history scholars saw their task as documenting women's contributions, but recently most have moved to more analytic scholarship. Unfortunately in entering the field of women's or gender history, Skocpol has come in at the bottom rather than standing on the shoulders of others. She produces an entirely celebratory account of the women's organizations she studies. She has no critique of maternalism.

Maternalism is, I think, a useful label for an orientation among women reformers, traceable back to the mid-nineteenth century and prominent in the Progressive era. It had varied and complex political implications, some more progressive and others more conservative. We can best define maternalism by contrasting it to an alternative stream of "welfare" thought in the Progressive era, social insurance. Social-insurance advocates, mainly male, sought programs to replace lost wages (e.g., for the aged, the unemployed, the disabled) for workingmen and their dependents. They wanted programs that would be entirely outside the tradition of charity and poor relief so that they would be without stigma. Indeed, they did not even want to orient their programs particularly towards the poor; they preferred insurance for (white) male wage-earners, including the secure and prosperous. They designed programs in which entitlements to provision would follow automatically from meeting clearly defined eligibility criteria, such as length of employment, as opposed to programs in which caseworkers would have discretion about whether and how much to give. I do not consider this approach paternalist, because it does not emphasize a parental, personal caretaking dimension. One could label it paternalist on the grounds that this stratum of professional men sought a structural relation of social control between themselves and the poor, but this social-control relation was distant, not individually supervisory. Nevertheless, while not primarily fatherly, this social-insurance strategy was definitely male in content as well as personnel, assuming wage labor to be the fundamental source of entitlement, devaluing unpaid domestic labor, and lacking the women's vision of a personal, caring welfare state.

Most of the woman-dominated groups agreed with these men on the basic premise that public provision should support the family wage, i.e., the principle that a man alone should be able to earn enough to support a family without help from wife or children. Their faith in a family wage became weaker over the period Skocpol discusses as the economic necessity for married women's work became more evident, and as cases of the unreliability of men as supporters seemed to mushroom. Moreover, the acceptance of married women's economic dependence on their husbands was a racial pattern, far more characteristic of white than of Black women.[4] Nevertheless, within the group of prosperous white reformers who are the subject of Skocpol's narrative, virtually none, whether male nor female, argued for replacing the family wage with married women's economic independence.

Still, many of the women reformers did, for most of the period Skocpol covers, adapt that family-wage assumption to a maternalist perspective, but we must carefully define what this means. My definition has three parts. First, embedded in maternalist policy proposals was a conviction that these reformers should function in a motherly role towards the poor. The women came from a charity and social-work tradition that combined genuine pity for the poor with social-control impulses, particularly for children and for mothers alone. Their reform perspective contained some of the heritage of "friendly visiting" of the nineteenth century and its conviction that the poor needed moral and spiritual as well as economic help. The "maternalist" aspect of their vision thus required supervision of the morals and mental "hygiene" of the poor, with rehabilitation where they deemed it necessary; this stream became "casework" to the newly professionalized social workers of the early twentieth century.

The second component of the maternalist vision was the women's belief that it was their work, experience and/or destiny as mothers that made women uniquely able to lead in the campaign for public social provision and made others deserving of help. This venerable view reached a peak of politicization in the nineteenth and early twentieth centuries. In the earliest campaigns for state intervention, in the mothers' pension drive and also in the briefs for wage, hours, and safety regulation of women's labor, maternalist feminists argued that women needed protection because of their responsibility as mothers of future generations. This argument was sometimes biological, sometimes social, but always expressed a commitment to gender differentiation. It is difficult to understand this view outside its political context, which included another feminist orientation that was directly critical of this emphasis on male-female difference. Skocpol ignores this context. The equal-rights feminists of this period feared that special protections for women would ultimately undermine women's advancement, and many emphasized the fundamental similarities of men and women.[5] Only in contrasting maternalism to another, distinctly non-maternalist but equally feminist political stance can we clarify the precise content of maternalism.

A third aspect of maternalism was the women's interest in giving money directly to women, through mothers' aid programs as opposed to proposals for family-allowance programs to give money to children through their fathers. These maternalists' highest priority was aid to single

mothers, particularly widows and deserted wives, rather than women with
husbands present. One can interpret this emphasis in different ways, as it
had ambiguous meanings. The mothers' aid campaign called attention to
the inadequacy of relying on men and to the existence and legitimacy of
female-headed households. At the same time it refused support to permanent or universal child benefit programs which might have undermined
male-headed households.

   One reason for Skocpol's missing these gendered meanings of
welfare strategies is that she is uninterested in ideas or ideology. Of course
ideology is affected by other forces: for example, Skocpol is absolutely
right that, once established and institutionalized and routinized, administrative arrangements shape future options. However, it is equally true that
traditional, noninstitutionalized patterns of social helping also affected
social policy proposals, as did social, economic, and political ideologies.
The maternalist reformers inherited charity, moral reform, and women's-
rights ideas which profoundly shaped their notions of what was possible
and desirable for the state to do for the poor.

   These failures of specification and definition function within a
larger vagueness resulting from Skocpol's failure to ground her concept of
gender in questions of male and female power. Gender is, after all, not
merely a neutral or benign difference; it is a difference, or rather a set of
meanings culturally constructed around sexual difference, in a context of
male domination. In the entire book there is no discussion of male power
in general or in its specifics — or, to put it inversely, of the fact that the
forms of political power with which Skocpol is so concerned are shaped
by their maleness. Equally important, she does not discuss the fact that the
maternalist outlook was a strategy developed in adaptation to lack of
political power in relation to men. This silence is the more noticeable
because the very concepts paternalism/maternalism refer to an inequity of
power, combining in their reference both gender and generation.

   The point here is that maternalist legacies of thought and strategy,
and gendered perspectives in general, were as influential as the contemporary organizational forms that the women's reform campaigns used.
Excluding the social and cultural deforms and impoverishes the history.
Perhaps even more limiting is Skocpol's resolute exclusion of class relations from the picture she draws. I am not by any means calling for fidelity
or attention to any traditional mode of class analysis, and would welcome
some unconventional thinking on this question. But it is unsatisfactory not

to offer some analysis of the role of different social and economic positions, perspectives, and power.

Skocpol does not apparently think that welfare ideas or strategies had a class content or were conditioned by societal power relations. The power of "business" is at one point described thus: "Multiple points of access [to the state] . . . give well-organized and resourceful groups such as business many opportunities . . ." — hardly an adequate characterization of the source of capital's relation to state power (p. 54). She describes the fathers of social insurance as "reformist professionals," as if their class and masculinity was irrelevant. (Obviously their professional positions are an important aspect of their status, but there is no analysis of the power of professionals either.) Later she considers a class interpretation of these reformers and dismisses it by caricaturing it; that is, she considers only a rather extreme theory which sees them as "agent[s] of capitalist interests" (p. 183). "Nor is there evidence that any of the wealthy donors ever successfully pressed his or her views on an otherwise reluctant AALL," she writes (p. 183). This interpretation of how the powerful impress their class interests on others is simplistic in relation to current class-analysis scholarship. Once we have, rightly, rejected the notion that Progressive reformers were mere pawns of some other group, we must still examine the class content in their own standpoint. There is a thick historical literature about this issue, which Skocpol surely knows (and no doubt a sociological literature as well, which I may not know), and it is by no means so simple as Skocpol's argument suggests. Historians like Gabriel Kolko and James Weinstein have argued that the Progressive-era achievements of these professional reformers served the interests of enlightened capitalists; this is by no means as easy to disprove as Skocpol implies. Historian Robert Wiebe retorted that the Progressive reformers were not tools of capitalists but sought their own, professional, class interests, an argument Skocpol does not address. Since then several historical interpretations, like those of Alan Dawley and Martin Sklar, advance complex class arguments. It will not do to dismiss class arguments by presenting them in their most simplistic form and then denying their applicability.

Sometimes Skocpol's lack of interest in even the most obvious class relationships makes her seem naive, which she is not. For example, we learn that states with relatively high proportions of child labor in manufacturing were slow to enact mothers'-pension laws. Since mothers' pensions were designed in part to obviate the necessity for children to be employed, it makes sense to hypothesize that employers of children used their influence against these laws, or that their influence contributed to a climate in which women reformers were less hopeful about campaigning for these reforms. But she offers no interpretation of this finding, perhaps because a polity-centered explanatory model does not stimulate questions about economic interests (p. 464).

Failure to discuss class is equally debilitating in the discussion of the "maternalist" reformers. It is as if, for her, gender and class were two mutually exclusive categories of analysis, with the result that women have no class identities. Skocpol has done a great deal of research into several key organizations — e.g., the National Consumers' League (NCL), the National Congress of Mothers (NCM), the General Federation of Women's Clubs (GFWC) — but she does not distinguish their perspectives and programs. In fact, the outlook and membership of these groups were quite different as were the roles they played in "maternalist" state-building, and these differences expressed race and class perspectives, although not in a simple, linear fashion. Skocpol has apparently studied most closely the groups pushing for mothers' aid laws, notably the NCM and GFWC, which were more conservative and less professional in orientation than the NCL. The NCL, by contrast, was to the "Left" of the other groups, and had in some ways a European social-democratic outlook, but was at the same time more professional and perhaps even more elite than the other two groups. The NCL was relatively unimportant in the mothers' aid agitation, and devoted itself primarily to protective labor legislation. The agendas of these groups were different, particularly in their social-control and women's-rights agendas. Of course Theda Skocpol knows this; I am not correcting "mistakes." Rather I am arguing with her implicit view that such issues are not important. She generalizes about these "maternalists" as if they were manifestations of some universal female principle. They did share some fundamental beliefs and assumptions about the proper role of government and the proper construction of families, but Skocpol identifies these commonalities no more than their differences.

Her story also neglects the implications of the power differential between the maternalist reformers and their designated "clients" or recipients of help. There exists considerable scholarship on social control as motive and function of these welfare programs and there is no reason for Skocpol to feel obliged to go over this material again. But one aspect of the question of social control intersects directly with her argument, for the distance between these women reformers and the women they sought to help contributed to constructing their outlook and their influence in a male state. Thus class is important also for the way it connected men and women. In *Protecting Soldiers and Mothers*, the male and female reformers appear virtually separate. I would argue, rather, that the effectiveness of each set of organizations depended in part on their mutual support or at least cooperation through a mutually agreeable division of labor. Women had to persuade male legislators to introduce and support their legislation; male reformers often relied on women to do the fact collecting and statistical presentations that argued for their programs.

Skocpol's book mentions not one person or group who isn't white and ignores race as a dimension of analysis. Yet Black women's organizations in this period, for example, were actively developing institutions and programs to provide for their people, based on a perspective that was in its way as "maternalist" as the white one. Conversely, the racial character of the white proposals was also marked, not only in relation to African-Americans but also in relation to many immigrants who were then considered by elite whites to be of a different "race."

The general result of the book's neglect of fundamental social divisions of class, race, and sex is a mystification of power. Skocpol is attentive to bureaucratic, governmental, and pressure-group power but remains unable to explain phenomena that result from social and economic power relations or from the ideas and ideology. For example, she erroneously writes that "welfare" always had a pejorative connotation. This is not so: once an extremely positive term for well-being, "welfare" in the period of this book referred primarily to regulation of the workplace.[6] The subsequent stigmatizing of welfare cannot be adequately explained on the basis of polity-centered analysis; that stigma resulted also from society-centered power relations, including those of class, race and sex. Certainly her version of a polity-centered analysis, tracing policies and policy feedback from veterans' pensions to Social Security, cannot explain why Social Security old-age pensions have become honorable, an entitlement, nonwelfare, while payments to single mothers raising children have become dishonorable, charity, welfare in its most pejorative sense. To explain this we need to examine the meanings of single motherhood, including the fact that it was female, and the meanings of being a veteran, including the fact that vets were mostly male. As Theda Skocpol knows well, at the beginning of the New Deal it was not yet the case that old-age pensions were widely perceived as more deserved than mothers' aid. To understand how some welfare programs were constructed as honorable, others as dishonorable, we require social as well as political analysis. In discussing the hostility to welfare, she frequently begs the question. For example, in comparing popular government aid to schools to unpopular aid to the "dependent," she simply asserts that "social policies for dependents were not broadly popular" (p. 92). But the question is precisely why these policies were unpopular, how "dependents" became stigmatized; or to put it another way, why some recipients of government money are classified as dependents while others are not.[7]

The most central single example of the relative absence of power from Skocpol's interpretive world is her consistent exaggeration of the influence of historically pre-existing state structures on social policy. To cite but one example of such an overstatement: "The leitmotif of U.S. politics during the early twentieth century was the effort to overcome the 'corruption' of patronage democracy . . ." (p. 355). In previous work she placed particular emphasis on the legacy of Civil War pensions; in this book she has effectively shown how the legacy of those pensions intersected with numerous other political factors, e.g., "institutional arrangements such as sovereign courts, federalism, the absence of civil service bureaucracies and parliamentary linkages between executives and legislature, and the absence of social-democratic labor consciousness and a political alliance between male reformers and working-class groups." But the neglect of social-structural power relations continues to weaken her explanations, as when she analyzes the debate about mothers' pensions. I would suggest that the gendered content of that discussion was as influential as the fear of corruption, with opponents anxious about a possible weakening of men's authority and responsibility as heads of families or of encouraging women to seek independence.

What is going on here is that, as some scholars have neglected the influence of "long-run processes of state formation" (p. 39), Theda Skocpol is now bending the stick the other way. There's nothing unusual in this, as it is often the way that old scholarly paradigms are challenged and replaced. Still, we ought to bear in mind that our goal ought to be an integration of political and social factors.

III.

One of Skocpol's important scholarly contributions has been to raise the status of historical sociology within sociology, a discipline dominated by empiricist assumptions. Her choice of methods may in part be determined by this strategic aim. Over the past decade she has begun to operate more like an historian, accepting the interpretive role of the scholar working with evidence that is inevitably partial and unverifiable, however plentiful. Nevertheless, she continues to rely at times on quantitative methods, and attempts to replicate with "soft," qualitative evidence the kinds of comparisons and precise measurement social scientists perform with quantifiable information. To a non-social scientist historian like myself these methods rarely seem useful and at times appear distorting. Consider two examples. In her discussion of early advocates of workingmen's insurance, Skocpol offers a table which lists the men's social background, education, career, organizational affiliations, major publications and auspices of the investigations. This *seven-page* table about seven men yields nothing important to the argument; its findings are summarized in one introductory paragraph informing us that the authors were well-educated men who became social scientists — hardly a claim that requires an elaborate defense.

Later, Skocpol considers at length the "policy diffusion across the states" of mothers' pensions. This project illustrates well not only my objection to her methods but also how these express larger theoretical problems. She wants to account for the difference between the states that provided mothers' aid early, between 1911 and 1915, and those that did so later, in the late 1920s and early 1930s. Why, we may ask, is the question important? That virtually every state in the US passed mothers' aid laws within about 20 years, 28 of them within four years, is significant; why should the contingencies that determined the timing of each be of interest? To this Skocpol has said that looking at differences in timing can lead us to finer determinations of causality. But let us examine the results actually generated by this study. The main conclusion is that the key factor in the passage of mothers' aid laws was the pressure of women's organizations. But historians have stated this for at least twenty years as have the participants in the campaigns for mothers' aid.[8] Nor has there been any revisionist challenge to this conclusion which might suggest a need for reconsideration. Another conclusion, which hardly requires a study as it is evident from one look at the dates of mothers' aid laws, is that all southern states passed them late. But it is well known to historians of the U.S. that the southern states had particularly small public assistance (poor relief) programs and weak women's movements, while states with strong women's movements almost all established these programs early (except

Connecticut and Rhode Island). She also found that the most important general predictor of early passage of mothers' aid laws was literacy. But what's the connection? Skocpol writes that it is because "the presence of more people able to read could well have facilitated the communication of ideas about mothers' pensions through newspapers, women's magazines, and the networks of women's clubs" (p. 461). This is dubious, as mobilization for and against mothers' pensions usually included only a minority, and that minority (legislators, professionals, [social workers in particular], women's-club members) was always literate. We also learn that states with stricter child labor laws and high per capita public-school expenditures in 1910 enacted mothers' pensions sooner. It may be nice to see this spelled out but it is hardly surprising that states with established welfare programs were quicker to expand them. Equally important is what this method does not reveal: even accepting for the moment Skocpol's preference for excluding social power from her analysis, there must have been a myriad of political factors in every state that affected the history of mothers-aid proposals and bills. Did the relevant lobbying groups have other priorities? Were there particularly effective leaders? Were the private charities (almost always opposed to mothers' aid) particularly strong? Had there been newsworthy, dramatic cases of needy single mothers or exploited, suffering child workers dramatizing the issue? Such questions are potentially infinite. We have no way of knowing whether such contingent factors were not more influential than any of the general factors Skocpol considers.

Is this quibbling? I think it is important. I am aware that I am challenging here not only Skocpol's but dominant sociological methods, which often produce a scholarship in which method and content are not well integrated. Often it seems that method is in control and becomes the master procedure driving the analysis. The analysis is done because it is possible to do it, without asking whether there is reason to believe it will reveal something new and important. Similarly, questions about whether the method is appropriate to the nature of the evidence do not seem to get asked. The result is false precision, an illusion of definitiveness which the "soft" historical evidence does not allow.

More important, the method is often extremely ahistorical, insensitive as it must be to the contested social and cultural construction and reconstruction of the concepts in play. For example, one of the strongest arguments for the influence of veterans' pensions would be that they affected the general understanding of what "pension" means and its connotation of entitlement, of a deserved recompense for service. ("Pension" did not originally have such connotations but meant simply a payment, stipend, or, later, wage.) Some mothers'-aid advocates deliberately referred to their assistance plan as "pensions" in order to draw on this positive sentiment, and argued that single mothers were servants of the state, like veterans, because they were raising future generations of citizens. One of the fundamental questions that must be answered in explaining the failure of the "maternalist" line of welfare programs is how and why that attempt to create a honorable status for single mothers failed. This is not a question that can be answered solely from politics, as Skocpol attempts to do. The answer requires also a society-based analysis of changing gender, class, and family relations as well as, for example, the influence of mass immigration from abroad and African-American migration from south to north.

Were I simply reviewing *Protecting Soldiers and Mothers* my comments would have been far different, and I would have spent much of my space discussing the considerable insights the book affords. My purpose here is not that of a review. I have tried to delineate and clarify areas of difference in order to contribute to a critical consciousness about how the past should be interpreted. In writing this I also became aware of another motive, to try to convince Theda Skocpol to incorporate more social structure, including more sensitivity to social power relations, in her future work, and not to waste her time and skill specifying and measuring slippery and partial artifacts of the past. That motive expresses, of course, my sense of the great value, influence, and intelligence of her work.

NOTES

1   See my introduction to *Women, the State, and Welfare* (Madison: University of Wisconsin, 1990) for a critical review of welfare scholarship. There is another full-length book, Mimi Abramovitz's *Regulating the Lives of Women: Social Welfare Policy from Colonial Times to the Present* (Boston: South End Press, 1988), but this bends the stick very far in another direction — positioning women rather exclusively as the victims of

male-constructed social policy and missing their contributions to public provision.

2   Thanks to Allen Hunter, Gwendolyn Mink, Ann Orloff, Alan Wolfe and Erik O. Wright for helping me to clarify my thinking on these points.

3   This lack of conceptual clarity exists also in Sonya Michel and Seth Koven, " 'Womanly Duties': Maternalist Politics and the Origins of Welfare States in France, Germany, Great Britain, and the United States, 1880-1920," *American Historical Review* 95, 4 (October 1990): 1067-1108.

4   On the influence of race among social reformers see Linda Gordon, "Black and White Visions of Welfare: Women's Welfare Activism, 1890-1945," *Journal of American History* (Sept. 1991): 559-590.

5   Equal-rights feminists in the early twentieth century, notably the supporters of the ERA, were the first to adopt the term "feminist" and some historians, such as Nancy Cott, have argued that it is best to limit the term to this more specific historical usage. I am convinced, however, that we would do well to comply with the more popular use of "feminist" as a generic term for those who sought the advancement of women, in order to be able to identify the continuity and diversity of the women's-rights legacy.

6   Kathryn Kish Sklar, "The Historical Foundations of Women's Power in the Creation of the American Welfare State, 1830-1930," in Seth Koven and Sonya Michel, eds., *Women and Welfare States*, forthcoming, typescript pp. 6-7.

7   Nancy Fraser and Linda Gordon, "A Genealogy of 'Dependency:' A Keyword of the US Welfare State," *Signs*, (forthcoming).

8   E.g., J. Stanley Lemons, *The Woman Citizen: Social Feminism in the 1920s* (Champaign: University of Illinois, 1973). for example.

SOLDIERS, WORKERS, AND MOTHERS:

GENDERED IDENTITIES IN EARLY U.S. SOCIAL POLICY

THEDA SKOCPOL

Protecting Soldiers and Mothers tells some startlingly new stories about the history of social policy in the United States. Few people realize that in 1910 over a quarter of all elderly American men were receiving regular old-age pensions from the federal government. How could this have happened so long before the New Deal of the 1930s, when "social security" for the elderly supposedly was enacted for the first time? Most people do not know, either, that some of the most impressive legislative victories ever achieved by U.S. women's groups occurred during the 1910s — *before* the vast majority of women had the right to vote. At that time, American women organized and spoke not as modern-style "feminists," but as civic mothers concerned to make government more caring. How could women who did not enjoy the right to vote have persuaded the federal government and forty-some U.S. state legislatures to enact laws intended to help mothers, children, and women workers?

Because my book asks fresh questions and offers innovative answers about what happened in the American past, reactions to it are bifurcated. *Protecting Soldiers and Mothers* is seen as fascinating and important by readers open to new perceptions about American politics. As Rosalind Rosenberg put it in the *New York Times Book Review*:

> *Protecting Soldiers and Mothers* is a monumental study that
> will likely become a classic. . . . [It] convincingly shows
> that nothing in either American individualism or the nature
> of industrial development prevented the United States Gov-
> ernment from creating innovative social policies, even
> before the New Deal. . . . Indeed, *Protecting Soldiers and
> Mothers* is a fundamentally optimistic work, aimed at illu-
> minating the possibilities for generous social provision that
> lie buried in the American past. If only Americans could tap
> into and build on those traditions, Ms. Skocpol seems to
> suggest, they might overcome the divisions of class and race
> that currently impede social planning.[1]

At the same time, my book arouses consternation among scholars who are
deeply committed to the orthodox view — held by modernization theorists
and Marxists alike — that the United States was (and is) a mere "laggard"
on the evolutionary, European road to what they call "*the* modern welfare
state." As Alan Wolfe acknowledged in the *The New Republic*, if
"Skocpol's analysis is correct, historians and social theorists" will have to
revise many cherished assumptions about the emergence of an "active
state" and the preeminent role of the working class in "political progress."[2] Wolfe quickly proceeds to explain that he, for one, doesn't intend
to rethink anything; he will stick by what he calls "the traditional interpretation." Skocpol tells us nothing new, Wolfe declares, nothing "that forces
us to reconsider the way the welfare state eventually came to the United
States . . . in the form of the New Deal."[3] Wolfe then proceeds to make
fun of me as an unsophisticated and inconsistent "theorist," and concludes
by arguing that Linda Gordon explains U.S. social policy better than I do.

Readers of the preceding article by Linda Gordon will know that
she has taken the same tack as Alan Wolfe. And no wonder! As a leading
scholar in U.S. women's history, Gordon has recently moved from studying the regulation of sexuality and family violence toward fashioning a
grand theory about male and female "styles of thought" as determinants
of the types of programs included in the Social Security Act of 1935.[4] She
is already deeply committed to assumptions and historical conclusions that
are in certain ways directly contradicted by the new evidence and arguments offered in *Protecting Soldiers and Mothers*. She therefore has a stake
in persuading people that my book offers little that is really new — at least
on issues pertaining to gender and social policy, which Gordon claims as

her turf. Gordon has very little to say about the overall historical sweep and political analysis of my book; she aims her criticisms at the parts overlapping her own scholarship, without ever taking on the whole of what I have to say.

Many important matters are at issue between Linda Gordon and me. She presents scholarship on gender and U.S. social policy as evolving in a single intellectual direction, but I hold that there are several alternative tendencies; and I see my book as reinforcing an alternative to her preferred approach. Gordon interprets politics in terms of gender and class domination, but I espouse a historical-institutional approach that includes social relationships but refuses to reduce government and politics to social domination. Gordon's account of gender in early U.S. social policy opposes male and female "styles of thought," while I explain the rise and fall of gendered political alliances that contended over social policies for soldiers, workers, and mothers. Gordon uses statistics to illustrate preconceived categories, while I use them to test hypotheses. Finally, Gordon sees American women's contributions to social policy as embedded in a restricted social work tradition. In my view she overlooks the most important contributions of past female reformers and women's associations. I hold that the differences between us go to the heart of how we are to understand the workings of U.S. politics and public policymaking down to the present day.

In this rejoinder, I explain each of these areas of disagreement. I do so in the belief that political analysis and American history can only benefit from an explicit yet respectful debate between two scholars who have taken seriously the challenge of incorporating gender into the understanding of U.S. policymaking.

THREE PERSPECTIVES ON HOW GENDER MATTERED IN EARLY U.S. SOCIAL POLICY

"Unfortunately," writes Gordon, "in entering the field of women's or gender history, Skocpol has come in at the bottom rather than standing on the shoulders of others." This tells us something about Gordon's conception of her specialty, women's history. She apparently sees scholars and their ideas as arrayed in a hierarchy — and it is not hard to imagine who she believes to be at the top. Or perhaps Gordon sees scholarship on gender (like "the" welfare state itself) as an evolutionary phenomenon. A few years ago, Gordon published an informative essay on "The New Feminist Scholarship on the Welfare State."[5] This included a useful discussion of different viewpoints about women, gender, and U.S. social welfare policy. Yet the points of view were arranged in what Gordon called "stages," forming an evolutionary path culminating in her own preferred approach. (All of us, including me, engage in a certain amount of this sort of thing, comparing our ideas to those of others in ways that make us look best. But I have rarely seen such hierarchical metaphors as those that Gordon uses.)

No doubt some feminist scholars will follow Gordon's suggestion to relegate *Protecting Soldiers and Mothers* to a primitive stage "undeveloped in relation to the theoretical level of much scholarly gender analysis today" (which would make it safe to set the book aside without too much thought). But broad educated audiences — including the readers of *Contention* — should not be fooled into imagining that scholarship on gender in early U.S. social policy is monolithic. Actually, there are lively theoretical and empirical debates — exactly as there should be in a vital area of inquiry. Contrary to any notion of a single evolutionary ladder, there are at least three major coexisting approaches: I shall discuss in turn what I call the *patriarchal* approach, the *social service* approach, and the *women's civic action* approach. Each of these perspectives itself encompasses important differences of opinion and historiographic emphasis (these are *not* "schools" of thought); yet the differences among them are clearly recognizable and important.

One tendency includes feminist scholars who see social policy developments around 1900 as reorganizations of *patriarchal domination* of women by men. These scholars view the growth of "the modern state" as an inexorable march of bureaucratization, professionalization, and corporate capitalism. Emergent governmental actions, including social policies, are portrayed as functioning to rework (while maintaining) male domination of women. As Eileen Boris and Peter Baradaglio explain in their aptly entitled essay, "The Transformation of State Patriarchy," the

> nineteenth and early twentieth centuries . . . saw not the decline of patriarchy but its transformation from a familial to a state form. . . . Laws and public policies — as well as governmental institutions and professional supervision by doctors, educators, social workers, and other so-called fam-

ily experts — developed as part of a larger support system
that reproduced patriarchal social relations. Consequently,
male-dominated — even male-headed — families became
less important to the maintenance of male domination in the
social arena outside the family. . . .

[I]ncreasingly egalitarian legal relations in families were
counterbalanced by the continued economic exploitation of
women at home and in the workplace.[6]

In a slightly different patriarchal formulation, Mimi Abramovitz argues in
Regulating the Lives of Women that U.S. social policies during the early
1900s functioned to enforce a "family ethic" about women's proper roles,
encouraging part-time, low-wage work when it was "needed" by the
economy, yet also rewarding "women whose lives included marriage,
motherhood, and homemaking" while penalizing women who did not, or
could not, choose such pursuits.[7]

A second scholarly tendency in the gender and U.S. welfare literature constitutes the *social service* approach. Included here are Robyn
Muncy, Barbara Nelson, and — most prominently — Linda Gordon
herself.[8] These scholars are uncomfortable with the functionalist styles of
theorizing usually engaged in by scholars of the patriarchalist persuasion.[9]
More to the point, they are critical of any presumption that women were
simply victims, merely objects of male oppression in the historical process
of modern welfare state building. Women are seen as intermediaries of
power, too. As Gordon has explained, it

is clear that an accurate welfare history must not only
incorporate racial and gender relations of power as fundamental but must also register the agency of these subordinated groups in the construction of programs and policies.
It must recognize the "relative autonomy" of the welfare
state from direct control by a unified ruling group and
register instead the state as an arena of conflict with a
particularly influential role played by social service professionals.[10]

To be sure, scholars within the social service tendency share many
basic presumptions with patriarchal theorists. Both groups take it as
axiomatic that policies for women and children are inherently inferior to
those for male workers; much theoretical energy is directed to proving why

this must be so. Both groups tend to see the growth of "the modern state" in unilinear evolutionary terms, paying virtually no attention to cross-national variations in governmental institutions, political party systems, and social movements. The distinctive history and forms of U.S. government and democracy are ignored in both the patriarchal and social service accounts. Equally important, both sets of theorists view the welfare state primarily in terms of ever-increasing professional and bureaucratic regulation of families and workplaces, rather than in terms of government spending for social benefits. Both groups of scholars focus above all on what they consider to be relations of class and racial domination — partly domination of workers by capitalists, but mainly domination of welfare clients by charity workers or professional social workers.

Nevertheless, what sets Gordon (and others of the social service persuasion) apart from the patriarchalists is emphasis on an indisputable fact: around 1900 (as now) most social service providers were not men. They were women, many of whom were becoming professional social workers. These female social-service providers were, as Gordon stresses, engaged in ambivalent and inherently conflictual relationships with "clients" — seeking at once to help and to supervise the lives of impoverished people (who were often single mothers of dependent children).

As she readily acknowledges, Gordon is modelling her ideas about women in U.S. welfare on what she discovered about social workers and clients in her previous studies of family violence.[11] Yet Gordon is not content to talk only about social services. By contrasting male professionals to female charitable and social service providers, Gordon fashions an encompassing, vocationally grounded theory of the gendered origins of the American welfare state.

During the entire period from the 1890s to 1935, Gordon maintains, the U.S. reformers who advocated social insurance were primarily male professional academics, while those who advocated public assistance programs were usually "social workers" (i.e., either volunteer charity workers or paid service providers) who were predominately women. Both male and female reformers "shared a fundamental premise: a welfare state should protect the family-wage system," in which, ideally, male breadwinners could provide for their wives and children.[12] Beyond that, however, males and females tended to have different outlooks within a "division of labor in welfare thought."[13] The advocates of social insurance, Gordon argues, used "rights talk" to propose universal and automatic social insurance benefits for citizens of all classes.[14] They spoke and wrote in terms that were abstract, actuarial, and market-oriented; and they did not show much concern for social needs, personal situations, or philosophical considerations. Meanwhile, according to Gordon, the predominantly female promoters of public assistance spoke of social "needs," and were concerned about reforming as well as aiding impoverished individuals. Concerned to distinguish the "worthy" from the "unworthy" poor, these charity and service workers preferred discretionary, individualized benefits accompanied by casework supervision of the clients of public assistance.

As the empirical basis for her discussion of male and female welfare reformers, Gordon examines the social backgrounds and ideas of 76 white men and 76 white women. (Those who have just read Gordon's criticism of me for not discussing African-American reformers in my book should note that Gordon also omits African-Americans in her study of public policymaking. She does this for the same reason that I did, arguing that "African Americans were concentrated in the South, overwhelmingly disenfranchised, with little influence on government at any level. As a result their campaigns for improving the welfare of blacks took different forms — more often building private institutions, because their campaigns for public provision were much less successful.")[15] Gordon focuses on people she calls "leading national advocates for public welfare or government officials responsible for welfare programs who were also important advocates of welfare" between 1890 and 1935.[16] Methodologically, much depends on who Gordon selected to study in her "collective biographies," and how. No random or formal selection was made, Gordon explains; instead she created what she calls "snowball samples" by tracing out the mutual references that appeared in the correspondence and personal papers she studied "during several years of research on welfare campaigns...."[17] This is a remarkably vague way to describe something called a "sample." Gordon nevertheless makes a daringly strong claim for the *representativeness* of her sets of names: "on the methodological principle of saturation, I doubt that my generalizations would be much altered by the addition of more individuals."[18]

Of the reformers that Gordon describes, the men tended to be higher-educated, hailing either from privileged North European Protestant families, or else from less privileged, including immigrant, Jewish families. The women came mostly from privileged, Protestant Eastern or Midwestern families. Most of the women had attained very high levels of education, and they pursued vocations, if not careers, as either reform-minded charitable volunteers or social workers. The women Gordon studied often remained single (or else became single during their periods of welfare activism), while the men were usually married. Gordon's women were affiliated with urban social settlements — such as Hull House in Chicago and the Henry Street Settlement in New York — or with New York City-based, staff-led reform associations such as the National Consumers' League, or with female-dominated bureaus in Washington D.C., especially the U.S. Children's Bureau and the U.S. Women's Bureau. Gordon acknowledges that 68 percent of her female activists "worked primarily in the New England and mid-Atlantic states — hardly surprising since the national headquarters of the organizations they worked for were usually located there. Moreover, 57 percent had worked in New York City during the Progressive Era or the 1920s" — something that Gordon also finds unsurprising, because she believes that "New York City played a vanguard role in the development of public services and regulation in the public interest . . ."[19]

Later, I will say more about the shaky empirical foundations of Gordon's work on the ideas of male and female reformers in the early twentieth century. For now, it is enough to note the logical creativity by which Gordon has extended the social service approach into a general theory of gender in all of U.S. social policymaking between the 1890s and the 1930s. Even if Gordon is wrong — and I think she is — she has made a bold attempt.

The third tendency within current feminist scholarship on gender and early U.S. social policy focuses on *women's civic action*. Here I would place such historians as Paula Baker, Kathryn Kish Sklar, and Seth Koven and Sonya Michel.[20] There are, to be sure, important differences among these scholars, especially in the subject matters they study: Sklar approaches the period through a biography of Florence Kelley; Baker has written about female voluntary styles of politics as a response to exclusion from male electoral politics; and Koven and Michel study early twentieth-century "maternalist" welfare movements in cross-national perspective. But some crucial ideas and methods tie these civic action theorists together, and differentiate them rather sharply from both patriarchalists and social service theorists.

In the civic action perspective, women are not only intermediaries of larger "structures" of class, racial, and gender power. Reformist intellectuals like Florence Kelley, Jane Addams, and Julia Lathrop are treated as major national civic leaders in their own right, not stand-ins for larger interests. Nor is there any attempt to locate all females active in social politics within occupations (even emerging occupations like social work). Voluntary *associations* run by married women outside the paid workforce are seen as unusually influential in early U.S. social policymaking. The female ideas emphasized by civic theorists are not just charitable urges to regulate, control, and "improve" clients. Although such orientations are acknowledged when present, civic action theorists place more emphasis on the conviction — widely held among women — that caring, domestic values should be extended into the public sphere. Not just charity workers and social service providers, but large numbers of middle-class and elite women regardless of vocational circumstances, believed that governments should take special responsibility for protecting mothers, children, and families.

Civic action scholars use distinctive explanatory strategies as well. To say why female intellectuals and voluntary groups were so influential for a time in American social policymaking, emphasis is placed on cross-nationally distinctive U.S. social, cultural, and institutional conditions. Civic action scholars note that women gained much earlier and more extensive access to higher education in the United States than in other nations, and that women were more prominent in the U.S. social settlement movement than in the British movement. These scholars stress the gendered bifurcation of nineteenth-century U.S. politics: men were enfranchised across class lines (even African-Americans for a time), while all women were excluded from the suffrage. At the same time, American politics allowed more "space" for women's voluntary politics, in contrast to nations where established churches, bureaucratic states, and working-class movements held sway. Some civic action scholars argue that there was an unusually vibrant "women's political culture" in the United States, conducive to welfare-state-building for mothers, children, and families. Significantly in my view, civic action scholars are the only feminists studying early U.S. social policy who refuse to accept a general, evolutionist conception of "the modern welfare state." Implicitly or explicitly, these scholars describe and explain U.S. politics with the aid of comparisons to developments in other nations.

Where does my work fit in? I am not primarily a women's historian, and my book contributes most fundamentally to the study of American political development, broadly conceived. Still, Part III of *Protecting Soldiers and Mothers* uses insights from all three of the above perspectives. It is especially influenced by aspects of the civic action scholarship of

Paula Baker and Kathryn Kish Sklar. What is more, the empirical findings of my book greatly bolster the case for approaching issues of gender in early U.S. social policymaking very much as scholars of the women's civic action persuasion tend to do: by using cross-national comparisons and understanding the distinctive features of U.S. social and political institutions.

THEORETICAL UNDERPINNINGS

My approach to analyzing American politics is historically and institutionally oriented; thus it contrasts sharply to Linda Gordon's loosely Marxian theoretical orientation. Gordon's approach to making sense of U.S. social policymaking consists of, first, identifying very broad categories of what she calls "social structure" — she advocates attention to categories of gender, class, race, and especially professional occupation — and then looking for central tendencies in the styles of thought of individual persons sorted into those categories. In turn, Gordon suggests that the styles of thought led to public policy outcomes. Her conception of policymaking is thus very elitist: reformers with certain characteristics and ideas "network" with one another, lobby governments, and gain access to key federal agencies, from which they in turn shape social legislation.[21] Gordon has nothing to say about voters and electoral processes, or about legislatures, courts, political parties, trade unions, business associations, or organizations other than professional, staff-led policy organizations. For her, American social policymaking has been something that takes place in, and among, New York City, Washington D.C., and a few other Eastern or Midwestern metropolises.

In contrast, for me the "polity" includes governmental institutions, electoral procedures and party organizations, as well as all politically active social groups (whether based on identities of class, gender roles, race, or ethnicity, or occupation). Over stretches of historical time, changes in patterns of politics and policymaking occur not only because of transformations of values, modes of economic production, or gender relationships — although such social transformations are important and I *do* discuss them. Changes in politics and policymaking also occur because of changes in the organizational arrangements of government and political parties. For the purpose of understanding U.S. social policymaking from the 1870s to the 1920s, I place a great deal of emphasis on the transformation of U.S. political structures *from* a nineteenth-century U.S. federal state featuring cross-class male democracy, competitive patronage-oriented political parties, weak bureaucracies, and strong courts and legislatures, *to* an early twentieth-century federal state featuring weakened political parties, less competitive elections, stronger executives, partial and fragmentary bureaucratization at all levels of government, and the rise of associational styles of legislative lobbying. I argue that such structural changes in U.S. politics differentially influenced the prospects of major social groups — including industrial labor and middle-class women — to achieve political self consciousness and leverage on processes of public social policymaking.

Do I leave "class" out of my analysis? Not at all. My book has much to say — more than Gordon's publications on social policy — about business, labor movements, and the relationships of reformist professionals to capitalism. Gordon engages in much handwaving about "class power," but she apparently does not want to explore empirically the actual influences of class relationships and interests on particular groups, legislative battles, and policy outcomes. The assertions that Gordon makes about my book's treatment of class are just plain wrong (as is her amazing claim that I do not deal with "ideas," when much of the book is about them). Business influences on legislative campaigns are assessed in every chapter of *Protecting Soldiers and Mothers*. An entire section of chapter 3 is devoted to analyzing the interests of reformist professionals — and I come to the same conclusion that Gordon does, arguing that professionals accepted the broad outlines of capitalism, yet pursued their own career and organizational interests within it. All of chapter 4, plus parts of other chapters, are devoted to the analysis of working-class politics at the turn of the century, and to detailed discussions of the roles of national and state-level trade union federations in campaigns for various sorts of social legislation. Finally, Gordon is wrong to claim that I do not interpret a (minor) statistical finding about the delaying influence of high levels of female and child labor on state-level mothers' pension enactments. On pages 462-64 of my book, I offer the same interpretation that Gordon does, arguing that labor-force conditions discouraged early enactments in some states.[22] My polity-centered frame of reference allows room for class relationships and actors to influence political processes; it simply does not assign them the automatically determining role that Marxist theories do. If that makes Linda Gordon unhappy, so be it.

The theoretical ideas used in *Protecting Soldiers and Mothers* are not at all in contradiction with the "state-centered" ideas I advocated earlier. Both Linda Gordon and Alan Wolfe imply that such a contradiction exists, but they are both juxtaposing the present Skocpol book *not* to the arguments I made at earlier points, but to simplified stereotypes each of them had formed about my work. Gordon and Wolfe are discovering that the real Skocpol is not as simple-minded as they had imagined. This makes them uncomfortable, so they attribute "contradictions" to me! But it is poppycock for anyone to say that I ever focused only on administrative bureaucracies or only on official state actors. My 1979 book, *States and Social Revolutions: A Comparative Analysis of France, Russia, and China* has been much dissected in the pages of *Contention* magazine, so faithful readers may recall that it analyzes monarchical states in triple relation to international contexts, to landed upper classes, and to the local social and political arrangements of peasant communities.[23] Revolutions were treated as conjunctures of social protests from below and state breakdowns triggered from above.

As a "theorist," too, I have always advocated a relational, state-society approach to analyzing politics — as those who reread my 1985 essay, "Bringing the State Back In," can remind themselves.[24] That essay calls for simultaneous pursuit of a "Weberian" line of analysis, treating states as historically formed institutions and organizational sites of potentially autonomous official action, along with a "Tocquevillian" line of analysis, examining ways in which both states and social relations affect the identities, goals, and capacities of politically active social groups. *Protecting Soldiers and Mothers* takes the theoretical advice I gave myself and others in 1985. Because my new book explains, not violent revolution in monarchies, but peaceful policy reforms in a democracy, it naturally places more emphasis on "Tocquevillian" than on "Weberian" arguments. But both lines of analysis are there, just as both were there in 1979.

One more bit of theory: Linda Gordon and I clearly differ on how gender should enter the analysis. She claims that what I do is not gender analysis. But of course it is. I simply do a different kind of gender analysis than the sort Gordon prefers. While Gordon examines gender in terms of the styles of thought of male and female welfare reformers, I focus on *gendered policies and gendered inter-group political alliances*. In the United States, such alliances were historically constructed between the 1870s and the 1920s around the male identities of the veteran soldier and the breadwinning wage-earner, and the female identity of the mother. I do not bifurcate gender identities into "male" and "female." Instead, I inquire into the changing historical conditions for the cultural and political construction of *alternative possible* male and female identities as objects of honorable forms of public social provision.

THE HISTORICAL ARGUMENT OF PROTECTING SOLDIERS AND MOTHERS

Why did U.S. public social provision from the 1870s to the 1920s protect and honor males as veteran soldiers and females as mothers, but not (for the most part) males as breadwinning wage-earners? Each part of my book focuses on a specific sort of gendered social policy, and analyzes the institutionally conditioned political alliances associated with making — or attempting to make — that type of policy.

Part I of *Protecting Soldiers and Mothers* explores why benefits for Union veterans of the Civil War expanded from the mid-1870s through the 1910s into de facto disability and old-age pensions for a very high proportion of Northern men (and into survivors' benefits for many women and children as well). I stress the workings of competitive, patronage-oriented political parties, embedded in the cross-class U.S. male electorate. A coalition of voters, male party politicians (especially Republicans), and local veterans' clubs federated into the Grand Army of the Republic came together, I show, to create what was, by international standards, an unusually generous social spending regime for former Union soldiers and their surviving dependents.

In Part II of *Protecting Soldiers and Mothers* the focus shifts to explaining the *failure* of cross-class coalitions that attempted to achieve benefits and regulations to help breadwinning workingmen and their dependents. Some reformers and trade union leaders, I show, hoped during the early 1900s to build on the precedent of Civil War pensions, creating old-age pensions for all needy elderly Americans, social insurance for wage-earners, and general labor regulations covering male as well as female wage-earners. But reform-minded male academics in the American Association for Labor Legislation often found themselves at ideological and organizational cross-purposes with male trade unionists in the American Federation of Labor and the state federations of labor. The U.S. polity was undergoing massive structural changes in the early twentieth century.

Elite and middle-class Americans were preoccupied with overcoming the "corruption" of patronage-oriented political parties, and they would not support new forms of social spending for masses of male workers and voters. There were no strong bureaucracies to implement social insurance programs. Also, the U.S. courts tended to block administrative regulations that would interfere with employers' rights to make "free contracts" with adult male laborers. After a period of unsettled judicial doctrine, it turned out by 1908 that the courts (and particularly the U.S. Supreme Court) would accept protective labor regulations for women workers understood as potential mothers, but not those applicable to most adult male workers.

Part III, the section of *Protecting Soldiers and Mothers* that is of most interest to women's historians, explains why so many U.S. social policies that targeted women as actual or potential mothers were enacted during the 1910s and early 1920s. As I have noted above, there is a genuine mystery to be unravelled here, because these maternalist laws (as I call them) were enacted by dozens of male-dominated state legislatures and the federal Congress mostly at times when U.S. women did not have the right to vote. Individual chapters in Part III reveal the precise — and varied — coalitions of women's groups, labor unions, business groups, reformers, and public officials — that struggled for and against state-level women's hour laws, state-level minimum-wage laws, state-level mothers' pension laws, and the establishment of the U.S. Children's Bureau and the expansion of its mission through the 1921 Sheppard-Towner Act. I go much further than any previous scholar toward gathering systematic information on these matters across all 48 U.S. states.

This is an important thing to do if one is studying social policymaking during the early twentieth century in the United States, because most of the legislative and political action occurred, not in Washington D.C., but in dozens of state capitals across the vast nation. Many sorts of legislative reforms were debated during the early 1900s, but the only ones likely to pass in the states or in Congress were those that had *simultaneous and very widespread* local and state-level support from educated middle-class public opinion and from legislators regardless of party affiliation. I argue in *Protecting Soldiers and Mothers* that American women's voluntary groups were uniquely positioned during the early 1900s to engage in nationwide, moralistic public education and agitation. Women's groups were the chief early welfare-state builders in the United States, acting in the absence of the centralized bureaucracies and programmatic political parties that shaped early paternalist welfare states in Europe and Australasia.

But not just *any* women's voluntary groups were the key to maternalist legislative enactments. Part III of *Protecting Soldiers and Mothers* makes a telling contribution to resolving a difference of opinion among U.S. women's historians. Patriarchal and social-service theorists of gender and social policymaking — including Linda Gordon — write as if the major organizations active in U.S. social policymaking during the 1910s and early 1920s were the Northeastern and Midwestern urban-based social settlements, the Women's Trade Union League, and the National Consumers' League — all of which were certainly important loci of activity for highly educated, mostly single, female reformers. I, too, write about the importance and the precise contributions of all of these staff-led organizations in my book. Yet my systematic, national evidence gives much more support to the position about women and politics outlined in Paula Baker's pathbreaking article on "The Domestication of Politics: Women and American Political Society, 1780-1920."[25] Baker points to the importance of locally rooted voluntary women's groups, associated into national federations such as the Women's Christian Temperance Union and the General Federation of Women's Clubs. Evidence amassed in Part III of my book shows that two of what I call *widespread federated associations* — the General Federation of Women's Clubs, and the National Congress of Mothers — were crucial to the legislative campaigns for social policies targeted on mothers and potential mothers in the early twentieth-century United States. Without the remarkable capacities of these federations of mostly middle-class married ladies to engage in *simultaneous* moral education and policy agitation in local communities and states across the entire nation, there would have been no mothers' pensions and no Sheppard-Towner Act; and the spread of protective labor laws for women workers would probably have been restricted to just a few states.

Much as I respect the efforts of Jane Addams and other female and male social settlement reformers, the efforts of Florence Kelley, Josephine Goldmark and others in the National Consumers' League, and the efforts of Julia Lathrop, Grace Abbott and their co-workers at the U.S. Children's Bureau, I am arguing that the effectiveness of these professionals as advocates of legislative enactments was extremely dependent on their ability to work cooperatively with ordinary married women politically mobilized through thousands of local clubs — particularly those federated nationally into the General Federation of Women's Clubs and the National Congress of Mothers.

Here was a truth that the first Chief of the U.S. Children's Bureau, Julia Lathrop, understood perfectly — as I show in my analysis of her "state-building" strategies in chapter 9 of *Protecting Soldiers and Mothers*. Lathrop understood that the Children's Bureau under her guidance could achieve the same kind of alliance with local women's voluntary groups that the U.S. Department of Agriculture was at that time forging with local farmers' voluntary groups. Lathrop realized that in the U.S. federal polity, where Congress plays a make or break role for federal agencies and programs, such an alliance was crucial to the survival and expansion of her Bureau. Lathrop did not imagine that she could get anywhere in U.S. politics by spending her time "networking" with friends in the Consumers' League or the social settlements! She may have corresponded mostly with these women professional friends (thus creating the archives that would later create certain misimpressions among historians). But Lathrop was a sufficiently astute politician to know that she had to direct her public and policymaking energies toward much broader and more grass-roots audiences all across the United States.

SKOCPOL AND GORDON: DISAGREEMENTS ABOUT HISTORY AND METHODOLOGY

In contrast to some other feminist scholars, neither Gordon nor I is willing to interpret early U.S. social policies for mothers merely as "patriarchal" impositions on women; we both feel that women themselves were important actors in creating these policies. Gordon and I agree, moreover, that male and female reformers in the early 1900s idealized the family wage, and wanted public policies, where possible, to support the complementary roles of male breadwinner and female homemaker. We both argue that female reformist professionals often thought of themselves as "public mothers" who made special efforts on behalf of welfare programs to aid mothers and children, as well as workers. Finally, too, Gordon and I agree that most of the pioneering U.S. advocates of social insurance were male social scientists with careers in universities and academic disciplines. Despite these nontrivial areas of agreement, however, there are equally important facets of early twentieth-century U.S.

social politics that Linda Gordon and I see quite differently — in part because we use different methodologies.

The intellectual content of early male professional writings about social insurance is a consequential matter about which Gordon and I disagree. While doing research for Part II of my book, I became intimately familiar with the contents of the first seven books about social insurance in the United States published between 1893 to 1913, and also with dozens of early 1900s articles. Based on these sources, I can confidently say that, whatever the relevance of Gordon's "rights talk" characterizations to U.S. social insurance writings after the early 1920s, she is dead wrong about the themes in these writings from the 1890s to the early 1920s. Early books and articles all focused on "workingmen's insurance," not on anything faintly resembling "universal" social insurance.[26] The early writings discussed at length the "needs" of workers and their families, and the policy proposals they put forward were justified not just with actuarial abstractions or dry statistics, but with explicit philosophical arguments about the desirability of "ethical statism" and about the need for social solidarity to limit pure market principles in a democratic industrial society. Most of the pioneering American social scientists who advocated workingmen's social insurance had received higher degrees in German universities, and they were inspired by German philosophical and ethical theories about the responsibility of the state in industrial society.

What is more, early male advocates of social insurance (in both the United States and Europe) were just as concerned as Gordon's female reformers to separate the "deserving" from the "undeserving" poor. They were not at all willing to give benefits "automatically," as Gordon claims. Male advocates of social insurance obsessed about the need to use tests of employment or readiness to accept waged employment as criteria for eligibility. It is not incidental that early employment insurance proposals were always explicitly linked to calls for the establishment of public employment exchanges. Reformers were unwilling to consider the prospect of giving out-of-work benefits, unless there were public offices to which the unemployed would have to report regularly to demonstrate their readiness to accept any available jobs. Workmen's compensation claimants, moreover, had to accept supervision by doctors — something that trade union leaders bitterly complained about during the 1910s.

Supervisory paternalism — along with the sense that professionals and the state should do something "for" workers, to meet their needs as the market could not — suffused early ideas about workingmen's social insurance. That is why I label these ideas "paternalist" — just as many of the reformers themselves did. One of the leading early U.S. advocates of social insurance, Isaac Max Rubinow, wrote in 1913 that "social insurance . . . has been decried as rank paternalism, and this indictment must be readily admitted. For social insurance, when properly developed, is nothing if not a well-defined effort of the organized state to come to the assistance of the wage-earner and furnish him something he individually is quite unable to obtain for himself."[27]

Linda Gordon and I also disagree fundamentally about female social policy activism in the early twentieth century. Here the disagreement is not just about how to characterize ideas but, more fundamentally, about *who* the most relevant female leaders and women's organizations actually were. As we have seen, Gordon holds that "national" female welfare activists consisted of mostly privileged, mostly single, women who worked in major cities as charity reformers, social workers, and public officials. Gordon believes that New York City was in "the vanguard" of reform. While including in her study many single social workers active strictly in New York city or state politics, Gordon inexplicably leaves out many non-careerist married clubwomen who were the actual leaders of nationwide drives for maternalist legislation. She leaves out the leaders of the interstate campaigns conducted by the General Federation of Women's Clubs and the National Congress of Mothers for protective labor laws, mothers' pensions, and the establishment of the U.S. Children's Bureau and the Sheppard-Towner program. She omits such key non-Eastern figures as Industrial Commissioner Katherine Philips Edson, who constructed the alliance of 53 women's groups that successfully campaigned for mothers' pensions, strict hours laws, and the minimum wage in California.[28] Most of the important national reform leaders that Gordon ignores in her study were married women, living outside the East, who did not pursue professional careers. Thus, Gordon's conclusions about the individual social characteristics of female reform leaders would have been different if her "sample" had been more truly representative of the national leadership she purports to analyze.

The nub of the difference between Gordon and me has to do not so much with individual women leaders, as with organizations and alliances. My research shows that — if we are talking about the women who actually helped to bring about new kinds of legislative reforms during the 1910s and early 1920s — we must highlight *alliances* between urban-based professional reformers, on the one hand, and widespread federated associations of local married women's voluntary clubs, on the other. We must also think about the entire nation, not just the East. The one part of the United States that was unequivocally "in the vanguard" for all types of maternalist social legislation was not New York City, but California. The West and Midwest were generally ahead of the East as well as the South, in terms both of how quickly they passed legislation, and of the qualitative characteristics of their laws.

At one point in her comment on *Protecting Soldiers and Mothers*, Gordon pokes fun at my ponderous "sociological" use of unnecessary statistics to prove points that are, she says, already well known to historians. (This sort of disciplinary chauvinism is not only unbecoming in a scholar of Gordon's stature; it is, in fact, unusual among practitioners of women's history, who usually celebrate interdisciplinary cooperation.) Gordon failed to note that statistics take up only five pages out of forty-five in my chapter about mothers' pensions. (Most of the chapter is devoted to qualitative descriptions of the ideas and arguments used by supporters of these new benefits.) Nor did Gordon accurately describe my key statistical finding — that the timing of mothers' pension enactments across the 48 states is powerfully predicted by the timing of endorsements of such laws by major women's federations in each of the 48 states. This finding is a solid statistical confirmation of the qualitative argument I make about the importance, not just of "women's groups" in general, but about the State Federations of Women's Clubs and the state Branches of the National Congress of Mothers in particular. What is more, I show that the states that enacted mothers' pensions very late, or not at all, were not just southern states. I transcend the South/non-South divide by specifying other factors — about labor force characteristics, public schooling, and women's group actions — that more meaningfully explain what was really going on politically.

Gordon not only misleadingly describes but also dismisses my statistical findings, claiming that historians have always known that "women's groups" (which ones, she conveniently does not specify) were the key supporters of mothers' pensions. In documentation of this, Gordon cites just one book, Stanley Lemons's *The Woman Citizen* — a study of the 1920s *that does not say one word about mothers' pensions*, which were mostly enacted during the 1910s. In fact, as Gordon surely knows, the charitable and social-work organizations that she cites as in the vanguard of maternalist social policymaking were mostly very strongly *opposed* to the initial enactment of mothers' pensions — and nowhere more opposed than in New York. The best study of the state-level enactments is a 1973 article by Mark Leff.[29] This article has many sound findings, but it did not pin down exactly how and why the federated married women's associations that I stress were the decisive actors in the interstate campaign for mothers' pensions.

The key methodological point is this: I use statistics to *test* my hypotheses in relation to those put forward by other scholars. This way of using numbers stands in sharp contrast to Gordon's use of numbers to *illustrate* her pre-given "theoretical" categories of analysis. In the case of the argument about mothers' pensions that appears in *Protecting Soldiers and Mothers*, I first worked out the analysis qualitatively, using traditional historical documentary sources. Then I put my hypotheses on the line, testing them against a huge number of alternative arguments (including all of those that Gordon lists). My entire argument could have fallen apart if the statistical tests had proved me wrong. But they didn't — and the full multivariate analysis (not included in the book, so as not to burden it with too many numbers) will appear in the September 1993 issue of the *American Political Science Review*.[30]

Why doesn't Linda Gordon herself go beyond merely illustrative uses of statistics? Why doesn't she improve her samples of reformers, and then use some statistical tests to put her own arguments on the line compared to the arguments of others? Her answer seems to be that to do this would somehow violate the integrity of historical writing. But obviously this is nonsense. Social historians have been using combinations of qualitative and statistical techniques for some time — and there is nothing to stop women's historians from doing this, too.

My statistical work was not wasted energy: As political scientists who study the spread of legislation across the U.S. states know very well, mothers' pensions are an important *exception* to the usual rules that laws take about forty years to spread across most states, and that large, wealthy, urban and industrial states are normally in the lead (with laws slowly diffusing to smaller, less urban and industrial states). The truly surprising patterns and tempos by which mothers' pension laws suddenly spread in the 1910s can, however, be perfectly well explained — once we understand the crucial role of the married women's club federations.

Gordon chooses to ridicule a small point I make in passing: that adult literacy rates were correlated with how soon states enacted mothers' pensions. Gordon suggests that I claim "literacy" caused mothers' pensions to be enacted. But that is not true. I point out that the most literate states during the 1910s were *not* primarily the urban and industrial states that Gordon treats as central. Many quite rural and non-industrial states were among the more literate, especially where women were concerned. These same states tended to have great densities of local women's clubs and more readers of mass-circulation women's magazines; and such states were often the leaders in enacting maternalist social policies. The point is not literacy as such; it is the strong presence of local women's clubs linked into the General Federation of Women's Clubs and the National Congress of Mothers.

Linda Gordon is often wrong about the ideas, as well as the groups, that lay behind maternalist legislation during the 1910s and early 1920s. Many of the characterizations that Gordon offers of female welfare thought are seriously biased by the overrepresentation of Eastern charity leaders and social workers in her research. Contrary to what Gordon argues, for example, the chief arguments used by women's groups in favor of mothers' pension legislation were designed sharply to differentiate these benefits from poor relief or charity.[31] Mothers should be honored, it was argued, for their service to the nation and the community. The term "pension" was meant to invoke some of the same ideas of an honorable reward for service to the Nation that had been previously invoked by Civil War pensions. The soldier, it was said, serves by giving his life in battle, while the mother serves by giving birth to and educating new citizens. The original advocates of mothers' pensions were trying to establish the civic value of motherhood, rather than primarily trying to supervise the poor, as Gordon suggests.

By trying to reduce female welfare activism to charity and social work traditions, Gordon also misses the fact that the first major American advocate of true "universalism" in social legislation was not a male professional at all. It was Julia Lathrop of the Children's Bureau, who argued that the Sheppard-Towner programs should be non-means-tested, "open to all" mothers across classes, races, and regions of the United States. Lathrop was explicit in arguing that universal access was necessary to make maternal health education programs honorable. She pointed out that programs limited to those unable to pay would soon "degenerate into poor relief."[32] Not only was Julia Lathrop politically astute in understanding that professionals had to work with local voluntary groups to further the cause of public programs for mothers and children in the United States. She also understood — well before the framers of Social Security arrived at the same conclusion — that universal, cross-class social policies are much more politically viable in U.S. democracy than programs targeted on the poor alone.[33]

Why does all of this matter? Linda Gordon's mischaracterization of the ideals and political strategies of male and female reformers is not of merely "academic" historical interest. Gordon obviously does not mean to celebrate male reformers while denigrating females. But she should take note of what others end up doing on the basis of inaccuracies in her work; and she should realize the possible implications for present-day policy debates. Citing Gordon as his authority, Alan Wolfe declared in the *New Republic* that male reformers have been the sole carriers of universalist "social citizenship" ideals in American social politics.[34] (This, of course, conveniently forgets that the framers of Social Security excluded or marginalized most women and virtually all African-Americans, leaving them out of initial social insurance programs. Like Wolfe, I think highly of the Social Security framers, but there is no need to pretend that they were full "universalists.") Not content to over-idealize men, Wolfe also dismisses the policy achievements of U.S. women reformers as "feudalistic," and asserts that American women cannot validly make simultaneous claims for equal political rights and social protections for mothers, children, and families.[35] Is it incidental, I ask myself, that the same *New Republic* a few weeks later published an issue prominently featuring attacks on the policy advocacy of Hillary Rodham Clinton and Marian Wright Edelman?[36] These women reformers of the 1990s are, after all, leaders of the Children's Defense Fund, which is the clearest contemporary voice for ideals similar (though of course not identical) to those espoused by female social policy advocates in earlier periods of U.S. history.

THEN AND NOW

In closing, let me comment briefly on the relevance of maternalist politics during the 1910s and 1920s for thinking about U.S. social politics today. To avoid any possible misunderstanding, I should stipulate that, when it comes to the social politics of the 1990s, I am not a maternalist! I do not want to carry into the present any of the "separate spheres" notions about men and women that were so prevalent around the turn of the century. Today's social policies, as I have written, should aim to help working families with both single or dual wage-earners. Ideally, a new Family

Security Program in the United States should blend concerns for individual rights with an emphasis on socially responsible caring, including responsible care of children by working parents.[37]

While times — not to mention gender roles — have certainly changed since the 1910s and 1920s, there nevertheless may be some valuable lessons to learn from certain aspects of the maternalist social politics of those times. One lesson to learn is that politics, especially in the United States, is not only about voting in elections. It is also about voluntary groups educating broad publics — for example, to appreciate the need to sustain and honor families, not just wage-earners. Another lesson is that the key to success in U.S. politics lies not merely in sending a few intellectuals to Washington D.C. to lobby or run federal agencies. In short, for those who hope to improve U.S. family policies during the 1990s, having Donna Shalala and Hillary Clinton in the nation's capitol will be helpful, but far from sufficient.

Americans in the present who would like to extend the best principles of Social Security to working parents and children should consider imitating, *not* the thinking, but the *broad political alliances* forged by women's groups during the 1910s and early 1920s. Progressive forces in America today need, once again, to find ways for educated professionals and local community groups to work together, furthering programs to meet the shared needs of parents and children across all of social classes, racial and ethnic groups, and geographical regions of our vast nation. *Protecting Soldiers and Mothers* is, historiographically speaking, a book entirely about the past. Yet I hope that it can contribute to a retrieval of lessons relevant for the future. Some of these lessons can be inspired by the best political achievements of organized American supporters of maternalist social policies in bygone days.

NOTES

1   Rosalind Rosenberg, "How the Safety Net Got Torn," *The New York Times Book Review* (January 31, 1993): 16.
2   Alan Wolfe, "The Mothers of Invention," *The New Republic* (January 4 & 11, 1993): 30.

3   Ibid., 35.
4   Linda Gordon, "Social Insurance and Public Assistance: The Influence of Gender in Welfare Thought in the United States, 1890-1935," *American Historical Review* 97, 6 (February 1992): 19-54. This is the article to which Alan Wolfe refers.
5   Linda Gordon, "The New Feminist Scholarship on the Welfare State," in *Women, the State, and Welfare*, ed. Linda Gordon (Madison: University of Wisconsin Press, 1990), pp. 9-35.
6   Eileen Boris and Peter Bardaglio, "The Transformation of Patriarchy: The Historic Role of the State," in *Families, Politics, and Public Policy: A Feminist Dialogue on Women and the State*, ed. Irene Diamond (New York: Longman, 1983), 72-73.
7   Mimi Abramovitz, *Regulating the Lives of Women: Social Welfare Policy from Colonial Times to the Present* (Boston: South End Press), 4.
8   In addition to the works by Gordon already cited, see Robyn Muncy, *Creating a Female Dominion in American Reform, 1890-1935* (New York: Oxford University Press, 1991); and Barbara J. Nelson, "The Gender, Race, and Class Origins of Early Welfare Policy and the Welfare State: A Comparison of Workmen's Compensation and Mothers' Aid," in *Women, Politics, and Change*, ed. Louise A. Tilly and Patricia Gurin (New York: Russell Sage Foundation, 1990), pp. 413-35.
9   See the discussion of functionalism in Gordon, *Women, the State, and Welfare*, 23.
10   Ibid., 28.
11   Ibid., 26, referring to Linda Gordon, *Heroes of Their Own Lives: The Politics and History of Family Violence, Boston, 1880-1960* (New York: Viking/Penguin, 1988); and Linda Gordon, "The Frustrations of Family Violence Social Work: An Historical Critique," *Journal of Sociology and Social Welfare* 15, 4 (December 1988).
12   Gordon, "Social Insurance and Public Assistance," 20-21.
13   Ibid., 21.
14   Ibid., 28, where Gordon clearly states that "Male influence on welfare thought" was registered "through a new concept, introduced at the turn of the century, social insurance. Its basic principles were government provision, based on compulsory participation and automatic (not means or morals-tested) benefits for covered groups. Indeed, social insurance programs were not exclusively directed at the poor; one of their selling points was that they benefited all classes." As I discuss below, this characterization of social insurance ideas in the period up to the 1920s is

dead wrong. Having seen an earlier draft of my response to her ideas, Gordon has now changed her position in her preceeding essay — but she does it without acknowledging that her February 1992 article was wrong on a point pivotal to its entire argument about "male" and "female" styles of welfare thought.

15   Gordon, "Social Insurance and Public Assistance," 22-23. At various points in *Protecting Soldiers and Mothers*, I discuss how African-Americans were treated in various public social programs.

16   Ibid., 51. Labor leaders and male politicians were, however, left out of Gordon's study.

17   Linda Gordon, "Black and White Visions of Welfare: Women's Welfare Activism, 1890-1945," *The Journal of American History* 78, 2 (September 1991): 562. (In this article, Gordon offers further information about her methods and her "white women reformers." I refer to it only in connection with these matters.)

18   Ibid.

19   Ibid., 572.

20   Paula Baker, "The Domestication of Politics: Women and American Political Society, 1780-1920," *American Historical Review* 85, 3 (June 1984): 620-47; Kathryn Kish Sklar, "The Historical Foundations of Women's Power in the Creation of the American Welfare State, 1890-1930," forthcoming in *Mothers of a New World: Maternalist Politics and the Origins of Welfare States*, ed. Seth D. Koven and Sonya Michel (London and New York: Routledge, 1993); and Seth Koven and Sonya Michel, "Womanly Duties: Maternalist Politics and the Origins of Welfare States in France, Germany, Great Britain, and the United States, 1880-1920," *American Historical Review* 95, 4 (October 1990): 1067-1108.

21   In "Social Insurance and Public Assistance," 22, 26, Gordon presents her white women leaders as a "network" of persons who wrote memos and letters to each other. Scattered throughout this article and "Black and White Visions" are descriptions of the lobbying techniques and the inter-personal and inter-organizational networking efforts that constitute Gordon's only descriptions of *how* her male or female reformers influenced public policymaking.

22   A thorough and more nuanced analysis and discussion of the factors that worked against early advocacy of mothers' pensions in the states appears in Theda Skocpol, Christopher Howard, Susan Goodrich Lehmann, and Marjorie Abend-Wein, "Women's Associations and the Enact-

ment of Mothers' Pensions in the United States," forthcoming in the *American Political Science Review* (September 1993).

23   Theda Skocpol, *States and Social Revolutions: A Comparative Analysis of France, Russia, and China* (Cambridge and New York: Cambridge University Press, 1979).

24   Theda Skocpol, "Bringing the State Back In: Strategies of Analysis in Current Research," in *Bringing the State Back In*, ed. Peter B. Evans, Dietrich Rueschemeyer, and Theda Skocpol (Cambridge and New York: Cambridge University Press, 1985), pp. 3-37.

25   See the full citation in note 20.

26   See Gordon, "Social Insurance and Public Assistance," 28; and the comment in note 14 above.

27   I.M. Rubinow, *Social Insurance, With Special Reference to American Conditions* (New York: Arno and the New York Times, 1969; originally 1913), p.11.

28   See *Protecting Soldiers and Mothers*, pp. 386, 410, 415, 416, and 453.

29   Mark Leff, "Consensus for Reform: The Mothers'-Pension Movement in the Progressive Era," *Social Service Review* 47, 3 (September 1973): 397-417.

30   Skocpol et. al., "Women's Associations and the Enactment of Mothers' Pensions."

31   Contrast the way Gordon presents the ideas behind mothers' pensions in "Social Insurance and Public Assistance" to my extensively documented presentation of the original arguments for these benefits in *Protecting Soldiers and Mothers*, chapter 8.

32   For the full quote and citation, see *Protecting Soldiers and Mothers*, p.500.

33   See Theda Skocpol, "Targeting within Universalism: Politically Viable Policies to Combat Poverty in the United States," pp.411-36 in *The Urban Underclass*, edited by Christopher Jencks and Paul E. Peterson (Washington D.C.: The Brookings Institution, 1991).

34   Wolfe, "Mothers of Invention," 34.

35   Ibid., 34 (for "feudalistic"), and 32-33 for the discussion of political versus social rights. Wolfe clearly believes, however, that organized industrial workers are entitled to have both political rights and special social protections at the same time.

36   Mickey Kaus, "TRB from Washington: Thinking of Hillary," and "The Godmother," in *The New Republic* (February 15, 1993): 6; and 21-25.

37   An explanation of how a new Family Security Program might improve contemporary U.S. social provision, while building on the best tendencies from the past, in my article "Sustainable Social Policy: Fighting Poverty without Poverty Programs," *The American Prospect* 1, 2 (Summer 1990): 58-70.

Response to Theda Skocpol

LINDA GORDON

I do not intend to add anything here to my critique of *Protecting Soldiers and Mothers*. Puzzled readers can find the book and decide for themselves. But in her response, Theda Skocpol refers frequently to my article in a recent *American Historical Review*, "Social Insurance and Public Assistance." I find hers a quirky reading of it and would like to correct the record.

Theda construes the article's main points in a direction almost opposite to its argument. The article begins and ends with the assertion that male and female welfare reformers worked within substantially the same gender system, the same set of assumptions about proper family life and the proper spheres for men and women. I argue *against* understanding gender as necessarily constructing opposite or sharply differing patterns, and show that the fundamental premise of *both* men and women welfare advocates was the family wage.[1] Within that larger agreement, I show that there were considerable differences in male and female welfare thought, the core of which was the women's commitment to casework. Theda Skocpol summarizes the article without mentioning casework and claims that my larger framework is one that emphasizes difference when the opposite is the case.[2]

Theda refers to my analysis of the male/female differences I found as "vocationally grounded." While I did indeed argue that men's far greater access to professional identification in the early twentieth century produced an orientation towards increasingly technical, "objective," and nonphilosophical presentation of ideas, I suggest many sources of this difference in the article, including women's-rights ideas, the practice of the "woman movement," class, ethnic, and family influences.

I was particularly puzzled by Theda's criticism that I, like her, omit African-American welfare work from my analysis. I wrote a separate article on Black women's advocacy, which Theda also cites. I will assume she forgot this, as well as the fact that the articles are part of a forthcoming book which sets as one of its main tasks integrating African-American history in the history of Aid to Families with Dependent Children (AFDC). The "Social Insurance and Public Assistance" article explains that I wrote separately about the national, elite, white leadership precisely in order to "control" for class, race, and region and thus allow a specific focus on gender.

I am equally bewildered by Theda's comment that my conception of policymaking is "elitist." I think that those who know my work would agree that it has been marked by an unusual degree of interest in bottom-up influence. The article she is criticizing is a study of an elite group; that topic does not make my approach elitist.

My sample of welfare reformers, which Theda finds "inexplicable," is explained in the article, albeit not to her satisfaction. Starting with the US Children's Bureau, which was the national center of women's agitation for federal welfare programs, I looked at the papers of the leaders of that Bureau in the National Archives and other collections. I traced their network of contacts through their correspondence, memoranda, etc., and did rudimentary biographical work on these women. To get into my network they had to be *national* leaders (defined in the article). The article also explains that, and why, I excluded women primarily working for protective labor legislation. I may have missed many women (and men) but I have not yet heard any evidence to alter my general claims about the women's group as a whole, including the high proportion of unmarried women and presence of strong homosocial bonding among them. (By contrast, Theda found — and I would not disagree — that the state-level leaders were mostly married women. What I missed in the book was an examination of how their marital status influenced their advocacy and helped shape their identities and ideas.)

I also stand by my claim that New York City played a vanguard role in the Progressive era and the 1920s in developing welfare programs. I was led to New York not by a study of various localities but by discovering something new to me: the high proportion of women in national public-welfare leadership who had worked in NYC in this period, and strengthened their network at the same time. In making this claim for New York's role I was thinking of housing codes, pure milk inspection, adult education, or public health education, for example. But I am open to being shown by some evidence that other locations produced as much, and nothing in my argument rests on this finding.

In a bizarre footnote (#31), Theda calls upon the reader to contrast her "extensively documented" presentation of mothers' pensions to mine. It feels foolish to have to point this out, but: Theda is contrasting a 500 page book to a 30-page article — and the article does not discuss mothers' pensions! The footnote seems connected to her claim that I "mischaracterize" the arguments for mothers' pensions. Here I'm just mystified: my article doesn't discuss them, and I am in entire agreement with Theda and earlier historians about the fact that this program was intended to separate its beneficiaries from others who collected poor relief.

Theda also claims that I "missed the fact that the first major American advocate of true 'universalism' was not a male professional" but Julia Lathrop, first head of the Children's Bureau. My article did not mention Lathrop in this regard, and the question of who was the first such advocate was not my concern; nevertheless, the article does point out exactly what Theda is arguing, that women were prominent in proposing universal benefits: "Nothing about this approach [universalizing benefits] differed from that of the social work tradition. Edith Abbott argued passionately at the beginning of the New Deal for seizing the opportunity to create one universal program of public assistance without stigma" (pp. 45-46).

I am feeling somewhat embarrassed as I defend myself against these criticisms, disappointed that we are not debating more substantial issues. The problem arises, I think, from the fact that Theda has spent too much of her response trying to find fault with an article of mine and too little trying to respond substantively to the larger issues raised in my review — for example, what she means by "polity-centered," or what she sees as the influence of gender, class, ideology, or ideas.

Theda may well be right that I use statistics primarily to illustrate, not to test hypotheses. Indeed, I generally don't use "statistics" at all in its recent meaning, but only report simple numbers and proportions. I learned in doing quantitative research for my study of family violence that statistical work makes no sense when the "data" are fragmentary, subjective, unreliable. Ironically, however, in the article to which she refers I did not simply "illustrate" but rather counted certain biographical features of the group; these produced several "findings" about the welfare networks of which I was not aware until I added up the numbers, such as the high proportion of unmarried women or the relatively large minority of Jews among the men. Usually the questions I ask are not susceptible to quantitative answers, and I therefore don't quantify information. (My criticism of the quantification in Theda's book is that it is applied to the wrong questions, those better answered by qualitative and even narrative information.)

As to my creating a "hierarchy" of women's and gender scholarship, Theda may also be right here if one can discount her loaded language. I do believe that some historical work is better than others, and I do think that the field has, on average, progressed in sophistication and complexity in the last two decades. Work that generalizes about women and women's organizations is less developed than work that distinguishes among women; work that uses the category "gender" only about women has been transcended by work that examines masculinity as well; work that assumes a single, universal gender system has been challenged by work that recognizes variety in gender systems and explodes binary constructions.

Finally, Theda has charged that I am "already deeply committed to assumptions and historical conclusions that are in certain ways directly contradicted by the new evidence and arguments" in her book. To this I can say only that if she will point out to me which of my assumptions and conclusions she refers to, and by what they are contradicted, we can have a sensible discussion. In fact, there isn't much in her book with which I disagree; rather I think that her explanatory framework is too restricted.

As to contemporary issues: Theda is absolutely right that one cannot conclude from her book, as James Kloppenberg did at the AHA, that she supports maternalism today. On the other hand, it seems to me that if we are to avoid the negative aspects of maternalism today, we could fruitfully begin with a critical analysis of the strengths and limitations of maternalism in the past. Indeed, we can only learn from the past if we are critical in examining it. Celebration or commemoration of the women reformers of the past is of limited value. But we must also avoid evaluating the past against presentist values and possibilities. Theda's approach yields material that is at once more and less celebratory than the approach I would use. Failing to contextualize their proposals in the constraints of their time — e.g., social/economic conditions, the standpoint of the reformers, the feminist debate surrounding them — she can neither honor nor evaluate their contributions historically.

NOTES

1   From the introduction to the article: "In identifying the influence
of gender, I do not argue that these visions were dichotomized between
men and women. . . . My purpose is not so much to distinguish male from
female as it is to illustrate the importance of asking questions about gender,
questions that illuminate similarity as well as difference" (p. 19). From the
conclusion: "While this article pleads for the value of gender analysis, it
also tries to demonstrate the inaccuracy of dichotomizing men and
women. . . . Welfare reformers, whether men or women, shared many
values, and these shared values were often themselves part of the gender
order . . ." (p. 50).
2   This representation of my approach seems particularly wrong-
headed given that I have several times written explicitly and even more
often implicitly against the emphasis on gender *difference* that characterizes some women's-studies scholarship (e.g., Linda Gordon, "On Difference," *Genders* 10 (spring 1991): 91-111; Linda Gordon, "The Peaceful
Sex?" *National Women's Studies Association Journal* 2, 4 [Autumn 1990]:
624-34).

D. Marxism and Women's History

Is Marxism Still a Useful Tool of Analysis for the History of British Women?

DEBORAH VALENZE

Many historians of women, particularly those whose specialty is Britain, maintain a kind of schizophrenia with regard to Marxist history. They often derive many of their fundamental assumptions from the legacy of the eminent school of British Marxists historians, yet they pursue quite different enterprises, some of them at sharp variance with those earlier projects. Professional meetings expose this split between conceptual loyalties and methodological practices. At the Ninth Berkshire Conference on the History of Women in 1993, for example, many participants showed an interest in a panel with a title similar to that of this essay, though different reasons for attending quickly became apparent. Historians of women are now pursuing questions of race, as well as gender, and many have employed the paradigms of Marxism in charting new directions of research in areas of sexuality, ethnicity, and national identity. In part, the diversity of their interests grows out of a wider inclusion of voices within the profession, which has encouraged the articulation of difference as a new frontier of debate. But underlying this development is a thornier issue having to do with political realities. With the disappearance of Marxist socialism as it existed in Eastern Europe, the Marxist critique of contemporary society and its history has come under scrutiny and attack. If historians are in fact on the brink of a new age in <u>historiography,</u> are any 史料編集(法) of the originating assumptions of Marxist scholarship still useful?

Contention, Vol. 4, No. 3, Spring 1995

As the putative home of industrial capitalism, Britain was also the birthplace of groundbreaking Marxist historiography. The pioneering work of Rodney Hilton, Christopher Hill, Eric J. Hobsbawm, John Saville, and E. P. Thompson formulated histories that went far beyond the economism of an earlier generation, opening up the study of class struggle through examination of culture and society. Popular movements of protest, customary practices, rituals, and religion revealed a fuller sense of the ways in which the growth of capitalism shaped class struggle. Exploitation and resistance, key processes in a Marxist conception of historical change, could be located in a greater variety of settings and guises. These developments cleared a path for the discussion of gender. Women could be identified among the rebellious crowds of history, the ranks of the proletariat, and the practitioners of popular culture and religion. Bolstered by the simultaneous interest in "history from below," historians of British women launched into fertile territory. It was here that female subjects of Marxist history could be found, as urban workers, women Chartists, domestic servants, and in a multitude of other settings.

But Marxist histories of women were destined to be more than just compensatory. Simply adding women to the picture, without changing the lineaments, color, and design of the project, was impossible. How were Marxists to explain the oppression of women? Did the sources lie in relations of capitalism, or further back, in the primary relationship between men and women? Conflict erupted in all quarters, producing a literature dense with theoretical implications. British feminists were at the forefront of debate, setting to work with energy and inspiration. Journals like *Feminist Review*, *Spare Rib*, and, at a later point, *History Workshop Journal* sustained a network of activists and scholars committed to working out the relationship between feminism and Marxism. Out of these circles came innovative, definitive scholarship, including Sheila Rowbotham's *Women, Resistance and Revolution* (1972) and *Hidden from History* (1973). Despite considerable ideological differences among historians of primarily feminist and primarily Marxist commitments, an uneasy alliance (or, in the memorable phrase of the period, "an unhappy marriage") was struck between Marxism and feminism.[1]

The political activism of the 1960s and 1970s had much to do with sustaining these collective endeavors. In retrospect, it is startling to note how many works of scholarship at that time, Marxist and otherwise, took as their founding premise the need to address existing social injustices and conditions of inequality. With a critique of capitalism at the center of their projects, Marxist historians of women held a key to a transformative process, an understanding of a historical movement away from the way things were, toward a socialist order. Capitalism made women wealthy or poor, powerful or enslaved; it had situated them in powerful country estates or back-to-back housing in Manchester, and endowed them with variable means of expressing their dissatisfactions. The implicit alliance between a study of the past and working in the world gave Marxist feminists an important place in wider discussions of progressive political strategies and social reforms. Women were clearly essential to the advance of capital, yet they were disempowered in society and politics. Marxist feminists made the case that the oppression of women worked to the detriment of all society, impeding the move to a more just system of production and distribution. Even if historians could not agree on the origins of capitalist patriarchy, a Marxist trajectory toward the future welded together a remarkable array of historians.

What did Marxist historians of women accomplish? Some practitioners set out to historicize the concept of patriarchy within the history of capitalism: they demonstrated the centrality of reproduction and the family, which enforced the authority of men and expropriated the labor of women as housekeepers and providers of care for the young and infirm. In contributing to the study of the working class, historians of women broke open the subject of a surplus labor force, endlessly available and exploitable, that was often female.[2] Dorothy Thompson prompted historians to think about the disappearance of women from nineteenth-century radical political movements. Leonore Davidoff's study of the psychological relationship between servant Hannah Cullwick and a barrister, Arthur Munby, highlighted the complexities of class oppression when intertwined with sexual fantasy. And Barbara Taylor's *Eve and the New Jerusalem* (1983) forced all historians to take note of the road not taken, the feminist alternative offered by Owenite socialists, when the future of capitalism seemed subject to revision.

As the profession of history grew to accommodate historians of women, so, too, grew the power of feminist history. By 1982, the significance of this intellectual forum convinced the editors of *History Workshop Journal* to alter its subtitle to "a journal of socialist and feminist historians" in order to include work that had "clearly moved onto the frontiers of progressive historical writing."[3] The editors admitted that not all socialists were feminists, and not all feminists focused on socialist history; but the two branches of endeavor were committed to working together. Writing feminist history was seen as a bona fide part of the socialist struggle.

The fissures in this alliance nevertheless remained apparent, particularly given the theoretical implications of many feminist critiques. With innovations emanating from many fields, current Marxist history has come to look very different than it did in the halcyon days of the 1960s and 1970s. Without reviewing the large literature produced since then, I would like to isolate instances contributing to the present state of research, as a number of historians of women appear to be working out a new rapprochement with Marxist scholarship. Major changes in the political landscape have obviously impinged on the writing of Marxist history. Probably the most salient has to do with the challenge to class as an agent of historical change.[4] One might expect historians who have privileged gender over class to celebrate the demise of a theoretical adversary, but for British historians, the sense of anomie arising from this particular development has yet to dissolve. Years of Thatcherite policies rendered historians on the left protective of notions of class, even as voting behavior contradicted cherished models of political allegiance. In any case, historiography lagged behind or resisted political reality, and as theorists proclaimed the death of class, many British historians remained preoccupied with revising its meaning.

As part of this project, the middle class became a more serious focus of research. Situated in the context of the eighteenth and nineteenth centuries, during the days of middle class formation, the new contributions left at least part of the Marxist terrain undisturbed. Leonore Davidoff and Catherine Hall produced a massive testimonial to the gendered nature of class in *Family Fortunes: Men and Women of the English Middle Class, 1780-1850* (1987). With each foray into the material reality of middle-class life — property ownership and the maintenance of status, religious and domestic life, and political affiliations — Davidoff and Hall found interlocking spheres of female and male influence, replete with prescriptive definitions of appropriate behavior for women and men. *Family Fortunes* revealed the nineteenth-century triumph of the British bourgeoisie as a gendered joint venture in the name of class. While remaining loyal to an implied narrative about class struggle and cultural hegemony, the book gave that legacy an important feminist twist.

In the world of labor history, with its emphasis on the formation of class consciousness, the organization of labor, and political conflict, the "story" of British history was rendered open to serious revision. Studies of gender relations within the labor movement revealed a past fraught with conflict over women's demands for employment. Historians of women have located new linkages between labor and the state that suggested collusion as well as conflict. In *Limited Livelihoods: Gender and Class in Nineteenth-Century England* (1992), Sonya Rose depicted the antagonism between male and female workers over employment as workers realized that their competition was driving down wage levels. Rose went beyond studying isolated arenas of family or factory and, in a more ambitious analysis, revealed fateful discussions of Parliamentary commissioners and male labor unionists who converged in their opinion that workers' homes would best be served by restricting the hours and conditions of female factory employment. Rose's study suggests that the terrain of the working class as a category, though fiercely contested by women, was masculine by the end of the nineteenth century.

Women historians have persisted in forcing the issue of gender in areas where old class verities have died hard. A good example can be found in the work of Ellen Ross, whose investigations of working-class motherhood in London have contradicted assumptions about "class experience" preserved in a sentimental corner of leftist history. If most labor and working-class historians have not completely ignored the subject of motherhood, they have been guilty of what Carolyn Steedman has called the celebration of "a kind of psychological simplicity . . . lived out in [Richard] Hoggart's endless streets of little houses."[5] The seemingly timeless image of the self-sacrificing "mum" of the slum, responsible, hard-working, and long-suffering, has maintained a hold on the historical imagination since the appearance of Hoggart's *The Uses of Literacy* in 1957. Ross's *Love and Toil: Motherhood in Outcast London* (1993) sets out to recover the complexity of London working class mothers' lives through voices and actions hitherto obscured beneath blanket generalizations about experience. These women are not viewed through the rose-colored lens of sons recollecting their mothers but rather through painstaking reconstructions of interactions between spouses, mothers, and children, and working-class women and middle-class observers. Issues of childcare emerge as perilous decisions impinging on how to survive, quite literally, in the face of material deprivation; simple household concerns become the forum for strenuous negotiations over authority and money among family members. Ross's nuanced explorations show women fully integrated into "public" neighborhood networks and state interventions that prove crucial to family maintenance. Working-class mothers display the backbone to defy middle-class philanthropists and the cerebral capabilities to wrench hard responsibilities out of errant family members. *Love and Toil* has contributed to wholly new understandings of agency embedded in class identities.

Yet with the possible exception of Barbara Taylor's work on feminism within the Owenite movement, the dominant narrative of British history (and the historians supporting it) yielded little to the analytical pressure of feminist historians. Many scholars continued to assume that the subject of women existed separately from the real world of politics and work, despite relentless professional conference time devoted to the demolition of the boundary between public and private. It is not surprising that historians of women mounted overt challenges to the usual choices of subject matter and methodology. Innovations in the profession, most notably poststructuralist discourse theory, encouraged analyses of hitherto unexplored realms of consciousness, as well as the area of consciousness itself. As old concepts of class were dismantled, some historians developed perspectives of gender from the vantage point of culture and sexuality. Sexual identity and experience became a means of opening up new discussions, such as the role of desire and consumption. The new spate of studies evolving now are not strictly materialist in focus but instead deal with the study of consciousness and behavior in the realms of personal identity and culture, where Marxists share efforts with many different kinds of historians.

This trajectory best fits the work of Judith Walkowitz, whose earlier work *Prostitution and Victorian Society* (1980) analyzed the way sexual reform could unite women and men of different classes against state regulation of Victorian prostitution. More recently, Walkowitz turned from a revision of conceptualizations of class oppression and political struggle for an adventurous exploration of more "modern" identities in late nineteenth-century London. In *City of Dreadful Delight* (1992), she excavated a multitude of competing narratives — of streetwalkers, New Women, spiritualists, and socialists — in an effort that was reminiscent of a former generation's project to locate the voices of the marginal and oppressed. But unlike earlier reclamation projects, this work deconstructed the unitary concept of agency. The actions of individuals became more fissiparous; rather than being caught up in finding their political niche in the struggle against capitalism and the state, these women (and men) were busy challenging and transgressing the boundaries of their sex in the context of a highly diverse urban life. Their activity was aimed not only at changing the world around them (indeed, this aspect of desire takes a subsidiary role), but also at constructing a self that was multidimensional. Walkowitz's subjects, as a result, became recognizably gendered, human (that is, full of contradictions), and modern.

More than any other recent work of British history, Walkowitz's *City of Dreadful Delight* was in tune with post-Marxist theoretical positions on the Continent. In a famous testimonial, Ernesto Laclau and Chantal Mouffe had already proclaimed the death of the "Jacobin imaginary," an illusive revolutionary goal that presumed a singular locus of power against which a unified class-based opposition poses its assault.[6] With the disappearance of really existing socialism, the implied narrative of Marxist historiography had almost entirely dissolved. Social changes in Britain (and America) only furthered the collapse of a coherent political left. The relative political quiescence of the late 1980s and early 1990s appeared to confirm a view of human nature that was less concerned with renouncing capitalism and more absorbed in the politics of identity. By definition pluralistic, new political agendas have driven activists in disparate directions, dividing feminists as well as Marxists according to new allegiances.

Yet these developments have not precluded a viable future for Marxist historical studies of women. The crux lies in the search for a common endeavor, which at the moment remains insufficiently theorized. I would like to propose one avenue of exploration, the study of domination and the goal of understanding the material origins of oppression contributing to relations of power. As Stanley Aronowitz has pointed out, discourses of domination remain key to a Marxist understanding of the past, even though the transhistorical principles that early theory relied upon are no longer viable.[7] New technologies have confounded Marx's notion of power, dispersing the sources and the foci of oppression. It is clear that the ranks of the industrial working class, which are not swelling in disproportion to other groups, have come to focus more on the pleasures than on the drawbacks of capitalism. Yet deep social and cultural inequalities persist and can be traced back to critical differences in the ownership of wealth, property, and authority that are specific to conditions under capitalism. Many people continue to nurture grievances against capitalism, albeit in ways not necessarily aimed towards activism. The very innovations in historical scholarship that challenged Marxist history may turn research in new, fruitful directions. A Marxist history of women can now explore problems of consciousness, sexual relations, consumption, religion, and more, and still ask questions about economic arrangements that generate differences in wealth and power.

In searching for capitalism's discourses of domination, historians inevitably turn into the path of the history of race relations. As a form of oppression linked to the advance of capitalism from the sixteenth century, histories of racism have remained more closely tied to a historical materialist approach than those focusing strictly on gender. Catherine Hall's recent effort to rescusitate British Marxist history with a simultaneous infusion of both categories of race and gender stands as a major example. In her work on missionary activity in Jamaica following the abolition of slavery in 1834, she shows how hierarchical understandings based on ethnicity, race, gender, and class proliferated, in spite of the enlightened intentions of Baptist women and men. Insisting on the instability of any one set of relationships, Hall elaborates on historical circumstances that converged to produce specific hierarchies and oppressions.[8]

Feminists have also called attention to the internalized dimension of capitalism's discourses of dominance, helping to make the category of psychology a legitimate area of exploration for both Marxists and feminists. In a study of ideologies of racial superiority, Vron Ware deftly interweaves analysis of twentieth-century understandings of race with historical accounts of British women to show how a psychological and social sense of white racial superiority established a foothold in the social relations of Europe and North America.[9] She juxtaposes a historical discussion of racism with the nineteenth-century abolitionist movement, revealing the limited accomplishments of the antislavery movement. Slavery as an institution was abolished in the British colonies in 1833, but assumptions of white domination of others continued and were even bolstered by the moral righteousness of anti-slavery advocates. As Nancy Stepan has pointed out in a study of scientific understandings of race, "The war against racism was being lost. The Negro was legally freed by the Emancipation Act of 1833, but in the British mind he was still mentally, morally and physically a slave."[10] Ware's work reminds us of how the theoretically outmoded attitudes of racial domination persist in contemporary experience.

Recent events in Europe continue to raise philosophical questions for Marxist historians of women. New forms of oppression have emerged in the "new world disorder" that now affects Europe. Native Europeans face the competing claims of migrant populations drawn from all parts of the world into Europe looking for employment, shelter, or simple rescue from collapsed economies and repressive polities. The tendencies that Marxist European historians traditionally noted — the power of capitalism to accumulate capital at the expense of inordinate masses of labor, its myriad ways of pitting worker against worker, its power to reify relations that distort and deny — have taken on new coloration in the light of political changes and movements of population. The response has been a multitude of racial and sexual oppressions by states as well as individuals.[11] At the same time, an efflorescence of nationalism has thrown a monkey-wrench into the frameworks of Marxism and, perhaps more stunningly, Western-style liberalism. Religious fundamentalism has created new divisions and dissolved old alliances. It is in our interest not only to understand these new constellations of power, but also to foreground the resulting forms of oppression, keeping both halves of the human population in the picture.[12]

The time may be particularly right for an intervention by feminists inspired by specific aspects of Marxist theory. With the demise of Marxism as a current political vision in Europe, commentaries have poured forth with pronouncements on the triumph of capitalism. Identity politics, including certain strands of feminism, sit in uneasy relation to this development. Late capitalism has facilitated the quest for a new emancipated self, which recognizes the importance of desires, pleasures, and the role of material consumption. The neoliberalism buttressing triumphant capitalism of recent years gives lip service to notions of democracy and equal opportunity. No one would deny that capitalism has done a better job of reinforcing the exercise of individual freedoms than old-style socialism. But western society still badly needs a corrective to liberalism. An understanding of the self without a correlated exploration of relations of domination can lead to conservative, not emancipatory, ends. Historically, Marxism has provided a means of critiquing the liberal self. With the help of feminism, it may still help to connect analysis focusing on individual identities to institutions and states that help to produce them.[13]

An alliance between feminism and Marxism ultimately exposes the underlying ethical considerations of Marxism, an agenda that can be informed by theory, but not wholly determined by it. The revolutionary aim of Marxism, after all, was to create a better society for all people. That human beings are entitled to basic subsistence in a society of plenty remains an important insight sustained by Marxist inquiries. In charting the historical empowerment of individuals in their struggle for self-realization, Marxism showed how organized collective action was a necessary response to social ills. More generally, the Marxist perspective still contains a viable recognition of the need to address the overall structure of society and the philosophical assumptions that govern it. A short step lies between that approach and the present need to identify a progressive vision for all of society.

New movements of liberation require the perspectives of both Marxism and feminism, each in its own way seeking to redefine and redirect agency toward liberatory ends. I am aware that by saying this, I open myself to the charge of superimposing a "soft" teleology, now severed from really existing socialism, upon empirical evidence. Yet historians may possess knowledge of the past that can puncture current cynicism and arrest the tendency to consider only the options in front of us now. Beyond the construction of multivalent selves and identities, historians must make a stronger case for larger social values and collective identities. These may assume new forms in the future, different from the family, community, and religious affiliations of the past. Is it too much to ask that women, who so often in history have borne responsiblity for others, be alert to potential connections among the agents of a new historical era?[14]

NOTES

The author wishes to thank Michael T. Gilmore, Peter Weiler, Ruth Smith, Nikki Keddie, and an anonymous reader for comments on earlier drafts of this essay, and Iris Berger, Mary Blewett, Sucheta Mazumdar, Teresa Meade, and Louise Tilly for their contributions to a panel at the Berkshire Conference on the History of Women in June, 1993, from which this essay originated.

1   See Zillah Eisenstein, ed., *Capitalist Patriarchy and the Case for Socialist Feminism* (New York: Monthly Review Press, 1979); Heidi Hartmann, "The Unhappy Marriage of Marxism and Feminism: Towards a More Progressive Union," in *Women and Revolution: A Discussion of the Unhappy Marriage of Marxism and Feminism*, ed. Lydia Sargent (Boston: South End Press, 1981), 1-41. On the British side, see the exchange between Sheila Rowbotham and Sally Alexander and Barbara

Taylor, *People's History and Socialist History*, ed. Raphael Samuel (London: Routledge and Kegan Paul, 1981), 364-73.

2   The activism as well as the published work of Sally Alexander and Anna Davin played an important part in developing these areas of research in Britain.

3   "Editorial: *History Workshop Journal* and Feminism," *History Workshop Journal* 13 (1982): iii.

4   The latest contribution on this point is Patrick Joyce, *Visions of the People: Industrial England and the Question of Class, 1848-1914* (Cambridge: Cambridge University Press, 1991).

5   Carolyn Kay Steedman, *Landscape for a Good Woman: A Story of Two Lives* (New Brunswick, NJ: Rutgers University Press, 1987), 7.

6   Laclau and Mouffe, *Hegemony and Socialist Strategy: Towards a Radical Democratic Politics* (London: Verso, 1985). See also the helpful introduction to Wai-chee Dimock and Michael T. Gilmore, eds., *Rethinking Class: Social Formation and Literary Studies* (New York: Columbia University Press, 1994).

7   Stanley Aronowitz, *The Crisis in Historical Materialism: Class, Politics and Culture in Marxist Theory*, 2nd ed. (Minneapolis: University of Minnesota Press, 1990), xvi.

8   See especially "Missionary Stories: Gender and Ethnicity in England in the 1830s and 1840s," in her *White, Male and Middle Class: Explorations in Feminism and History* (New York: Routledge, 1992), 205-54.

9   Vron Ware, *Beyond the Pale: White Women, Racism and History* (London: Verso, 1992).

10   *The Idea of Race in Science: Great Britain 1800-1960* (Houndmills: Macmillan, 1982), 1, quoted in Ware, *Beyond the Pale*, 108.

11   Benedict Anderson, "The New World Disorder," *New Left Review* 192 (May/June, 1992): 3-13.

12   See the helpful discussion of these questions in Eric Hobsbawm, "The Crisis of Today's Ideologies," *New Left Review* 192 (March/April, 1992): 55-64.

13   As Stanley Aronowitz has pointed out, Marxism is "a mode of discovery of the ways in which desire is transformed as compulsory sexual and social morality, imposed by ideological institutions of domination as an order from on high." *Crisis in Historical Materialism*, 172.

14   See Cornel West, *The Ethical Dimensions of Marxist Thought* (New York: Monthly Review Press, 1991); Kate Soper, "Socialist Human-

ism," in *E. P. Thompson: Critical Perspectives*, ed. Harvey J. Kaye and Keith McClelland (Philadelphia: Temple University Press, 1990), 204-32; Leszek Kolakowski, *Toward a Marxist Humanism* (New York: Grove Press, 1968), especially his "Permanent vs. Transitory Aspects of Marxism," 173-87.

Marxism and Women's History:

African Perspectives

IRIS BERGER

Although Marxism has left a strong imprint on academic discourse during the past three decades, its position has not gone unchallenged. Just as feminists pushed for their own form of "marriage," however unhappy and unstable, between Marxism and feminism, scholars in both the West and the former colonial world forcefully emphasized that race, too, was a partner in this relationship. And, during the 1980s and 1990s, as multiculturalism and identity politics have moved to the forefront of scholarly interpretation, Marxism and class analysis, if not forgotten entirely, are often portrayed in a kind of New Age polygynous union with multiple, equally powerful and independent partners.

While the metaphor of polygyny may seem appropriately Afrocentric, the image of multiple partners also is a useful reminder that for most historians of the "non-Western world" Marxism always required modification, based as it is on nineteenth-century Western models of social transformation that were written into the past as universal patterns of change. Thus, feminism has not been the only force pushing to recast the terms of the marriage contract.

Nonetheless, despite the wide acceptance of the idea that Marxism had to be revised in order to represent African realities, Marxist theory has been more central to African historiography than to that of the United

States. Whether reflected in the underdevelopment theories and the "mode of production" debates of the 1970s or in the work of the social historians and sociologists who have dominated the writing of South African history for the past two decades, Marxism and Marxist-influenced scholarship have provided much of the language of African historical writing, and postmodernism has been slow to win acceptance.[1] This Marxist idiom is extremely eclectic, however, drawing as often on the insights of Ester Boserup, Claude Meillassoux, Andre Gunder Frank, or Gramsci as on those of Marx himself.

During its pioneering years in the 1960s, African historiography assumed a strongly nationalist perspective. Historical writing on the precolonial era focused on the state and, for the colonial period, on undifferentiated "African" struggles against oppression and exploitation. This emphasis grew from two contemporary concerns: the impulse to disprove the common Western assumption (even among scholars) that the continent had no real "history" and the effort to reverse the colonial representation of Africa's past as a narrative of the exploits and contributions of Europeans.[2] As in most scholarship of the period, women were noteworthy primarily for their absence as historical actors.

Beginning in the 1960s, several alternative paradigms were developing, however. If nationalist historiography was a product of the short-lived optimism that followed independence for many countries of West and East Africa, the new writing was a response to a growing realization that "flag independence" did not affect the continent's continued economic dependency. Thus "radical historians" (either self-consciously Marxist or influenced by Marxist ideas) turned their attention particularly to the social and economic dimensions of the past. For those interested in precolonial societies and their transition to capitalism, the insights of French Marxist anthropologists such as Claude Meillassoux, Emmanuel Terray, and P.P. Rey generated a lengthy (and, in the end, somewhat scholastic) debate over the characteristics of an African "mode of production" and its "articulation" with capitalism. Heavily influenced by dependency theory, other scholars focused on tracing the continent's underdevelopment from the era of the slave trade to the present. Finally, class analysis and an emphasis on the materialist foundations of historical transformation strongly shaped emerging national historiographies in South Africa and Tanzania. Through strong British connections, the social history of Edward Thompson and the Oxford-based History Workshop also permeated South African history in important ways.[3]

Scholarly interest in Marxism was closely related to political developments on the continent. In some countries, radical scholarship emerged in conjunction with national efforts to implement socialist economic policies; in others, in conscious opposition to capitalist-oriented development programs. Southern Africa experienced a different dynamic. The high level of industrialization and the growing militancy of working-class protest in South Africa lent support to a traditional Marxist vision of the past. For Mozambique, Angola, and Zimbabwe, the experience of armed struggle and (especially in Mozambique) revolutionary reconstruction lent a Marxist orientation to both political and intellectual life. Everywhere, the language of socialism retained a subversive cast in the context of the Cold War mentality that dominated international relations during the first three decades of African independence. Both intellectuals and politicians turned to Marxism as a counterpoint to efforts at Western hegemony. Indeed, even some of the most Western-oriented governments clothed their early economic plans in the language of "African socialism" as a symbolic means of asserting their autonomy from former colonial rulers and the United States.

Because the high point of Marxist-influenced historiography coincided with the birth of African women's history in the 1970s, studies of women were strongly shaped by the analytical language of the period.[4] Thus the nascent women's history assumed a distinct class orientation and rarely discussed "women" as a single unified group. Analyses of class and race paid close attention to people's material circumstances, seeking to understand consciousness primarily in relation to political action. The concept of identity with its more fluid underpinnings and implications had not yet entered historical discourse.

The identification of many women's historians with the "radical" strain of African scholarship has produced an historical tradition that, while not necessarily overtly Marxist, is highly attentive to the social and economic nuances of women's place in a given social structure or labor process. Whether the women in question are Muslim dance society participants in Mombasa, traders in Accra or the markets of Sierra Leone, garment workers and petty bourgeois pass resisters in South Africa, elite women in Lagos, or Kenyan peasants in the Land and Freedom Army, participants in social movements are rarely divorced from the economic, political, social, and religious forces that have created the context for their lives.[5]

Furthermore, because class analysis has so strongly permeated African historiography during the past two decades, women's historians have not usually conceptualized Marxism and feminism as antagonistic. Rather, many have sought to reframe selected aspects of Marxism in an effort to create a new synthesis. In doing so, they usually have relied not only on archival sources, but also on extensive interviews with African women. Thus, perceptions of class and its meaning often come through in women's own words, rather than echoing the perceptions or misperceptions of outside observers.

South African sociologist Belinda Bozzoli, steeped in the Marxist tradition of both local and exiled scholars of the 1970s, sought such a theoretical merger in her innovative article "Marxism, Feminism and Southern African Studies."[6] Reacting against scholars who analyzed women's oppression solely in terms of its functional relationship to capitalism, Bozzoli developed the twin concepts of "internal domestic struggle" (within the household) and "external domestic struggle" (between the household and the wider capitalist society) in order to expand the Marxist concept of struggle to include gender relations. She then applied this theoretical model to explain the gendered patterns of proletarianization among different racial and ethnic groups in the nineteenth and twentieth centuries. Pointing to the inadequacies of both Marxist and feminist scholarship, her aim was "to demonstrate the two-way interaction" between them.

As a member of the inner circle of white academics in South Africa, Bozzoli was critical of her male contemporaries. Describing the tendency to collapse female oppression into the capitalist mode of production, she argued:

> It is a tendency which has suited the indigenous left, reluctant as it is to consider the implications of its own internal sexism. It appears to be far more comfortable for the left to absorb feminist struggles, or indeed subordinate them into the general struggle against capitalism, than to begin to consider the vast implications of admitting the relative autonomy of female oppression.[7]

In the introduction to *Women and Class in Africa*, Claire Robertson and I sought a similar integration of Marxist and feminist theory. We were reacting to a body of literature that ignored or obscured the position of women, conveying the impression that female members of a household always shared the class position of related men. In order to address these problems, we outlined the concept of "access to critical resources," modifying "control over the means of production" in a way that better fit the experience of African women.[8] This broader, more flexible concept allowed us to understand women's class status as a product both of their own resources and of those they attain through their relationships with men. By promoting a fuller and more accurate understanding of women and class, we also hoped to explain the widespread feminization of poverty in Africa during the twentieth century.

Luise White, another North American historian, also addressed the conjuncture of Marxism and feminism in her award-winning book *The Comforts of Home: Prostitution in Colonial Nairobi*.[9] By reconceptualizing prostitution as another form of domestic work, she used the concept of labor to challenge accepted academic perspectives. Although these perspectives were strongly shaped by feminist scholarship, she felt that many feminists had not freed themselves sufficiently from moralist interpretations. She asks: "If this book challenges any of the conventional assumptions about prostitutes' degradation and victimization, is it because Nairobi is unlike anywhere else on earth, or because those assumptions are flawed and based on information generated by attacks on prostitutes?"[10] Rather than writing the history of a "deviant" subculture, White located prostitution as a form of capitalist labor, observing: "Prostitution is a capitalist social relationship not because capitalism causes prostitution by commoditizing sexual relations but because wage labor is a unique feature of capitalism: capitalism commoditized labor."[11] In addition to her emphasis on labor, Marxist-feminist approaches also shaped her concern with how prostitution reproduced both male energies and the prostitutes and their dependents.[12]

Examining the experience of precolonial African women, Nakanyike Musisi, a Ugandan scholar based in Canada, reassessed the development of Buganda in her article "Women, 'Elite Polygyny,' and Buganda State Formation."[13] She analyzed class and state formation in this East African kingdom from an innovative perspective, looking at political history through the lens of gender rather than simply including women in her discussion. Although she did not explicitly identify her approach as Marxist, Musisi acknowledged her debt to Karen Sacks's study *Sisters and Wives: The Past and Future of Sexual Equality*,[14] noting, "It is in fact her materialist, historical evolutionary approach to understanding women's past that I found most relevant to this study."[15] Musisi's contribution to the dialogue between class analysis and feminism is primarily methodological, showing how the two approaches combined can illuminate the difficult and often-neglected field of precolonial women's history.

Thus, for most historians of African women, whether self-consciously Marxist or not, class power and class conflict, labor, the impact of capitalism, and the notion of struggle have occupied central places in the historical landscape. The strength of this writing lies in connecting women's individual and collective lives with broader processes of social transformation. Whether the women in question were peasants or factory workers, petty traders, prostitutes, nurses, or teachers, historical analysis has drawn on a wide range of interdisciplinary work, including individual life histories, to contextualize their experience in terms of the joint forces of capitalism, colonialism, and local patriarchal traditions.

Although African women's history emerged and matured in close conjuncture with the "radical" and Marxist scholarship of the past two decades, differences of emphasis mark the two scholarly traditions. Key to women's history has been an effort to understand not only (for the colonial and postcolonial periods) the world created by capital and the state, but also its close and changing links with the world of household and family. Women's historians also have tended to perceive the household as a potential site of conflicting interests and have begun to explore the themes of domesticity and childbirth that have long occupied historians of Europe and North America.[16]

While many women's historians have shared the interest of their contemporaries in "resistance" to colonial rule and to postcolonial states, women's history has developed its own emphasis. By underscoring the gender differences in anticolonial movements, by bringing to light the careers of women's leaders, and by showing the ways that female solidarity operated in times of political and economic crisis, this new field often has challenged accepted ideas about the character of African social movements. Prior to the work of Susan Geiger, for example, historians credited a group of Western-educated middle-class men for the successful nationalist movement in colonial Tanzania (then Tanganyika). Geiger's research uncovered the powerful mobilizing efforts of female Muslim traders, who successfully turned their dance societies into advocates of freedom from colonial rule.[17]

The relatively smooth, though not altogether peaceful, "marriage" between Marxism and feminism in historical studies of Africa (as compared to the United States and Western Europe) merits comment. The works discussed above acknowledge the shortcomings and silences of traditional Marxist analysis with regard to African women: its male-oriented construction of concepts such as class and labor, its tendency to ignore the domestic realm and the casual economy that sustains so many women on the continent, and its habit of subsuming other analytical categories under the rubric of class. Yet, whereas historical work on Europe and the United States often seems to take capitalism for granted, it is not possible to do so in studies of modern African history.[18] In a period when new economic, social, and cultural relationships originating in Europe were being imposed and selectively adopted throughout the continent, historians simply could not ignore the rhythms and contours of capitalist intrusion as critical, if not always determining, in all aspects of society, including gender relationships.

An additional factor also may be important, though. Much of the earliest writing on African women's history was the scholarly product of outsiders, both black and white (or, in the case of South Africa, of local whites). For these writers, criticizing or even drawing attention to indigenous patriarchal patterns was a more sensitive issue than for historians of the United States and Europe who were tracing the past of their own societies. Cloaking critiques of unequal gender relations in the garb of capitalist domination may have helped to frame sensitive issues in a language that local intellectuals could share more easily. Indeed, a class-conscious vision of society has inspired the African male writers most vocal in their critiques of women's position.[19]

Over the past two decades, however, the context for feminist analysis of Africa has shifted as more African women have created their own movements and their own concepts of feminism. Although many of the scholars involved come from disciplinary backgrounds other than history, their work has greatly enhanced studies of the past, often from a Marxist or Marxist-influenced perspective.[20] In addition, the rich and growing body of African women's fiction has added a wide range of voices and idioms to the dialogue over women's shifting place and its representation. Portraying the dilemmas of women caught in a nexus of conflicting cultural expectations, these writers focus on the personal and family relationships that are at the core of most women's worlds. By privileging women's vision, they decenter the political and economic arena that sets the stage for most histories. Concerned instead with childbearing and infertility, spouses and co-wives, and the personal tensions between autonomy and community, these writers sketch paths that many women's historians have begun to follow in an effort to reconceptualize the past through women's eyes.[21]

The economic and political emphasis of work in African women's history has the strength of not isolating women from their broader social context; but it also has drawbacks. Many aspects of culture, including sexuality, are rarely explored, and women are inserted into a narrative that rests on gender-neutral notions of political and economic change. Furthermore, the history of women in precolonial, precapitalist Africa has received relatively little attention[22] and, with a few notable exceptions, the new voices of postmodernism have gone largely unheeded or unheard, including the tendency to pay greater attention to gender and to gendered meanings. In her critique of existing research in African women's history, Nancy Rose Hunt wrote in 1989, "It is surprising . . . how many themes and analytic approaches which have been developed in European and American women's history are barely broached in African women's history."[23]

As postmodernism has begun to permeate African women's studies in recent years (not always through the work of historians), its main impact has been to widen the perception of gender as a category, showing how its flexibility in many African societies makes perfect sense of concepts strange to Western ears, such as "male daughters" and "female husbands." This writing suggests the need to focus on particular female roles, "diverse, overlapping, and paradoxical" as they might be, rather than to generalize about the category "women" (particularly in opposition to "men").[24]

Some examples of this challenge have come from African scholars. A Nigerian sociologist with a London University doctorate, Ifi Amadiume wrote *Male Daughters, Female Husbands*[25] in part to explain these common African relationships and the gender system that produced them. In her analysis, both "male daughters," women who have been accorded male status in the absence of a son in order to safeguard their father's line and property, and "female husbands," wealthy women who acquired "wives" to assist them in their economic pursuits, were evidence of a gender system more flexible than in the West. While not ignoring class, she underscores the need to understand the workings of gender in a society in which biological sex and ideological gender did not necessarily correspond, thereby significantly broadening the roles that women might play.

Similarly, sociologist Oyeronke Oyewumi, Nigerian born and now teaching in the United States, argued that the construction of "women" as a category was erroneous in application to precolonial Yorubaland.[26] She observed instead that "females were not defined as antithetical to men. They were not the *other*. The genitalia and biological sex did not constitute the basis of distinction."[27] In precolonial Yorubaland, instead of "women," there were females in various roles, and, for women and men alike, seniority within lineage structures was the main form of social differentiation. She concludes, "No doubt gender has its place and time in scholarly analyses, but its place and its time is not precolonial Yoruba society. The time of 'gender' was to come during the colonial period."[28]

From a somewhat different perspective, Linzi Manicom, in her article "Ruling Relations: Rethinking State and Gender in South African History,"[29] calls for an understanding of the role of state discourses and practices in producing gender, race, and class subjectivity. Previous research, she argues, has simply taken that subjectivity for granted and then examined the impact of state policies on particular groups of people. A South African teaching in Canada, she is also concerned with understanding the gendered assumptions of such categories as "worker" and "African."

While this reassessment of the meaning of gender does not necessarily undermine the concept of class, it does highlight the importance of understanding African conceptions of status differentials and their operation, and of examining how social categories (including class and gender) are produced, reproduced, and transformed. It also raises questions about the common assumption that male/female opposition as a primary principle of social organization necessarily applies to all societies.

These new analytical paradigms coincide with the contemporary challenge to Marxism following the collapse of the Soviet Union. Since shifts in African history during the past three decades have closely reflected changes in the political and economic fate of the continent, it is important to consider the possible import of this transformation for African women's history.

For Africa in general the new era in global history has had contradictory results. With an end to Cold War rivalries and decreasing external support for authoritarian rulers, democratic movements have gained strength in many countries. Yet Marxist movements have not totally disappeared; in South Africa, for example, the Communist Party remains a vital political force. Simultaneously, IMF/World Bank structural adjustment policies have imposed new forms of privatization and have forced governments to reduce state subsidies for many social services.

How these transformations will affect the writing of women's history is difficult to predict. Might we expect, for example, a new interest in women's past participation in government and politics, as women in countries with recently developed democratic systems strategize about how to make the best use of their own traditions? Will electoral politics or democratic prospects lead to enhanced ethnic polarization, as has been the case elsewhere in the world (as well as in Africa)? If so, will historians develop a new interest in the historical relationships among ethnicity, gender, and class? How will greater privatization translate into new forms of stratification, and what will the results be for women in particular? Will this period of transformation strengthen an interest in understanding the gendered and class implications of other eras of rapid change? Or does the degree of crisis in some African countries, and often the resulting devastation for women, lead attention away from the study of history to a concern with issues that seem more immediate and pressing?

This question is not abstract speculation - nor is it relevant to Africa alone. There is little doubt that African historiography during the past three decades has closely reflected contemporary political and economic preoccupations. Nancy Hunt is uneasy at this trend, expressing her fear that African women's history "risks becoming a department of the literature on women and development."[30] From a slightly different vantage point, I was struck by the virtual absence of interest in the past at a recent conference on African women's studies. As speakers from across the continent outlined the state of research in their respective countries, history was mentioned only rarely, and then usually as a hypothetical baseline for change. Indeed, given the upheavals in some African universities, research of any kind sometimes risks becoming a luxury. While Marxist-oriented analysis of African women may thrive under these conditions, the implications for women's *history* may be substantial.[31]

In conclusion, it seems clear that Marxist-influenced historians have contributed significantly to the development of African women's history and that, given the current unstable, economically fragile state of many African countries, their concern with a materialist perspective, with class analysis, and with the shifting impact of global capitalism on gender relations is not likely to disappear. Yet equally apparent is the need to continue to integrate new perspectives in order to address issues outside the concern of Marxist discourse and to raise questions about the dominant narrative inherent in Marxism. This means developing a fuller understanding of changing African categories of social analysis and their implications for gender studies and, without losing the economic grounding of earlier work, deepening our historical insights into a wide range of topics in social history, from health and healing to childbirth, childhood, marriage, sexuality, family life, and religion.[32] In providing the material to reconstruct women-centered histories, this research may raise questions about the ability of a capitalist-centered Marxist historiography to capture fully the experience and viewpoints of African women. Some of this work has begun, and the eclecticism of African history leaves me little doubt that it will continue; but, given the very different context for historical work in Africa than in the North, the direction of this trend remains uncertain.

Finally, another issue is also pertinent to this discussion. If Marxist interpretations of African women's history have focused in large part on class analysis and on the impact of capitalism on women's lives, the political practice of Marxism and feminism also have contributed to shaping visions of the future, particularly in revolutionary settings such as Mozambique during and immediately after the war of liberation and in South Africa since the 1980s.

While the historical realities of the twentieth century have punctured any simple connection between socialism and women's liberation or between revolutionary struggles and the creation of egalitarian states, it is also apparent that current policies in Africa and elsewhere are reshaping and reinforcing class, gender, and other social tensions and inequities. Thus, the political collapse of "communism" notwithstanding, it seems unlikely that the impulse that created Marxism and socialism will diminish. As Irving Howe observed in 1985, "Whatever the fate of socialism, the yearning for a better mode of life, which found expression in its thought and its struggle will reappear."[33] I might add that whatever the fate of women's history, one hopes that it, too, will remain part of that struggle.

NOTES

My thanks to Ron Berger, Nalova Lyonga, Karen Sacks, and an anonymous reviewer for their comments on earlier drafts of this article. I am also grateful to Nikki Keddie for seeing the possibilities of transforming a talk delivered at the Berkshire Conference on Women's History in June 1993 into a more detailed article.

1   See, for example, Jan Vansina's highly critical article, "Some Perceptions on the Writing of African History, 1948-1992," *Itinerario* 7, no. 1 (1992): 77-91.

2   These issues are outlined more fully in Bogumil Jewsiewicki and David Newbury, eds., *African Historiographies: What History for Which Africa?* (Beverly Hills: Sage Press, 1986).

3   In addition to Jewsiewicki and Newbury, see Bogumil Jewsiewicki, "African Historical Studies: Academic Knowledge as 'Usable Past' and Radical Scholarship," *African Studies Review* 32, no. 3 (December 1989): 1-76. Jan Vansina's new book, *Living With Africa* (Madison: University of Wisconsin Press, 1994) provides a personal appraisal of changing trends in the historiography of Africa. See especially 203-206 for his critique of Marxist history as applied to Africa.

4   It is important to note that, apart from the work of French anthropologists, which often portrayed women passively as part of the currency of social relationships, much of the "radical history" was as gender-blind as its more traditional counterparts. Women are scarcely mentioned in either of the historiographical works cited above. One important exception to this silence is Charles van Onselen's writing on the social history of Johannesburg.

5   I refer here, in order, to the following works: Margaret Strobel, *Muslim Women in Mombasa, 1890-1975* (New Haven: Yale University Press), 1979; Claire Robertson, *Sharing the Same Bowl: A Socioeconomic History of Women and Class in Accra, Ghana* (Bloomington: Indiana University Press, 1984); E. Frances White, *Sierra Leone's Settler Women Traders: Women on the Afro-European Frontier* (Ann Arbor: University of Michigan Press, 1987); Iris Berger, *Threads of Solidarity: Women in South African Industry,1900-1980* (Bloomington: Indiana University Press, 1992); Julia Wells, "Why Women Rebel: A Comparative Study of South African Women's Resistance in Bloemfontein (1913) and Johannes-

burg (1958)," *Journal of Southern African Studies* 10, no. 1 (October 1983): 55-70; and Cora Ann Presley, *Kikuyu Women, the Mau Mau Rebellion and Social Change in Kenya* (Boulder, CO: Westview Press, 1992).

6   *Journal of Southern African Studies* 9, no. 2 (April 1983): 139-71. This section is not intended to be a complete review of all historical scholarship on African women, but rather highlights works that have self-consciously addressed the relationship between Marxism and feminism.

7   Ibid., 142. Bozzoli is equally critical of "rectificatory" scholarship on women's resistance for insufficiently explaining the material base of such movements.

8   Claire Robertson and Iris Berger, eds., "Introduction: Analyzing Class and Gender — African Perspectives," (New York: Holmes and Meier, 1986).

9   *The Comforts of Home* (Chicago: University of Chicago Press, 1990).

10   Ibid., 2.

11   Ibid., 11.

12   Ibid., 12.

13   *Signs* 16, no. 4 (1991): 757-86.

14   *Sisters and Wives* (Westport, CT: Greenwood, 1979).

15   Nakanyike B. Musisi, "Women, 'Elite Polygyny,' and Buganda State Formation," *Signs* 16, no. 4 (summer 1991): 766, nt. 29.

16   Karen Tranberg Hansen has drawn together some of this work in *African Encounters with Domesticity* (New Brunswick, NJ: Rutgers University Press, 1992).

17   Susan Geiger, "Women in Nationalist Struggle: TANU Activists in Dar es Salaam," *International Journal of African Historical Studies* 20, no. 1 (1987): 1-26.

18   On the naturalization of capitalism in U.S. history see Joyce Appleby, Lynn Hunt and Margaret Jacob, *Telling the Truth about History* (New York: W. W. Norton, 1994), 120-21.

19   I am grateful to Nalova Lyonga for drawing my attention to this point with reference to the work of Mongo Béti, Sembène Ousmane, Nuruddin Farah, and Ngũgĩ wa Thiong'o.

20   Some of these works include: Monica Munachonga, "Women and the State: Zambia's Development Policies and their Impact on Women," in *Women and the State in Africa*, eds. Jane Parpart and Kathleen Staudt

(Boulder,CO.: Lynne Rienner Publishers, 1988); Maud Shimwaayi
Muntemba, "Women and Agricultural Change in the Railway Region of
Zambia: Dispossession and Counterstrategies, 1930-1970," in *Women and
Work in Africa*, ed. Edna G. Bay (Boulder, Colo.: Westview Press, 1982);
Achola Pala Okeyo, "Daughters of the Lakes and Rivers: Colonization
and the Land Rights of Luo Women," in *Women and Colonization*. eds.
Mona Etienne and Eleanor Leacock (New York: Praeger, 1980); Harriet
Sibisi, "How Women Cope with Migrant Labor in South Africa," *Signs* 3,
no. 1 (Autumn 1977): 167-77; and Ruth Meena, ed., *Gender in Southern
Africa: Conceptual and Theoretical Issues* (Harare, Zimbabwe: SAPES
Books, 1992). For West Africa, see: Simi Afonja, "Changing Modes of
Production and the Sexual Division of Labor Among the Yoruba," *Signs*
7, no. 2 (1981): 299-313; Bolanle Awe, "The Iyalode in the Traditional
Yoruba Political System," in *Sexual Stratification: A Cross-Cultural View*,
ed. Alice Schlegel (New York: Columbia University Press, 1977); Chris-
tine Oppong, ed., *Female and Male in West Africa* (London: George Allen
& Unwin, 1983); Filomena Chioma Steady, ed., *The Black Woman Cross-
Culturally* (Cambridge, MA.: Schenkman Publishing Co., 1981); and M.
Ramphele, "The Dynamics of Gender Politics in the Hostels of Cape
Town," *Journal of Southern African Studies* 15, no. 3 (1989): 393-414.
Biographies and politically oriented works also are important. Among
these are: Asma El Dareer, *Woman, Why Do You Weep? Circumcision and
Its Consequences* (London: Zed Press, 1982); Ellen Kuzwayo, *Call Me
Woman* (San Francisco: Spinster's Ink, 1985); Emma Mashinini, *Strikes
Have Followed Me All My Life: A South African Autobiography* (London:
The Women's Press, 1989); Awa Thiam, *Black Sisters Speak Out: Femi-
nism and Oppression in Black Africa*; and Olayinka Koso-Thomas, *The
Circumcision of Women: A Strategy for Eradication* (London: Zed Books,
1987).

21   Some of the most influential fiction writers include Bessie Head,
Mariama Ba, Buchi Emecheta, and Flora Nwapa. Nalova Lyonga's forthcoming book, *African Women and Feminist Theories*, addresses both
African women's writing and their representation in the works of male
writers across the continent.

22   The popularity of precolonial history waned in the 1970s, with the
heavy emphasis on understanding the roots of current problems. While
studying earlier periods is always challenging because of the need to rely
heavily on unconventional sources, there are now graduate students using
linguistic techniques and material culture to explore problems of women's

history. In the process, they are also challenging the entire field of pre-colonial history and its prior preoccupation with political structures.

23   Nancy Rose Hunt, "Placing African Women's History and Locating Gender," *Social History* 14, no. 3 (October 1989): 369.

24   See especially Oyewumi, "Inventing Gender: Questioning Gender in Precolonial Yorubaland," in *Problems in African History: The Precolonial Centuries*, ed. Robert Collins, (New York and Princeton: Markus Wiener, 1993) which (p.250) is the source of the short quotation in this sentence.

25   The full title is Ifi Amadiume, *Male Daughters, Female Husbands: Gender and Sex in an African Society* (London: Zed Press, 1987).

26   See footnote 24.

27   Ibid., 244.

28   Ibid., 250.

29   *Journal of African History* 33 (1992), 441-65.

30   Hunt, "African Women's History," 372.

31   Another theme that became apparent at the conference was the importance of donor agencies in funding research. Since most are concerned primarily with development projects, history is not likely to have high priority.

32   See Diana Jeater, *Marriage, Perversion, and Power: The Construction of Moral Discourse in Southern Rhodesia 1894-1930* (Oxford: Clarendon Press, 1993) for a well-regarded example of a new approach to African women's history that is particularly concerned with changing gender identities. Rather than beginning her study of change with new production opportunities, she surmises that perhaps the greatest upset that colonialism introduced was the possibility of women in particular thinking of their sexuality outside the context of family authority. Another important earlier work is Kristin Mann, *Marrying Well: Marriage, Status and Social Change among the Educated Elite in Colonial Lagos* (Cambridge: Cambridge University Press, 1985).

33   *The Nation*, 31, May 1993, 721.

Response to Valenze and Berger

PHILIPPA LEVINE

A reconsideration of Marxism in the mid-1990s is a complex business. Large parts of the world have moved steadily to the right. The wholesale rejection of Marxism throughout Eastern Europe brought innumerable communist parties in nonsocialist nations to the brink of extinction and gave many a gleeful commentator the opportunity to proclaim, from a profoundly Eurocentric perspective, the death of Marxism. Meanwhile, Asia remains deeply divided between the principles of communism and the practice of capitalism. And, as Iris Berger points out in her contribution to this debate, in Africa the Marxist model "always required modification" from its European and nineteenth-century origin. Certainly in the late twentieth century Marxism has seldom been without its detractors, its champions, and its embellishers, and feminists have occupied all three of these roles.

Deborah Valenze focuses on the strong and rich tradition of Marxism in Britain and on the significant impact feminist socialists have had on that heritage. Indubitably, the dominant mode of academic feminism in the United Kingdom has been a socialist feminism that has found less favor in other English-speaking countries, where different strands of feminism — identity politics, sexual preference, postmodernism — have gained greater currency. In North America, more especially in the United States, Marxist interpretations are far less the academic norm. The point is, as Iris Berger's article points out so well, that Marxism cannot be understood without its specific explanatory context. It derives much of its meaning not from the systemic interpretation of the world it purports to offer, but from its own situation in specific cultural spaces and places. The visibility of academic Marxism in Britain derives in large part from the specific historical circumstances of Britain's early shift to industrial capitalism, which Marxist interpretations have sought to explain. Thus, the very history that Valenze sees British Marxist feminists bringing to life is one steeped in a preoccupation with the struggles of labor and of class. Marx's confidence that Britain would be the cradle of the first proletarian revolution may have been mistaken, but it did make sense in the context of the harsh capitalism of the mid-nineteenth century. And the subsequent historiographical tradition derived from the Marxist perspective has in Britain focused largely on the manifestations of the conflict between labor and capital.

It seems redundant to point out that the histories that explain African varieties of Marxism and of feminism are of a wholly different stripe, given the interplay of colonialism — and its corollary of a nationalism born from that experience — with an older precolonial history. Lineage rather than labor, at least in precolonial Yorubaland, offers historians the key to understanding that society (Berger): neither Marxism nor feminism in their Western garb can adequately account for the social and political structures of Africa, especially before the advent of the European imperial adventure. And Berger makes the telling point that it is with the imposition of capitalism under colonial rule that assumptions about class and gender begin to approximate Western meanings. Implicitly, then, in historicizing both Marxism and feminism, Berger questions how far they can go in explaining historical developments in non-Western arenas.

Yet even in the West, the birthplace of Marxism, there has been considerable resistance to its influence. The palpable failure of a Marxist politics in the U.S. is — not surprisingly — reflected in American academic fashions and concerns. In the U.S., grassroots politics means something wholly different than it does in Britain or Africa, and its manifestation in AIDS activism, abortion protests (pro and anti), or in the civil rights movement of the 1960s owes little to the precepts of Marxism or to the trade unionism on which socialist hopes were so long pinned. The materiality of economic circumstance clearly played and plays an enormous role in such campaigns, but Marxist readings of that materiality have clearly been found wanting. Alternative analyses and strategies abound, and few leave the door open for a Marxist position in contemporary America.

Feminism, meanwhile, has attempted to cast a broad net, and if the naiveté of early enthusiasm insisted that all women shared the same experience of oppression, women who saw themselves doubly marginalized by notions of "global sisterhood" — lesbians, women of color, Jews, Muslims, to name but a few — were there to demand a recapitulation of so inadequate an analysis. In its early days, modern feminism was thus forced to understand the limitations of a claim to universality. As a result, one of the most powerful and distinctive hallmarks of late-twentieth-century feminism has been its challenge both to the claim of universality and to the logical and equally flawed corollary of a binary worldview that naturalized such divisions as masculine/feminine or white/black as given truths. And while Valenze and Berger demonstrate that in Africa and the United Kingdom, feminists have sought intellectual rapprochement with an older Marxist tradition — and often have been at least partially successful in demasculinizing the concerns of that tradition — there have been just as many feminist scholars less eager to seek out and develop that alliance.

This is not to belittle the significance or the importance of the association between Marxism and feminism, but rather to understand its historical specificity. To deny the profound impact of Marxism on historical scholarship and on modern incarnations of feminism would be foolhardy. Moreover, the insights Marxism has offered us into the many and brutal methods of domination and division have enriched and furthered our understanding and appreciation of the history of resistance and of agency. Marxism has offered generations of historians a tool for learning to listen to the voiceless; it has given us the language of class; and for many around the world, it has held out the hope of a brighter, more just future.

Valenze, while acknowledging the importance of postmodernism for feminist historians of Britain (where, incidentally, she might well have drawn equal attention to such skilled proponents as Mary Poovey or Jenny Sharpe in addition to Judith Walkowitz, whom she discusses at length), nonetheless seeks to sustain a place within feminist thinking for a Marxist perspective. Pointing to the strength of Marxism in insisting upon the liberating powers of collective agency, Valenze sees Marxism as still viable and relevant as we approach a new century. Yet I remain unconvinced, not only because "the struggle for self-realization and economic justice" (Valenze) is hardly unique to Marxism, but because the fundamental underpinnings of that tradition cannot escape an ultimately static, because universalizing, model of social structure and of change, antithetical in the breach to the most basic tenets of precisely those feminisms with which it has sought the closest allegiance. Ironically, some of the most vigorous opposition to essentialism and universalism within the feminist movement has come from socialist feminists who nonetheless remain committed to finding meeting points between their materialist feminism and their Marxist reading of history. This concentration on material historical change as the analytic motor of development has been one of the firmest bases of feminism's uneasy alliance with Marxism, yet the latter rests on an analysis that, while it pays its dues to historical specificity, is still identified with a "capitalist-centered historiography" (Berger) and a transhistorical notion of domination centered above all on class.

Thus, when Valenze calls for a humane Marxism-feminism that keeps "*both* [my emphasis] halves of the human population in the picture," I see emerging in that vision an unremittingly binary reading of the world inherent in the Marxist narrative, and ultimately dangerous for feminism. After all, Berger's discussion of male daughters and female husbands suggests that what in the British context Mary Poovey has dubbed the "ideological work of gender" is a good deal more complicated than a world divided into two uncontested subspecies of man and woman.

Yet Berger, too, employs a Marxist vocabulary. When she lists for us the dazzling variety of women who have participated in African social movements, the most striking feature of her roster is that the women she describes are defined almost exclusively by occupation and by class. We are presented with traders and marketers, garment workers and peasants, with the bourgeois women of South Africa and the elite women of West Africa. These are definitions of women that depend upon class, in which women seem to derive their identity and their very meaning from what they do and from where it places them in a vertical social system. Yet Berger argues that the "context for their lives" is a tapestry of social and religious as well as economic and political forces. If their identification for the historian rests wholly on class and occupation, as it does here, then how do we read those social and religious forces? Would it not make as much sense to define them through religious association as through class? We can no more assume a collectivity of class interest in the light of substantial historical evidence to the contrary than we can assume that religious affiliation will bind its activists or proponents to a single politics. Valenze's rueful admission of the gap between political reality and a vision of the future in contemporary Britain is a valuable barometer of the danger of assuming common interests on the basis of such categories as class. As Valenze acknowledges, in the Thatcherite Britain of the 1980s and 1990s (and I would argue, much earlier), "voting behavior contradicted cherished models of political allegiance."

And it is that very notion of political allegiance that we need to examine more critically, especially since it lies at the very root of the Marxist perspective. The divisive issue of race — finally receiving mass recognition from scholars after years of relative neglect in the mainstream — cuts across longstanding notions of Marxist solidarity in profound ways. It was a cherished belief among British Marxists for the greater part of this century that racism was a weapon wielded by the establishment and foisted cynically upon white British workers to divide them from their "natural" proletarian allies and to divert attention from capitalist injustices. The ruling class, Marxists argued, did not share these racist preconceptions; they simply used them as powerful tools of division and diversion. In reality, of course, racial intolerance is no more classbound than is, say, marital violence, fragmenting once more any fleeting temptation to nail down hard and fast categories of sodality or, indeed, of class behaviors.

Class remains a critically important analytical tool, but it neither subsumes divisions emanating from race, ethnicity, gender, or a multitude of other distinctions nor operates alike in different historical landscapes. Race, indeed, might be said to have had a profound impact in shifting the identification of class identities under imperialism. In the case of the British overseas, it was whiteness rather than birth that very often brought with it the privileges and lifestyle more usually associated with the British elite. Class identification, clearly critical to colonials overseas, seldom operated in ways that would have made sense in the "metropole." While the high-born continued to enjoy the fruits of their longstanding privilege, many whose lives in Britain would have borne the stamp of "commonness" found that in the colonies their white skins conferred upon them power and status to which they could have had no access at home. Their class identification thus became inseparable in crucial ways from their racial identification to produce a complex web of status markers unique to the workings of colonialism, but subtly affecting domestic class issues into the bargain. And the operation of gender, too, took on more complex meanings in so racialized an environment, where the attributes of masculinity or of femininity — invisibly white in the British context — jostled with those of competing if subordinated cultures.

We neither can nor should assume that all women share a common vision or that the working class has somehow been "corrupted" by the lure of camcorders and central heating, or even — in less affluent countries — by a sack of grain. Feminist activists have worked hard to expose such hubris, just as Marxists have had to come to terms with the apparent lack of proletarian enthusiasm for socialism in many countries. Valenze praises Judith Walkowitz for giving us in her recent writings subjects humanized sufficiently to be not only gendered and modern but "full of contradictions." It is this unpredictability, this contradictoriness, the element of surprise (and not always of pleasant surprise) that surely keeps us, as historians, alive and attuned to the nuances of our unfolding history. By all means let us use all and any of the intellectual tools available to us in our quest to make sense of those contradictions, but let us not commit ourselves to any single system of model-building that will quash the potential for undreamed-of change in the future. Contradiction necessarily undermines the search for universal solutions, and it remains the wild card of excitement for historians.

Historiographically, we can trace among historians, and not just in the West, the gradual shift from an attention to high politics to an interest in class and labor, from there to gender and latterly sexuality, and then, if belatedly, to race. Feminism and Marxism have served to broaden the range of legitimized historical pursuits and to force consideration of hitherto marginalized interests on the profession. Their attention to and association with a politics and commitment that go beyond the academy have set them apart in some respects from other developments in the field. With the collapse of communism in Eastern Europe, the backlash against the feminist gains of the past two or three decades, and the media hysteria over a mythical onslaught of "political correctness," huge challenges face us academically and politically in the future. I simply hope that we will have the sense to keep our options open, to absorb the critical lessons of the failure of authoritarian Marxism, and to build a future sensitive to the changing, diverse, sometimes unpalatable, and all-too-often contradictory demands of the voices now so passionately and fiercely "unsilenced."

E. THE UNDEBATED

Life-Story, History, Fiction: Reflections on Simone de Beauvoir's Wartime Writings

SUSAN RUBIN SULEIMAN

... it is when one has been able to reach the moment of opening oneself completely to the other that the scene of the other, which is more specifically the scene of History, will be able to take place in a very vast way.

Hélène Cixous

I think it is good for thoughts to be shaped by experience; at any rate, that is the path I have always followed.

Simone de Beauvoir

I.

In the spring of 1990, my fancy often turned to thoughts of Simone de Beauvoir. Forced to stay home for a week to recover from an eye operation, I spent my time alternating between the rare luxury of daytime sleep and the equally rare luxury, in a teaching year, of long hours of reading in bed. One eye was bandaged, but the other one raced down the pages of Deirdre Bair's massive biography of Beauvoir.[1] Over 700 pages of life-story, told in scrupulous detail from beginning to end: I read the book conscientiously, in the pre-publication proofs I had been sent by the *Atlantic*, which had asked me to review it. But mingled with the profes-

sional obligation was a deep sense of personal pleasure, as memories of
when I first read Simone de Beauvoir's life-story kept surfacing and
crisscrossing with this reading. *Memoirs of a Dutiful Daughter*, *The Prime
of Life* — I had read those books in Paris (the second was not even
translated yet), during the year I spent there after graduating from college.
Propped up on pillows on the bed in my room at the Cité Universitaire, I
would dream about Beauvoir and Sartre, the Sorbonne during the twenties,
Paris during the Occupation, the Resistance. This was spring 1961, a
season of crisis over the Algerian war. The newly founded terrorist group
O.A.S., as a last-ditch effort to maintain "l'Algérie française," was plant-
ing bombs in strategic Parisian places (or in France) associated with
opposition to the war and support for Algerian independence. Naturally,
the office of Sartre and Beauvoir's journal, *Les Temps Modernes*, was on
their list, as was Sartre's apartment. The previous fall, Sartre and Beauvoir
had both signed the *Déclaration des 121*, the intellectuals' manifesto
calling for active resistance to the war, including military insubordination.

For a number of years, Sartre and Beauvoir had been associated
with left-wing causes: anticolonialism, support for Castro, goodwill trips
to China and the Soviet Union. Although new intellectual movements such
as structuralism would soon be challenging their dominance, in 1961 they
were still (at least, they appeared to me to be) at the height of their celebrity
and influence. They were *engagé* writers, taking the weight of the world
on their shoulders. They were my idols, individually and as a couple.

A few years earlier, Simone de Beauvoir had won France's most
prestigious literary prize, the Prix Goncourt, with her autobiographical
novel about post-war French intellectuals, *The Mandarins* (1956); some
years before that, she had earned both local notoriety and a permanent
place in modern intellectual history by publishing *The Second Sex* (1949),
a work of immense erudition and passion that would become one of the
founding works of contemporary feminism. To me, however, during that
year in Paris, she was most important as an autobiographer. She had just
published *La Force de l'âge* (*The Prime of Life*), the fat book I was reading,
whose second half covered the years of the war and the beginning of her
career as a writer. Projecting backward, I endowed the story she told there,
about her life during the 1930's and 1940's, with all of her political and
intellectual prestige of the 1950's and 1960's. "My life would be a
beautiful story, which would become true as I told it to myself," she had
written in *Memoirs of a Dutiful Daughter*, describing her first dreams of
becoming a writer.[2] In *The Prime of Life*, she recounted how her personal

"belle histoire" had collided with, and been forever changed by, the collective history of France during the war. "Not only had the war changed my relations to everything, but it had changed everything . . . After June 1940, I no longer recognized things, or people, or moments, or places, or myself."[3] The only thing that hadn't changed, and wouldn't change, she implied, was her relation of mutual love and commitment to Sartre.

The heroine of her autobiography, she was also my heroine: a character I felt close to and would have liked to emulate. "That was almost thirty years ago," I told myself as I read Deirdre Bair's biography. "You were naive then." In fact, I had gone through quite a few stages in my understanding of Beauvoir since those heady days of reading at the Cité Universitaire; nowadays, my appreciation of her life and work was a great deal more realistic. I knew about her evasiveness and her self-deceptions, especially where her personal relation to Sartre was concerned; about her complicated intellectual and emotional relations, over the years, to feminism and to "other women"; I had even written about some of the contradictions in her self-conception as a (woman) writer.[4] My days of idealizing identification were long past.

Considering all this, it would be inaccurate to say that I was disillusioned by the cold light brought to bear on some aspects of Beauvoir's life in Bair's carefully documented narrative. No, it was not disillusionment but a curious sense of separation I experienced when I learned that in October 1940 Simone de Beauvoir had signed the oath required by the Vichy government from all teachers, attesting to the fact that she was neither Jewish nor a Freemason; and that in 1943, after being dismissed from her teaching post because of an official complaint from the mother of her young friend Nathalie Sorokine (Lise in *The Prime of Life*), she accepted a job at the German-controlled radio station, Radio-Paris. Bair goes into great detail about this, explaining that Beauvoir's job was in no way political but consisted merely in selecting material for a cultural program on "Historical Music," and also explaining Beauvoir's own position that she had done nothing wrong but merely bowed to the necessity of earning a living. And yet, Bair notes, "No matter how she explained it away, she was uneasy about this work. She glossed over it in her memoirs, always resented being questioned about it, and was furious whenever she learned of a scholar or journalist who wrote about it" (p. 307).

For me, reading Bair's account, it was not a matter of judging Simone de Beauvoir. She did no worse than many others at the time, and certainly did better than many; although she later omitted some facts or glossed over them in *The Prime of Life*, she told no outright lies; to judge her for not having been heroic would have been sheer hypocrisy. The sense of separation I felt, however, was a different matter; it came, quite simply, from my realization that had I been in her place, I would not have had the choice of signing the oath or working for Radio-Paris. Nor could I have frequented the Café Flore, whether it was a favorite hangout of German officers (as Bair says historians claim) or whether it was shunned by them (as Beauvoir claimed in *The Prime of Life*). My choices, as a Jewish woman, even if I had been a self-identified *French* Jewish woman, would have been very, very different.

Just as I was mulling this over, the French publishing scene brought me more food for thought. Almost at the same time as the Bair biography appeared in the United States, Beauvoir's war diary, *Journal de guerre* (covering the period between September 1939 and January 1941) and her supposedly "lost" but suddenly "found" letters to Sartre (two volumes covering the years 1930 to 1963) were published in Paris.[5] I threw myself at them, looking for I knew not exactly what (perhaps there would be a diary entry in October 1940, mentioning the oath?). Concentrating only on the war years, what I found were not revelations — unless one considers the confirmation of Beauvoir's bisexuality, long denied by her, a revelation; rather, a network of paths leading to other texts, which now demanded to be reread, or read for the first time. These hitherto private works, then, provided a way of opening up, or a new way of entering, a whole series of other, public works: Sartre's letters to her, for example, published several years earlier, as well as Sartre's own war notebooks (symmetry *oblige*); *The Prime of Life*, indeed all of Beauvoir's autobiographical writings, including interviews about herself; and most obviously, the published works that she conceived and wrote entirely during the war years. These include her second novel, *The Blood of Others*, about which she began jotting notes in her diary in January 1941 and which she finished in 1943; her only play, *Les Bouches inutiles* (*Who Shall Die?*), staged in Paris in November 1944; and her first philosophical essay, *Pyrrhus et Cinéas*, which she wrote at the invitation of Jean Grenier (who was an editor at Gallimard) in 1943.

I cannot follow all of these paths here, but I will try to gesture toward a few. The one that especially interests me is the path that leads through the diary to *The Blood of Others*, a novel that had a huge success at the time of its publication but is rarely discussed today, and that Beauvoir herself belittled in her autobiography.[6] Following this path allows one to see how Beauvoir negotiated the complicated interactions between life-story, history, and fiction; and it obliges one (I should say, in this case, me) to experience in a particularly vivid way what otherwise might remain only in the realm of theory: the increasingly vexed issue in current feminist thought, regarding the relative importance of gender, race, ethnicity, and class as analytical and critical categories.

II.

Sartre to the Castor ("Beaver," his term of endearment for Beauvoir), somewhere in Alsace, 6 January 1940:

> I've just read Heine's biography, and it inspired some curious thoughts in me. Since I praised him to myself for having succeeded in assuming his condition as a Jew, and saw with brilliant clarity that Jewish rationalists like Pieter or Brunschvick [two of his fellow soldiers] were inauthentic by thinking of themselves as men first, not as Jews, I was forced to conclude, logically, that I had to assume my own condition as a Frenchman; it was without enthusiasm, and above all it had no meaning for me. Nothing more than an inevitable and obvious conclusion. I wonder where it all leads and I'm going to put my mind to it tomorrow.[7]

Castor to Sartre, Paris, 8 January 1940:

> I don't know whether we have to assume ourselves as French, I'll think about it until tomorrow; in part yes, certainly . . . Didn't we talk about that at the "Rey" once, how we couldn't feel as much solidarity with the persecuted Jews in Germany as we would with Jews in France, and that the fact of being "situated" *en situation* necessarily involved the sense of frontiers? I'll think about it (but it seems to me that this assuming doesn't lead to patriotism any more than assuming the war leads to warmongering); it's a matter (or not?) in that case of attaining universals, ideas, works, etc., through a singular historical position.[8]

Note Beauvoir's use of the contrary-to-fact conditional ("as we would with
Jews in France") to talk about the persecution of French Jews: the Vichy
anti-Jewish decrees were still in the future. Note also that she seeks to allay
Sartre's worries about what it would mean for him to assume his condition
as a Frenchman. It would not entail "patriotism," a value they don't hold
high; it would still allow one to reach the level of universals, albeit from
a singular historical position. Clearly, at this point she (and she assumes
the same for him) is interested in transcendance not as a movement toward
other human subjects, but as a direct accession to universals, "ideas,
works, etc."

The day after his letter to her, Sartre tells her he has written 39
pages in his dark blue notebook on his relation to France.[9] I rush to his war
diary, the *Carnets de la drôle de guerre*: alas, that notebook was lost. The
day after her letter to him, Beauvoir celebrates her 32nd birthday (a fact
she mentions to Sartre but fails to note in her diary for that day); she will
not return to the question of frontiers, France/Germany, or the question of
the relation between singular and universal, or the question of Jews *versus*
non-Jews, until much later — after June 1940. Instead, on January 9 she
tells Sartre, among other details, about her latest potential "conquest" at
the *lycée*: "the brunette from H[enry] IV [another *lycée*] who sent me a
letter at the beginning of the year; I contemplated cheating on Sorokine
with her, but she put on a red wig after speaking to me and some people
warned me that she was a rotten apple."[10]

The liberty, one might even say the locker-room quality, of
Beauvoir's amorous confidences to Sartre, as well as the details of her
sexual encounters with Nathalie Sorokine and another ex-student, Louise
Védrine, as told to him and in her diary, are among the revelations (after
all) of these volumes. All references to this aspect of her life were carefully
edited out of the diary passages reproduced in *The Prime of Life*. Beauvoir
told Alice Schwarzer in 1978 that she wished she had given, in her
autobiography, a "frank and balanced account of [her] own sexuality. A
truly sincere one. . . ."[11] But she seems to have been unable to give a frank
account even after that admission; when, in a later interview (1982),
Schwarzer asked her point blank: "Have you never had a sexual relationship with a woman?" Beauvoir lied: "No. I have had some very important
friendships with women, of course, some very close relationships, sometimes close in a physical sense. But they never aroused erotic passion on
my part."[12] One could, I suppose, construe this to mean, casuistically, that
her sexual relationships with women "didn't count" since there was never

any real erotic passion, and therefore conclude that she was not lying. I mention this because, as we shall see, Beauvoir was not above a certain casuistry when dealing with embarrassing questions. The fact is that, passionate or not, she did have sexual relations with women, and she wrote about them frankly and in detail both to Sartre and in her diary.

Some of the critical reactions to these volumes, in Paris in 1991, were extremely negative; almost as if the critic felt betrayed, like a jilted lover: "How is one to read these *Lettres* and this *Journal*? What do we learn from them?" asked Marianne Alphant in a long review in the liberal newspaper *Libération*. "That *The Prime of Life* is a trumped-up story? That we have been duped . . . ? Undoubtedly. But also that the philosopher didn't have time to think. . . . That the pioneer of feminism only liked women who were submissive to her domination. That this austere muse had the fantasies of a shopgirl (*des états d'âme de midinette*)."[13] As one reads Marianne Alphant's pitiless accumulation of quotations to support her claim (in the style of "she told me I was very beautiful to look at, which flattered me, I like the way I look these days, it's because of my earrings and the turban, they look as beautiful to me as if I were someone else" — p. 167), one has to admit that she may be right about the "états d'âme de midinette," in any case.

My own feeling, as I read the *Journal*, floated somewhere between admiration and disbelief. Was it really possible — especially for an intellectual, a teacher of philosophy who read the newspapers and listened to the radio — to live in Paris from September 1939 to June 1940 *as if nothing had changed?* Evidently, it was. Not for nothing was this called the "phony war" — it was as if it did not exist at all. Beauvoir's days, reported in all their "chronological banality" (Marianne Alphant's phrase), consisted of working on her novel (*She Came To Stay*, her first published work) in a café in the morning, usually at Le Dôme or La Coupole; writing to her soldiers, Sartre and "le petit Bost" (Jacques-Laurent Bost, Sartre's former student, who had become her lover on an outing they took in the Alps the previous year) in another café, lunching in a third, teaching in two different *lycées*, occasionally correcting student papers, reading a lot, doing her nails, going to concerts, movies, and the opera with various young women friends, mediating the disputes that arose (often over who got to see her and for how long) among those friends — and, of course, writing in her diary. There is an entry for every single day, without fail, from September 1, 1939 to February 23, 1940. If she misses a day, she makes up for it the next day, or even several days later — never by quickly summarizing what has happened, but always by writing what looks like that day's account, usually in the present tense. In early September, she spends a few difficult days getting used to Sartre's absence — she saw him off at the train, with other draftees, on September 2. On September 7, she is still feeling sad: "I go to the hairdresser, he makes me a beautiful *coiffure*, I feel sad at not having anyone to show myself to" (p. 31). By September 26, on a trip to visit Louise Védrine in Brittany, she feels better. She spends a day by herself exploring the Pointe du Raz: "It's as beautiful as everything I'd been told about it. . . . [Despite the war] I feel an immense joy in the present, no matter what the future will bring" (p. 62).

Reading this, I am filled with a kind of admiration: a spunky woman, nothing can faze her for long. In early November, she manages to wangle a travel permit to visit Sartre in Alsace for a few days, pretending she has to visit a sick relative. He skips out of his barracks to see her several times a day; waiting for him in her room, she feels "plunged into the world of war, it fills me up — I feel poetic and happy" (p. 121). Twice on the preceding days, she uses the word "adventure" to describe how this trip feels: "I'm beginning to have a real feeling of adventure" (p. 116); "The feeling of adventure continues . . ." (p. 117). A few weeks earlier, when Sartre was suddenly transferred and she had had to cancel her trip to visit him, she had cried, but soon felt better: "I have another good cry and fix my make-up as well as I can. Then I go and eat some fries and crêpes at the *crêperie* while finishing Agatha Christie" (p. 80).

Is this spunkiness or blind egotism? Is she indomitable or unconscionable? For her, the question never arises; the possibility that others might find the life she is leading smug or self-centered never crosses her mind. To condemn Beauvoir for her apparent blindness during this period, as one may be tempted to do (and as some critics obviously did), is understandable; it was my own first impulse as well. But it is an anachronistic judgment, based on what we know now to have happened later. If one tries to imagine what it was actually like to live as a civilian in Paris during the winter of 1939-1940, *without knowing what was in store*, it becomes easier to understand Beauvoir's apparent insensitivity, her selfish pursuit of pleasure even as catastrophe is about to strike. Over the new year, she goes skiing and loves it; she takes private lessons and makes good progress. In late January, Sartre arrives in Paris on a ten-day leave and she is happy. A few days after he leaves, it's Bost's turn.

Then, after the entry of February 23, a sudden break. The next notebook, number VI, is dated "9 June-18 July."[14] Unlike the previous notebooks, this one is fragmented, irregular, with great gaps between entries. The first 27 pages consist of a retrospective account, written in Paris at the end of June, of Beauvoir's exit from Paris on June 9, shortly before the Germans entered the city; her stay at La Pouèze, near Le Mans, with her and Sartre's friend Mme Morel; and her return to the capital after the Armistice, first in a car with other returning Parisians and then, after the car ran out of gas, in a German truck. The trip back to Paris took two days: "Rarely have I spent more interesting and heady days [*jours plus intéressants et forts*] than those two" (p. 315). In Le Mans, while they were waiting for gas, she had a chance to look closely at the German soldiers:

> Many were young and looked appealing. . . . There were many soldiers all smiling and happy and young and often quite handsome . . . and I could feel what a wonderful adventure it must be for a young German to find himself in France as a conqueror . . . — it was crushing to see them with their beautiful ambulance wagons, their neat appearance, their confidently polite manners, whereas France was represented by hundreds of fearful and ragged refugees who had only those handsome soldiers to rely on for food, gas, transportation, a remedy to their current misery (p. 317-318).

At this point, my attempt at historical empathy begins to fade. I cannot help but feel my *difference* from Beauvoir, and to judge her. Does she still see only the adventure, is she still finding her days "interesting"? Those "handsome soldiers" she saw in Le Mans, and with whose superiority she clearly identified rather than with the "fearful and ragged French refugees," will soon be rounding up Jews and hunting down Resistants. Has this woman no soul? (I am suddenly reminded of the despicable pharmacist in Marcel Ophuls's film about that period, *The Sorrow and the Pity*. "You understand, one had to look out for oneself," he tells Ophuls with his cynical smile, explaining that his family managed quite well by "not getting involved".)

One thing in her favor: in the middle of the paragraph describing her feelings in Le Mans, she inserts a sentence that refers to the present (the time of writing in Paris), which I omitted in quoting that paragraph above: "All those [soldiers] I see right now in Paris with their cameras and rosy faces look like such imbeciles that I hesitate — but the day before yesterday at Le Mans, they looked totally different to me and I felt what a wonderful adventure. . . ." At least she is no longer taken with them. But my discomfort persists: what if the German soldiers in Paris had looked intelligent?

The rest of this notebook produces a mixed effect. Life starts again, with Sorokine and other friends. She buys a bicycle and proudly learns to ride it, using it to get to the *lycée* and to take pleasure rides. Things still "interest" her — but she no longer identifies with the German soldiers. She even notes scornfully, on July 2: "The newspapers are loathsome, exhorting the French to be moral, to be more like the Germans, etc." (p. 334). On July 11, listening to the radio, she hears good music; "but it was interspersed with dreadful German homilies (against foreigners, Jews, for work, etc.)." She has begun seriously reading Hegel at the Bibliothèque Nationale, and finds that comforting — it reminds her of her student days. Around this time, she writes a letter to Sartre (he had been captured by the Germans and was in a prison camp in southern France) in which she finally returns to the question of universals and the individual, left in abeyance since January:

> I remember a conversation at the "Louis XV," where we discussed whether we thought of ourselves in terms of the limits of a human life, and wondered whether it made any sense to speak from the point of view of universal life. . . . It seemed to us then that that point of view reduced everything to a kind of absurd indifference. But I no longer believe that: in the end, that point of view is *real* and the joint influence of Hegel and what's happening now [*les événements*] are making me adopt from the inside, for the first time in my life, that attitude close to Spinozism which had always been so foreign to me. (p. 182).

The joint influence of Hegel and "les événements." Does the war seem real to her at last?

The notebook for this period stops on July 19, interrupted after the date entry as if she could not bear to continue. The next one begins on September 20: "This is a letter I am beginning for you — maybe you'll receive it in a year." (p. 355). She doesn't know where Sartre is, where she can write to him. He has been transferred to a prison camp in Germany, but she doesn't know that yet. Finally, she is beginning to suffer. The second entry, quite short, is dated October 1, a big gap:

> My sweet darling — I haven't kept up this little notebook
> — I didn't have the morale — each time I stop to speak to
> you, I begin to cry. I'm moody [*instable*], with a great many
> moments of anguish and agitation. And even when I'm
> calm, when a few days pass that feel rich and peaceful, it's
> always against a background of nothingness [*néant*], it's
> soul-wrenching. As if my whole life were between paren-
> theses . . . (p. 357).

On October 17 she is able to start writing to him again for real, to Germany, and regains some of her optimism: "All is going very well for me"; October 18: "People, concerts, a lot of work, you see it's an honest life."[15] Not a word, to Sartre or in her diary, about having signed the Vichy oath; it evidently caused no crisis of conscience.

Still, something is not quite right. Her diary remains fragmentary, with rare entries: November, January. On January 9, 1941, she reads the current issue of the literary journal *La Nouvelle Revue Française* (the first one to appear since the Occupation, under the new collaborationist editor-ship of Pierre Drieu La Rochelle) and finds it "ridicule et odieux"; she thinks about how fascism reduces the human to its animal, biological aspect, and realizes that since she too is human, "it's really *I* who am involved [*en jeu*]. I feel that to the point of anguish." She no longer finds comfort in Hegel, "that historical infinite in which Hegel optimistically dilutes everything. Anguish . . . solitude, as complete as in the face of death. Last year, I was still with Sartre — now I live in a world in which Sartre is absent, muzzled. Psychologically, I was stupidly proud sometimes to feel myself so solid and to manage so well. But today, those superficial defenses are no longer a help. I feel dazed" (pp. 361-362). Then, suddenly, a metaphor:

> To make oneself an ant among ants, or a free consciousness
> before others. A *metaphysical* solidarity that is a new dis-
> covery for me, I who was a solipsist. I cannot be a con-
> sciousness, a mind, among ants. I realize in what ways our
> antihumanism fell short. To admire man as a given [as in
> the "classic" humanism she and Sartre scorned] is stupid
> — but there is no other reality than human reality — all
> values are founded on it. And it's the "that toward which it
> transcends itself" which has always moved us and which
> orients our individual destiny, each one of us (p. 362).

Reading this passage on one of the last pages of the *Journal de guerre*, my pulse quickens: what is happening here? Deprived of Sartre's presence, alone in front of death, she seems to be discovering, *for the first time*, the historical and ethical existence of others. Sartre had never been an "other" for her, he had been her second self. With him, she could still be a solipsist, living a *solipsisme à deux*. To see the other (not Sartre, but a "real" other) no longer as a consciousness to be annihilated (recall the epigraph from Hegel, placed at the head of *She Came To Stay*: "Each consciousness seeks the death of the other") but as "that toward which human reality transcends itself," is nothing less than a major philosophical leap — one that, by an extraordinary coincidence, Sartre was making at the same time in his German stalag. "His experience as a prisoner marked him deeply: it taught him solidarity," wrote Beauvoir about him in *The Force of Circumstance*.[16] But she too discovered solidarity, in her own way, while he was in prison. January 21, 1941:

> How short-sighted my old idea of happiness seems to me! It dominated ten years of my life but I think I'm almost completely through with it. . . . My novel [*She Came To Stay*]. Rushing to finish it. Rests on a philosophical position that is no longer mine. The next one will be about the *situation of the individual*, its ethical significance and its relation to the social (p. 363).

Eight days later:

> I would like my next novel to illustrate the relation to others in its existential complexity. It's a fine subject. *To suppress the consciousness of the other is a bit puerile.* The problem attains the social, etc., but it must exist starting from an individual case. I must find a relationship of subject-object, probably an unrequited love, simply (p. 365).

With that entry, the *Journal* proper ends, followed by a few pages of notes devoted to the new novel she is planning.[17] It is a matter of finding the right "individual case" to illustrate her point:

> Possible scene: the exodus [the flight of refugees in June 1940], seen through the woman's eyes, with the temptation to give up on herself; she would have lost her love at that point, feeling injured. And then she recovers, maintains her

value as an individual — a destiny linked to that of the
world. Throws herself into antifascist activity. (But what an
ungrateful task, to deal with the social, and how to avoid
the appearance of preaching? [*comment éviter que ça ne
fasse édifiant et moralisateur?*]) (p. 368)

III.

The Blood of Others, finished in the spring of 1943, had to wait
until 1945 to be published because of its antifascist theme. Read as a
"novel of the Resistance," it was an immediate and huge success. Later,
Beauvoir judged it harshly, accepting Maurice Blanchot's assessment that
it was too illustrative, too much of a *roman à thèse*. (Her discomfort was
already indicated by the parenthetical remark about "preaching" quoted
above). The *thèse* it illustrates, she explains in *The Prime of Life*, is not so
much political as existential: the main subject is not the Resistance, but the
relation of individuals linked by free choice in a common project.[18]

Still, the public of 1945 was not wrong to see in *The Blood of Others*
a novel about the Resistance. The hero, Jean Blomart, is a bourgeois who
has joined the working class and become a union organizer. Once the war
breaks out, his problem is whether to engage as a leader in terrorist
activities against the Nazis, knowing that his actions will inevitably cause
the death of both his own comrades and innocent civilians whom the Nazis
will kill in retaliation. Whence the title of the book, indicating Blomart's
ethical dilemma. The more interesting protagonist of this novel, however,
especially in my present perspective, is Hélène, the young woman who
falls in love with Jean before the war and manages, by the sheer force of
her own love, to convince him that he "should" marry her. (The war breaks
out before they can get married.)

For the greater part of the story, Hélène recalls the two main female
characters of *She Came To Stay*: her youthfulness and her unabashed
pursuit of the man she loves are traits she shares with Xavière; with
Françoise, the heroine, she shares a determination to find individual
happiness and to let nothing stop her, certainly not any ethical considerations about community or solidarity. Hélène is a solipsist, and unashamed
of it. Even after the war breaks out, she does not change: after Jean is
mobilized, and contrary to his express wishes, she manages to take advan-

tage of his family connections and have him transferred to a "safe" job in Paris. When Jean tries to dissuade her by evoking his solidarity with his buddies, "les copains," she answers "with desperation": "I don't give a damn about the others . . . I don't owe anything to anybody . . . I'll kill myself if you die, and I don't want to die."[19] His response is to break off with her and reenlist as a soldier.

Clearly, Beauvoir put a lot of herself into Hélène (one example among many: in several places in the *Journal*, Beauvoir mentions that she will not continue living if Sartre is killed). But the really interesting thing is what she left out, or on the contrary exaggerated; and now that we have the *Journal de guerre* and the letters to Sartre, it is possible to offer some hypotheses about that, of more than merely anecdotal interest.

The chief thing Beauvoir left out is intellect, or more exactly intellectualism. Hélène is not an intellectual; she is not interested in ideas and she does not write. She is the manager of a candy store who paints and draws in her spare time (perhaps an allusion to Beauvoir's sister, an artist whose name is also Hélène). Her chief preoccupation is her love for Jean, who provides her with a sense of purpose and being. Although Hélène is not a full-fledged version of "the woman in love" as painted in *The Second Sex* — a figure Beauvoir found both fascinating and repulsive — she comes close to it.

If Beauvoir deprived Hélène of her own intellectual drive, she compensated in other ways. The most important of these is that in the end Hélène not only discovers her solidarity with other human beings, including persecuted Jews, but becomes an active member of the Resistance. Her change is shown to occur gradually, in stages: first, during the exodus and then the return to Paris, she gives up her seat in the car in which she has been traveling to a woman and her child while she herself finds a place in a German truck (Beauvoir did no such thing — she abandoned the car she shared with returning Parisians out of impatience, after it ran out of gas). Then, even though she has the chance to advance her career as a designer and become rich by doing business in Germany, Hélène changes her mind at the last minute and decides to remain with her fellow countrymen. Finally, one day when her Jewish friend Yvonne is about to be arrested by the Vichy police, she helps her escape. That same day, crossing the Place de la Contrescarpe, she sees some parked police buses and women and children being herded toward them. One of the policemen forcibly separates a little girl from her mother, who cries out after her as Hélène stands by, horrified and helpless. No date is given for this incident, but "la rafle du Vél d'hiv" of July 1942, in which thousands of Jews were rounded up and turned over to the Nazis, seems to be the historical reference.

This is the experience which definitively tips the balance for Hélène. "I was watching History pass by! It was my story [*mon histoire*]. All of this is happening to me" (p. 215). (I think here of Beauvoir's journal entry of January 1941: "it's really *I* who am involved"). Hélène goes to find Jean, asking for his help in getting Yvonne to safety and offering to join his group. Beauvoir makes a point of emphasizing, here, that love is no longer the motive for Hélène's actions: she earns Jean's real love this time, but it is a "bonus." What is foremost is their common action of resistance.

Shall we call this a compensatory fantasy on Beauvoir's part — she who signed the Vichy oath in 1940 with so few qualms that she didn't even bother to mention it in her diary? She who never, in fact, participated in any Resistance activity during the war and who accepted, a few months after finishing *The Blood of Others*, to work for the German-controlled Radio-Paris? Perhaps. It is worth emphasizing, in that case, that Hélène pays for her heroism and her personal fulfillment with her life — indeed, from the opening page of the novel she is on her deathbed. The story is told entirely in flashbacks, as Jean sits by her bedside. On the previous night's mission, she was shot by the Nazis; in the morning, as the novel ends, she dies.

Was this ending Beauvoir's way of settling the score with her own compensatory fantasy? One of her last notes for the novel in 1941 reads: "(Something moralizing and asshole-ish [*con*] about this subject)."[20] If her heroine went so far in her sense of solidarity with others as to actually risk her life, she only got what she asked for. As for Beauvoir, she writes to Sartre from the Alps, where she is on a skiing vacation with "le petit Bost" in January 1944:

> Here I am, sore all over and very happy. I've already got a long day [of skiing] behind me and I had a fantastic time. I'll tell you all about it in order. First, on Monday I went to the radio . . . — it was a lot of fun to see a program [being made] and what's especially interesting to me is that Jacques Armand offered me a job as a technical producer [*metteuse en ondes*], he'll teach me the job and after that I'll record my programs myself, it must pay quite well, and if

it takes a lot of time I'll leave more of the other work [gathering the material] to Bost.[21]

Curious, isn't it? She told Deirdre Bair that her job consisted exclusively in gathering material, not in actually working at the radio station. In *The Prime of Life*, she had written: "The writers in our circle had tacitly adopted certain rules. One must not write in the newspapers and magazines of the Occupied Zone, nor speak on Radio-Paris."[22] Less than twenty pages after this passage, when she has to deal with the unpleasant subject of her dismissal from the *lycée*, she writes: "My only problem was, how to earn a living. I don't know by what connection I got a job as 'metteuse en ondes' at the national radio; I have already said that, according to our code, it was all right to work there: everything depended on what one did."[23] In fact, she did not say earlier that "it was all right to work there," but that it was *not* all right to speak on the air. Technically, she did not speak on the air: the job of *metteuse en onde* evidently involved everything *but* speaking on the air. Here is a case of Beauvoir's casuistry, if ever there was one. Her letter to Sartre speaks of "mes émissions," "my programs" or "my broadcasts." The idea for the program was hers ("a colorless program: reconstitutions, spoken, sung, and with sound effects, of ancient festivals from the Middle Ages to our own day"[24]). Presumably, her name was mentioned on the air, but it was not her voice that mentioned it. Could it be that she referred to "radio nationale" in the second passage instead of "Radio-Paris" to make the casuistry less glaring?

IV.

We have come full circle, back to the personal issues raised by my reading and rereading of Beauvoir. But in fact we have never left them, for this whole essay has been an attempt to give an account of (and to account, at least in part, for) the conflicting responses elicited in me by that experience. How does one think again about an author who has played a significant role in one's life? Beauvoir's private writings not only cast a new light on her other works, especially on her autobiography, which turns out so obviously to have been "edited" (as if we didn't know that all autobiographies are public self-portraits, carefully posed). They have also forced me to consider from a personal perspective the importance of differences, rather than similarities, among individuals belonging to the same broad category. Potentially, every genuine reading experience is a life-changing encounter, even though few individual books can be said to have truly transformed one's life. The transforming effects are cumulative, each new work contributing its own small parcel. Reading Beauvoir's war diaries, rereading some of her other works, I find myself confronting issues of personal identity: What really determines the shape and texture of a life?

For a long time, feminists assumed that gender is by far the most important determining factor in a person's life. This may in fact be true, in a general way; and as a founding assumption, it can lead to a positive sense of solidarity among women, over and above other divisions. But as the recent emphasis on differences, both in feminist thought and in cultural theorizing in general, has made clear, such an assumption can also lead to a mythical universalism — or, in more hostile terms, to the hegemony of a single dominant group which seeks, even if unconsciously, to assimilate all others. Many white middle-class feminists in the United States have learned, over the past few years, that the designation of their race and class can serve as a marker of separation and even, occasionally, of hostility and conflict in their relation to other women, even though they may all consider themselves feminists.[25] As Joan Scott has remarked, "it becomes clear that in certain circumstances gender is far less central than race, ethnicity, or class in the construction of personal identity."[26] (It may not be merely coincidental that this observation occurs à propos of the war diaries of Anne Frank and Ettie Hillesum, two young Jewish women who did not survive the war). The issue for feminist theorists is not only methodological or analytic; it is also, in a very real and sometimes painful sense, personal and existential. If gender is a category that unites women, will the others have the effect of driving them apart? (On an even more general level, one can ask a similar question about the category of "human being." Is it, like its onetime synonym, "man," a mythologizing universal that elides significant differences and their political consequences? That argument has been made more than once, and persuasively. Yet in some circumstances, for example in cases of torture and other violations of what are rightly called "human rights," one wants to affirm the general category.)

Although the question about the primacy of gender has surfaced only recently *within* feminism, it was for a long time thrown *at* feminism by orthodox Marxists. Beauvoir refused to call herself a feminist for a long time because she believed that gender as an analytic category was less central than class. As she explained to Alice Schwarzer in 1972:

> At the end of *The Second Sex* I said that I was not a feminist
> because I believed that the problems of women would
> resolve themselves automatically in the context of socialist
> development. By feminist, I meant fighting on specifically
> feminine issues independently of the class struggle . . . I am
> a feminist today, because I realized that we must fight for
> the situation of women, here and now, before our dreams of
> socialism come true.[27]

By contrast, whether because of another change of mind or because she
considered History as transcending both class and gender, in 1984
Beauvoir insisted that certain collective experiences took precedence over
gender in the patterning of a life. When asked, by Hélène Wenzel, whether
she found that "there are well-marked stages in a woman's life that are
different from those in a man's," Beauvoir answered: "No, I don't think
so. I don't think it's due to sex, it's due obviously to politics, events; . . .
the Resistance, Liberation, the war in Algeria. . . . That's what marked the
big epochs in our lives, it's the historical events, the historical involve-
ments one has in these larger events. It's much more important than any
other kind of difference."[28]

This statement, especially when read after the *Journal de guerre*
and its associated texts, elicits a whole series of responses. Surely, the
emphatic "No" is wrong. There *are* well-marked stages in a woman's life
that are different from a man's. Yet, she is right about the importance of
collective events. But collective events are experienced in very different
ways, depending on who one is. Her insistence on the shared experience
of "Resistance, Liberation" among French people is dishonest, for it elides
the differences in the way those events were experienced, not only between
Jews and non-Jews, but between, say, women intellectuals who did or did
not actively participate in the Resistance.[29] On the other hand, to deny a
certain bedrock of shared historical experience leads to ever greater
fragmentation and to its own kind of dishonesty. How does one define
exactly who one is? Where do the significant differences begin, or end?

More questions than answers, as I conclude these reflections. Still,
of one thing I am certain. It took courage and a gritty honesty for Beauvoir
to authorize the publication, even posthumously, of writings that she surely
knew would cast her in a less than heroic light. There is its own kind of
heroism in daring to reveal one's human weaknesses and imperfections.
Beauvoir's wartime writings contain no revelations nearly as troubling as

those that have recently come to light about certain other intellectual heroes like Martin Heidegger or Paul de Man. Maybe it was because her "imperfections" were relatively minor that she found it easier to save for publication the private writings that document them. (Heidegger and de Man, significantly, kept silent to the end, and it does not appear that they left behind any diaries for posthumous publication). Still, Beauvoir made a choice that could not have been a simple or easy one. Without glossing over her failings or eliding our differences, as a reader I cannot but feel grateful for her generosity.[30]

NOTES

1   Deirdre Bair, *Simone de Beauvoir: A Biography* (New York: Summit Books, 1990).

2   *Mémoires d'une jeune fille rangée* (Paris: Gallimard, 1958), p. 168. Unless otherwise indicated, all translations from the French are my own.

3   *La Force de l'âge* (Paris: Gallimard, 1960), p. 613.

4   See my essay, "Simone de Beauvoir and the Writing Self," *L'Esprit Créateur*, 29:4 (Winter 1989), pp. 42-51.

5   Simone de Beauvoir, *Journal de guerre* (Paris: Gallimard, 1990); *Lettres à Sartre*, 2 vols. (Paris: Gallimard, 1990). As of this writing (May 1991), neither has been published in English.

6   See *La Force des choses* (Paris: Gallimard, 1965), p. 50. (The English title of this book is *The Force of Circumstance*). There is a good brief discussion of *The Blood of Others* in Elaine Marks, *Simone de Beauvoir: Encounters with Death* (New Brunswick: Rutgers University Press, 1973), chapter 6. Marks refers to passages from the war diary that were inserted into *The Prime of Life*; however, a comparison with the complete version which is now available shows that these excerpts were heavily edited by Beauvoir.

7   Jean-Paul Sartre, *Lettres au Castor et à quelques autres*, vol. II (Paris: Gallimard, 1983), p. 21.

8   Beauvoir, *Lettres à Sartre*, II, p. 26.

9   Sartre, *Lettres*, II, p. 22.

10   Beauvoir, *Journal de guerre*, p. 29. Other page references will be given in parentheses in the text.

11   Alice Schwarzer, *After "The Second Sex": Conversations with Simone de Beauvoir*, trans. Marianne Howarth (New York: Pantheon Books, 1984), p. 85.

12   *Ibid.*, pp. 112-113.

13   Marianne Alphant, "Abus de Beauvoir," *Libération*, 22 February 1990), p. 21.

14   Sylvie Le Bon de Beauvoir, the editor of these volumes, gives no explanation for the gap in the *Journal* between February 22 and June 9. The letters to Sartre continue through March 23, then stop as well. Sartre was in Paris on leave in April, and correspondence in May was impossible because of the German invasion. She starts writing to him again on July 11, when Sartre is in a prisoner of war camp in southern France.

15   Beauvoir, *Lettres*, II, pp. 192, 193.

16   Beauvoir, *La Force des choses* (Paris: Gallimard, 1963), p. 16.

17   It is not clear why Sylvie Le Bon de Beauvoir decided to end the *Journal* in 1941. She writes in her brief introduction that Beauvoir kept a diary all her life, intermittently, and that the *Journal de guerre* is but a small part of a much vaster whole. She does not indicate, however, whether more diaries exist for the war years — and if so, whether they will be published. One can only hope that the negative reactions to the *Journal de guerre* and the *Lettres à Sartre* will not prevent publication of the rest of Beauvoir's private writings in the near future.

18   See Beauvoir, *La Force de l'âge*, pp. 555-561.

19   Beauvoir, *Le Sang des autres* (Paris: Gallimard, 1945), p. 163. Other page references will be given in parentheses in the text.

20   Beauvoir, *Journal de guerre*, p. 368.

21   Beavoir, *Lettres à Sartre*, II, p. 246.

22   Beauvoir, *La Force de l'âge*, p. 528.

23   *Ibid.*, pp. 554-555.

24   Beauvoir, *La Force de l'âge*, p. 555.

25   See, in this regard, the recent volume edited by Marianne Hirsch and Evelyn Fox Keller, *Conflicts in Feminism* (New York and London: Routledge, 1990).

26   Joan W. Scott, "Rewriting History," in *Behind the Lines: Gender and the Two World Wars*, ed. M. Higonnet, J. Jenson, S. Michel, M. Weitz (New Haven: Yale University Press, 1987), p. 25.

27   Schwarzer, *After the "The Second Sex"*, p. 37.

28   Hélène Vivienne Wenzel, "Interview with Simone de Beauvoir," *Yale French Studies*, 72 (1986), p. 25.

29   A comparative reading of diaries and memoirs by French women intellectuals of Beauvoir's generation would be extremely enlightening. Dorothy Kaufmann's current work on Edith Thomas, a novelist and active member of the Resistance who also kept a diary during the war (to date unpublished) is one case in point.

30   I wish to thank the following people for their helpful comments on an earlier version of this essay: Dorrit Cohn, Natalie Davis, Dorothy Kaufmann, Nikki Keddie, Gerald Prince.

THE MALE'S SEARCH FOR A NEW IDENTITY

THEODORE C. KENT

Approximately one and three quarter billion years ago there were only ladies living on our youthful planet. In those ancient days of muck, water and slime, nature had not yet invented males. The responsibility for species' survival fell on single-celled mothers who split themselves into two separate organisms to create daughters identical to themselves. This method of propagation, called mitosis, still exists today among single-celled plants, protozoa and some lower invertebrates.

Asexual reproduction — reproduction without sex — may have been devoid of romance but it had other advantages. Mitosis avoided the danger of embryonic maldevelopment and, barring mutations, enabled organisms to pass on their genetic characteristics unaltered to the next generation. Except for accidental deaths and the ever-present danger of being eaten alive, mother and daughter enjoyed immortality since dividing took the place of dying. Obviously, male chauvinism was nonexistent in those halcyon days.

Nevertheless, it seems that nature got bored with the *status quo* and after a while sought excitement by inventing sex. The idea caught on and soon sex played a major role in life's unfolding drama. It evolved exotic mating dances among fowl and certain reptiles. It produced flowers with bright colors and alluring smells to attract bees that would distribute pollen. Sex also promoted horn-butting and male rivalry among four-footed animals and was responsible for a host of weird behaviors among humans. Internally, the sex process involved reducing the genetic material by half during the formation of sex cells. This enabled parental gene pools to mix and made possible individuals who differed from their parents and each other. As a gesture of good will nature provided the participants in the sex act with a hitherto unknown kind of fun.

There were advantages and disadvantages to possessing either male or female physiologies. As could have been expected, a few biological shrewdies, like some starfish and jellyfish, played unfair by seasonally alternating from female to male and back. One species of spider settled the matter of sex advantages among themselves for all time. It programmed into the female spider an instinct to devour her male lover immediately after copulation. The results were illuminating — no chauvinistic males, no complaints about males failing to do their part!

Male versus female superiority was never really an issue until Homo sapiens arrived a mere couple of million years ago. Even humans didn't give the matter much thought until they became agriculturalists and began to domesticate animals ten to fifteen thousand years ago. Before that people lived in nomadic bands and men did the hunting while women did the gathering of wild berries and fruit. After humans adopted a sedentary way of life, children were helpful as field hands and animal herders. They could assist their parents in doing chores in the villages where people now lived in permanent dwellings. Men who fathered lots of children gained macho reputations.

Since the advent of agriculture and animal domestication, big game hunters and bow-and-arrow makers no longer were necessary to sustain human life. During their new found leisure men ruminated about their lost status. It seems that one of the topics they thought about was the increased value of having offspring in the age of farming and herding. It hit them now with full force that the human race would quickly become extinct were it not for women giving birth to children. This led them to consider their own worthlessness now that agriculture made surplus food available. The pain and hassles of pregnancy and delivery notwithstanding, it seemed unfair that gestation and birthing children was an inviolate woman's prerogative. Just the idea that women could do something super-important that males couldn't, irked men in their state of mind at this time. However, men's pride would never allow them to leak out their feeling of deprivation. It was better to pretend that men played a more important role in giving birth to children than women did. Health professionals call it using the ego-defense of denial.

I will introduce the fraud that was called couvade by quoting from the New Columbia Encyclopedia:

COUVADE, imitation by the father of many of the concomitants of childbirth at the time of his wife's parturition. The father may go to bed, retire into seclusion and observe taboos and restrictions. . . . in extreme form, men may mimic the pain and process of childbirth. While the woman in labor lay ignored in a corner of the hut, the medicine man, accompanied by anxious well-wishers, performed a variety of rites to assuage her groaning husband's pain.

Could men really pull this off? I quote the Encyclopedia: "The practice of couvade has been noted since antiquity into modern times and in such widely dispersed places as Africa, China, Japan, India, and among the Indians of both North and South America."

When men were finally called to task to explain such irrational behavior, they could hardly be expected to confess. Instead, they justified couvade by saying it served to distract the devil from entering a woman's body while she was in labor. Even young children not wishing to attend school invent better stories to explain their aches in the absence of physical disease. Yet the devil explanation is accepted in some places to this day.

I have used the practice of couvade to illustrate the male's easily aroused sense of inferiority because it reveals its unpublicized origin so dramatically. Throughout written history there are, also, other methods used to impress the weaker sex with their spouses' importance. The most audacious of these is the legend that women and children must be protected from males of other tribes or villages. Word was spread that without protectors women would be dragged off, raped and enslaved. The rumor became self-fulfilled prophecy.

It is easy to see why this absurd idea caught on. Since males in other villages suffered from the same malaise as all males at the time, they cooperated by making organized killing a normal part of life. At first there were only raiding parties. They justified painting faces and bodies to look fierce. With the increase of population full-scale wars took place. During the fighting, women and children huddled in fear and their gratitude for the sacrifices their defenders made for them was unbounded. Men savored their roles as saviors while at the same time, according to some theorists, unknowingly heeded nature's grim call for birth control. Women made people, men killed people — war, it seemed, satisfied everyone.

But even engaging in ceaseless war wasn't enough to make up for the indignity men suffered by their minuscule role in creating new human beings. To redress the balance men had to be better than women in everything else — governing, healing, dispensing wisdom and communicating with the spirit world. Accordingly, when they were too old to be warriors men became patriarchs, law givers, wise old men and elders.

When couvade was kaput, what would replace it? Psychoanalytic ingenuity. To bolster the male ego in our century, along came Sigmund Freud, the psychoanalytic father of the ego-defenses that include projection. With a straight face he successfully declared that penis envy was driving women crazy. Men needed that boost. Because men were soon thereafter to learn that their Y chromosome for maleness was the tiniest of the human 46 and that the double Xs the female has in place of the male's XY enables them to avoid giving their daughters the genetic diseases they give to their sons when they — the females — are the carriers! Unfairness didn't stop there. Men learned that nature makes an average young male create 120 million spermatozoa every few days to contribute to the gamete, while the female only has to release one ovum every twenty-eight days. Alas, there was no glory in numbers — the single ovum carries the food supply! Obviously something drastic had to be done. The gauche answer was male chauvinism, often aided and abetted by a touch (a well-chosen word) of female harassment here and there. The resulting status quo remained in force until the modern advent of female liberation.

The descendants of the pragmatic women who once had to tolerate males' fictitious superiority to save their skins now found protection from the courts and the police. In the late twentieth century the males' game was up. Women won the freedom to prove that they could do anything men could do, including going to work and to war. As before, men were physically bigger and stronger than women, but the gun is called the great equalizer for a good reason.

The male dilemma triggered by the loss of big game hunter status twelve thousand years ago is presently mirrored in the confused self-images of Neolithic men's modern counterpart. The challenge of gaining equal opportunity gave women a goal and a purpose. Men got nothing in return except the loss of their reputation as breadwinners and their dethronement as kings in their castles. To date we have not solved the problems created on earth when nature invented sex. Men, smarting (of course, never admitting it) from their exclusion in the drama of giving birth, unlike some species of birds, can't even take turns sitting on the eggs.

History is played out in a spiral, not a straight line. The circular development of male destiny has today reached its periodic stumbling block. After their bubble of superiority was pricked and the air that kept it inflated escaped, men again asked themselves — who are we? And what are we good for in a new world where women are fighter pilots and share men's hardships in the trenches? Their self-pity was manifested in silent dispair. We have lost our last stronghold — the humble right to die for women even now still vouchsafed for some male spiders!

Female liberation brought with it simple solutions to men's loss of status. Men should diaper babies, wash the family's dishes, do the laundry, clean the house, and do chores previously contemptuously labelled by them as women's work. It was a modern version of couvade. With some men it didn't seem to work. Something else males needed was missing. It would be totally unfair, incorrect, and, in fact, dangerous to theorize that in their frustration men increasingly turned to crime, child molestation, wife beating, and mass murder. Yet, I have heard this travesty whispered in dark caves and wine cellars.

In the present search for solutions to the male dilemma, the books that stroke the modern males crushed egos are selling well. Their authors agree that a compensatory macho of displaced hunters living in a super-market world is self-defeating. Robert Bly's best-selling book, *Iron John* (Vintage 1992), describes the masculinity of today's males as a Wild Man in the woods, imprisoned beneath the water of a lake and rescued by a little boy. Bly seems to think that modern males suffer from what sounds to me like Freudian castration anxiety hidden beneath layers of social compliance. Let the Wild Man out, he advises. But there is another way to do it no one has mentioned. The ability to manipulate the human genome is just around the corner. As soon as molecular biologists learn what genes to shuffle around on the Y chromosome, the Iron John problem will be solved for all eternity.

Barring this, clearly, it will take something of a breakthrough to restore men's self-respect. I disagree with all the published reports on the need for males to get in touch with their inner caved-in cave man. The whole issue should be kept on a higher plane. I insist that modern males' redemption can be gained only by their discovery of their unsuspected, divine spirituality that they always have had hidden within themselves. When that happens men can assume their rightful role as benevolent gods proudly striding the earth and making right everything that is wrong with it. However, in doing so they must be careful not to antagonize the real God who rules both Heaven and Earth. She might resent it.

PART TWO

SEXUALITY: FREUD, FOUCAULT, AND AFTER

A. FOUCAULT AND SEXUALITY

Is Foucault Useful for Understanding Eighteenth and Nineteenth Century Sexuality?

ROY PORTER

In 1976, Michel Foucault's projected multi-volume analysis of Western sexuality began to appear with the publication of *La volonté de savoir*. Two further volumes came out, *L'usage des plaisirs* (1984), and *Le souci de soi* (1984), translated as *The Use of Pleasure* (1985) and *The Care of the Self* (1986).[1] A further volume, *Les aveux de la chair* (*Confessions of the Flesh*), was largely complete at the time of the author's death in 1985, and is supposedly being prepared for publication. My brief account will focus upon the three published volumes, above all the first (translated as *The History of Sexuality*, vol. 1, *Introduction*), though I shall also draw upon some of his other writings. I do not pretend to be offering an analysis of all aspects of Foucault's thinking on sexuality. I will make no effort to situate Foucault's writings on sex in context of the wider development of his thought or the intellectual currents of the 1970s; nor shall I attempt an assessment of the project's theoretical coherence.[2] Instead, my restricted and somewhat polemical aim is to examine the pertinence of Foucault's views to historical readings of Western sex and sexuality. In the light of Foucault's revisionism, how far must our historiographical orthodoxies be abandoned? Or, on the contrary, do historical evidence and interpretations cast doubt upon Foucault's recension?[3]

ORTHODOXY CHALLENGED

The History of Sexuality is a brilliant enterprise, astonishingly bold, shocking even, in its subversion of conventional explanatory frameworks, chronologies, and evaluations, and in its proposed alternatives. Its strengths are beyond dispute. On many specific issues — for example the intricate interweaving of incest, oedipality, psychoanalysis, in context of the late Victorian bourgeois family — Foucault is dazzlingly penetrating. (pp. 130ff.) He is surely right to deny that it is useful to talk about *sex* in history, in the sense of some protean biological force, a hydrostatic equilibration of pressures and resistances, insisting instead that our proper study must instead be *sexuality*, i.e., the inscription of desire within discourse. Sexual identities are not innate, but are the products of labelling and negotiation processes, and the creation of subjectivities, within wider economies of discursive practice. Thus the Freudian assumption that we have, at long last, recognized — that is, ceased to deny — that sex is the ultimate secret, the key to our innermost nature, must itself be problematized: what is it that has made us propose sex as the real thing?[4]

Foucault, moreover, brilliantly exposed the Whiggishness of standard histories of sex, with their heroic, but finally complacent, tale of liberation from sexual ignorance, negativism, and hypocrisy through the crusades of enlightened Bohemians, free-thinkers, doctors, and, finally, historians. Such histories are likewise problematized by Foucault.[5]

Not least, Foucault challenged our categories and orthodoxies. We — that is, the right-thinking liberal intelligentsia of a mainly Freudo-Marxian hue and a mainly male gender — we believe that sexuality is a healthy, pleasurable drive, repressed down the centuries by the powers-that-be, for long the killjoy Christian Churches, but latterly the dominant politico-economic order, committed to suppressing, or at least sublimating, libido in the cause of social discipline, ordered production and reproduction, respectability, and sobriety. We believe that sex has been stifled and penalized, all too often at the cost of hypocrisy or neurosis. We believe certain groups — deviants, prostitutes, hysterical women, perverts, homosexuals — have been pilloried by pulpit, press, police, and parliaments, all engaging in surplus repression, and perhaps even thereby safely finding release for their own inadmissible, unspeakable urges. We believe that, in the course of the Christian centuries, our culture was drilled into compulsory sexual ignorance, morbid erotic fears, hatreds, prohibitions, and displaced desires — though, thankfully, we believe, the anti-sexual strait-jacket has been belatedly relaxed this century, partly through exposure of this shameful legacy in the theoretico-historical readings of Sigmund Freud, Havelock Ellis, Wilhelm Reich, Herbert Marcuse, Norman O. Brown and all their followers, and partly (if more ambiguously), through the rise of modern permissive narcissism as a dimension of consumer capitalism: loosened, that is, until the advent of AIDS and its accompanying puritanical and homophobic backlash.[6]

    This credo of ours is not, however, contends Foucault, the authentic history, sociology, or "truth", of sexuality: it is, rather, a misleading and mystifying mythology. Empirically, Foucault claims, and with reason, it is false on many specifics — for instance the transformation of sexual imperatives is not chronologically isomorphous with the stages of capitalism (pp. 5-6). Worse, it is blatantly self-serving: modern historical theorists have shamelessly conferred upon themselves the crown of liberators. Above all, it promotes a fundamental misconstrual of the realities of Western sexuality. For the keynotes of the story, Foucault contends, are not, in actuality, censorship, silencing, frustration, and criminalization — or, in a word, *repression*. The truth of our civilization over the last few hundred years is the reverse: there has been, argues Foucault, ever more varied and vociferous talking about sex, a greater emphasis on sex in every dimension of all our lives, and a variegation and intensification of libidinous pleasures (not least, the pleasures of knowing and talking about sex). It is preposterous, he argues, to claim that we have been, and continue to be, repressed, or at least that "repression is . . . fundamental and overriding": the pertinent question, rather, is what makes us feel such a need to insist on that patently phony assertion (p. 53).

REPRESSION EXPLODED

    Foucault's assertions amount to a stunning slaughter of the most sacred cows of the liberal recension, and I believe it is worth quoting Foucault *in extenso*, just as a reminder of the force and degree of his repudiation of what he has damned as the "repressive hypothesis". For one thing, not silencing but garrulity: "This is the essential thing: that Western man has been drawn for three centuries to the task of telling everything concerning his sex; that since the classical age [by which

Foucault means the seventeenth century] there has been a constant optimization and an increasing valorization of the discourse on sex . . . the
boundaries of what one could say about sex [were] enlarged" (p. 23); or,
again, on what he calls the "discursive explosion" (p. 38), "rather than the
uniform concern to hide sex, what distinguishes these last three centuries
is the variety, the wide dispersion of devices that were invented for
speaking about it" (p. 34).

Such practices and apparatuses, Foucault contends, involve "less
a principle of inhibition than an inciting and multiplying mechanism" (p.
46). Hence, "we must therefore abandon the hypothesis that modern
industrial societies ushered in an age of increased repression" (p. 49);
rather the "opposite": "never have there existed more centres of power . . .
never more sites where the intensity of pleasures and the persistency of
power catch hold, only to spread elsewhere" (p. 49).

It is commonly said, admits Foucault, that "no society has been
more prudish". Not so! "Is sex hidden from us", Foucault asks, "kept
under a bushel by the grim necessities of bourgeois society?": "On the
contrary," he responds, lyrically, "it shines forth, it is incandescent"
(p. 77).

Addressing the issue of sexual regulation and socio-sexual control
(what is often called "policing the silences"), Foucault emphasizes, "I
have repeatedly stressed that the history of the last centuries in Western
societies did not manifest the movement of a power that was essentially
repressive" (p. 81). It is a mistake to decode the development of sexuality
in terms of coercion: "we must not look for who has the power in the order
of sexuality (men, adults, parents, doctors) and who is deprived of it
(women, adolescents, children, patients); nor for who has the right to know
and who is forced to remain ignorant" (p. 99). Rather sexual power has
been universally distributed, user-friendly, generally empowering; subjects have been erotically endowed within pervasive sign-systems, fabrics
of discourse, wherein power, knowledge and pleasure comprise a happy
trinity: "parents and children, adults and adolescents, educators and students, doctors and patients, the psychiatrist with his hysteric and his
perverts, all have played this game continually since the nineteenth
century" (p. 45).

More discourse, more pleasure, more permissions. This is a regime
which began with the Church, for Christianity, Foucault assures us,
employed "many ruses" to make us "love sex", and "to make the
knowledge of it desirable" (p. 159). It is an order which continued with

secularization, for, in the nineteenth century, "sexuality, far from being repressed . . . on the contrary was constantly aroused" (p. 148); "the mechanisms of power were in fact used more to arouse and 'excite' sexuality than to repress it" (p. 151).

Social historians have dwelt on conflict and exclusion, the censors and the censored, and have claimed to see a dominant Thou-Shalt-Notism battling against a counter, underground, Rabelaisian tradition of anarchic, popular subversion. But falsely. "We must not imagine a world of discourse divided between accepted discourse and excluded discourse, or between the dominant discourse and the dominated one" (p. 100). In particular, Foucault insists, "there is not on the one side, a discourse of power, and opposite it, another discourse that runs counter to it" (p. 101). So much for dogmatists who contend that the sexual economy has served the interests of those in the saddle, by validating patriarchal, conjugal heterosexuality, and stigmatizing non-procreative, recreational eroticism: "the idea that there have been repeated attempts, by various means, to reduce all of sex to its reproductive function, its heterosexual and adult form, and its matrimonial legitimacy, fails to take into account the manifold objectives aimed for, the manifold means employed in the different sexual politics concerned with the two sexes, the different age groups and social classes" (p. 103).

Moreover, just as the history of sexuality is not to be construed in terms of struggles between official and radical discourses, neither must it be seen as the policing of group by group, or class by class. Thus Foucault contends that "the working classes managed for a long time to escape the deployment of 'sexuality' " (p. 121), being hardly affected by the imperatives of ecclesiastical pastoral care in early modern times or subsequently by bourgeois morality. "It appears unlikely that there was an age of sexual restriction" (p. 122), imposed by the middle classes upon the lower orders. "Particularly in the first half of the nineteenth century," Foucault assures us, "there was anything but concern for [the working class] body and its sex" (p. 126). Indeed, insofar as the propertied and the polite exercised themselves to heighten sexual regulation, "they first tried it on themselves" (p. 122) — the reformation of sexuality was, thus, not the "enslavement of others, but . . . affirmation of self" (p. 123). In short, it is Foucault's thesis that what counted down the centuries was the "production of sexuality rather than the repression of sex" (p. 114).

These ringing assertions clinch the explosively radical quality of Foucault's revisionism. High time, he believes, to cease talking of interdictions and stigmatization, punitiveness and policing, social control, gender privileging and penalization, the ghettoization of deviants. Successively, through the disciplines of pastoral theology, medicine, law, psychiatry, and public opinion, sex grew more visible, audible, and, above all, more pleasurable, and it did so through the length and breadth of society.

Foucault certainly scores some palpable hits. Social historians and historical demographers alike would today endorse his onslaught against on the old notion, given a new lease of life by the Freudo-Marxists, and confidently reasserted in Marcuse's *Eros and Civilization*, that industrialization demanded erotic austerity.[7] Peter Gay and other recent students of nineteenth century morals and manners have confirmed his demolition of the hoary myth of the Victorian bourgeoisie as just a bunch of up-tight prudes.[8] More generally, Foucault is clearly right to remind us that Victorian denials must not be taken at face value: clearly they demand careful evaluation. Culturally, politically, and, if you like, psychodynamically, prohibitions presuppose and even multiply desire. The forbidden has been integral to desire at least since Sade if not since Eve. The proverbial frilly skirt veiling the piano legs eroticized what had hitherto been innocent items of joinery.[9]

"SPIRALS OF PLEASURE"?

All such insights are perceptive, and have doubtless helped, over the last decade, to shape key revisions in the history and historical sociology of sexuality.[10] I am, nevertheless, left overall unconvinced and perplexed. For one thing, Foucault, presumably for polemical reasons, habitually reduces the received tradition to gross caricature. Was the "repressive hypothesis" true? No, he responds, because down the centuries there has been a proliferation of sexual talk and writing, from the Counter-Reformation catalogue of sins to Krafft-Ebing's psychopathological zoo (pp. 43, 63).[11] Yet surely Foucault cannot be so naive (or so tendentiously question-begging) as to be implying that discourse itself could not be repressive — how else *would* you repress, except through words, ideas, and their protocols? For the "repressive hypothesis" to be plausible, it is not necessary to demonstrate that any and every mention of sex became unspeakable in the age of Bowdlerization, Grundyism, Victorian prudery and so forth.[12] No one ever claimed that total silence was imposed; what historians have been at great pains to demonstrate is that extraordinary quantities of anxious energy were applied to purifying, concealing, blaming, and banning, and that many people were actually silenced, shamed, and stigmatized by moral anathemas or the engines of the law, be they children and ladies, who had to be "protected" from carnal knowledge, or writers who had to be prevented from corrupting them. ("Is this a book that you would even wish your wife or your servants to read?" demanded the prosecution in the obscenity trial against the publishers of *Lady Chatterley's Lover* as late as 1960).[13]

Indeed, many of the books adduced by Foucault as proof of the crescendo of erotic discourse, including Krafft-Ebing, were themselves prosecuted, expurgated, or hidden from history in safe places such as the British Museum's private case. Other classics were castrated (one recalls that "Under the greenwood tree, Who loves to lie with Me", from *As You Like It*, was bowdlerized to "who loves to work with Me" — grist for the Freudo-Marxist mill, if ever it was needed.[14] The belief that carnal knowledge was too dangerous to be disclosed was no mere passing foible of a few quirky Victorian evangelicals. As recently as 1953, as Richard Davenport-Hines has reminded us, the *Kinsey Report* narrowly escaped Home Office presecution for obscenity. In 1989, the British Prime Minister, on record as an idolizer of Victorian values, vetoed the proposal of her own Department of Health and Social Security to survey her nation's sexual habits.[15] Concepts such as repression, marginalization, and policing must, it goes without saying, be deployed with sensitivity, discretion, and respect for evidence; but equally clearly it won't do for Foucault to imply that the mere presence of discourse refutes, out of hand, the "repressive hypothesis". (Otherwise we confuse words and realities: the same idealist logic would prove that South African Blacks must be free because there's so much talk about freedom in South Africa.)

What is surely at stake is not whether the silence was total, but the question of *who* was permitted to say *what*, and *who* was prohibited, or dissuaded, from saying *what*, and *who* had what kinds of powers to enforce the taboos. Isn't there something deeply disingenuous, or at least highly tendentious, in Foucault pointing to *My Secret Life* as a proof of proliferating sexualities in the nineteenth century - indeed claiming that its anonymous author might be more typical of his times than the Queen after whom they were named (pp. 21-22); or, put another way, that those whom Steven Marcus dubbed the "other Victorians" were, in reality, the true Victorians.[16] For only a few copies of *My Secret Life* were ever printed, and then only in circumstances of secrecy for private circulation — and, ever since its publication, the work has remained almost inaccessible.[17] Nobody would deny that there were pockets of libertinism; but there were also great terrains of sexual reticence in eighteenth and nineteenth century society. In short, Foucault is being tendentious, or, at least from the historian's viewpoint, irresponsibly selective in his choice of facts, and nowhere does he address himself to questions of typicality, cultural differentiation, or to the task of evaluating and interpreting contemporary testimony. Indeed, he seems programmatically to dismiss such issues by denying, out of hand, the differentiation of discourses into hegemonic and underground, high and low, or male and female registers (p. 99).

Above all, Foucault seems guilty of a spectacular elision. He adduces a proliferation of talk about sex. This may, I have suggested, require qualification. But true or not, it is not in itself a refutation of the "repressive hypothesis." It can just as easily be said to reinforce it, if much of that talk was indeed repressive, in intention and/or effect. And surely it was. It was one of the great aims of so many British and American writers on sex — educators, preachers, doctors, reformers — particularly in the wake of the French Revolution, to prevent other people finding out about sex, talking about sex, reading about sex, writing about sex, and above all engaging in sex (save under strictly specified circumstances).[18] Crusades were launched to humiliate sexual transgressors, pathologize them, psychopathologize them, lock them up, shut them up, and, occasionally, put them to death. (And it would be hardly decent for Foucault to retort that all this activity proved that sexuality was being expressed not suppressed, except by analogy with the preciousness of freedom to Lenin).

In any case, Foucault waxes lyrical about "*perpetual spirals of power and pleasure*" (p. 45); he ought, in conscience, to have made more of the perpetual spirals of power and pain, punitiveness and persecution, and invited a Benthamite pondering of such pleasures and pains in the balance. Alongside his sublimely meliorist vision of a "constant optimization and an increasing valorization of the discourse on sex" (p. 23), he might have noted the aggression, the guilty fears, the vituperative disgusts, so often recorded. It is all very well for Foucault to talk about the libidinous power/knowledge/ pleasure "game" played by doctors and patients, parents and children, but the stark truth, masked by Foucault's trivializing term "game", is that what we may, *pace* Foucault, call dominant discourses, such as institutional psychiatry, commonly resulted in delinquents — e.g. juvenile masturbators or unmarried mothers — being disgraced,

sequestrated, or hounded to death.[19] Foucault claims that with the proliferation of discourses, there was "a visible explosion of unorthodox sexualities . . . the proliferation of specific pleasures and the multiplication of
disparate sexualities" (p. 49). But this sunny view of the destinies of
deviants appears, to say the least, insensitive, flying in the face of massive
evidence during the last century of intensified police harassment, moral
marginalization and the like — indeed, seemingly incompatible with one
of his own examples, the simpleton, Jouy, from the village of Lapcourt (p.
49).

The ironically eponymous Jouy, one recalls, fell under the official
gaze in 1867 after, it seems, persuading a young girl to masturbate him in
the corner of a field. Following an intense investigation conducted by
police, magistrates and doctors, he was locked up in an asylum for the rest
of his days. As Foucault admits, sexual exchanges of the kind solicited by
Jouy had doubtless been going on time out of mind between dirty old men
and little girls. Only latterly did the official discourses and coercive
machinery which penalized such acts materialize. Foucault takes this as a
sign of the new nineteenth century "noisiness" about sex. Of course; but
it is a noise, an energy, rigorously devoted not to promoting spirals of
pleasure but to policing and punishing (and I take it that Foucault isn't
seriously suggesting that the spirals of pleasures he is discussing are wholly
the pleasures of sadistic persecutors and masochistic victims).[20]

One could proceed, instance by instance, to challenge Foucault's
odd refusal to go beyond the presence of sexual discourse and consider its
meanings and consequences — respecting class, respecting gender. There
is no space. One further example must suffice: Marie Stopes, most recently
discussed by Lesley Hall.[21] This prominent sex-educator and birth control
campaigner claimed — on the basis of direct, first-hand experience — that
sexual ignorance caused immense personal misery, and that the British
moral, religious and medical establishments were largely committed to
upholding it, convinced that ignorance was essential to "virtue". Stopes
received tens of thousands of pathetic letters from sexually ill-informed,
frustrated and desperate correspondents, many of whom claimed that their
doctors or priests, even when pressed, fed them no sexual information —
at best, disinformation — and, to add insult to injury, dished out humilia-
tion on top (so much for Foucault's denial of "the uniform concern to hide
sex" and insistence upon "the wide dispersion of devices . . . invented for
speaking about it") (p. 34). Now, of course, Foucault might interpret this
taciturnity as one of the jolly sexual games perpetually being played

between doctors and their patients; and he could, moreover, argue that the mere presence of Stopes and all those letters she received further corroborates his case. But this would surely be question-begging. What the social historian finds salient is that cultural configurations had come about in which — regardless of what sexological discourses were being uttered or muttered in certain quarters — large sectors of the population were being held in ignorance and denied access to sexual knowledge; wherein, indeed, a highly-educated palaeobotanist with a Ph.D. degree was unaware even that she had failed to consummate her own marriage. The absence of repression is not — *pace* Foucault — proved by the mere presence, somewhere in the system, of discourse. What is crucial is to address serious analysis to the implications of that discourse — for the powerless, the marginalized, those deemed deviant. And here I believe that Richard Davenport-Hines has done well, in his recently-published *Sex, Death and Punishment*, to insist that so much of the proliferating sexual discourse in Britain over the last few centuries has been a discourse of disqualification, targeted against the lower orders, the young, the aberrant, and, overwhelmingly, against women. Examine the torrents of misogyny and homophobia: where do we find the "spirals of power and pleasure"?[22]

Here lies the heart of the matter. Foucault seems to be claiming that the "repressive hypothesis" must be wrong, insofar as it involves the notion that some people were repressing others: men repressing women, parents children, psychiatrists their patients, judges offenders. Above all, he insists that the ruling classes were not seriously engaged in surveying and punishing the sexual morals of the laboring classes. These claims appear to me to be contradicted by contemporary eyewitnesses and by oceans of historical research. Any number of feminist scholars have demonstrated how, within the "separate spheres" and double standards ideologies to the fore in the eighteenth and nineteenth centuries, women were systematically rendered, to a greater or lesser degree, sexually impotent.[23] And what were moral purity movements — Societies for the Reformation of Manners and their successors — but movements for policing the morals, including sexual morals, of the poor?[24] Foucault blithely speaks of sexual regulation as something the upper orders first tried out upon themselves. Really? Recall Sydney Smith's characterization in early nineteenth century England of the Vice Society as a "Society for Suppressing the Vices of Persons whose income does not exceed £500 per annum."[25] Clearly, not everyone thought the upper classes kept their prohibitions to themselves.

We are finally forced to come to grips with a profound peculiarity in Foucault's account. Not silencing but a deafening, not repression but proliferation, collusive games between rich and poor, men and women, doctors and deviants: this is, obviously, a view which flies in the face of any social history which emphasizes difference and conflict. But this picture of the pluralistic multiplication and intensification of sexuality since the seventeenth century — is it not also utterly discrepant with the vision presented in the earlier *Madness and Civilization* of the "great confinement" of the poor and the mad in the same epoch.[26] In the former analysis, the imperatives of reason, absolutism, and bourgeois capitalism require the repression of what once had been free-range madness (Folly was thereby reduced to Unreason, alongside the idle, the ne'er-do-well, and sexual transgressors such as whores). In the later volume, by contrast, it appears that selfsame society had no investment in policing the sexuality (and, by implication, the behavior at large) of the lower orders.

It is, maybe, unsurprising that Foucault does not draw attention to this seeming paradox, or rather interpretative volte-face. But the problems it poses are presumably on his mind when he argues, in the *History of Sexuality*, that we must cease to think of power as something negative, an exclusionary interdiction descending from Above, and treat it rather as a general facilitation, providing grids of popular discursive possibilities throughout society.[27] In other words, if one may simplify rather brutally, whereas proto-Foucault, the Foucault of *Madness and Civilization*, and to some degree also of *Discipline and Punish*, saw knowledge-power operating to invalidate and sequestrate, deutero-Foucault saw power as the harbinger of possibility and pleasure. It is interesting, if idle, to speculate about the personal politics of this about-turn. Is it entirely fortuitous that *Madness and Civilization* was the work of an unknown scholar, researching in Uppsala, still troubled about his own sexual identity (the trigger of youthful suicide attempts), whereas the *History of Sexuality*, fulsome in praise of the pleasures conferred by power, adamant in its denial of alternative discourses, was written by a much-fêted professor at the Collège de France? (It would not be the first time that one esconsced in such a position penned an apologia denying the coercive nature of power: Foucault himself notes, I suspect slyly, that power, to exercise itself successfully, must necessarily be self-masking). Certainly proto-Foucault construed the mad as the silenced victims of modernity — and seemingly identified with them — whereas deutero-Foucault had possibly become so Olympian as to be attuned only to official discourses, and incapable of gazing beyond to probe the real implications of sexual penology or pedagogics for the lives, hopes, and fears of the miserable and the marginalized.

AN HISTORICAL DYNAMIC?

It is, however, beside the point to speculate upon Foucault's motives, to ask what his game was (and it would be stupid to underestimate his desire to provoke). What is relevant is whether he can plausibly account for the grip of the "repressive hypothesis" — he waves it aside as little more than late nineteenth century liberal and especially Freudian special pleading — and provide us with a coherent and true account of the sexual trajectory of the West. I remain unconvinced, on several scores.

First, if he is to dethrone the "repressive hypothesis", surely he needs at least to engage seriously with the fact that so many commentators, from the Enlightenment onwards, drew attention to what they deplored as a sick and vindictive puritanical streak, which was still, at the turn of the nineteenth century in Britain, sending sodomites to their death and, in developments new to Victorian times, surgically mutilating sexually-transgressive women. Were such protestors exaggerating, grinding their own axes, or should we take their witness seriously?[28]

Second, Foucault surely owes it to us to differentiate more fully between, on the one hand, the mere presence of sexual discourses, and, on the other, the values, the protocols for action, which they inscribed. Thus he is assuredly correct to contend that, over the last five centuries, an eroticization of marriage has been encouraged by religious and medical opinion. But shouldn't he equally stress that those selfsame writings have also been aiming to confine sexual activity essentially to conjugal relations, thereby producing a close fit between production and reproduction? For Western sexual science has been overwhelmingly concerned to condemn non-conjugal and, till very recently, non-reproductive coitus (masturbation, buggery, pre- and extra-marital liaisons) as immoral, pathological, and socially dangerous. That clearcut distinctions were drawn between conjugal eroticism, which was accorded guarded approval, and hedonistic and recreational sex, which was abominated, has been reaffirmed by scores of historians.[29]

It follows that Foucault is himself in need of a plausible alternative explanation as to why, over the last five hundred years, Western societies have produced such a proliferation of talk about sex. If not anxiety in the face of danger, not least the new threat posed by the advent of syphilis;[30] if not the demands for order and economy in early capitalism and nation states; if not the patriarchalist need to subordinate women and to discipline the Malthusian masses; if not the pervasive sense of pollution endemic to a Christian cosmology and church identifying sex as the original sin, prizing chastity or at least continence, radically distrustful of the flesh, and institutionally punitive of sexual transgressions — what?

In other words, can Foucault offer a plausible account of the development and transformation of Western sexual theoretical practices from Greco-Roman roots, through their Judeo-Christian trunk, up to the present? There is no unambiguous answer, for Foucault's death left a gaping chasm in his project, between the two volumes on Antiquity, and the *Introduction* volume which deals mainly, if inevitably sketchily, with developments from the eighteenth century.

I believe Foucault offers an illuminating reading of the articulation of sexuality in the writings of Antiquity. Greek sexual discourse (he argues in volume 2, *The Use of Pleasure*), prescribed the sexual pleasures, the sexual practices, appropriate to particular gender and social groups. Attention focused upon the free-born, affluent male citizen. It was proper for such an individual, while still a youth, to enjoy sexual contacts with his male peers; and, at a later stage, to engage in sexual relations with his wife (for the sake of procreation, honor, and family), with mistresses, concubines, and slave-girls (for the sake of pleasure), and with well-born youths (for the sake of love and friendship). All such connections were honorable and dignified, integral to the privileges of a good man, so long as they were pursued with moderation and decorum. Excessive activity, indulgence with debasing partners or any hint of addiction to sexual urges were condemned as degrading and threats to health.[31]

In the shift from the golden age of Greece through to the heyday of *Romanitas*, a growing sexual austerity may be seen, a shift marked in Foucault's titles, from *The Use of Pleasure* to *The Care of the Self*. The thinkers of late Antiquity grew more cautious about appropriate sexual expression. Attachments with boys fell under suspicion as undignified, while fidelity to one's wife became prized as specially conducive to tenderness and intimacy; not least, medical writings emphasized that sex could be a high-risk activity, orgasm a little death.[32]

If, over the course of half a millennium of Antiquity, eroticism grew more controlled, more guarded, this was not, Foucault contends, a defensive response to unfavorable external repressive circumstances (the arbitrariness and moral anomie of Imperial Rome). Nor was it because new theologies and philosophies banished or despised sex. It was because intrinsic persuasives within the value-systems of Antiquity (moral, political, domestic, medical, aesthetic) increasingly emphasized that virtuous and healthy living required disciplined regulation of the passions and drives, for the positive education and enhancement of the self.

In other words, we must not assume that the Greeks and Romans advocated and liberally indulged in orgiastic license, until some rigorous theological puritanism supervened to rescue them from Dionysus. To explain their erotic economy — one which seemingly became increasingly Apollonian — it is not helpful to imagine lustings after Bacchanalian debauch being checked, from outside, by the arm of the law, or from within, by the bugaboos of sin. Paramount was a positive philosophy of the welfare and dignity of the self. Antiquity did not operate upon a repressive model.

The crucial question, then, is how far these sexual values changed with the advent and uptake of Christianity. Is the popular picture — that Christianity flayed the flesh, imposing negative sexual prejudices and punitive protocols (eros was at its best when denied, especially absolutely in virginity) — just a grotesque caricature? No doubt, Latin Christendom was less hostile to carnal desires than were Gnosticism or Manicheism. Yet Foucault's comment that Christianity brought "many ruses" to make us "love sex" (p. 159) would not be easy to sustain as a balanced reading of the impact of the propagation of the faith (it certainly involves a novel reading of the Garden of Eden!) — particularly in the light of Peter Brown's recent emphasis upon the pervasive associations between chastity and eschatology forged in the early Church, and Jean Delumeau's richly-documented assertion that, from the late Middle Ages through the Reformation and Counter-Reformation, theology and pastoral care alike, while losing interest in sins such as gluttony, became ever more preoccupied with concupiscence as the epitome of sinfulness — something depicted in sermons and in religious art as especially gruesome.[33]

It seems that Foucault — son of a notably anti-clerical doctor — wishes neither to inculpate nor exonerate Christianity. He lays no special stress upon the significance of Commandments or the new sexual theology of sin; nor does he deny their role. For one who, in his early works, made much of epistemological discontinuities, he is notably diplomatic regarding the degree of rupture between Classical and Christian views. What he does accentuate, however — and here we return to the question of his explanation of the modern intensification of sexual discourse — is that the emphasis first on penance and then on confession within Catholicism (and its Protestant analogue, conscience) created an imperative to talk about sex, which led inexorably, when secularized, to nineteenth century sexology: the confessional as precursor of the couch. If God was an illusion, the future of that illusion was Freud (p. 158).

I don't find this account of Counter-Reformation Catholicism as the catalyst of modern sexual garrulity very convincing. It is a further sign of Foucault's selectivity with evidence that he attributes so much significance to the confession, as the agency for stimulating sexual discourse, while saying so little about the enormous investment of the Christian churches over the centuries in rendering sex polluting, sinful, in large measure unspeakable, and liable for punitive measures.[34]

In any case, I am far from sure that "the essential thing" — to revert to an earlier quotation — is indeed "that Western man has been drawn for three centuries to the task of telling everything concerning his sex" (p. 23). Read the diaries, autobiographies, and letters of even sexually active Christian folks — married and unmarried — in the seventeenth, eighteenth and nineteenth centuries. Disregard a score of notorious exceptions — Pepys, Boswell, Casanova — and we encounter a blanket of silence, or at least of self-censorship, magnified by the indefatigable excisions and Bowdlerizations of subsequent editors. The evasions, the interdictions, do not bespeak a great wash of sensual pleasures translated into discourse. Indeed, as Francis Barker in particular has contended, when diarists such as Pepys translate sex into text, it is typically furtive, guilty, and coded: no paeans to the joys of Eros.[35] Arguably, it might be truer to say, of the period up to the close of the nineteenth century, "that Western man has been drawn for three centuries to the task of veiling everything concerning his sex" — tasks of repudiation, and the projection of hatreds upon others: misogyny, homophobia, and so forth. Better still would be to discriminate between the few who talked and the many who held their tongue, and to examine those who upheld the silences.[36]

Of course, Foucault does not discuss these aspects. Thanks to his private feud with the Left Bank Marxist intelligentsia, and because of his post-structuralist affectation of the death of the author and the sovereignty of texts and discourse, he is driven into his bizarre refusal to treat sexual discourse as ideology, typically recruited into the service of coercive power. If Richard Davenport-Hines's recent survey is flawed because, while foregrounding the punitive and pathological pronouncements of press, preachers and politicians, he cannot explain their phobias, Foucault's work is far more deeply vitiated by its denial — one resists the temptation to say "repression" — of the class and gender dynamics of public sexuality.

Contrary to both these inadequate readings, in my opinion the best scholarship in women's studies over the last twenty years — from Carol Smith-Rosenberg through to Lynne Nead, Cynthia Russett, Elaine Showalter, Ludmilla Jordanova, and many others — has been properly sensitive to the brute realities of sexual and class politics — the real capacity of some authorities in a patriarchal class society to control the sexuality of others, imposing identities, attitudes, and actions; and it has been no less sensitive to the complexities and ambiguities of those realities. (And, it needs to be stressed, the most catastrophic absence in Foucault's *opus* is his apparent indifference to the role of sexual discourse in the management of women, and the politics of gender.) It is these models, not the wayward idiosyncrasies of Foucault, which signal ways forward.[37]

NOTES

1   Michel Foucault, *Histoire de la sexualité*, Vol. 1, *La volonté de savoir* (Paris: Gallimard, 1976); Vol. 2, *L'usage des plaisirs* (Paris: Gallimard, 1984); Vol. 3, *Le souci de soi* (Paris: Gallimard, 1984). Volume 4, *Les aveux de la chair*, announced by Gallimard, remained unfinished. Translations, by Robert Hurley, have been published as *The History of Sexuality: Introduction* (London: Allen Lane, 1978), *The Use of Pleasure* (New York: Random House, 1985), *The Care of the Self* (New York: Random House, 1987). Almost all references in the text are to the English translation of the first volume, *The History of Sexuality: Introduction*; the page numbers given parenthetically in the text refer to this work.

2   All these enterprises have, of course, been attempted elsewhere. For a brilliant recent evaluation of the interplay of sexual and psychoanalytical criticism in Foucault, see John Forrester, *The Seductions of Psychoanalysis* (Cambridge: Cambridge University Press, 1990), "Michel

Foucault and the History of Psychoanalysis," pp. 286-315. Alan Sheridan, *Michel Foucault: The Will to Truth* (London: Tavistock, 1980), remains immensely helpful.

3 The following summary of Foucault's argument, as should be clear, is highly selective, spotlighting only aspects germane to my concerns, which are principally those of an empirical historian.

4 Sigmund Freud, *Three Essays on the Theory of Sexuality*, trans. James Strachey (New York: Basic Books, 1975).

5 In this category we might place popular works such as Gordon Rattray Taylor, *Sex in History* (New York: Vanguard, 1954); Reay Tannahill, *Sex in History* (New York: Stein & Day, 1980); and Wayland Young, *Eros Denied: Sex in Western Society* (New York: Grove Press, 1964). Such works depend heavily upon the researches of early twentieth-century sexologists such as Iwan Bloch, for whom see, for instance, *The Sexual Life of Our Time*, trans. M. Eden Paul (London: Rebman, 1909); idem, *Sex Life in England Illustrated: As Revealed in its Obscene Literature and Art*, trans. Richard Deniston (New York: Falstaff, 1934); idem, *Sexual Life in England Past and Present*, trans. William H. Forstern (London: Arco, 1958); idem, *A History of English Sexual Morals*, trans. W. H. Fostern (London: Francis Aldon, 1938).

6 For the kind of ideological and historiographical credo summarized here, see Paul Robinson, *The Modernization of Sex; Havelock Ellis, Alfred Kinsey, William Masters and Virginia Johnson* (New York: Harper & Row, 1976); Christopher Lasch, *The Culture of Narcissism: American Life in an Age of Diminishing Expectations* (New York: Norton, 1978), and especially Herbert Marcuse, *Eros and Civilization* (Boston: Beacon Press, 1966), and N. O. Brown, *Life Against Death* (London: Routledge & Kegan Paul, 1959) — these last being quite explicitly Freudian histories.

7 Herbert Marcuse, *Eros and Civilization* (Boston: Beacon Press, 1966).

8 Peter Gay, *The Bourgeois Experience — Victoria to Freud*, Vol. 1, *Education of the Senses* (New York: Oxford University Press, 1984); idem, *The Bourgeois Experience — Victoria to Freud*, Vol. 2, *The Tender Passion* (New York: Oxford University Press, 1986); idem, "Victorian Sexuality: Old Texts and New Insights," *American Scholar* 49 (1980): 372-377; Carl N. Degler, "What Ought to Be and What Was: Women's Sexuality in the Nineteenth Century," *American Historical Review* 79 (1974): 1467-1490; Wendell Stacy Johnson, *Living in Sin: The Victorian Sexual Revolution* (Chicago: Nelson-Hall, 1979); F. Barry Smith, "Sexuality in Britain,

1800-1900: Some Suggested Revisions," in Martha Vicinus, ed., *A Widening Sphere: Changing Roles of Victorian Women* (Bloomington: Indiana University Press, 1977), 182-198.

9   The work of Peter Gay mentioned in the previous note is especially sensitive to these issues.

10   I take it that this point is beyond dispute, and so I will not elaborate it further here. Most of the most exciting work of the last ten years has been fundamentally influenced by Foucault's reformulations. See, for the merest sample, Frank Mort, *Dangerous Sexualities: Medical-Moral Politics in England* (London: Routledge & Kegan Paul, 1987); Alan Bray, *Homosexuality in Renaissance England* (London: Gay Men's Press, 1982); Jeffrey Weeks, *Sex, Politics and Society: The Regulation of Sexuality since 1800* (London: Longman, 1981); idem, *Sexuality and Its Discontents: Meanings, Myths and Modern Sexualities* (London: Routledge & Kegan Paul, 1985); Lawrence Birken, *Consuming Desire: Sexual Science and the Emergence of a Culture of Abundance, 1871-1914* (Ithaca & London: Cornell University Press, 1989).

11   Richard von Krafft-Ebing, *Psychopathia Sexualis*, trans. Franklin Klaf from 12th German edition (New York: Stein & Day, 1978).

12   For traditionalist and popular accounts of Victorian strategies with sex, see P. Fryer, *Mrs. Grundy: Studies in English Prudery* (London: Dennis Dobson, 1963); Ronald Pearsall, *The Worm in the Bud: The World of Victorian Sexuality* (Harmondsworth: Penguin, 1971); Fraser Harrison, *The Dark Angel: Aspects of Victorian Sexuality* (London: Sheldon Press, 1977); Eric Trudgill, *Madonnas and Magdalens: The Origins and Development of Victorian Sexual Attitudes* (New York: Holmes & Meier, 1976).

13   Many recent works explore these mechanisms. See especially Richard Davenport Hines, *Sex, Death and Punishment: Attitudes to Sex and Sexuality in Britain since the Renaissance* (London: Collins, 1989). For the trial, see p. 225.

14   Discussed in Lawrence Stone, *The Family, Sex and Marriage in England 1500-1800* (London: Weidenfeld & Nicolson, 1977), p. 674.

15   Davenport Hines, *Sex, Death and Punishment*, p. 274.

16   Steven Marcus, *The Other Victorians: A Study of Sexuality and Pornography in Mid-Nineteenth Century England* (New York: Basic Books, 1964).

17   Patrick J. Kearney, *The Private Case: An Annotated Bibliography of the Private Case Erotica Collection in the British (Museum) Library* (London: Jay Landesman, 1981); Alec Craig, *The Banned Books of*

England, and other Countries: A Study of the Conception of Literary Obscenity (London: George Allen and Unwin, 1962); Pia Pascal, Les livres de l'enfer: Bibliographie critique des ouvrages érotiques dans leurs différents éditions du XVIe siècle à nos jours, 2 vols (Paris: Coulet et Faure, 1978); Eberhard and Phyllis Kronhausen, Walter, The English Casanova (London: Polybooks, 1967).

18   In addition to the works cited above, see Muriel Jaeger, Before Victoria (London: 1956); Maurice Quinlan, Victorian Prelude: A History of English Manners, 1700-1830 (New York: Columbia University Press, 1941). Another way of putting this would be to emphasize the alliance between pornography and political dissidence. See I. D. McCalman, "Unrespectable Radicalism: Infidels and Pornography in early Nineteenth Century London," Past and Present 104 (1984): 74-110.

19   See for instance the work of Andrew Scull: Museums of Madness: The Social Organization of Insanity in Nineteenth-Century England (London: Allen Lane; New York: St. Martin's Press, 1979); idem, Social Order/Mental Disorder: Anglo-American Psychiatry in Historical Perspective (London: Routledge, 1989).

20   On the treatment of masturbators in the nineteenth century see Arthur N. Gilbert, "Doctor, Patient, and Onanist Diseases in the Nineteenth Century," Journal of the History of Medicine and Allied Sciences 30 (1975): 217-234; Robert H. MacDonald, "The Frightful Consequences of Onanism: Notes on the History of a Delusion," Journal of the History of Ideas 28 (1967): 423-431; J. Stengers & A. Van Neck, Histoire d'une grand peur: La masturbation (Brussels: University of Brussels Press, 1984); Tristram Engelhardt, "The Disease of Masturbation: Values and Concept of Disease," Bulletin of the History of Medicine 48 (1974): 234-248.

21   See Lesley A. Hall, "Medical Attitudes to the Sexual Disorders of the 'Normal' Male in Britain, 1900-1950" (Ph.D. diss., University of London, 1990); Ruth Hall, Marie Stopes: A Biography (London: Deutsch, 1977); E. M. Holtzman, "The Pursuit of Married Love: Women's Attitudes towards Sexuality in Great Britain, 1918-39," Journal of Social History 16 (1982): 39-51.

22   Davenport Hines, Sex, Death and Punishment, chs. 5 and 8.

23   See for instance Lynne Nead, Myths of Sexuality: Representations of Women in Victorian Britain (Oxford: Basil Blackwell, 1988); Leonore Davidoff and Catherine Hall, Family Fortunes: Men and Women of the English Middle Class, 1780-1850 (Chicago: University of Chicago Press,

1987). It is moreover highly question-begging for Foucault to aver that the hysterization of women rendered them sexually supersaturated.

24   Excellent recent discussions include Donna Andrews, *Philanthropy and Police* (Princeton: Princeton University Press, 1990), and T. C. Curtis and W. R. Speck, "The Societies for the Reformation of Manners," *Literature and History* 3 (1976): 45-64.

25   For a discussion, see Edward Bristow, *Vice and Vigilance: Purity Movements in Britain Since 1700* (Dublin: Gill & Macmillan, 1977).

26   Michel Foucault, *Histoire de la folie à l'âge classique* (Paris: Gallimard, 1972); trans. *Madness and Civilization: A History of Insanity in the Age of Reason* (New York: Random House, 1973).

27   See the admirable discussion in Alan Sheridan, *Michael Foucault: The Will to Truth* (London: Tavistock, 1980).

28   For Enlightenment sexual liberalism, see Peter Gay, *The Enlightenment: An Interpretation*. Vol 1, *The Rise of Modern Paganism* (London: Weidenfeld & Nicolson, 1967); Vol. 2, *The Science of Freedom* (London: Weidenfeld & Nicolson, 1969); Theodore Tarczylo, *Sexe et liberté au siècle des lumières* (Paris: Presses de la Renaissance, 1983); G. S. Rousseau & Roy Porter, eds., *Sexual Underworlds of the Enlightenment* (Manchester: Manchester University Press, 1987); Paul-Gabriel Boucé, "Aspects of Sexual Tolerance and Intolerance in Eighteenth Century England," *British Journal for Eighteenth Century Studies* 3 (1980): 173-8; Peter Wagner, *Eros Revived: Erotica in the Age of Enlightenment* (London: Secker & Warburg, 1988). For sodomites, see A. D. Harvey, "Prosecutions for Sodomy in England at the Beginning of the Nineteenth Century," *Historical Journal* 21 (1978): 939-948; for a sober account of Victorian sexual surgery, see Ornella Moscucci, *The Science of Woman* (Cambridge: Cambridge University Press, 1990).

29   For marriage in the earlier period see Jean-Louis Flandrin, *Families in Former Times: Kinship, Household and Sexuality*, trans. Richard Southern (Cambridge: Cambridge University Press, 1976); for more recent times, see John D'Emilio and Estelle B. Freedman, *Intimate Matters. A History of Sexuality in America* (New York: Harper and Row, 1988).

30   Syphilis is central to Davenport Hines's story, doubtless because of the analogue with AIDS.

31   Michel Foucault, *Histoire de la sexualité*, Vol. 2. *L'usage des plaisirs* (Paris: Gallimard, 1984); trans. Robert Hurley, *The Use of Pleasure* (New York: Random House, 1985); compare A. Rousselle, *Porneia* (Oxford: Basil Blackwell, 1989).

32   Michel Foucault, *Histoire de la sexualité*, Vol.3. *Le souci de soi* (Paris: Gallimard, 1984); trans. Robert Hurley, *The Care of the Self* (New York: Random House, 1987).

33   Peter Brown, *The Body and Society: Men, Women and Sexual Renunciation in Early Christianity* (London: Faber, 1989); Jean Delumeau, *Sin and Fear: The Emergence of a Western Guilt Culture, 13th-18th Centuries* (New York: St. Martin's Press, 1990); Sander Gilman, *Sexuality* (New York: Wiley, 1989).

34   See Delumeau, cited in ref. 67.

35   F. Barker, *The Tremulous Private Body* (London: Methuen, 1984). See also David Vincent, "Love and Death and the Nineteenth Century Working Class," *Social History* 5 (1980): 223-247, for parallel lower class sexual reticence.

36   For instance, into the twentieth century the *British Medical Journal* was still refusing to permit the advertisement of contraceptives. See Peter Bartrip, *Mirror of Medicine: The BMJ 1840-1990* (Oxford: Clarendon Press, 1990).

37   For a sample of recent works see Elizabeth Abel, *Virginia Woolf and the Fictions of Psychoanalysis* (Chicago: University of Chicago Press, 1989); Louise A. DeSalvo, *Virginia Woolf: The Impact of Childhood Sexual Abuse on her Life and Work* (Boston: Beacon Press, 1989); Ruth Brandon, *The New Women and the Old Men* (London: Secker and Warburg, 1990); Joan Jacobs Brumberg, *Fasting Girls: The Emergence of Anorexia Nervosa as a Modern Disease* (Cambridge: Harvard University Press, 1989); Donna Haraway, *Primate Visions: Gender, Race and Nature in the World of Modern Science* (New York and London: Routledge, 1990); Sheila Jeffreys, *Anti-Climax* (London: The Women's Press, 1990); Ludmilla Jordanova, *Sexual Visions: Images of Gender in Science and Medicine between the Eighteenth and Twentieth Centuries* (London: Harvester Wheatsheaf, 1989); Jeffrey Moussaieff Masson, *A Dark Science: Women, Sexuality, and Psychiatry in the Nineteenth Century* (New York: Farrar, Straus and Giroux, 1986); Lynne Nead, *Myths of Sexuality: Representations of Women in Victorian Britain* (Oxford: Basil Blackwell, 1988); Cynthia Eagle Russett, *Sexual Science: The Victorian Construction of Womanhood* (Cambridge: Harvard University Press, 1989); Londa Schiebinger, *The Mind Has No Sex? Women in the Origins of Modern Science* (Cambridge: Harvard University Press, 1989); Elaine Showalter, *The Female Malady: Women, Madness and English Culture 1830-1980* (London: Virago, 1987).

SEXUALITY AND DISCOURSE:

A RESPONSE TO ROY PORTER ON FOUCAULT

MARK POSTER

Roy Porter's essay, "Is Foucault Helpful for Understanding Eighteenth and Nineteenth Century Sexuality," is really about sexuality today. It poses the important and difficult political question about sexuality. If Foucault is right that sexuality was not repressed in the Victorian era but actually intensified and multiplied in the sense that the *discourse* on sexuality greatly expanded in that epoch, then (1) does not Foucault collapse the distinction between discourse and practice, ideas and behavior; (2) what is to be made of our strong sense of the squeamishness of Victorians about sex, their unsexuality; and (3) is it not clear that what may be called "the sexual liberation movement" has resulted in a change from a sex-negative attitude to a sex positive attitude, from an embarrassed, guilt-ridden minimal sexuality to a greater uninhibited, passionate sexuality? Porter is raising the troubling question that if one accepts Foucault's position on sexuality one gives up the seemingly emancipatory elements of the Freudo-Marxian or Reichian position. One loses the critical value of the norm of "healthy" sexuality, replacing it with an acritical analysis of different regimes of sexual discourse each of which contains elements of domination.

I admit to having been a Freudo-Marxist/Reichian/Fourierist. In courses on the history of sexuality and in writings on the subject[1] in the

1970s I enthusiastically supported the elimination of restrictions on sexual repression, agreeing with Freud in *Civilization and Its Discontents* that the Victorian era was the high water mark of sexual repression. A committed New Leftist, I regarded the critique of sexual repression as essential to the feminist movement, gay and lesbian rights, and part of the broad attack on bourgeois capitalist society in its various manifestations and nefarious elaborations. Capitalism was the denial of love, eroticism, sexuality in favor of an oppressive culture of instrumental reason.

Then I read Foucault's work of the 1970s — first *Discipline and Punish*, then *The History of Sexuality, volume 1*. I began to see that my New Left position left in place many aspects of white, male culture, even reinforcing them, that my supposed critical, emancipatory position did not go far enough. My earlier stance preserved aspects of bourgeois culture that I thought I had ruthlessly critiqued. Most notably the Freudo-Marxist critique of sexual repression reproduced a split between the subject and the object, between the autonomous rational theorist/historian/critic and the field of analysis. A binary opposition persisted in my New Leftism between the mind as rational agent and the body as object of pleasure. It conserved as well the understanding of emancipation as a lifting of oppressions, an unchaining, one that left as its freed residue a whole human being who had been there all along. In principle Victorians were as capable as we enlightened New Leftists of great sex if only they could tear away the veils of mystification, change the associated laws, they too, women and men alike, could enjoy the pleasures of the body. Yet both of these assumptions, the subject/object split and the view of emancipation as an unchaining also contained a deeper assumption that is the hallmark of Enlightenment critique: that humans are in essence and always individual rational agents who are also able instrumentally to deploy their bodies in sexually pleasureful acts. The fact that this position, this mode of constituting of the subject, was developed in discourses by white men especially in the midst of the movement of Enlightenment in the eighteenth century, a movement that excluded the voices of women and non-whites in an emerging free space or public sphere[2] — all of this began to trouble me a great deal.

Foucault's move to a model of discourse/practice has the advantage of disrupting the reproduction in discourse of the white male subject, centered and essentialized in reason, convinced that freedom means removing obstacles to an already fixed self. Foucault's critique of the repressive hypothesis is not intended as a simple reversal of the Freudo-

Marxist position, as Porter unfortunately assumes. Foucault does not, like Peter Gay, substitute sexy for uptight Victorians, a truly horrific mistake. What he argues is that practices of sexuality are in good part produced through articulated forms of language. Since human beings experience the world through the mediation of language their experience cannot be divorced from their formulations about it. While this position can lead to linguistic reductionism, it need not do so and Foucault makes every effort to avoid that unproductive intellectual strategy. He argues instead that sexuality is not simply a question of plus or minus, absence or presence, with the Victorians suffering an absence and we enjoying/struggling for a presence. Even though he refutes the repressive hypothesis he does not put in its place a picture of Victorian "free" sex, Henry Miller instead of Dr. William Acton. He depicts Victorian sexuality as dominated by four types of discourse ("the hysterization of women's bodies," "the pedagogization of children's sex," "the socialization of procreative behavior," and "the psychiatrization of perverse pleasure"), hardly a hedonist heaven.

The theme of discourse/practice, which I think Porter does not really grasp, decenters the definition of sexuality from its white male confine. It allows the development of critical discourses on sexuality from outside, from the Other of the enlightenment.[3] The Freudo-Marxist repressive hypothesis reproduces sexuality as a male gaze toward a woman/object. It presumes a movement of liberation as a telos of history in which a "natural" body emerges from the mystifying robes of Victorian prudery. And the body that appears naked and sensual is the woman's. In this way Foucault encourages a history of sexuality that is outside the metanarrative of repression/liberation, but remains nonetheless critical of the various configurations of discourse/practice that have emerged and disappeared in time. It allows us to see the historical drama of sexuality in relation to a politics of a new discursive regime, one that would promote a multiplicity of sexual practices/discourses each of which would remain an imposition, a constituting of sexuality but would escape the specific "technology of power" or "micropolitics" of Victorian modernity.

Porter concedes that he is ignorant of Foucault's intellectual impulses. He admits "I do not pretend to be offering an analysis of all aspects of Foucault's thinking on sexuality. I will make no effort to situate Foucault's writings on sex in context of the wider development of his thought or the intellectual currents of the 1970s; nor shall I attempt an assessment of the project's theoretical coherence." (p. 1) With this disarming confession, Porter goes on systematically to misconstrue Foucault's position on sex precisely by misunderstanding "the project's theoretical coherence." His humble admission of ignorance about "the intellectual currents of the 1970s" does not prevent him from making rather firm conclusions about its merits: ". . . because of [Foucault's] post-structuralist affectation of the death of the author and the sovereignty of texts and discourse, he is driven into his bizarre refusal to treat sexual discourse as ideology, typically recruited into the service of coercive power." (p. 25) Porter here thinks he knows enough about poststructuralism to conclude that its critique of the authorial function is an "affectation" but not enough to refute through argument, or apparently even to be aware of, Foucault's careful and to me convincing critique of the concept of ideology.

Porter concludes that Foucault's work "denies" "the class and gender dynamics of public sexuality." (p. 26) Frankly and sadly I think the left is in deep trouble at present because of the lazy ignorance of these kinds of statements. Porter doesn't take the trouble to learn about "the intellectual currents of the 1970s" that he easily condemns. But he feels defensive and threatened by them, that somehow they endanger the politics of class and gender. I see in Porter's critique of Foucault a symptom of the failure of left theory to come to grips with intellectual, cultural and social changes of recent decades. Foucault's critique of Marxism may be taken as a threat from outside, as Porter does, refusing to work to understand the critique, or as a new direction of critical thinking, one that may or may not prove incompatible with working class politics however that is currently understood. As long as the left responds to work like Foucault's in Porter's manner (and Perry Anderson's *In The Tracks of Historical Materialism*[4] is not less defensive), the left is hiding, ostrich-like, within its theoretical framework even as the world moves on to new forms of domination and new systems of control.

In the short space of a reply I cannot fully elaborate a Foucauldian treatise on the history of sexuality.[5] I wish only to point to the egregious misreading effected by Porter of Foucault's discussion of Victorian sexual discourse. Porter whips himself into no little frenzy when presenting Foucault's understanding of such discourse. He quotes Foucault's determination of a "constant optimization and an increasing valorization of the discourse on sex" (p. 13), misreading it as "his sublimely meliorist vision." If anything, of course, Foucault's text reads inversely as a pessimism over the increasing discourse/practice of sexuality that culminates in Freudian therapy, the ultimate discourse of the "truth" about sex. But Porter goes on misconstruing Foucault. He seems to think that Foucault applauds Victorian discourses on sexuality as found in psychiatry, medicine, criminology, etc. Yet Foucault was closely associated with intellectual leaders of the anti-psychiatry movement in France (Félix Guattari and Giles Deleuze) and wrote two books, *Madness and Civilization* and *The Birth of the Clinic*, as critiques of medicine broadly conceived. What is more, Porter seems to think that Foucault or his method prevents one from opposing the cruel treatment of gays, children who masturbate, all forms of sexual gratification at odds with Victorian sensibility. But of course Foucault himself was gay, died of aids, and, no doubt, masturbated as a child. Porter's capacity for miscomprehension is startling. His hysterical defense of victims of sexual restraints is totally misplaced. The object of Foucault's strategy on sexuality is precisely to broaden the basis of a critique of Victorian sexuality to include not only the punishments, persecutions, sequestrations, and violence against those determined to be "perverts" but also the play of power in language configurations, even those by the self-proclaimed enlightened ones, that extend the manipulating and shaping of sexuality to the level of subject constitution.

The *History of Sexuality, Volumes 1, 2 and 3* are a prehistory of a deployment of sexuality as we currently face it, in a culture which ostensibly revels in sexuality, whose discourses on it are ubiquitous in the field of everyday life, yet whose realization of tender, affirmative contacts between human beings are at best problematic. Foucault did not celebrate Victorian sexuality in any sense. Rather he sought a more comprehensive basis for its critique. Near the end of *The History of Sexuality, Volume 1* he wrote: "It is the agency of sex that we must break away from, if we aim — through a tactical reversal of the various mechanisms of sexuality — to counter the grips of power with the claims of bodies, pleasures, and knowledges, in their multiplicity and their possibility of resistance. The rallying point for the counterattack against the deployment of sexuality ought not to be sex-desire, but bodies and pleasures." (p. 157) In light of this passage, the real question posed by Porter's essay is why a well-intentioned Freudo-Marxist would so confound a reading of Foucault as to turn him into an enemy of sexual pleasure? And more importantly, why is it that Porter's view of Foucault is all too typical of many similarly inclined writers on gender and class? I pose this question for these people to urge them a moment of self-reflection.

NOTES

1   See especially *Critical Theory of the Family* (New York: Continuum, 1978).

2   Joan Landes, *Women and the Public Sphere* (Ithaca: Cornell University Press, 1988).

3   For a feminist use and critique of Foucault see Teresa de Lauretis, *Technologies of Gender* (Bloomington: Indiana University Press, 1987).

4   (Chicago: University of Chicago Press, 1983).

5   For a longer treatment of these themes see my *Foucault, Marxism and History* (New York: Blackwell, 1984), Ch. 5.

B. Freud, Sexuality, and Repressed Memory

THE ASSAULT ON JEFFREY MASSON

ROY PORTER

BOOKS MENTIONED IN THIS PAPER INCLUDE:

JEFFREY M. MASSON, *THE ASSAULT ON TRUTH:
FREUD'S SUPPRESSION OF THE SEDUCTION THEORY*
(New York: Farrar, Straus and Giroux, 1983; London: Faber
and Faber, 1984); *idem, A DARK SCIENCE: WOMEN,
SEXUALITY AND PSYCHIATRY IN THE NINETEENTH
CENTURY* (New York: Farrar, Straus and Giroux, 1986); *idem,
AGAINST THERAPY. WARNING: PSYCHOTHERAPY MAY
BE HAZARDOUS TO YOUR HEALTH* (London: Collins,
1989); *idem, FINAL ANALYSIS: THE MAKING AND
UNMAKING OF A PSYCHOANALYST* (London: Harper
Collins, 1991).

PAUL ROBINSON, *FREUD AND HIS CRITICS*
(Berkeley/Los Angeles/Oxford: University of California Press,
1993).

JOHN FORRESTER AND LISA APPIGNANESI, *FREUD'S
WOMEN* (London: Weidenfeld and Nicolson; New York: Basic
Books, 1992).

Nobody in the entire history of psychoanalysis, since Freud himself, has felt so misunderstood and maltreated as Jeffrey Masson. He gives

off a tormented sense of identification with the lost leader — consciously or not, Masson has portrayed himself as fulfilling the abandoned mission of his erstwhile idol; and this is hardly surprising, for the parallels are numerous. Similarities of self-image abound — both have entertained noble visions of their crusade against benightedness and bigotry. And they have shared a common rhetoric. Each has presented himself as a daring intellectual radical, a rebellious young Turk, iconoclastic and heretical, a dauntless upholder of truth, championing honesty and integrity in a world of falsehood and shabby compromise — Masson in particular has thundered with righteous indignation.[1] And each in his way has paraded as the protector of the disadvantaged and victimized, while arguably producing theories that demean those they would defend. It is not my intention here further to labor the resemblances between Freud and Masson; I allude to them merely to draw attention to a key aspect of Masson's work: like Freud, Masson is a master of self-dramatization, using rhetorical flair to inject objective issues with subjective urgency. In consequence, his impact has exceeded, or at least spread far beyond, the academic crux of his work. Masson has not merely made contributions to scholarship; he has created new climates of opinion and helped draw battle lines. His histrionic flair, his sense of destiny, have also provoked a backlash that may ironically distract attention from the theories he has fostered.[2]

MASSON'S RECEPTION

From the early 1980s, Jeffrey Masson has claimed in a string of publications that psychoanalysis, indeed psychotherapy as a whole, is founded upon bad faith — initially Freud's, and latterly that of the psychoanalytic establishment.[3] A budding Sanskrit professor who had retrained as a Freudian analyst, Masson became in the 1970s a favored son within influential North American psychoanalytical circles. He won the blessing and sponsorship of Kurt Eissler, director of the Freud Archives; Eissler soon designated him his heir apparent and appointed him projects director to the Archives, entrusting him with publication of the authorized edition of the sensitive Freud-Fliess correspondence.[4] At a meeting of the Western New England Psychoanalytic Society in 1981, however, Masson delivered a devastating paper, expounding iconoclastic theories about the origins of Freud's psychoanalytical doctrines. In the ensuing hubbub,

Masson displayed great aplomb as a publicist: The *New York Times* printed two articles detailing his views and ran an interview. The stunned Eissler fired him, and Masson retaliated with million-dollar writs, quickly becoming news, even notorious. In 1983, Janet Malcolm published in *The New Yorker* two lengthy features about the Masson affair, soon to be issued in book form as *In the Freud Archives*. Meantime, Masson remained engulfed in tortuous infighting with the psychoanalytic establishment, which, according to his autobiographical *Final Analysis: The Making and Unmaking of a Psychoanalyst* (1991), had no stomach for the historical truth about Freud, being concerned to protect comforting myths and avoid rocking the boat.[5]

Masson was thus in the throes of personal transformation, conversion even. At the same time, after reaching a peak of public favor in the fifties and sixties, Freudianism was under fire. The attack came from several fronts: from practitioners sympathetic to the anti-psychiatric crusade, not least Thomas Szasz;[6] from sundry academics and pundits;[7] and, increasingly vocally, from the women's movement. Though feminists like Juliet Mitchell argued that patriarchy should be criticized with the tools of Freudian theory, a militant chorus, including especially Kate Millett, Germaine Greer, and Shulamith Firestone, arose to condemn Freud as an agent of patriarchy, perhaps its most astute apologist:[8] for Millett, Freud was "beyond question the strongest individual counterrevolutionary force in the ideology of sexual politics," while Greer emphasized that "the revolutionary woman must know her enemy."[9]

These circumstances — Masson's apostasy coupled with growing public distrust of psychoanalysis, conspicuously amongst feminists — explain the mixed response prompted by Masson's first work, *The Assault on Truth: Freud's Suppression of the Seduction Theory* (1984), which received outspoken and enduring condemnation from reviewers within the psychoanalytic profession and their sympathizers. "Despite the sound and fury with which it appeared," judged Charles Hanly, *The Assault on Truth* "has come to signify, if not nothing, then very little indeed in the estimation of its reviewers. . . . This review can do little to alter that critical judgement but must agree with it."[10] *The Assault on Truth*, in Jenny Turner's later opinion, "reads as a loopy crochet of wilful misreadings, inept argument, and unconvincing moral bluster, held together only by parricidal spite."[11] Perhaps the most crushing verdict was that delivered by Anthony Storr. Assessing *The Assault on Truth*, "all that it and its author deserve," he commented, "is oblivion."[12]

Commentators have been incensed by Masson's supposed egoism
and self-promotion, and there has been a widespread tendency to conflate
the man and his message, leading to the ready supposition that Masson's
historical claims necessarily lack substance. Of course, implicit faith
should not be vested in Masson's assertions; but it would *prima facie* be
strange if the scholar who, as projects director of the Freud Archive, had
been granted privileged access to Freud's private papers did not possess
exceptional empirical mastery of the records. Nonetheless, numerous
rejoinders have blithely assumed, almost without further ado, that he must
have got his facts wrong or built his conclusions upon nothing but bile and
bluster. In *The Assault on Truth*, Masson noted that Freud's patient, Emma
Eckstein, had undergone severe hemorrhaging after Freud's friend,
Wilhelm Fliess, had bungled the nasal operation Freud had urged; Masson
showed that Freud subsequently gave the patient's bleeding a psychoanalytic interpretation.[13] Reviewing Masson's narrative, Charles Hanly countered, regarding Freud's view: "There is no suggesting that the
post-surgical hemorrhaging was hysterical. Freud says only that 'she saw
how affected I was by' the hemorrhaging."[14] But this is a case of a reviewer
being questionably impatient to dismiss Masson's scholarship. This is what
Freud in fact wrote to Fliess about his patient:

> I know only that she bled out of *longing*. She has always
> been a bleeder, when cutting herself and in similar circum-
> stances; as a child she suffered from severe nosebleeds;
> during the years when she was not yet menstruating, she
> had headaches which were interpreted to her as malingering
> and which in truth had been generated by suggestion; for
> this reason she joyously welcomed her severe menstrual
> bleeding as proof that her illness was genuine, a proof that
> was also recognized as such by others. She described a
> scene from the age of fifteen, in which she suddenly began
> to bleed from the nose when she had the wish to be treated
> by a certain young doctor who was present (and who also
> appeared in the dream). When she saw how affected I was
> by her first haemorrhage while she was in the hands of
> Rosanes, she experienced this as the realization of an old
> wish to be loved in her illness, and in spite of the danger
> during the succeeding hours she felt happy as never before.
> Then, in the sanatorium, she became restless during the

night because of an unconscious wish to entice me to go there; since I did not come during the night, she renewed the bleedings, as an unfailing means of rearousing my affection.[15]

Freud's own words thus all but explicitly identify the bleeding as hysterical. Responses such as Hanly's lend credence to Masson's charge that, while claiming to be a science of truth, psychoanalysis is often weirdly deaf to its discovery. This is seemingly borne out by another statement of Hanly's, which appears to imply that further research into the sources is bound to prove irrelevant to the understanding of psychoanalysis. "In the background," Hanly writes,

> is the question of the Freud archives and access to them. It can now be predicted that nothing of theoretical importance will be found in the archives. It can also be predicted that nothing of consequence will be uncovered concerning the history of the development of psychoanalytic theory and practice. What will be new will only be further information concerning the lives and personalities of the men and women who developed psychoanalysis.[16]

As a historian I cannot understand how it could be thought that "further information concerning the lives and personalities of the men and women who developed psychanalysis" could be regarded as disclosing "nothing of consequence" about "the history of the development of psychoanalytic theory and practice" — unless, of course, that history is axiomatically a kind of gospel story independent of merely human subjectivities.

If Masson has had a rough ride from the psychoanalytic community, he has received a warmer welcome from certain quarters of the women's movement. Self-respecting feminists might be expected to display mixed feelings about being rescued from the clutches of psychoanalysis by a womanizing deliverer who admits to having slept with almost a thousand partners before he was twenty-five; but his credentials as a campaigner against the psychoanalytic and psychotherapeutic abuse of women and children have won Masson a largely sympathetic hearing.[17] His work has notably been championed by Catharine A. MacKinnon, the anti-pornography campaigner.[18] In her preface to Masson's *A Dark Science* (1986), MacKinnon maintained that the psychoanalytic community's antagonism to Masson's writings betrayed its ingrained misogyny. Indeed, she claimed, "the truth about women did not matter to Freud. And neither the truth about women nor the truth about Freud now appears to matter to the Freudians."[19] Masson had been correct, she contended, to attribute Freud's "suppression" of the "seduction theory" in favor of the "fantasy theory" to a telltale flight of fantasy on Freud's part:

> Once one realizes that the abuse is real, it is the doctors' elaborate alibis for the perpetrators, and their fantastic theoretical reconstructions of the victims' accounts, that require the "lively imagination." The fantasy theory is the fantasy.[20]

In short, the Masson debate has proceeded along predictable lines. Till now, his work has fed prejudices more than it has initiated inquiry.

MASSON AND HISTORY

Masson's paradigm switch in reconstruing the history of psycho-analysis falls within a broader interpretative program developed in a series of works published since *The Assault on Truth*. His contention is that psychoanalysis — and, more broadly, all modes of psychiatry and therapy — are instruments of patriarchy deployed for the domination and debase-ment of women: therapy's promise of help is thus a cruel cheat, even an instrument of torture. "For Masson," one reviewer has glossed, "it is no exaggeration to say that psychiatric science is one long exercise in organ-ized medical misogyny."[21] These indictments are most comprehensively set out in *Against Therapy* (1988), where Masson argues that:

> Psychotherapy of any kind is wrong. [Its] structure is such that no matter how kindly a person is, when that person becomes a therapist, he or she is engaged in acts that are bound to diminish the dignity, autonomy, and freedom of the person who comes for help.[22]

The reason for this is that, from early in the nineteenth century, psychiatry had been forged as a quintessential tool of patriarchal exploitation. "From a historical perspective," Masson has recently asserted, "it is clear that Freud was perpetuating a tradition that did not begin with him. Its basic characteristics were that it was male-orientated, ethnocentric, sexist, and rigidly hierarchical."[23] Indulging in scapegoating enabled the mature and brow-beating Freud to escape the need for serious self and social criticism. "By blaming the victim," Masson argues, "Freud was able to unburden the society of any need for reform or deep reflection. Ultimately, Freud reaffirmed the male code, and did little to disturb the sleep of the world. That is why psychoanalysis fits so nicely into hierarchical structures."[24]

Yet, Masson has insisted, there had also been an earlier Freud, who had glimpsed the truth as a young man before rapidly deserting it. Thus, Masson's account of the founder of psychoanalysis is not a simple case of hero worship or Freud-bashing; it rather enshrines a more complex account of the play of truth and falsehood. It is Masson's aim to show that the traditional entrenched telling of the "birth of psychoanalysis" is incorrect, and also to advance a new explication of the motivation prompting Freud's change of mind. From the late 1880s, Freud grew extraordinarily interested in hysteria.[25] He arrived at the view that the women he treated fell sick because they had suffered childhood sexual abuse, generally at their fathers' hands. He later abandoned this seduction theory, contending that the women's "memories" were in truth infantile incestuous fantasies; it was the libidinous desire, followed by its guilty suppression, that triggered the neurosis. Thus hysteria, in Freud's later theories, was an unconscious defence against erotic drives rather than the product of memories of actual events.

Psychoanalysts have always viewed Freud's explanatory switch, involving as it did the "discovery" of the unconscious and of infantile sexuality, as the true birth of their science. Masson counterargues that the earlier seduction theory had been essentially correct — that is to say, based upon clinical evidence. Freud's abandonment of it was not a discovery of the truth but its betrayal. This resulted from bad faith on Freud's part. Freud forsook the seduction theory, Masson contends, partly because it reflected too badly on adult males like himself, and partly because its hostile reception by the Viennese psychiatric community convinced him that continued espousal of the theory would hamper his career. His motives for abandoning the seduction theory were thus discreditable.

Masson's *Assault on Truth* scrutinizes a few years in the 1890s. A brief summary of its arguments will suffice. For approximately four years during the mid-1890s, Freud was of the view that particular sorts of mental illnesses, notably hysteria, derived from early sexual traumas. His hysterical patients, he became convinced, had been subjected to pre-pubescent "seduction" (Freud's term: we would say sexual abuse); repressed mem-

ories of such assaults were the source of the patients' malady. Freud
characteristically identified a parent, standardly the father, as the source
of these childhood molestations, just as a daughter was the typical victim.
Freud first spelt out the seduction theory to Fliess in May 1893, and letters
in subsequent years exhibit his deepening faith in the hypothesis. On April
21, 1896, he publicized his hypothesis in a talk on "The Aetiology of
Hysteria," delivered to the Society for Psychiatry and Neurology in
Vienna; it was published shortly thereafter. The theory was also spelt out
in two other papers of 1896, "Heredity and the Aetiology of the Neuroses"
and "Further Remarks on the Neuro-Psychoses of Defence."

Barely a year later, however, on September 21, 1897, Freud wrote
to Fliess with remarkable tidings: "I no longer believe in my *neurotica*,"
that is, his seduction theory. Freud advanced several grounds for his new
scepticism, notably disbelief as to whether adult male perversion was as
frequent as the seduction theory presupposed:

> The surprise that in all cases, the *father*, not excluding my
> own, had to be accused of being perverse — the realization
> of the unexpected frequency of hysteria, with precisely the
> same conditions prevailing in each, whereas surely such
> widespread perversions against children are not very prob-
> able. The [incidence of] perversion would have to be
> immeasurably more frequent than the [resulting] hysteria
> because the illness, after all, occurs only where there has
> been an accumulation of events and there is a contributory
> factor that weakens the defense.[26]

Though privately abandoning the seduction theory, Freud did not publicly
concede his change of mind until eight years later, in the *Three Essays on
the Theory of Sexuality* (1905), and then only in rather equivocal terms.
He had reached the conclusion that his patients' accounts of seduction
typically began in fantasies: their footing lay not in the perverse deeds of
adults but in the instinctive sexual yearnings of infants. The casting aside
of the seduction theory thus facilitated the emergence of the hypothesis of
infantile sexuality, and in particular the notion of the Oedipus complex —
first mentioned in a letter to Fliess of October 15, 1897, a few weeks after
Freud first divulged his disowning of the seduction theory. The new role
attributed to fantasy magnified the significance of the unconscious in
Freud's conception of the life of the psyche. Those twin pillars of mature
psychoanalytic theory — the unconscious and infantile sexuality — thus

came into focus as a result of the opinion-shift Freud revealed in his September letter. Indeed, in later accounts of his intellectual growth, Freud and his biographers were to claim that had the error of the seduction theory not been recognized, had the theory itself not been abjured, psychoanalysis would never have been born. Freud would instead have remained marooned in erroneous environmentalist accounts of psychological development and would have failed to grasp the role of innate desire and the unconscious in psychic life.

Masson stands this conventional interpretation on its head. *The Assault on Truth* argues that Freud's original view was correct; his abandonment of the seduction theory was an error — not just a blameless blunder but a betrayal of the truth — and equally a betrayal of his patients. Yet it is at this point that Masson's case loses its plausibility. It is perfectly reasonable for Masson to lock horns with the conventional version, which holds that the shift from the seduction theory to the fantasy theory was an abandonment of error that requires no more explaining than the self-evident superiority of truth: truth is great and will prevail. After all, it has now become widely accepted amongst historians and sociologists of science that there must be symmetry in explanatory strategies: espousal of truth needs explanation no less than attachment to error.[27] Far from clear, however, are the grounds upon which Masson can be so positive of the disreputable motives for Freud's change of mind. Rock solid evidence is wanting. There is no documentation that decisively resolves the empirical question. No daily clinical records or case notes survive for the score or so neurosis cases mentioned in "The Aetiology of Hysteria" that initially fueled Freud's conviction and subsequently became the basis of his misgivings. And, in the absence of intimate private diaries and memoranda, how would one penetrate beyond Freud's former conviction that the tales he extracted from his patients were true and his later assurance that they were false?[28] With scanty evidence at our disposal, the question must be one of interpretation on the basis of a balance of probabilities. Masson's historical claim seems to assume that unambiguous events passed between Freud and his patients, and definite thoughts passed through Freud's mind; that these are available to fairly unproblematic historical recovery; and that he, Masson, holds the key.

In reality, things are more complicated and Masson's case cannot be substantiated; neither, however, should it be dismissed out of hand. There is every reason to suppose that the traditional accounts of Freud's leap into truth are no more, and perhaps a good deal less, satisfactory than

Masson's portrayal of his "suppression of truth." Something far more enigmatic was afoot. The evidence is fragmentary, the arguments highly intricate; it is unnecessary to rehearse them here, especially since they have recently been scrupulously evaluated in meticulous detail by Israëls and Schatzman.[29] Speaking simply, we cannot say with certitude for precisely which reasons Freud retracted the seduction theory and proposed the fantasy theory of hysteria's aetiology. The notion that moral cowardice or a failure of courage underlay the switch must, nonetheless, be profoundly implausible, since the fantasy theory, positing as it did infantile and childhood sexuality, would surely have appeared to Freud's elders and betters not a whit less scientifically rash and morally repugnant than the speculation it was superseding, that of the seducing or child-abusing father.[30] Hence, if Freud were conniving and careerist, such a move would have been out of the frying pan into the fire.

The case painstakingly expounded by Israëls and Schatzman carries greater plausibility. Freud was forced to the conclusion, they contend, that the conduct of analyses on the basis of the seduction theory had turned out to be therapeutically barren. Therapeutic failure presumably brought it home to him that the seduction theory had been but a daring supposition on his part, presumably suggested by the analyst to his patients rather than a truth they had spontaneously divulged loud and clear.[31] And so, in retreating from the theory, Freud did not so much suppress a truth as sensibly switch hypotheses when his first hunch seemed to be becoming disconfirmed.

Hence, it is unnecessary to posit shady personal and autobiographical reasons as to why Freud formulated the fantasy theory. In truth, he was growing more interested throughout this period, for numerous reasons and in a variety of ways, in exploring experiences of imagination, dreams, and fantasy.[32] He embarked upon extensive studies of the fairy-tale components of consciousness and became engrossed with daydreaming, with illusions and if-only's, with fabled ancestries and mythic destinies, with his patients' romances of illegitimacy and parental death — in short, with a multitude of often-masked or forbidden musings that grabbed the attention and informed desire. Freud began to argue that "wish fulfilment must meet the requirements of this unconscious defence."[33] Increasingly, on the basis of various inquiries, he took the view that fantasy and fiction were no less active than fact in producing symptoms. In this emergent theory, the three key components were memory fragments, impulses, and protective fictions. Fantasies ("unconscious fictions") serving as substitutes for memories began to assume in Freud's thinking the potential for explaining pathological defence. In short, in 1897 Freud found diverse preoccupations concatenating, in particular dream and fantasy analysis, and the salience of motive in symptom-formation: "Remembering is never a motive but only a way, a method. The first motive for the formation of symptoms is, chronologically, libido. Thus symptoms, like dreams, are the fulfilment of a wish."[34]

For Freud, therefore, it had become plausible to conceive of the language of seduction and the contents of fantasy as intimately entangled:

> Where does the material for creating the [family] romance
> — adultery, illegitimate child, and the like — come from?
> Usually from the lower social circles of servant girls. Such
> things are so common among them that one is never at a
> loss for material, and it is especially apt to occur if the
> seductress was a person in service. In all analyses one
> therefore hears the same story twice: once as a fantasy about
> the mother; the second time as a real memory of the maid.[35]

Thus, Freud's ripening intellectual preoccupations — rather than some personal crisis or opportunist leap — led him to grow absorbed in what he began to perceive as his patients' fantasies.

It is also worth keeping in mind, against Masson, that Freud never blatantly denied the reality of the seduction or abuse of children by adult figures. As Israëls and Schatzman have noted, it was simply the case that notions of childhood sexuality, fantasy, and repression were to attain prime significance within the structure of his theories.[36] "The charge that Freud abandoned the seduction theory (which, Masson implies, was right all along) is spurious," comments Sander Gilman "since he continued for most of the rest of his career to make a distinction between incestuous seductions and universal fantasies about such seductions. Freud does not discount the importance of actual molestation, but such cases were of secondary interest to him, since the main direction of his thought is away from a limited set of specific instances (in line with the positivistic science of his day) toward the universals of human behavior, a movement away from the pathological towards the normal."[37]

LASTING SIGNIFICANCE

There is nowadays a tendency to be dismissive of Masson's work. He has been widely accused of committing those very offenses with which he charges Freud. *Against Therapy* has been criticized for its "specious reasoning,"[38] and it has been supposed that Masson (like Masson's Freud) prefers rhetoric to veracity. Masson claimed Freud suppressed the seduction theory. With a *tu quoque*, a reviewer has responded that Masson "suppresses for his readers the fact of Freud's continued recognition of the sexual seduction of children."[39]

There are understandable reasons for this disdain. Masson is readily caricatured as a self-regarding and self-serving charlatan — the image projected by Janet Malcolm's waspish account of Masson as *enfant terrible* in *In The Freud Archives* (her book, *Psychoanalysis: The Impossible Profession*, 1982, had shown her to be no great admirer of orthodox psychoanalysis either). Masson appears to invite such readings. In his autobiographical *Final Analysis* (1991), he has chosen to expose himself chiefly in the comic mode — as a naive psychoanalytic acolyte in what proved to be a nest of vipers, a trusting Candide-like chap, all guileless candor, who for many years, out of innocence or natural benevolence, took psychoanalytic sucker punches on the chin.[40] He recollects (his recall is uncanny) being on the receiving end of daily verbal abuse from his Toronto analyst, Dr. Schiffer, who branded him a "filthy Nazi." "By the way, your wife's intelligence is not natural," Schiffer would tell him as he lay on the couch:

> "In fact, I find it disgusting. Because I know what it is really all about. And so does every other normal woman. Normal women don't want to be with your wife. They can't stand her. And you know why? Because they can tell that she is using her brain like a penis. Her mind is so developed because she is so filled with penis envy. She is so desperate for a penis that she has created one in her head. Her brain. Her huge brain is nothing but a substitute for her desire for a huge penis. Your wife has a cock for a brain, Masson, and you're getting fucked." He chortled in delight.[41]

Masson the analysand would meekly accept it, being "still very much under the influence of my own idealizing transference to Schiffer. . . . I maintained till almost the very end that he was a kind of genius."[42] Yet even he would take only so much. Finally, more sinned against than sinning, the worm turned, and he decided to break with the psychoanalytic Revelation, believing it was time to come clean and tell all.

Since he seemingly incriminates himself out of his own mouth, it has been easy not to take Masson seriously, on the supposition that he is little more than an intellectual buffoon whose work affords more showmanship than scholarship. Masson's reputation may decline still further as feminists perceive that the critique of psychoanalysis requires more sophisticated theoretical grounding, and if recognition grows that the so-called epidemic of child abuse may be a more enigmatic phenomenon than first met the eye.[43]

It would be unfortunate, however, if Masson's work were joked or jeered off the stage. For his work, and the controversy surrounding it, have stimulated a crucial awareness of how far our received "historical" account of Freud is not history at all, but an uncritical mishmash of memoir, memory, myth of origin, and psychoanalytic doctrine, chronologically laid out in convenient legendary mode.

What is essential is that, as research progresses, polemical and partisan altercations about Freud — lover of truth or its traducer? — should be transcended. It is vital that we acquire a more solid grasp of the formation of his opinions — not just in the 1890s (till now the overwhelming focus of attention) but throughout his long career. It is time for new research to set Freud more securely in context of the broader psychological and psychiatric speculations of colleagues, dissidents, and diverse schools, time that Freud ceases to be portrayed as the *fons et origo* of psychoanalytical science — or the spring of psychoanalytical poison! For far too long, Freud has been taken at his own evaluation, as the "only begetter" of the science he is still sometimes seen as having fathered through his self-analysis.[44] It is time to attend to wider terrains of obsessions and omissions in Freud's writings.[45]

Not least, serious examination is needed of what was lost from explorations of the psyche as a result of Freud's growing and overpowering urge to explain the economy of human consciousness and behavior in terms of inner, indeed infantile, events. Such a commitment entailed in Freud and his followers a mode of individualistic reductionism that blotted out and mystified wider cultural and socio-political domains. The stifling of politics by psychoanalysis dates right back to Freud himself. On this blind spot or suppression in Freud, Eugene W. Holland has recently had judicious

words to say. The 1950s were to witness, Holland notes, two attempts —
by Herbert Marcuse in *Eros and Civilization* and Norman O. Brown in *Life
Against Death* — to recover the political dimensions of psychoanalytic
theory, the politics of neurosis. That effort came to little, however, and the
restoration of the politics of Freud's work remains a desideratum.[46] As
Holland has observed, given Masson's intense concern with feminist
politics and child abuse, it would have been more helpful if, instead of
concentrating on conspiracies, censorship, and the problem of Freud's
integrity, he had directed attention to the tendency prominent throughout
Freud's mature work to turn psychoanalytic theory away from the actual
socio-political determinants of psychic life within family and community
and towards purely internal, universal elements. In Freudian theory, the
interpersonal dynamics of family and society are programmatically displaced onto infantile fantasy, and their political significance is thereby
dissipated. In this respect — in its preference for moral indictment and its
failure to repoliticize Freud — Masson's work perhaps represents a missed
opportunity. One hopes it will at least prove a halting step forward.

NOTES

1   On the projection of Freud as moral hero, there is a valuable
discussion in Kevin Piver, "Philip Rieff; or, the Critic of Psychoanalysis
as Cultural Theorist," in Mark Micale and Roy Porter, eds., *Discovering
the History of Psychiatry* (New York: Oxford University Press, 1994), pp.
191-215.
2   Many of these and the following points have been made more fully
and eloquently in Paul Robinson's elegant and erudite *Freud and his
Critics* (Berkeley/Los Angeles/Oxford: University of California Press,
1993). I was pleased to find many of my inchoate impressions luminously
developed by Robinson. It is important to note that other scholars have
advanced views on psychiatric abuse similar to those adduced by Masson,
without winning or soliciting equal publicity fanfares; see, for instance,
Alice Miller, *For Your Own Good: Hidden Cruelty in Child-Rearing and
the Roots of Violence* (London: Faber and Faber, 1983).

3   There are now many accounts of Masson's mission. The most witty, if scabrous, is Janet Malcolm, *In the Freud Archives* (New York: Knopf, 1984). Masson sued Malcolm for malicious misrepresentation. In 1993 he won his case, but the jury could not agree on damages. A judge then ruled that the whole case must be retried.

4   This appeared as Jeffrey M. Masson, ed., *The Complete Letters of Sigmund Freud to Wilhelm Fliess, 1887-1904* (Cambridge, MA: Harvard University Press, 1986).

5   The relevant works that explicate Masson's indictment against Freud, against psychoanalysis, and against therapy in general, are: Jeffrey M. Masson, *The Assault on Truth: Freud's Suppression of the Seduction Theory* (New York: Farrar, Straus and Giroux, 1983; London: Faber and Faber, 1984); *idem, A Dark Science: Women, Sexuality and Psychiatry in the Nineteenth Century* (New York: Farrar, Straus and Giroux, 1986); *idem, Against Therapy: Warning: Psychotherapy May Be Hazardous to your Health* (London: Collins, 1989); *idem, Final Analysis: The Making and Unmaking of a Psychoanalyst* (London: Harper Collins, 1991).

6   Thomas S. Szasz, *The Myth of Mental Illness: Foundations of a Theory of Personal Conduct* (New York: Paladin, 1961; London: Granada, 1972; rev. ed., New York: Harper and Row, 1974); see Richard Vatz and Lee Weinberg, "The Rhetorical Paradigm in Psychiatric History: Thomas Szasz and the Myth of Mental Illness," in Micale and Porter, *History of Psychiatry*, pp. 311-30.

7   For instance: E. Gellner, *The Psychoanalytic Movement* (London: Paladin, 1985); H. J. Eysenck, *The Decline and Fall of the Freudian Empire* (Harmondsworth: Viking, 1985); Paul Roazen, *Freud and His Followers* (New York: New York University Press, 1985); for shifting evaluations, see Elisabeth Young-Bruehl, "A History of Freud Biographies," in Micale and Porter, *History of Psychiatry*, pp. 157-73.

8   See Nancy Tomes, "Feminist Histories of Psychiatry," in Micale and Porter, *History of Psychiatry*, pp. 348-483.

9   Kate Millett, *Sexual Politics* (London: Rupert Hart-Davis, 1971), p. 178, quoted in John Forrester and Lisa Appignanesi, *Freud's Women* (London: Weidenfeld and Nicolson; New York: Basic Books, 1992), p. 455; Germaine Greer, *The Female Eunuch* (New York: Bantam Books, 1971), p. 10.

10   Charles Hanly, review of Masson, *The Assault on Truth, The International Journal of Psycho-Analysis* 67 (1986): 517.

11   Jenny Turner, review of Masson, *Final Analysis, New Statesman and Society*, 17 May 1991, 35.

12   Anthony Storr, review of Masson, *The Assault on Truth, New York Times Book Review*, 6 Feb. 1984, 35.

13   Masson, *The Assault on Truth*, 57ff.

14   Hanly, review of Masson, *The Assault on Truth*, 518.

15   Masson, *The Complete Letters*, Freud to Fliess, 4 May 1896, 186. See the balanced discussion in Forrester and Appignanesi, *Freud's Women*, 137.

16   Hanly, review of Masson, *The Assault on Truth*, 519.

17   See Nancy Tomes, "Feminist Histories of Psychiatry," in Micale and Porter, *History of Psychiatry*, pp. 348-483.

18   Catharine A. MacKinnon, Preface to Masson, *A Dark Science*. Regarding this Preface, Mark Micale has written: "A short preface to the book has been supplied by Katharine [sic] A. MacKinnon, author of the well-known work on the sexual harassment of working women. At times, MacKinnon's prosecuting fury is extraordinary. She characterizes nineteenth-century psychiatric practices as 'sexual atrocities' and sees the medical world of the time as 'a chamber of horrors for women,' 'a nightmare.' In the opening paragraph of the book, she likens the ill-treatment of women by doctors in the past to the prosecution of heretics during the Inquisition and the murder of the Jews during the Holocaust." (Mark Micale, review of Masson, *A Dark Science, Partisan Review* 54 [1987]: 487.)

19   MacKinnon, Preface, to Masson, *A Dark Science*, xiii.

20   MacKinnon, "Preface," to Masson, *A Dark Science*, xiv. Like Masson, MacKinnon offers a black-and-white picture in which Freud is an outright villain and women are passive victims. Not only does this view not make plausible history, it hardly offers a hopeful basis for feminism. A far more convincing reading of the complex dialectic of power and knowledge between Freud and his female clients is offered in Forrester and Appignanesi, *Freud's Women*.

21   Micale, review of *A Dark Science, Partisan Review*, 486.

22   Masson, *Against Therapy*, ix.

23   Masson, *Final Analysis*, 208.

24   Masson, *Final Analysis*, 208.

25   For context on *fin-de-siècle* understandings of hysteria and its historiography, see Mark Micale, "Hysteria and its Historiography — a Review of Past and Present Writings," *History of Science* xxvii (1989):

223-261, 319-351; *idem*, "Hysteria and its Historiography: the Future Perspective," *History of Psychiatry*, i, 1 (1990): 33-124; Elaine Showalter, *The Female Malady: Women, Madness, and English Culture, 1830-1980* (New York: Pantheon Press, 1986; London: Virago, 1987); Sander Gilman, Helen King, Roy Porter, George Rousseau and Elaine Showalter, *Hysteria Before Freud* (Berkeley: University of California Press, 1993).

26   Masson, *The Complete Letters*, 264.

27   See Barry Barnes, "Sociological Theories of Scientific Knowledge," in R. C. Olby, G. N. Cantor, J. R. R. Christie, and M. J. S. Hodge, eds., *Companion to the History of Modern Science* (London: Routledge, 1990), pp. 60-76.

28   For some musings upon how to read a scientist's mind, see F. L. Holmes, "The Fine Structure of Scientific Creativity," *History of Science* xix (1981): 60-70; Thomas L. Hankins, "In Defence of Biography: The Use of Biography in the History of Science," *History of Science* xvii (1979): 1-16; Susan Sheets-Pyenson, "New Directions for Scientific Biography: The Case of Sir William Dawson," *History of Science* xxviii (1990): 399-410.

29   Han Israëls and Morton Schatzman, "The Seduction Theory," *History of Psychiatry* iv (1993): 61-94. They list all the other recent scholarship. Israëls and Schatzman particularly show that there is no evidence that Freud's patients ever spontaneously revealed any childhood sexual abuse to him; in so far as they did, they indicate, it was as a result of his own suggestion.

30   As argued by Robinson's *Freud and his Critics*, 115: "Surely, however, the most powerful objection to Masson's thesis of moral cowardice is that Freud abandoned the seduction theory only to embrace an idea that was even more offensive to the prejudices of his culture, the theory of infantile sexuality." See also Peter Gay, *Freud, A Life for Our Time* (London: Dent, 1988), p. 751.

31   This point has also been made by Frank Cioffi, review of Masson, *The Assault on Truth*, *Times Literary Supplement* 6 (July 1984): 463: "Freud gave up the seduction theory because he realised that the theme of seduction had been introduced into the material of the analytic sessions by his own preconceptions. His problem was how to disengage from the theory without at the same time conceding the unreliability of psychoanalytic method."

32   Forrester and Appignanesi, *Freud's Women*, 129ff. The following paragraphs draw heavily on their illuminating account.

33   Masson, *The Complete Letters*, 226.

34   *Ibid.*, 251.

35   *Ibid.*, 317.

36   Israëls and Schatzman, "The Seduction Theory," 27.

37   Sander Gilman, review of Masson, *The Complete Letters*, *London Review of Books*, 20 June 1985, 11. Schatzman acknowledges this orientation in Freud (i.e., a preoccupation with the unconscious world of fantasy) while also recognizing its shortcomings; see Morton Schatzman, *The Story of Ruth: One Woman's Haunting Psychiatric Odyssey* (London: Duckworth, 1980).

38   Glenn Collins, review of Masson, *Against Therapy*, *New York Times Book Review*, 13 Nov. 1988, 20.

39   Hanly, review of Masson, *The Assault on Truth*, 517.

40   Masson presents himself as a bit of a buffoon. His chapter titles in *Final Analysis* include "The Worm Turns."

41   Masson, *Final Analysis*, 75.

42   Masson, *Final Analysis*, 77.

43   Masson has discussed the significance of his work for understanding modern child-abuse cases in *A Dark Science*, p. 4. A sensible case as to why current concern over child sexual abuse should not result in an orgy of Freud-blaming is to be found in Forrester and Appignanesi, *Freud's Women*, 472f., and John Forrester, *The Seductions of Psychoanalysis: Freud, Lacan and Derrida* (Cambridge: Cambridge University Press, 1990), 75f. See also David Healy, *Images of Trauma: From Hysteria to Post-Traumatic Stress Disorder* (London and Boston: Faber and Faber, 1993).

44   One of the great virtues of Frank J. Sulloway's *Freud, Biologist of the Mind: Beyond the Psychoanalytic Legend* (New York: Basic Books, 1979; London: Burnett Books, 1979) lies in its contextualizing of Freud as one of a cohort of thinkers developing new theories of brain/mind and reason/unconscious relations. On new approaches to Freud biography, the two key essays are now Elisabeth Young-Bruehl, "A History of Freud Biographies," in Micale and Porter, *History of Psychiatry*, 157-73; and John Forrester, "A Whole Climate of Opinion: Rewriting the History of Psychoanalysis," in *ibid.*, pp. 174-90.

45   Prospects for a fuller understanding are brightened by the appearance of works adducing new evidence and exploring new issues. One recent example of the former is R. Andrew Paskauskas, *The Complete Correspondence of Sigmund Freud and Ernest Jones, 1908-39* (Cam-

bridge, MA: Harvard University Press, 1993) — these letters provide ample ammunition to those like Masson who believe that psychoanalysis has much to answer for in respect to child abuse and sexual harassment. Jones migrated to Canada after *twice* being accused of indecency with children in the course of his medical duties. An instance of exploring new issues is Sander Gilman's *Freud, Race and Gender* (Princeton: Princeton University Press, 1993) — a work which, while avoiding sensationalism, penetrates into aspects of Freud often judiciously supressed, not least his Jewishness. For the more standard view that race and Jewishness do not form key elements in Freud's thinking, see Peter Gay, *A Godless Jew: Freud, Atheism, and the Making of Psychoanalysis* (New Haven and London: Yale University Press, Cincinnati: Hebrew Union College Press, 1987). For further historically sophisticated readings of Freud, see John Forrester, *Lying on the Couch: Truth, Lies and Psychoanalysis* (Oxford: Blackwell, 1993).

46   See Eugene W. Holland, "The Suppression of Politics in the Establishment of Psychoanalysis," *Salmagundi* 66 (1985): 156. The texts referred to are N. O. Brown, *Life Against Death: The Psychoanalytical Meaning of History* (London: Routledge & Kegan Paul, 1957); and Herbert Marcuse, *Eros and Civilization* (Boston: Beacon, 1966). In a unintentionally revealing comment — meant as a criticism but capable of being taken as a compliment — George H. Allison has remarked about Masson: "His essentially sociological focus is curious, coming from an individual who has had psychoanalytic training." (George H. Allison, *The Psychoanalytic Quarterly* 56 [1987]: 367.) See also, along similar lines, Russell Jacoby, *Social Amnesia: A Critique of Contemporary Psychology from Adler to Laing* (Boston: Beacon Press, 1975).

RESPONSE TO ROY PORTER'S "THE ASSAULT ON JEFFREY MASSON"

JEFFREY MOUSSAIEFF MASSON

What is distressing about Roy Porter's vitriolic review of my books and life is that he seems not to know much about either. He wonders how I can be so positive of the disreputable motives for Freud's change of mind. In fact, my books are not about Freud's motives at all. The little I say about it is pure speculation and labeled as such. I am curious about what led Freud to change his mind, but anything I have to say about that question is not really all that interesting. What is interesting, and what Porter does not address, are the documents discussed in my book which were new and that show, unequivocally, that the standard history on this matter is open to grave objections. *In fact*, there are several letters that Anna Freud did not publish in her first edition of Freud's letters to Fliess which make it crystal clear that for several years Freud was not at all certain that the sexual abuse women reported to him from their childhood was fantasy as opposed to reality. Until these documents are carefully integrated into the history of psychoanalysis we do not have a genuine history. The letters are all included in my edition of *The Complete Letters of Sigmund Freud to Wilhelm Fliess, 1887-1904*, published by Harvard University Press in 1985. (Though analysts clamored for the original texts, once they appeared this book went almost entirely unreviewed.)

We will never know, for certain, exactly why Freud changed his mind. What is certain is that several key documents to this history were kept back from psychoanalytic historians. The greatest part of my book was devoted to resurrecting those documents and attempting to interpret them. I expected further historians to bring to light other documents, and perhaps some that cast doubt on my interpretations. I still expect that to happen one day. But for the moment it has not. Roy Porter brings to light not a single new document, not a single new fact. It is all very disappointing. Surely there must be *some* scholars out there who can tear themselves away, even for a moment, from the preoccupation with how many women I slept with, to do some archival research and come up with something new. I am perfectly prepared to alter my views in light of new findings. Porter writes:

> The notion that moral cowardice or a failure of courage underlay the switch must, nonetheless, be profoundly implausible, since the fantasy theory, positing as it did infantile and childhood sexuality, would surely have appeared to Freud's elders and betters not a whit less scientifically rash and morally repugnant than the speculation it was superseding, that of the seducing or child-abusing father. Hence, if Freud were conniving and careerist, such a move would have been out of the frying-pan into the fire.

In a footnote he indicates that this is the view of Paul Robinson and Peter Gay as well.

But is it true that Freud's theory of childhood sexuality was as unpopular in the profession as his seduction theory had been? Analysts from Peter Gay to Kurt Eissler hold that Freud's *Three Essays on the Theory of Sexuality* (1905), which claimed that children *wished* for sexual contact with adults, that they *fantasized* them, that they were subject to *impulses* over them, in short, that they were the victims of their own sexual imaginations, was received with even more hostility than Freud's original thesis that children were sexually abused. There is nothing *inherently* improbable about this assertion with respect to the response on the part of the Viennese medical community, but the people who make it have done no research to determine whether it is true or not. I had not seen a single positive review of the earlier work, the work which stood by the reality of abuse. I decided to read through the German reviews of the *Three Essays* to see if they were as badly received as has been claimed. In fact, the vast majority of the reviews I saw had something good to say about Freud's book. The shift was well received; 50% approximately were positive.

Often they mentioned, with praise, that Freud had changed from the seduction theory back to the more commonly held views of psychiatry. A. Friedlander, in the *Journal für Psychologie und Neurologie* (10, 1907, pp. 201-213), for example, reviews all of Freud's publications to date. He is pleased, he says, to see Freud accept the view that of major importance is the "general neuropathic disposition" of the patient. In the *Berliner klinische Wochenschrift* (44, 1907, p. 1000), Placzek points out that Freud recognized that his earlier seduction theory was "unscientific." A. Eulenburg, the noted psychiatrist from Berlin, published a positive review of the *Three Essays* in the *Medizinische Klinik* (2, 1906, p. 740).

Speculation about human behavior and belief, however plausible, do not replace scientific inquiry. As Robert Fliess wrote in answer to a famous letter from Freud in 1897, in which Freud said that "it was hardly credible that perverted acts against children were so general": "What place has 'creed' in a science? The frequency of perverted acts against children is a subject for scientific exploration; and if they exceed, as they do, one's naive expectation, that is a fact of no more than quasibiographical value to the explorer" (*Symbol, Dream and Psychosis*, 1973, p. 209). He is correct: we need research and documents, not moral indignation.

Porter goes on to bring out another cliché from the analytic treasure trove: "Freud does not discount the importance of actual molestation." In an Afterward to the *Assault* I review every passage in Freud's writings where sexual abuse is mentioned: That review makes clear, and I believe a fair-minded critic will recognize, that once he renounced the seduction theory, Freud was simply no longer interested in real child sexual abuse. Even more telling is the following: If Freud had maintained an interest in the sexual seduction of children, as my critics widely claim, then surely one would find it written about in psychoanalytic publications during Freud's lifetime. Again, it has not occurred to any of my critics to actually read through the German literature. I did. In the *Internationale Zeitschrift*, edited by Freud, Ferenczi and Rank, from volume one in 1913 to volume 26 in 1941, there was *not a single article* on sexual abuse of any kind. In the *Jahrbuch*, edited by Freud, Bleuler and Jung, from volume one in 1909 to volume six, in 1915, there are no such articles either. And in the four volumes (1911-1915) of the *Zentralblatt*, edited by Freud and Stekel, there is nothing.

It never occurred to any analytic writer prior to the controversy over Freud's views unleashed by my book to claim that psychoanalysts always had an interest in sexual abuse. Now analysts are claiming that it is now and *has always been* a major concern within psychoanalysis. But if we look at the journals, we do not find this to be so. The cumulative index of the authoritative *Journal of the American Psychoanalytic Association*, more than 600 pages, contains the contents of the Journal from its inception in 1953 through 1974 — thus the heyday of psychoanalysis and its influence — and has five columns devoted to the words "Oedipus Complex." By contrast, the word "abuse" is not found in the index. Nor is there a single entry under sexual abuse. Under "violence" there is one reference to family violence, and that is to an article on dreams in latency. Under "rape" there are two entries, one about dreams, the other in an article on genital primacy. Under the term "father" there are such entries as "role in beating fantasies," "impotent," "killing of primal," and "quest for," but nothing under "abuse by," or "violence of." Under mother, on the other hand, there are eleven references to "seductive." So much for the interest of analysts in truth, at least until 1974. I have before me *The New Harvard Guide to Psychiatry*, with the contribution of many distinguished psychiatrists and psychoanalysts, dating from 1988. There is only a single reference to incest, and that is under "delusional disorders," and only one page on child abuse and neglect.

What I find astonishing although, at this point, perhaps I shouldn't, is that the actual issue of the sexual abuse of children is hardly mentioned by Porter, even though that has been the overriding concern of almost all my books. I really do not know how to engage with somebody who simply shows no interest in the real topic of the discussion. It was this very lack of interest that first alerted me to the fact that something was perhaps being avoided. In my training as a psychoanalyst (from 1972-78), the topic of the sexual abuse of children was raised only to be dismissed. We were never assigned any reading about it. When it was, in any given individual case, reluctantly recognized, the emphasis was put on what the child did to bring the abuse about. I do not believe that most psychoanalysts have significantly changed their views. I wish they would. I hope they do. I have never yet seen the major works on child sexual abuse by feminists such as Louise Armstrong, Florence Rush, Diana Russell, or Judith Herman referred to or reviewed in psychoanalytic journals. Most analysts appear completely unfamiliar with and uninterested in the scholarship in this area. Typical is the comment by Charles Rycroft, a psychoanalyst, in a review of the *Assault* in the *New York Review of Books* (April 12, 1984), when he writes: "Although Masson says that he is 'inclined to accept' the view that the incidence of sexual violence in the early lives of children may be as high as one in three in the general population and is 'undoubtedly higher among women who seek psychotherapy,' he gives no evidence or references to support his inclination." The major study was and remains, as anyone with the slightest familiarity with the area knows, that of Diana Russell: "The Incidence and Prevalence of Intrafamilial and Extrafamilial Sexual Abuse of Female Children" published in *Child Abuse and Neglect* 7 (1983), pp. 136-146. (See too her 1986 groundbreaking book *The Secret Trauma: Incest in the Lives of Girls and Women*.) Her conclusion that "over one-quarter of the population of female children have experienced sexual abuse before the age of 14, and well over one-third have had such an experience by the age of 18 years" has been corroborated by researchers across the United States (e.g., G.E. Wyatt, "The Sexual Abuse of Afro-American and White Women in Childhood," *Child Abuse and Neglect* 9 [1985]: 507-519). It is not as if the psychoanalytic and psychiatric world has tried to come to grips with this kind of research. They have avoided it, as has Roy Porter.

Missing the Point about Freud

FREDERICK CREWS

I

As a member of this journal's editorial board and an interested observer of Freud studies, I was eager to accept Nikki Keddie's invitation to offer some reflections about the issues debated by Roy Porter and Jeffrey Moussaieff Masson in the Winter 1994 issue of *Contention*. We live in a moment when carefully nurtured myths about the birth of psychoanalysis are finally being debunked by independent scholars, who are bringing to light both logical and empirical absurdities, to say nothing of outright falsehoods, in Freud's founding leap from "seduction" to fantasy in 1897. Unfortunately, however, neither Masson nor Porter appears to appreciate what is taking place. While some of their remarks about each other's misconceptions are on target, both writers leave the key question — namely, whether Freud discovered *anything at all* about his hysterical patients in the 1890s, either before or after choosing to regard them in an oedipal light — largely unaddressed.

Masson's failure in this respect is not much of a surprise, since he has already passed up a decade's worth of opportunities to repair the patent naiveté of the book that helped to make him a celebrity, *The Assault on Truth* (1984).[1] His latest statement suggests that, instead of learning from the reviews and early critiques of that work, he has taken refuge in grandiose self-portrayal as a courageous pioneer surrounded by envious nonentities. ("Surely there must be *some* scholars out there who can tear themselves away, even for a moment, from the preoccupation with how many women I slept with, to do some archival research and come up with something new.") By contrast, Roy Porter's essay actually cites important work on the seduction theory, notably the newest and most decisive study of that episode in Freud's career. Yet Porter then makes an abrupt about-face, retreating into obfuscation of an all too familiar kind.

Let me begin with Jeffrey Masson — who, I should say straight off, has made one invaluable contribution to our understanding of psychoanalysis. This is his publication of a complete and reliable edition of the Freud-Fliess letters, replacing the shamelessly bowdlerized version that Marie Bonaparte, Anna Freud, and Ernst Kris foisted upon an unsuspecting world in 1950.[2] Masson's edition gave a notable boost to a movement of Freud revisionism that (as he still refuses to admit) was already well under way, and whose evolving portrait of the founder was and remains more nuanced than his own.[3]

A remarkable lapse of memory, however, prevents Masson from replying effectively to Roy Porter's charge that he went beyond the record, in *The Assault on Truth*, when he ascribed Freud's abandonment of the seduction theory to cowardice. Masson cannot recall having made any such claim, except perhaps in a speculative aside or two. What he is forgetting is nothing less than the thesis of his book. In his own words from his concluding chapter, "Freud gave up this theory, not for theoretical or clinical reasons, but because of a personal failure of courage."[4]

Freud's motives apart, the argument of *The Assault on Truth* rests on two glaring fallacies. First, Masson assumed (and still assumes) that there are only two possible interpretations of Freud's change of heart about "seduction." Either Freud had found good clinical reasons, in 1897, to blame his patients' adult neuroses on their repressed infantile fantasies — the gospel psychoanalytic version of events — or he must have been right the first time: the patients had been rendered hysterical by early sexual abuse. Masson was overlooking an obvious third option that has come to seem more plausible with every passing year, namely, that Freud was guessing wildly in both instances. And second, Masson assumed that if Freud's patients were telling the truth about having been molested, that fact in itself would secure the seduction etiology. Again, the mistake is elementary: without a great deal of further proof, the existence of a given episode in someone's past hardly guarantees the power of that episode to bring about a specific form of illness.

Masson's way of establishing that Freud's patients were indeed molested in early childhood was unconvincing as well. Having scant access to their actual histories, he fashioned an elaborate circumstantial argument about Freud's exposure to *other* cases of abuse, going all the way back to his visit to the Paris morgue in 1885. Of course, such examples had no defensible bearing on the traumas suffered or not suffered by the hysterics who visited Freud's consulting room, much less on the causes of their neuroses. What Masson was actually doing, it seems, was assimilating Freud's hysterics to the modern epidemic of child abuse that he now chides Roy Porter, bizarrely, for having overlooked. One-quarter of all American females, Masson tells Porter, have been molested by age fourteen, and one-third by age eighteen. According to Masson, these figures have been "corroborated by researchers across the United States." Characteristically, he omits to report that they have also been *disputed* by researchers across the United States.[5]

Masson does not seem to care that data from modern America — even better data than his own — are irrelevant to turn-of-the-century Vienna. Nor is he bothered by the thought that such a high incidence of abuse, if it indeed obtained in Freud's day, would have been unpropitious for the assigning of a definite etiological role. (A phenomenon as widespread as he alleges molestation to be fades into the background of factors too common to be considered causative of such a limited effect as hysteria.) Nor does the virtual disappearance of hysteria in the twentieth century sit well with what Masson himself regards as the unabated virulence of its "cause," sexual abuse. If none of this matters to Masson, the reason is that his primary aim is not to solve a historical problem but to align himself with radical feminists in their denunciation of a brutal and uncaring patriarchal society — the same society that made his melodramatic book a best seller. It was Masson's good fortune to have fallen upon some sensational evidence of Freud's insensitivity to women's feelings, but now that the dust has settled, perhaps we can all agree that *The Assault on Truth* tells us nothing whatever about the actual roots of hysteria.

Masson did, however, discover a piece of evidence bearing on the question of whether or not at least one of Freud's early patients had suffered a "seduction." In a note to his edition of the Freud-Fliess letters, he cites a passage by Freud's contemporary Leopold Löwenfeld, a Munich psychiatrist who astutely challenged the seduction theory on the grounds that Freud's patients "were subjected to a suggestive influence coming from the person who analyzed them." Löwenfeld added:

> By chance, one of the patients with whom Freud used the analytic method came under my observation. The patient told me with certainty that the infantile sexual scene which analysis had apparently uncovered *was pure fantasy and had never really happened to him.* It is difficult to understand how a researcher like Freud . . . still could maintain toward his patients that the pictures that arose in their minds were memories of real events. However, it is still more difficult to understand that Freud thought that he could consider this assumption to be completely proven in each single case of hysteria.[6]

Interestingly, Masson neglects to mention this pertinent item in *The Assault on Truth*, published just a year before the Freud-Fliess letters, even though he there quotes the same work of Löwenfeld's in another context (p. 129).

In a passage that Porter quotes from *Against Therapy* (1988), Masson registers his conviction that "[p]sychotherapy of any kind is wrong." Holding that view, Masson ought to take a lively interest in our current national debate about child abuse, since unscrupulous and fanatical psychotherapists are the parties most responsible for the zany tales of satanic ritual violation that have befuddled American juries and landed a number of innocent citizens in prison.[7] A genealogical line extends from Freud's bullying technique of interrogation (both before and after 1897) to that of these debased successors, who typically override their patients' initial denials of having been molested and end by imbuing them with sinister "memories" that then take on a mischievous life of their own. Masson, however, ignores all such evidence, perhaps because it could only jeopardize his dubious estimates of virtually ubiquitous child abuse.

Roy Porter correctly points out that Masson should not have charged Freud with cowardice in abandoning the seduction theory, since Freud had acquired solid grounds for doubting that all or even most of his patients had been molested in their early years. As his momentous letter to Fliess on September 21, 1897, made clear, the seduction theory had proved to be therapeutically valueless and intellectually burdensome. The suspicion may have even crossed Freud's mind — he explicitly voiced it much later, in 1925 — that he himself "had perhaps forced" the seduction scenes upon his reluctant patients.[8] As I will indicate below, and as I have argued in more detail elsewhere, that is not just a possibility but a demonstrable fact.[9]

To be sure, Masson does show in *The Assault on Truth* that Freud continued to search for corroboration of the seduction theory in the months immediately following his apostasy. Such behavior, however, scarcely convicts Freud of having backed away from instances of early molestation that he knew to have occurred. Rather, it seems clear that he was casting about for some way, any way, of salvaging prematurely sanguine claims of therapeutic success that had now vanished along with many of his disgruntled patients. There is no shortage of cowardice in *this* (post-1897) record, which includes Freud's duplicitous public reassertion of the full-blown seduction theory a year after he had privately lost faith in it and a failure even to hint publicly at his mistake until 1905 or to make a full admission of it until 1914. *Contra* Masson, however, Freud's cravenness had nothing to do with "assaulting the truth" of verified molestation in the early lives of his patients.

II

But now let us turn to Roy Porter's own problems with reconstruction of the past. As a prelude, we should recognize that the standard story of the emergence of psychoanalysis requires us to embrace two quite independent propositions, which I will call A and B. First, as we have seen above, we must agree (Proposition A) that *Freud found a good basis for doubting his own hasty inference that all of his hysterics had been molested in early childhood.* The utter recalcitrance of those patients to treatment as "survivors" provided Freud with just such a basis; he would have been an even greater prevaricator than he already was if he had followed Masson's preferred path of stonewalling with the seduction theory. But then there is proposition B: that *Freud also possessed compelling clinical reasons for deciding that his patients' alleged tales of molestation derived from the repression of their own sexual fantasies.* Clearly, this cornerstone of the psychoanalytic edifice in no way follows from proposition A. On the contrary, it calls to mind a host of pressing questions to which Freud provided either lame answers or none at all.

For example, if the fantasies of Freud's patients were repressed, how had he gained reliable access to them? How had he safeguarded them against contamination by his own influence? Had he, in fact, refrained from coaching and cajoling his now fully psychoanalytic patients, as he had surely coached and cajoled those same people about seduction a few months earlier? How could he be sure that the recovered fantasies dated from early childhood? Even if they did, by what combination of observation and reasoning could he have determined that the fantasies were causally operative as pathogens? By what mechanism had the hysterics' early traumas lain dormant for so long and suddenly flared up in their adulthood? What exactly was repression, and where was Freud's evidence that it played a cardinal role in every child's development? Did Freud's patients eventually agree to, or otherwise convincingly confirm, his suppositions? Could he perhaps have mistaken their repugnance toward his prurient insinuations for proof that he had struck home? Did the patients really get well, and did they stay well? By what means could another investigator corroborate *any* of Freud's new claims? And if the fantasy etiology rested on the same clinical procedure as the erroneous seduction theory, about whose curative effects Freud had lied to his colleagues, why should we take Freud's word about the results of that procedure on its second try?

These are not unreasonably demanding questions dating from a time of more rigorous scientific standards than those that prevailed in Freud's day. Most of them were raised by well-informed colleagues who continually challenged the epistemic foundation of psychoanalysis throughout the first two decades of its existence — until Freudianism got the last laugh by becoming the chic international parlor game of the Jazz Age. But the doubts have returned with redoubled force now that we find ourselves in possession of biographical documents showing, for instance, that Freud was being deserted by the very patients he boasted of having cured and that there was scarcely any interval between his private admission of defeat and his "discovery" of psychoanalysis. The Freud-Fliess letters strongly imply that Freud's overnight shift to an oedipal outlook was not a therapeutic breakthrough, as he later maintained, but a mere adjustment of perspective deriving partly from his subservience to Fliess, partly from muddled musings about his own infancy, and partly from his desperate need for a theory that could at once rescue his favorite notion of repression from the seduction debacle and locate the ultimate causes of neurosis in a region remote enough from observation to be inaccessible to skeptical researchers.

Where does Roy Porter stand with respect to all this? Squarely on both sides of the fence. With one voice he tells us that there is "every reason to suppose that the traditional accounts of Freud's leap into truth are no more, and perhaps a good deal less, satisfactory than Masson's portrayal of his 'suppression of truth.' " But a scant paragraph later, another voice says that "Freud did not so much suppress a truth as *sensibly* switch hypotheses when his first hunch seemed to be becoming disconfirmed" (italics added). If we want to know what, exactly, was sensible about causally linking adult neurosis, based on a sample of mostly female patients, to a male baby's hypothesized desire to fornicate with one of its parents and spare its penis from the knife of the other, all we get from Porter is a smoke screen of vague and disembodied language. Freud's theoretical turn, he unhelpfully suggests, was made "on the basis of various inquiries"; he "found diverse preoccupations concatenating"; there was, for Freud, a "salience of motive in symptom-formation"; "it had become plausible" for him to match real seductions with fantasized ones; and notions of childhood sexuality, fantasy, and repression "were to attain prime significance within the structure of his theories."

The effect of all this hand waving is to decouple psychoanalysis from clinical validation while nevertheless hinting that the new theory was on the right track simply because its author had so very much on his mind. Before Porter is through, the image of Freud as Deep Thinker, standing beyond the reach of criticism, has been largely reassembled. Freud's confused, self-protective hedging of his bet against seduction now comes out looking like the fruit of a refined judiciousness: "Freud does not discount the importance of actual molestation, but such cases were of secondary interest to him, since the main direction of his thought is away from a limited set of specific instances . . . toward the universals of human behavior, a movement away from the pathological towards the normal." This is how Porter implements his belief that, as he says, the time has come when altercations about Freud "should be transcended." A less polite way of putting it would be to say that Porter wants to sweep Freud's scientific failings under the rug.

I will not speculate about Porter's motives for rushing to the defense of an etiology that even most psychoanalysts have abandoned by now, except to say that if Masson is against it, Porter evidently feels obliged to step forward as its advocate. I can, however, show where Porter has let his logical guard down. His assent to Proposition A — that Freud had good reason to ditch the seduction theory — has left him uncritical of Proposition B — that the fantasy theory was cogent. Since, as Porter says, there was no "moral cowardice" in Freud's abandonment of seduction, there must also have been none in his embracing of oedipal fantasy. A historian of medicine should know better than to resolve issues of fact in this deductive manner. Though only a minority of scholars have as yet realized it, moral cowardice was precisely the signature trait of Freud's entire psychoanalytic career, and never more so than in the combined surreptitiousness and bluffing that attended his movement's entry into the world.

What makes Porter's sublimation of history especially puzzling is his acknowledged acquaintance with the best study of the seduction theory to date, Han Israëls and Morton Schatzman's recent article in *History of Psychiatry*.[10] Porter wisely accepts Israëls and Schatzman's conclusion that therapeutic failure was the chief determinant behind Freud's desertion of his pet idea, but he overlooks a more consequential if less conspicuous implication of their work, explicitly developed in an earlier article by Schatzman alone.[11] This is that *Freud's hysterics never told him about childhood "seductions" at all*. As his papers from the 1890s make clear, it was Freud himself who hypothesized that those patients had been molested as toddlers and who then scripted their "repressed" early scenes and tried to browbeat them into fleshing out his "reconstructions." Even those patients who humored him in that effort ended, as Freud confessed, with "no feeling of remembering the scenes."[12] Freud's later insistence, in the teens and twenties, that "almost all [of his] women patients told [him] that they had been seduced by their father" was at best a convenient trick of misremembering, at worst a contemptible lie.[13] Porter, however, joins Jeffrey Masson in referring ingenuously to "the sexual abuse women reported to [Freud] from childhood" (Masson) and "his patients' accounts of seduction" (Porter).

Now, why does this misperception matter for a grasp of the origins of psychoanalysis? The answer is that psychoanalytic theory was introduced as *a better way of accounting for Freud's patients' stories of having been abused in early childhood* — stories that were absolutely nonexistent in anyone's mind but Freud's. It thus begins to dawn on us that psychoanalysis took its cue from an error so egregious as to smack of delusion. Having failed to implant false memories in his patients' psyches, Freud decided that those fictitious narratives *of his own* were to be explained by repressed infantile fantasies *of theirs*.[14] It is as if I were to accuse someone of murder and then, realizing that he was innocent, hypothesize that my idea must have been generated by bloody thoughts that *he* had entertained at age two. We can only surmise how clouded, perhaps with cocaine,

Freud's thought processes must have been in 1897 to permit such a farcical misstep.

Later, certainly, Freud became competent enough to cover his traces with brilliant sophistries, enthrallingly self-flattering anecdotes, elegant allusions, and brazenly mendacious claims of healing power. Only during the past generation have a significant number of scholars begun to slash through the thickets of his rhetoric and break into his secret temple, which is turning out to be the very palace of Oz. It is a pity that Roy Porter, for whatever reason, has lost his taste for that adventure.

What Porter prefers instead, a mere "repoliticizing" of Freud's thought to supply the interpersonal dimension that is indeed sadly missing from it, strikes me as a relatively tame and equivocal project. Why allow oneself to be goaded by Jeffrey Masson into a halfhearted rehabilitation of the psychoanalytic Freud? And why seek to add balance to a theory that has been shown to be not simply one-sided but unnecessary and perverse? Porter, I think, needs to bear in mind a friendly warning that Freud himself once issued about making compromises with his system of thought. "It might be said of psycho-analysis," said the man who knew this hypnotic doctrine best, "that if anyone holds out a little finger to it[,] it quickly grasps his whole hand."[15]

NOTES

1   Jeffrey Moussaieff Masson, *The Assault on Truth: Freud's Suppression of the Seduction Theory* (New York: Farrar, Straus and Giroux, 1984). The most astute review of *The Assault on Truth* was Frank Cioffi's "The Cradle of Neurosis," *Times Literary Supplement* (London), 6 July 1984, 743-44. In Cioffi's words, Masson had achieved "the remarkable feat of concocting an account no less tendentious and unreliable than Freud's own" (p. 743). I myself discussed Masson's errors in an essay, "The Freudian Way of Knowledge," that was published in 1984 and reprinted in my *Skeptical Engagements* (New York: Oxford University Press, 1986); see pp. 46-47. I also appeared in two public forums with Masson in Berkeley, California, attempting unsuccessfully to draw his attention to the vulnerability of his argument.

2   *Aus den Anfängen der Psychoanalyse: Briefe an Wilhelm Fliess, Abhandlungen und Notizen aus den Jahren 1887-1902*, ed. Marie Bonaparte, Anna Freud, and Ernst Kris (London: Imago, 1950); translated as *The Origins of Psycho-Analysis, Letters to Wilhelm Fliess, Drafts and Notes: 1887-1902*, trans. Eric Mosbacher and James Strachey (New York: Basic Books, 1954). The uncensored edition is *The Complete Letters of Sigmund Freud to Wilhelm Fliess, 1887-1904*, ed. Jeffrey Moussaieff Masson (Cambridge: Harvard University Press, 1985).

3   It is commonly forgotten — and both Porter and Masson continue to forget — that a vigorous critique of Freud's methodological transgressions had already been mounted in the 1950s by philosophers such as Sidney Hook, Ernest Nagel, and Karl Popper. As for biographical understanding, the long chapter on Freud in Henri Ellenberger's *The Discovery of the Unconscious* (New York: Basic Books, 1970) set a standard that contemporary scholars are still trying to match — and that Porter and Masson would be well advised to study before saying more about Freud.

4   Masson, *Assault*, 189. Lest anyone take this to be a minor point, it is repeated on the dust jacket: "That [Freud] abandoned his seduction theory, Masson argues, was a failure of courage rather than a clinical or theoretical insight."

5   For an excellent summary of the unsettled state of knowledge surrounding child abuse, see two articles by Bruce Bower, "Sudden Recall: Adult Memories of Child Abuse Spark a Heated Debate," *Science News*, 18 September 1993, 184-86; and "The Survivor Syndrome: Childhood Sexual Abuse Leaves a Controversial Trail of Aftereffects," *Science News*, 25 September 1993, 202-4.

6   This passage is quoted and discussed on pages 43-44 of the Israëls and Schatzman article cited below, note 10. The italics are mine.

7   On this point, see the discussion and the citations at the end of my review essay, "The Unknown Freud," *New York Review of Books*, 18 November 1993, 55-66.

8   See *The Standard Edition of the Complete Psychological Works of Sigmund Freud*, 24 vols., trans. James Strachey (London: Hogarth Press, 1953-1974), 20:34.

9   See Crews, "The Unknown Freud," 61-62.

10   Han Israëls and Morton Schatzman, "The Seduction Theory," *History of Psychiatry* 4 (1993): 23-59.

11   Morton Schatzman, "Freud: Who Seduced Whom?" *New Scientist*, 21 March 1992, 34-37.

12   Freud, *Standard Edition*, 3:204.
13   Freud, *Standard Edition*, 22:120.
14   This point has been made most clearly by Allen Esterson, *Seductive Mirage: An Exploration of the Work of Sigmund Freud* (Chicago and La Salle, Ill.: Open Court, 1993), 133.
15   Freud, *Standard Edition*, 15:193.

Response to Frederick Crews's "Missing the Point about Freud"

JEFFREY MOUSSAIEFF MASSON

The major error of Crews's review is to insist that I claim to have said something in *The Assault on Truth* about the "actual roots of hysteria."[1] I did not then, and I do not now, believe that there *is* any such entity as "hysteria," and, therefore, I have no interest in its roots. I believe that there is such a thing as human unhappiness (and I think that "unhappiness" is not a completely unfair translation of Freud's early use of the word "hysteria" though I realize that he would have disputed this[2]), and I think that sexual abuse in early childhood has a good claim on being the source of a great deal of later human suffering, especially for women. That is the heart of our dispute. Crews is not interested in child sexual abuse; he is interested in this fictive thing he and psychiatry call "hysteria." I am more interested in the reality of child sexual abuse. I am not an expert in its long-term effects. Other people are and have written about them persuasively. Nor am I an expert on the statistics of child sexual abuse, having done no original research of my own. I have, however, read the major literature, and I venture to say that *all* serious scholars in this field accept the authoritative figures given by Diana Russell and others. She has her critics, but these critics have not undertaken any statistical research of their own as Diana Russell indisputably did. The people who deny the significance of her work are clearly motivated by political considerations. Crews speaks of "the zany tales of satanic ritual violation that have befuddled American juries and landed a number of innocent citizens in prison." This is moving us back a hundred years. Tales? How does Crews decide this? Zany? Is this because Crews thinks they did not happen? Was he there? Innocent citizens? Judge and jury, all in one professor of English. Amazing. How familiar it all is: the Freudian repudiation of the reality of abuse played out over and over again. There is still a whole hierarchy of those who find it impossible to believe children — from the perpetrators to their friends in high places, from the naive man on the street to the ignorant professor in the university.

It is true that we do not know the true figures of child sexual abuse in Vienna or anywhere else before the modern studies I mentioned were undertaken. And I suppose we never will know. So the best evidence we have is still, surprisingly, to be found in the complete letters between Freud and Fliess. They do not provide statistics, certainly, but they definitely prove that Freud, for some time at least, believed what his patients were telling him about child sexual abuse. Crews cannot even believe that the patients *were* telling Freud about abuse. He says that it was at best a convenient trick of misremembering, at worst a contemptible lie. Well, it is impossible now to know for sure exactly *what* Freud's patients told him and how sexual abuse came up in the analytic sessions. But I do know for sure (based on testimonies to me) that many thousands of analytic patients in modern times have *tried* to tell *their* Freudian analysts about their abuse, only to be met with at best benign agnosticism ("we'll never know, will we?"), at worst denial on the part of the analyst ("you only imagined it"). At least this was true through the 1970s. Time are changing rapidly, and it is the rare therapist today in 1994 who would tell his female patient that she is fantasizing her abuse. But this newly found belief makes me nervous. Permit me a degree of skepticism when belief comes from people who for the better part of their careers denied the reality of child sexual abuse and now claim to be experts in its cure. Nonetheless, that is still a step beyond Crews, who seems stuck in some prehistoric period of — and now at last I have found a use for the word — antifeminist hysteria.

NOTES

1   Crews is obsessed with a "gotcha" mentality. And so he quotes a passage from a book by Löewenfeld that I cited in my notes to the Freud/Fliess letters, then claims that I deliberately did not mention this passage a year earlier in *The Assault on Truth*. As I explained in the letters, I had only *just* found this passage. As far as I know, nobody else had ever noticed the passage, or at least had not brought it to the attention of Freud scholars. In the Harvard edition, p. 413, I state: "This passage may have played a role in Freud's abandonment of the seduction theory." How, then, can Crews claim that I left this "refractory testimony" out of account? By the way, Crews is wrong when he asserts that I quote the same work of Löewenfeld in another context. I pointed out in the letters that the book I am quoting *there* is an 1899 edition, and the one I referred to in *Assault* is from 1904. Obviously, there are major differences in the two books, but I did not know it until I came across the earlier edition and was able to compare the two.

2   I am amazed that Crews is incapable of quoting me correctly. I did not say that Freud abandoned the seduction theory because of "cowardice." That is simply not a word I used. What I referred to was a "failure of courage." They are not interchangeable phrases. Cowardice is a state, a trait. A failure of courage is something one does or that happens. Who Freud *is* is not the same as what he *did*.

On the Abuses of Freud:

A REPLY TO MASSON AND CREWS

JEFFREY PRAGER

The November 29, 1993, issue of *Time* positioned a picture of
Freud on its cover but with the upper portion of his head removed. Freud's
face was presented like parts of a picture puzzle being taken apart, the
message being that what once had been whole was now, piece by piece,
being dismantled. To the left of Freud was the question, "Is Freud Dead?"
Time was devoting its cover story to an assessment of what, if anything,
remains of the Freudian legacy. The story itself, written by Paul Gray,
acknowledged Freud's extraordinary cultural contribution to the twentieth
century but argued that several elements of that bequest are being recon-
sidered, suggesting that "it may someday become necessary to imagine
our world without him." The main focus of Gray's article was some recent
critical scholarship on Freud and psychoanalysis, including a new book by
Adolf Grunbaum — perhaps psychoanalysis's most effective positivistic
critic — that challenges the status of psychoanalysis as a science. *Time*'s
cover story was followed by a lengthy article on the recovered memory
movement, one of the cultural preoccupations of the moment. The tone
was highly skeptical of those therapists who claim to have uncovered
repressed memories of childhood abuse through techniques of guided
imagery, hypnosis, and body massage. Yet the recovered memory movement itself, and not the skepticism toward it, was understood in *Time* as

Contention, Vol. 4, No. 1, Fall 1994

part of Freud's legacy. The recovered memory movement, the president of *Time* insisted, was "a practical application of Freudian theory." As it happens, these two articles express the twin shoals of the contemporary attack on Freud and psychoanalysis: on the one side, a view that psychoanalysis suffers from an inability to be scientifically validated; and, on the other, a view that Freudian thought — particularly its interest in the unconscious — somehow obscures our capacity to see things clearly, and for what they are.

Now, on a somewhat more lofty plane and for a different audience, *Contention* engages these same issues, with various authors leveling similar kinds of challenges. In a recent issue, Roy Porter offers a defense, if not of Freud himself, then of psychoanalysis more broadly at a time when few have much good to say of either. And befitting the contemporary skepticism toward Freud and his legacy, Porter's defense is a tempered and, I might say, reasonable one. But Jeffrey Masson in the same issue and Frederick Crews in a subsequent one bask, like the *Time* articles, in this season of anti-Freudianism. Each happily sees himself moving in to hammer in the last nails of Freudianism's coffin; neither gives Freud nor his followers the opportunity to breathe. Masson pounds from the left, decrying psychoanalysis's political irrelevance and its hostility to women and children. Crews hammers from the right, incensed at its scientific laxity. And both insist that psychoanalysis is dead at the core: Document Freud's personal fallibility, they maintain, and the edifice of psychoanalysis — the entire cultural legacy — rightfully shrivels.

But when we think of the "God is dead" trope from which *Time* borrowed, we quickly appreciate how much more the "death of God" discourse reveals about the cultural moment in which the sentiment is expressed — when Nietzsche first articulated it in the European *fin de siècle*, for example, and when it became *au courant* again during our cultural revolution of the 1960s — than about God's actual fate. In the same way, I suspect that this current challenge to psychoanalysis and its founder reveals more about the time in which we are living, our cultural moment, than the actual death knell of psychoanalytic theory and the clinical insights that Freud advanced. To be sure, Freud and psychoanalysis have been the subject of many cycles of attack, but typically over different issues and concerns than those of today. Now, Masson may summon left-wing populist and feminist criticisms of Freud, and Crews may resort to right-wing appeals to impose scientific standards of proof and demonstration, but both share in what might be called a culturally reactionary theme, each identifying in the Freudian legacy the source of what they perceive to be a contemporary cultural crisis. Each, in his earnest quest for the truth about Freud, expresses just how reactionary these times seem to be.

When we consider the question of the moment, that is, childhood abuse and repressed memory, we see just how much at odds Crews and Masson are in their predictable approaches to the topic. At the same time, both conclude that their position unequivocally demonstrates Freud's culpability either in obscuring just how widespread real abuse is or in generating an "abuse industry" by a fraudulent psychotherapy. The evidence on repressed memory and abuse, of course, is more complicated and less clear than either Crews or Masson cares to acknowledge. Currently, there is a considerable amount of research being conducted on the topic by cognitive psychologists, neurobiologists, and sociologists. Not surprisingly, the findings are mixed. A substantial research study, for example, by Linda Williams interviewed young adult women about childhood memories. Each of these women had been documented to have been admitted to a hospital 17 years earlier, having suffered from sexual abuse. Upon being interviewed about these incidents, more than one third of these women had no recollection at all about them.[1] Such studies give credibility to those impressed by the mind's power of repression.[2] Yet, at the same time, equally provocative research efforts have focused on the striking impact that suggestibility holds upon memory. Elizabeth Loftus's work, for example, demonstrates just how malleable memory is even to those who have eyewitnessed a given event.[3] From this research has emerged a conception of "false memory"; the False Memory Syndrome Foundation, in fact, has been organized composed of academic researchers interested in these problems of suggestion, and professionals and parents who claim to have been falsely accused of sexually abusing their children. The Foundation has placed at center stage the intense battles being fought about the veridicality of memory: the director of the Foundation, who has a Ph.D. in psychology, has gained prominence in part because of charges of sexual abuse leveled by her daughter, herself a prominent and outspoken poet, against her father, the director's husband.

The tricky issues of operationalizing these concepts of trauma, memory, repression, and suggestion and the problems of measurement validation and generalization have generally prevented social scientists from drawing definitive conclusions concerning the implication that their research has on the broader social questions being addressed. What seems to be clearly emerging from this body of research, as I read it, is that the question of repressed or coerced memory cannot be decided, even discussed, independently of the specific contexts — how and with whom — in which memory is uncovered. Memory and the contemporary settings where it occurs are, in fact, inextricably linked.[4] While these topics have stimulated research and generated creative experimental strategies, they certainly have not resulted in any broadly based consensus toward the conflicting poles of repression or suggestion in understanding these issues. But to read either Crews or Masson, one would think that the question is open and shut: Masson has it that it is sexual abuse that has been repressed; Crews has it that manipulation and suggestion by charlatan therapists has brought us to this point.

As Paul Robinson in *Freud and His Critics* has persuasively argued, the "Freud is dead" position today, represented in these pages by Crews and Masson, expresses an extreme discomfort with contemporary conceptions of subjectivity, that is, with our current appreciation of the complex, multivalent, conflictual, and malleable forces coexisting within a single self. While not always in agreement, Crews and Masson share a nostalgia for a pre- (or early) Freudian world (at least as they imagine it) — a world where things are precisely as they appear, always reflecting a hard, obdurate reality that can be easily and readily perceived. No interpreting self, no unconscious one. What happens happens, and there is no mystery as to how one processes, interprets, and gives meaning to those occurrences.

This unease with a contemporary understanding of the self captures Masson's interest, in the one case, in recovering an early Freud who thought that specific traumatic events generate psychoneurotic illness later in life. Introducing the possibility that individuals have the capacity at certain times and for specific psychic reasons to imagine seduction both captures a twentieth-century, Freudian-inspired understanding of subjectivity and also enrages Masson. Masson clearly yearns for what we might call a narrowly defined experientially driven theory of the self, one defined and determined by the specific things (especially traumatic ones) that materially happen to the person, and, in this way, Masson is riding the crest of a (counter-) cultural tidal wave. Our contemporary preoccupation with demonstrating the prevalence of childhood molestation, with a growing interest in the existence of satanic cults that engage in ritualized forms of abuse particularly directed at children, and even a growing respectability for those who believe in alien abductions and the trauma experienced by the abductees are all, I believe, in the service of establishing this unequivocal correspondence between real trauma and adult dysfunction. Culturally, we are witnessing a powerful movement toward this traumatic theory of neuroses, a theory that Freud first embraced, along with Pierre Janet and others, and only later moved away from, with his insistence upon a psychic reality that is not identical with physical reality. But now, Masson rejects the "revisionist" Freud, and, partly as a result of Masson's own efforts, Freud's *Studies on Hysteria* (with Breuer) holds more currency as his *Interpretation of Dreams* holds less. Masson and others promote a "smoking gun" approach to adult psychology: identify the early traumatic event and explain the subsequent pathology. When Masson writes that "I think that sexual abuse in childhood has a good claim on being the source of a good deal of later human suffering, especially for women," he invokes this materialist, antipsychological psychology. It is, I believe, a disturbing line of argument because, even as Crews points out, it presumes a one-to-one correspondence between a given episode in a person's life and a specific form of illness. Subjectivity is stripped of its significance, and the meaning-making, interpretative process that undoubtedly makes its own contribution to illness is deprived of its consequentiality. While it should go without saying that I, too, condemn child abuse, deplore its prevalence, and believe that it can produce devastating subsequent consequences, I believe that to construct a discourse about the self that relies so heavily on real trauma as its constituent basis surely reveals a wish to "tame" subjectivity, to make it more manageable.

And if, in the name of disempowered women and children, Masson attempts to resurrect a late-nineteenth-century, pre-Freudian conception of trauma and pathology to subdue subjectivity, Crews, for his part, is attempting to revive a similarly outdated conception of positivist science to achieve the same end. Freud's striving for a science of the unconscious expressed his desire to break out of an epistemological stance that prevented exploration of a psychic world that challenged logic, rationality, and measurement as traditionally conceived. And yet Freud's efforts, part of a broader attack on positivism in *fin de siècle* Europe, become the basis upon which Crews attempts to undermine psychoanalysis. In his slavish obeisance to the data on Freud and his motivations, for example, he presumes that in the documents we can discover "the truth" about Freud, the "unknown" Freud. "Facts" speak for themselves, he implies; Crews attempts to present himself, through his diligent research, only as a conduit revealing what Freud was truly about. Even more to the point, Crews imputes great significance to the fact that while Freud himself aspired to the canon of scientific neutrality and objectivity he failed, nonetheless, to transcend either self-interest or certain cultural presumptions. But instead of helping to situate psychoanalytic science within a broader cultural frame as historians and sociologists of science have been doing to science in general for at least the past decade, these findings (granting for purposes of argument their accuracy) generate, instead, Crews's outrage and indignation. Invoking an idea of empirical validation that has little resonance with our current understandings of science, psychoanalytic or otherwise, Crews insists upon a kind of positivism already under sharp attack in Freud's day. By impugning Freud, we can dismiss all of psychoanalysis; the result, Crews imagines, is that we all might be able to return to a simpler understanding of scientific "truth," and of science, as Masson characterizes Crews's approach, that proceeds via a "gotcha" mentality.

For Masson and Crews, then, the question of the past is paramount in their assessment of the adequacy of Freud and psychoanalysis. For Masson, the issue is whether Freud or psychoanalysis has anything to contribute to those who have really suffered and who continue to struggle with the consequences. For Crews, the question is whether there is any demonstrable relation between what happened in Freud's past and the current world of psychoanalysis and psychotherapy that he helped create. Both make an assault on what they consider to be the original founding "myth" of psychoanalysis, believing in the possibility of replacing truth in place of what they insist to be fiction. And what is striking about both is their certain naive faith in our capacity to "know" the past, either our own or Freud's, and to understand its consequences for the present. Masson, for example, suggests that Freud's abandonment of the seduction theory has been influential in a wholesale victimization of women and children. He shares with Judith Lewis Herman the following sentiment: "Out of the ruins of the traumatic theory of hysteria," Herman writes, "Freud created psychoanalysis. The dominant psychological theory of the next century was founded in the denial of women's reality."[5] Crews takes his turn and, in a quite remarkable passage, argues that Freud is responsible for all those charlatan therapists who today wrongfully and coercively elicit false memories from their clients. "Freud is the true historical sponsor," Crews writes recently in the *New York Review of Books*, "of 'false memory syndrome.' "[6] In *Contention*, he reiterates this sentiment when he writes, "a genealogical line extends from Freud's bullying technique of interrogation (both before and after 1897) to that of these debased successors, who typically override their patients' initial denials of having been molested and end by imbuing them with sinister 'memories' that then take on a mischievous life of their own."

To achieve each of their broadsides on Freud and psychoanalysis, Crews and Masson resort, in the end, to a simple-minded understanding of historical truth, seemingly unmindful of the ways in which our present needs (and theirs) help to shape, color, give form to, construct the past. The American sociologist George Herbert Mead, not Freud, wrote that "the past is an overflow of the present." Why is it so imperative, we can rightfully ask, to rewrite so profoundly the history of Freud and of psychoanalysis by invoking a new myth of its origin — this time, psycho-analysis as the antihero invoked to elide real trauma and to obscure self-interested charlatanism — without acknowledging the contemporary motivations for such a rewriting? And why, in so offering an alternative account of psychoanalysis, do they imagine that Freud and Freudianism might forever disappear?

The answer, I believe, derives from Crews and Masson's discom-fort in their own relation to their past: Both would like to believe that their own scholarly commitments today have no relation to who they were in their earlier lives. But what we know about each of these writers, and their own complex and complicated relation to Freud and psychoanalysis, already reveals the limitations of this simple search for truth. They would like us to think that, while Freud's intellectual pursuits were hopelessly contaminated by personal and suspect motivations, theirs is simply schol-arship, as pure as the driven snow. It is remarkable how unreflective both writers are in understanding their anti-Freud animus: Here are two men who had been intimately and intensely involved with Freud and his legacy — Masson as a Freudian analyst, Crews as a Freudian literary critic — who now challenge the orthodoxy for both its intellectual and moral bankruptcy. Though I can only speculate as to the reasons behind the virulence of Crews and Masson's disdain for Freud (and insistence that he is *the* cultural icon that must be destroyed), it must have something to do with their own sense of themselves having been betrayed, their insistence of reconstructing the "true" Freud linked to their feelings about having once been seduced by him. They write more like jilted lovers than dispas-sionate scholars, and we, as readers, now have to suffer their rage, indig-nation, and hyperbole, being asked to read their prose *as if* all they are really after is the truth, and not vindication. But when each, in their own way, finds a way to argue that Freud himself is responsible for much of the

pain and suffering of the current age, we become aware how much they
have gone over the top, confirming for us Freud's insight that love and hate
sometimes occupy overlapping psychic terrain. But — I suppose we can
thank Freud for this — the wish to escape one's past, to pretend that it
never happened, results instead in a kind of sequestering of those feelings
and experiences, discovering its expression in often strange and distorted
ways. This is how I have come to understand the peculiarly passionate
scholarship that Crews and Masson have come to exemplify.

This has been perhaps the most profound insight of contemporary
thinking about our relation to the past: An understanding of the past
requires an investigation into the properties of consciousness itself. And it
is this insight that provides the most thorny problem for the contemporary
scholar as well as the currently practicing psychoanalyst. The problem of
the moment, we might say, is that of social construction: of imagining a
past, a history, an identity, a myth of origin that is putatively true (i.e.,
objective) but that necessarily is also constructed to service our current
subjective needs and desires. Can we distinguish between the world as it
is and the world as we want it to be? And this is the challenge of
contemporary scholarship: Now that we are aware of how suffused objective knowledge is with subjectivity, the proper scholarly stance is to be
humbled in the face of an extraordinarily complex reality and to resist the
impulse to simplify it. To suggest that the "truth" about Freud lies in his
deceitfulness or in his specious reasoning is to scurry for cover in the face
of the multiple realities and ambiguities of the origins of psychoanalysis.
Or to impute that in real childhood abuse we find *the* explanation for adult
pain and suffering is to seek solace in a world that defies such simple or
easy answers.

Like the scholar who appreciates that the world is more than a
morality play, the practicing psychoanalyst similarly assumes the position
of not-knowing in the face of an individual life, extraordinarily rich and
complex, that resists simple, formulaic interpretation. The supreme challenge for the psychoanalyst is to suspend knowing, to subordinate the
"knowledge" of the truth for an ever more careful and open *search* for it.
The task in psychoanalytic treatment, I would argue, is to avoid the
premature closure of psychic realities by too quickly settling on a story
line of what happened. It is a difficult position to maintain but a necessary
one: The search for the truth, and my experience as an analyst I believe
bears this out, oftentimes yields greater results than the settling on a
particular rendering of truth. Both those stances toward objectivity and

truth are products of the current moment; it has been a hard won battle to insist both on an objective world and, given the autonomy of a psychic reality, a world extremely difficult to apprehend. For those who, like Crews and Masson, long for an objective world with sharper edges and squarer corners, these positions become the focus of their counterattack. They remain deeply suspicious and fearful of according subjectivity its voice. But this challenge to subjectivity, despite the persistence and stridency of those who engage in it, is well worth resisting. In withstanding these kinds of assaults, we are able to continue to explore the many ways in which subjectivity shapes both our own experiences as well as our knowledge of the world.

NOTES

1   Linda Williams, "Recall of Childhood Trauma: A Prospective Study of Women's Memories of Child Sexual Abuse," *Journal of Consulting and Clinical Psychology* (in press).

2   Other examples of research that sustain a view of repressed memory are John Briere and Jon Conte, "Self-Reported Amnesia for Abuse in Adults Molested as Children," *Journal of Traumatic Stress* 6 (1993): 21-31; Judith Herman and Emily Schatzow, "Recovery and Verification of Memories of Childhood Sexual Trauma," *Psychoanalytic Psychology* 4 (1987): 1-14.

3   Elizabeth Loftus, *Eyewitness Testimony* (Cambridge: Harvard University Press, 1979); also, idem, "The Reality of Repressed Memories," *American Psychologist* 48 (1993): 518-37.

4   D. Steven Lindsay and J. Don Read, "Incest Resolution Psychotherapy and Memories of Childhood Sexual Abuse: A Cognitive Perspective," *Applied Cognitive Psychology* (in press).

5   Judith Herman, *Trauma and Recovery* (New York: Basic Books, 1992), 14.

6   Frederick Crews, "The Unknown Freud," *New York Review of Books*, 18 November 1993, 66.

REPLY TO JEFFREY PRAGER

FREDERICK CREWS

In his response, the sociologist and psychoanalyst Jeffrey Prager presents himself as someone attuned to a deep contemporary insight, the unavailability of any objective knowledge. With his patients, Prager tells us, he eschews "a particular rendering of truth" and takes pride in his "position of not-knowing in the face of an individual life." And on the basis of this up-to-date cognitive indeterminacy, he chides Jeffrey Masson and me for our "naive faith in our capacity to 'know' the past, either our own or Freud's." Yet in a remarkable turnabout, Prager goes on to disclose, as he puts it, "what we know" about the histories, loyalties, and warped psyches of those same two zealots Masson and Crews. Even though he may never have laid eyes on either of us, our innermost selves are evidently transparent to him. I wonder: could it be Freud alone, in Prager's scheme of things, who is truly off-limits to psychological understanding?

Prager's show of humility serves as a fig leaf for reckless biographical speculations. In my own case, he begins by misidentifying me as a right winger, a positivist, and a cultural reactionary. Then he peers into my heart and finds it to be suffused with rage. Nor does he stop there; my rage is that of a "jilted lover" who irrationally pursues Freud out of a sense of betrayal. The very idea that someone who was once "intimately and intensely involved with Freud and his legacy" could now "challenge the orthodoxy for both its intellectual and moral bankruptcy" strikes Prager as pathological. And since the rantings of the emotionally disturbed needn't be assessed for their propositional content, Prager feels entitled to dismiss out of hand my entire reasoning about Freud and psychoanalysis.

The generic name for such discourse is *ad hominem* argumentation, but the peculiarly patronizing form it takes here — namely, a diagnosis of unconscious conflict that must have hobbled the thought processes of one's adversary — is a specialty of the psychoanalytic tradition. It originated in Freud's announcements that first Fliess and then Jung, Adler, Rank, and Ferenczi, just as soon as they dared to dispute his authority, were all deranged. Prager's assessment of my mental trouble is less grave, but its rhetorical purpose is the same: to "medicalize" opposition and thereby not just to disarm it but also to pass it through the very meat grinder of motivational reductionism that it was trying to protest.

Readers who have followed my tortuously gradual, but eventually adamant, disaffection from Freudianism over some twenty-five years will surely smile at one of Prager's forays into armchair analysis. This is his claim that the intellectually disastrous "sequestering" (i.e., repression) of my "feelings and experiences" as a Freudian must stem from my "wish to escape [my] past — to pretend that it never happened." If that has been my intention, I have chosen a most peculiar way of actuating it, repeatedly exploring in print both my early attraction to psychoanalysis and the doubts about it that finally became unanswerable. Unconscious cover-up? A more plausible charge might be that I have made a career out of penitence on this topic.

Prager's logic as applied to Jeffrey Masson and me would dictate that no one who changes his mind in a fundamental way need ever be taken seriously. Paul, despite himself, would have to remain forever Saul. The Arthur Koestler who became an ardent foe of Stalinism, the Malcolm X who began preaching that white people aren't necessarily devils, even the Freud who trashed his own seduction theory would all be self-exposed as "cases." But of course Prager has no intention of making such a sweeping claim; only apostasy from psychoanalysis, his personal creed, triggers his recourse to symptomatic explanation.

I must say that I was initially startled to find a tenured sociologist stigmatizing a concern for evidential considerations as inherently "right wing." But perhaps I shouldn't have been surprised. Prager's highly selective subjectivism — for he tacitly exempts Freudian doctrine from his belief that "the truth" will always elude us — is recognizable as a vulgarized Kuhnianism of the sort that Thomas Kuhn himself, in the second edition of *The Structure of Scientific Revolutions*, took pains to disavow.[1] If Prager rereads that book with care, he will see that even Kuhn, writing from an epistemological perspective that gives full due to the sociology of knowledge, associates himself with objective criteria by which one theory can be judged preferable to another. And if Prager, instead of merely using "positivism" as a term of abuse, ever learns what positivism actually was, he will realize that there is nothing positivist about either my own or Adolf Grünbaum's insistence that a theory of mind be accountable to the garden-variety demands of cogency and corroboration that obtain in the daily practice of science.

Prager's philosophical confusion is manifested in his fancy that, though armed with Freudian theory and Freudian rules of interpretation, he listens to his patients without any presuppositions about the sources of their disturbance. To be sure, nothing much *is* seriously the matter with most people who now meet the selection criteria for analytic treatment; and as psychoanalysis has come under increasingly withering attack from all quarters, its adepts have been discarding classic Freudian notions at an accelerating rate. Thus some contemporary analyses do approach Prager's seeming ideal of a (very protracted, very expensive) colloquy during which little if anything gets determined. Still, neither Prager nor any other Freudian is free to reach just any old conclusions about his patients; and research has established that clients in all types of psychotherapy get coached to produce the kind of "evidence" highlighted within their therapist's theory. The Freudian clinical setting is notoriously rich in effects that would interest a sincere inquirer into epistemic contamination. It is all too obvious, however, that Prager's appeal to cognitive uncertainty is meant only to discredit findings that could embarrass psychoanalysis itself.

Prager's essay is not just *ad hominem*; the figures it presumes to psychoanalyze are men of straw. It is not the case, for example, that I hold Freud accountable "for much of the pain and suffering of the present age"; it is Prager himself who goes "over the top" in making such a charge. Again, according to Prager, Crews and Masson think they can bring down psychoanalysis merely by "document[ing] Freud's personal fallibility." This is patently false to the Masson of *Against Therapy*,[2] and it is no less inaccurate about me.

Prager has evidently not taken the trouble to check my book *Skeptical Engagements*, which dwells extensively on weaknesses in psychoanalytic theory that stand quite apart from Freud's personality. Yet he does say that he has read my *New York Review* article of last November and the two exchanges of letters that followed it. In the first of those rounds, addressing the very misapprehension that Prager advances here, I explicitly stated that "I object to Freud's doctrine not because Freud himself displayed certain weaknesses of judgment and character but because his theoretical and therapeutic pretensions have been weighed and found to be hollow."[3] Insofar as it applies to me, Prager's whole response constitutes an evasion of that plainly stated position.

Even in the one substantive area that he does broach, false memory syndrome, Prager fails to address my specific claims. One would gather from his comments that I ascribe all reports of early sexual abuse to the charlatanry of therapists influenced by Freud. Thus, for example, Prager makes a show of opposing me by citing the mixed state of current research about the genuineness of such reports. Yet in my original response to Porter and Masson, I myself offered a citation to the same effect. As I have repeatedly made clear, the key points for me are quite different ones: first, that *some* recent "memories" of molestation must be artifacts of therapeutic malpractice; and second, that such malpractice is ultimately traceable to two precedents, Freud's bullying technique of interrogation and his belief in the commonness of undegraded, "photographic" retrieval of very early memories. Prager could have challenged either assertion, but instead he has chosen to express a generalized amazement at "the virulence of [my] disdain" for Freud and to dwell on truisms ("Memory and the contemporary settings where it occurs are . . . inextricably linked") that have no bearing on my actual argument.

Finally, there is Prager's unsupported claim that I wish to turn back the scientific clock, restoring us to "a world where things are precisely as they appear." Coming from an advocate of a movement that is rapidly vanishing from the scene, that is a strange accusation indeed. Nothing could be plainer than that psychoanalysis has shown itself incapable of satisfying the generally accepted scientific standards of our own time. Those standards make full allowance for "the interpreting self" that Prager finds so impressive, but they do not fetishize that self in Prager's style. As he apparently has yet to learn, science is an *inter*subjective enterprise — one that relies crucially on the testing of claims like Freud's against rival hypotheses in the same domain.

Thus the only nostalgic in this quarrel is Prager himself, who hopes that he can spare Freudianism from its doom by appealing to such ineffabilities as "the complex, multivalent, conflictual and malleable forces coexisting within a single self." Such rhetoric might have sounded convincing in the heyday of Lionel Trilling and Norman O. Brown, when Freudianism and mental complexity were widely considered to be synonymous. Today, however, increasing numbers of people are coming to realize that Freud's allegory of the psychic underworld was a bizarre collage of dubious second-hand notions, outright errors, and personal fantasies writ large. Given this massive shift of judgment, mere diagnostic snideness toward critics of psychoanalysis will no longer suffice to keep the leaky Freudian vessel afloat.

NOTES

1   See Thomas S. Kuhn, *The Structure of Scientific Revolutions*, 2d ed., rev. and enl. (Chicago: University of Chicago Press, 1970).
2   See Jeffrey Moussaieff Masson, *Against Therapy: Emotional Tyranny and the Myth of Psychological Healing* (New York: Atheneum, 1988).
3   See Frederick Crews, *Skeptical Engagements* (New York: Oxford University Press, 1986); "The Unknown Freud," *New York Review of Books*, 18 November 1994, 55-66; response to letters, *New York Review of Books*, 3 February 1994, 38-43 (the quotation above is from p. 38); and further response, *New York Review of Books*, 21 April 1994, 67-68.

CONTRIBUTORS

IRIS BERGER is Professor of History, Africana Studies, and Women's Studies at the University of Albany, State University of New York, where she also directs the Institute for Research on Women. Her books include *Threads of Solidarity: Women in South African Industry, 1900–1980; Religion and Resistance: East African Kingdoms in the Precolonial Period;* and *Women and Class in Africa,* co-edited with Claire Robertson.

RUTH H. BLOCH is in the history department at UCLA and specializes in early American religious, intellectual, and women's history. In addition to articles and essays, her publications include a book, *Visionary Republic: Millennial Themes in American Thought, 1756–1800.*

FREDERICK CREWS is Professor Emeritus of English at the University of California, Berkeley, and a member of the American Academy of Arts and Sciences. His most recent book are *The Critics Bear It Away: American Fiction and the Academy* (1992) and *The Memory Wars: Freud's Legacy in Dispute* (1995).

ELIZABETH FOX-GENOVESE is Eleonore Raoul Professor of the Humanities at Emory University and the author of *Feminism Without Illusions: A Critique of Individualism* and *Feminism Is Not the Story of My Life* (1996).

LINDA GORDON is Florence Kelly Professor of History at the University of Wisconsin, Madison. Her books include *Woman's Body, Woman's Right: A History of Birth Control in America; Heroes of Their Own Lives: The Politics and History of Family Violence;* and *Women, State, and Welfare.* Her most recent book is *Pitied But Not Entitled: Single Mothers and the History of Welfare, 1890–1935.*

SANDRA HARDING is Professor of Philosopy at the University of Delaware and Adjunct Professor of Philosophy at the University of California, Los Angeles. She is author of *Whose Science? Whose Knowledge? Thinking from Women's Lives* and editor of *The "Racial" Economy of Science: Toward a Democratic Future.*

NICKY HART, mother of three and Associate Professor of Sociology and Medicine at the University of California, Los Angeles, is author of *When Marriage Ends.* From 1977 to 1980, she served as Research Fellow to the Inequalities in Health Working Group, Department of Health and Social Security, London. Her article "Gender and the Rise and Fall of Class Politics" appeared in the *New Left Review* #175.

NIKKI R. KEDDIE is Professor of History at the University of California, Los Angeles, and author of several books, including *Iran and the Muslim World: Resistance and Revolution* (1995), and co-editor of *Women in Middle Eastern History.*

THEODORE C. KENT is a Fellow of the American Psychological Association. He has doctoral degrees in both psychology and physical anthropology. He is emeritus from the University of Southern Colorado where he headed the Department of Behavioral Science.

BARBARA LASLETT is Professor of Sociology at the University of Minnesota. She has written extensively on the historical sociology of gender, social reproduction, and the family. Her recent work has focused on feminist analyses of academic knowledge, including the history of American sociology and feminist scholarship. She edited *Contemporary Sociology* from 1983 to 1986, and *Signs: Journal of Women in Culture and Society* from 1990 to 1995.

PHILIPPA LEVINE is the author of *The Amateur and the Professional: Historians, Antiquarians, and Archaeologists in Victorian England 1838–1886; Feminist Lives in Victorian England: Private Roles and Public Commitment;* and *Victorian Feminism, 1850–1900.* She teaches history at the University of Southern California.

JEFFREY MOUSSAIEFF MASSON is the author of *Against Therapy* and *My Father's Guru,* and, most recently, co-author, with Susan McCarthy, of *When Elephants Weep: The Emotional Lives of Animals.*

JULIET MITCHELL, psychoanalyst and social critic, is author of *Psychoanalysis and Feminism* and *Women, the Longest Revolution: Essays on Feminism, Literature, and Psychoanalysis.*

ROY PORTER is Senior Lecturer at the Wellcome Institute, London. Among his many books are *Mind Forg'd Manacles* and the *Faber Book of Madness.*

MARK POSTER is Professor of History at the University of California, Irvine, and the author of *Critical Theory and Poststructuralism; The Mode of Information: Poststructuralism and Contexts;* and *The Second Media Age.*

JEFFREY PRAGER is Associate Professor of Sociology at the University of California, Los Angeles. He is also Research Psychoanalyst at the Southern California Psychoanalytic Institute and is in private practice. He is the editor, with Michael Rustin, of *Psychoanalytic Sociology,* and is currently working on a book, *Memory in Its Contexts,* to be published by Harvard University Press.

THEDA SKOCPOL is Professor of Government and Sociology at Harvard University and the author of numerous books, including the award-winning *States and Social Revolutions: A Comparative Analysis of France, Russia, and China* and *Protecting Soldiers and Mothers: The Political Origins of Social Policy in the United States,* which has won five major scholarly awards.

SUSAN RUBIN SULEIMAN is Professor of Romance and Comparative Literatures at Harvard University. Her books include *Authoritarian Fictions: The Ideological Novel As Literary Genre; Subversive Intent: Gender, Politics, and the Avant-Garde;* and *Risking Who One Is: Encounters with Contemporary Art and Literature.* Her memoir of Budapest, *Excerpts from the Motherbook,* will be published in 1996.

DEBORAH VALENZE is Assistant Professor of History at Barnard College, Columbia University. She is the author of *Prophetic Sons and Daughters: Female Preaching and Popular Religion in Industrial England* and *The First Industrial Woman.*